Basic Income Guarantee and Politics

Exploring the Basic Income Guarantee

Basic income is one of the most innovative, powerful, straightforward, and controversial proposals for addressing poverty and growing inequalities. A Basic Income Guarantee (BIG) is designed to be an unconditional, government-ensured guarantee that all citizens will have enough income to meet their basic needs. The concept of basic, or guaranteed, income is a form of social provision and this series examines the arguments for and against it from an interdisciplinary perspective with a special focus on the economic and social factors. By systematically connecting abstract philosophical debates over competing principles of BIG to the empirical analysis of concrete policy proposals, this series contributes to the fields of economics, politics, social policy, and philosophy and establishes a theoretical framework for interdisciplinary research. It will bring together international and national scholars and activists to provide a comparative look at the main efforts to date to pass unconditional BIG legislation across regions of the globe and will identify commonalities and differences across countries drawing lessons for advancing social policies in general and BIG policies in particular.

Series Editors:

Karl Widerquist is a visiting associate professor of Philosophy at Georgetown University-Qatar.

James Bryan is an associate professor of Economics at Manhattanville College.

Michael A. Lewis is an associate professor at Hunter College School of Social Work.

Basic Income Reconsidered
Simon Birnbaum

Alaska's Permanent Fund Dividend
Edited by Karl Widerquist and Michael W. Howard

Basic Income Guarantee
Allan Sheahen

Basic Income Guarantee and Politics
Edited by Richard K. Caputo

Basic Income Guarantee and Politics

International Experiences and Perspectives on the Viability of Income Guarantee

Edited by

Richard K. Caputo

palgrave
macmillan

BASIC INCOME GUARANTEE AND POLITICS

First published in 2012 by
PALGRAVE MACMILLAN®
in the United States—a division of St. Martin's Press LLC,
175 Fifth Avenue, New York, NY 10010.

Where this book is distributed in the UK, Europe and the rest of the world, this is by Palgrave Macmillan, a division of Macmillan Publishers Limited, registered in England, company number 785998, of Houndmills, Basingstoke, Hampshire RG21 6XS.

Palgrave Macmillan is the global academic imprint of the above companies and has companies and representatives throughout the world.

ISBN: 978–0–230–11691–7

Library of Congress Cataloging-in-Publication Data

Basic income guarantee and politics : international experiences and perspectives on the viability of income guarantee / [edited by] Richard K. Caputo.
p. cm.—(Basic income guarantee)
Includes bibliographical references.
ISBN 978–0–230–11691–7 (alk. paper)
1. Guaranteed annual income. 2. Income maintenance programs.
I. Caputo, Richard K.

HC79.I5B342 2012
331.2′36—dc23 2011050320

A catalogue record of the book is available from the British Library.

Design by Newgen Imaging Systems (P) Ltd., Chennai, India.

First edition: August 2012

10 9 8 7 6 5 4 3 2 1

Printed in the United States of America.

To

My Dearest Friend and Lovely Wife Mary

In Memory

Emily and Salvatore Caputo, My Parents

Philip Caputo, My Uncle and Social Policy Sparring Partner

Previous Publications

U.S. Social Welfare Reform: Policy Transitions from 1981 to the Present (2011).

Advantage White and Male, Disadvantage Black and Female: Income Inequality, Economic Well-Being and Economic Mobility among Families in a Youth Cohort, 1979–1993 (1999).

Welfare and Freedom American Style II: The Role of the Federal Government, 1941–1980 (1994).

Welfare and Freedom American Style: The Role of the Federal Government, 1900–1940 (1991).

Management and Information Systems in Human Services (1988).

Challenges of Aging on U.S. Families: Policy and Practice Implications (2005, Editor).

Contents

Acknowledgments ix

Part 1 Introduction

1 Hopes and Realities of Adopting Unconditional Basic Income Guarantee Schemes 3
Richard K. Caputo

2 On the Political Feasibility of Universal Basic Income: An Analytic Framework 17
Jurgen De Wispelaere and José Antonio Noguera

Part 2 Hopes

3 The Best Income Transfer Program for Modern Economies 41
Eduardo Matarazzo Suplicy

4 An Anniversary Note—BIEN's Twenty-fifth 55
Guy Standing

Part 3 Realities
European Union Countries

5 Finland: Institutional Resistance of the Welfare State against a Basic Income 63
Markku Ikkala

6 Germany: Far, though Close—Problems and Prospects of BI in Germany 83
Sascha Liebermann

7 Ireland: Pathways to a Basic Income in Ireland 107
Seán Healy and Brigid Reynolds

8 The Netherlands: Final Piece of the Welfare State Is Still to Come 125
Michiel van Hasslet

9 Kingdom of Spain: Basic Income from Social Movements to Parliament and Back Again 135
Daniel Raventós, Julie Wark, and David Casassas

Other OECD Countries

10 Australia: Will Basic Income Have a Second Coming? 153
John Tomlinson

11 Canada: A Guaranteed Income Framework to Address Poverty and Inequality? 177
James P. Mulvale and Yannick Vanderborght

12 Japan: Political Change after the Economic Crisis Introduces Universalist Benefit 203
Toru Yamamori

13 Mexico: The First Steps toward Basic Income 217
Pablo Yanes

14 The United Kingdom: Only for Children? 235
Malcolm Torry

15 United States of America: GAI Almost in the 1970s but Downhill Thereafter 265
Richard K. Caputo

Other Countries

16 Iran: A Bumpy Road toward Basic Income 285
Hamid Tabatabai

Notes on Contributors 301

Index 307

Acknowledgments

I wish to thank the Rabbi Arthur Schneier Center for International Affairs at Yeshiva University whose Faculty Summer Research Fellowship award program made it possible for me to extend and sustain my scholarly interests in the ethics and economics of basic income as an aspect of social welfare provisioning. Michael Howard, Michael Lewis, Steve Pressman, and Karl Widerquist also get thanks for inviting me to brainstorm with them about the prospect of approaching Palgrave Macmillan with the idea of a book series about basic income and for encouraging me to undertake this book as a contribution to that series. I am thankful to each of the contributing authors for their thoughtful chapters and reflective responses to editorial comments and to the Palgrave Macmillan staff (Tiffany Hufford, Lauri Harting, Samantha Hasey, Leila Campoli, and Joel Breuklander) and Newgen Knowledge Works staff (Deepa John), who oversaw and helped me negotiate the production and copyediting process. Thanks also go to Sheldon Gelman, Carmen Hendricks, Jade Docherty, and Ann Persaud who afforded me sufficient "space" given my responsibilities for administering the doctoral program at the Wurzweiler School of Social Work (WSSW). Their commitment to creating and maintaining an environment conducive to faculty scholarship within WSSW as a whole enabled me to worry less about day-to-day programmatic needs of the doctoral program and to do what was necessary for the successful completion of this book. Finally, I thank my wife Mary who enhances all the good things in my life, of which this book is one, and to whom the book is dedicated.

PART 1

Introduction

CHAPTER 1

Hopes and Realities of Adopting Unconditional Basic Income Guarantee Schemes

Richard K. Caputo

Proposals for basic income schemes, whether in the form of a single lump sum or a regular lifelong income stream, have been around for several centuries, finding little political traction until the latter part of the twentieth century when national- and municipal-level legislative bodies considered them (Caputo 2006; Cunliffe and Erreygers 2004). In the 1970s, for example, national-level legislative bodies in Canada and the United States deliberated specific basic income proposals, and social experiments or demonstration projects were conducted that aimed to test the effects of guaranteeing a cash income stream with little or no strings attached on primarily among low-income individuals and families. Neither country adopted a guaranteed annual income plan at the time; for all practical purposes, it seemed that unconditional basic income guarantees would disappear from the political radar screen. The 1980s, however, nurtured a revival, of sorts.

As Guy Standing highlights in chapter 4, what began as a fledging workshop in 1986 among a small group of scholars and activists *to discuss* the idea of basic income, shortly thereafter self-organized into the Basic Income European Network (BIEN) as nonpartisan, nonpoliticized loosely affiliated organizations to deliberate not only about the idea but also inform each other about efforts in their respective countries to promote the idea and get related measures on the political agenda. Subsequently, BIEN bloomed into a networked array of national organizations that holds biannual international conferences, and in 2004, it officially changed its name to the Basic Income Earth

Network and is currently comprised of 17 members. Many articles and several books emerged from the subsequent biannual congresses of BIEN over the years, including an edited book by van der Veen and Groot (2000a) whose contributors, among other things, also addressed the feasibility of getting unconditional basic income schemes on the political agenda.

Prior Assessments of Adopting Basic Income Schemes in Europe

Van der Veen and Groot's book (2000a), comprising revised papers from the Seventh International Congress of the BIEN (Amsterdam, September 1998), addressed a series of practical issues facing primarily European countries seeking reforms in welfare state provisioning throughout much of the 1990s. Such reforms included paring down benefits, making them "leaner and meaner," allowing them to survive global market competition and more intense EU competition for advantageous tax regimes; finding new ways to maintain basic features of the European welfare state in the face of such challenges; inactivity traps besetting means-tested welfare arrangements, the persistence of long-term unemployment among low-skilled persons, and the intractability of poverty despite the relative affluence of European countries; increased reliance on flexible work arrangements, the decline of breadwinner families along with increased female labor force participation, especially those with young children, and the greater difficulty of combining work and family responsibilities.

Contributors to the second half of van der Veen and Groot's book discussed the political chances of adopting a basic income scheme any time soon in their respective countries as the twentieth century came to its close. The overall prospects seemed mildly optimistic or hopeful to downright bleak or "dead on arrival." In their own contribution about Netherlands, for example, van der Veen and Groot (2000b) expressed guarded optimism, with basic income viewed as an extension of social legislation tied to tax-reform efforts. The hopeful chances for adopting unconditional basic income in the Netherlands began to unravel between 1975 and 1985 and never fully recovered through 2001. This was the case despite studies examining the economic feasibility of a basic income scheme, a social-liberal coalition coming to power in 1994, and a pragmatic turn beginning in 1997 which suggested that the prospects of adopting and implementing an unconditional basic income scheme might be advanced in a piecemeal fashion, perhaps by stealth, with components embedded in and its fate tied to other social legislation related to tax reform. Andersson (2000) reported that the idea of basic income found favorable political traction in Finland in the 1990s but very little in Sweden. Despite support from four political parties (the Centre Party, the Left-Wing Alliance, the Green Party, and the Young Finns) for a basic income scheme, opposition by the Social Democratic Party, which never accepted proposals close to a basic income scheme and favored the "work principle" (one should either work, be looking for work, or study) over the "income-maintenance principle," and by the conservative National Coalition Party was not overcome. Andersson was notably silent about future prospects.

In van der Veen and Groot's book, Seán Healy and Brigid Reynolds (2000) reported only marginal success in getting basic income on the political agenda as a viable policy option in Ireland during the 1990s. After ten years, during which the Irish government negotiated with employers, trade union, and farmer's organizations to develop a three-year national plan, in 1997, the newly elected government committed only to producing a green paper on "basic income" by 1999. As if to throw cold water on the faces of basic income advocates at large, Lessenich (2000: 247) summarized his short story about Germany thus: "there is no good news from Germany concerning the basic income matter." Despite broad intellectual debates about minimum-income provisions, publically rewarded "civic work," negative income taxes in the form of a citizen's income, and public subsidies for low-income jobs, the bottom line in Germany was that none of the proposals that remotely came close to unconditional basic schemes made it into public, political debates.

In Denmark, basic income never got onto "the agenda of practical politics" (Christensen and Loftager 2000: 257); in France, basic income also appeared to be a nonstarter for formal political debate despite support from some associations and unemployment groups (Euzéby 2000). Finally, in Belgium, the two-year old and barely notable political party VIVANT won 2 percent of the votes in 1999 on a platform almost solely devoted to the introduction of an unconditional basic income (Vanderborght 2000). Despite this "victory" of sorts, attributed primarily to the media's attention to the personality of Roland Duchâtelet, Vanderborght concluded that the emergence of VIVANT on the political scene contributed little to public discussion of the unconditional basic income, which dropped out of public attention after the election.

On the whole, on the basis of contributors to van der Veen and Groot (2000a), a case could be made for mildly optimistic or hopeful to downright bleak prospects for adoption and implementation of basic income schemes with the best hope embedded in more piecemeal income-maintenance schemes targeting specific vulnerable groups rather than universal coverage. A subsequent assessment of political viability of basic income schemes that took into account developments in the early 2000s reaffirmed the guarded optimism, suggesting outright that an incremental or "stealth" approach might make the most sense to increase its likelihood of gaining political traction (Caputo 2007).

The Altered Socioeconomic Environment

Since the late 1990s, many of the socioeconomic problems faced by European welfare states have deteriorated and extended beyond the EU, particularly with global-wide recessions and the housing and financial crises in the first decade of the 2000s, exacerbated in part by highly speculative mortgage-and-credit-related practices in the United States (Gross 2009; Hyman 2011). Most of the early 2000s were characterized on the one hand by rising and longer-term unemployment and increased income inequality and on the other hand by national priorities focused on deficit and tax reduction: in 2010, for example, gross government debt as a share of GDP exceeded 100 percent in Greece (143 percent) and Italy (119 percent), with the United States (96 percent) and the Eurozone (85 percent) not too far behind; and budget deficits as a share of GDP exceeded 10 percent in Ireland (32.4 percent), Greece (10.5 percent), and Briton (10.4 percent), with Spain (9.2 percent), Portugal (9.1 percent), and the United States (8.9 percent) not far behind (Bowley and Alderman 2011). Many countries across the globe were reported to have expenditures exceeding revenues (Central Intelligence Agency 2011).

Over the past decade or two, there has been a notable shift in how these socioeconomic issues are cast in industrialized countries, affecting the boundaries of acceptable or viable policy responses. Culpability is cast at the level of individual responsibility vis-à-vis consequences of systemic socioeconomic conditions, whether, for example, in regard to poverty resulting from individual behavior of welfare recipients (Lens 2000) or intermittent low-wage work for members of the working class (Jones 2011). Social responsibility is thereby minimized. Market values that stress individual choice and responsibility have increased their saliency while government has been denigrated in the public eye (Draut 2005).

Longtime policy analysts of the US welfare state Theodore Marmor and Jerry Mashaw (2011) observed that the political rhetoric favoring government responsibility for ensuring shared risk and mutual obligations that had characterized earlier welfare-state reform efforts in the United States and elsewhere has been eclipsed by rhetoric emphasizing individual choice, agency, and preferences; national governments or the state are cast as an alien presence standing between citizens and realization of individual ambitions. The overriding rhetoric on the global-level concern on budgeting emphasized the need for national governments and by extension provincial and other levels of government to live within their means, thereby shifting what had been viewed as collective responsibility for ensuring economic well being and medical care access across family structural types to individuals and families themselves. The chapters in this book were written against this backdrop of global socioeconomic uncertainty and generalized reluctance by national governments to expand welfare state functions, despite efforts by members of BIEN network affiliates and others.

What to Expect in This Book

In chapter 2, De Wispelaere and Noguera construct an analytical framework that affords a systematic way of thinking about the political feasibility of adopting and implementing an unconditional basic income scheme. De Wispelaere and Noguera wrote their chapter while other authors were preparing their chapter contributions. Nonetheless, as will be noted in my summaries and commentaries below, many of the concerns raised by De Wispelaere and Noguera's framework are interwoven throughout each of the chapters.

De Wispelaere and Noguera create a typology of political feasibility, namely strategic, institutional, psychological, and behavioral, varying by dimensions—reflecting on the one hand two types of agency and on the other hand two types of constraints. Types of agency contrast discreet (identifiable political actors with distinctive interests, roles, capacities, and intentions) vis-à-vis diffuse (an amorphous set of actors with little or no apparent coordination or collective action); types of constraints, prospective (those that affect the probability of a policy's adoption) vis-à-vis retrospective (those that affect the functioning and resiliency of adopted policies). Strategic and institutional forms of political feasibility are associated with discreet agency; psychological and behavioral forms of political feasibility are associated with diffuse agency; strategic and psychological, with prospective constraints; and institutional and behavioral with retrospective constraints.

With the aid of the aforementioned typology, De Wispelaere and Noguera recommend where advocates of basic income should focus their efforts to increase the likelihood of getting onto the political agenda and adopting related legislation. For example, strategic feasibility can be enhanced by further discussions about and analyses of efforts to building enduring political coalitions. The related discussion of the problem of "cheap political support" is most useful in this regard. Institutional feasibility suggests that implementation of a basic income scheme whole cloth is more problematic than advocates claim, given political and financial commitments to the existing array of social welfare policies and programs in many countries. As will be seen in several of the contributions to this book, such as Brazil (Suplicy, chapter 3) and the

Netherlands (van Hasslet, chapter 8), piecemeal approaches might have greater success. Psychological feasibility focuses on framing Basic Income Guarantee (BIG)-related issues so as to obtain broad social support and offset seemingly embedded dispositions such as those for reciprocity. Finally, behavioral feasibility refers to how basic income schemes will affect labor incentives and labor-force participation. What percentage of a country's population can become "surfers" (living off an unconditional basic income with no other substantive contribution to society's productive capacity) without eroding the economic surplus necessary to support them?

Parts Two and Three follow: Hopes and Realities. Part Two, Hopes, comprises of two chapters whose authors contend that the aforementioned deterioration of socioeconomic conditions across the globe increases the political prospects for adopting an unconditional basic income scheme. The perennially optimistic Brazilian senator Eduardo Suplicy was instrumental in passage of unconditional basic income legislation in Brazil in 2004 (Suplicy 2005), the only adopted national-level legislation to date (though unfunded). In chapter 3, Senator Suplicy contends that basic income guarantees make political and economic sense in underdeveloped countries at this particular historical juncture of increased global competiveness. As evidence, the senator highlights income transfer programs in developed countries, such as the Earned Income Tax Credit in the United States and more importantly the Alaskan Permanent Fund both of which are noted below and further elaborated in chapter 15. In chapter 4, BIEN cofounder Guy Standing (also elaborated elsewhere: 2011) portends dire consequences of social unrest, particularly in more affluent countries as working and middle class citizens experience declines in their economic well being and an erosion of social protections.

The 11 chapters of this volume that make up Part Three, Realities, are case studies that highlight political prospects of adopting and implementing unconditional basic income schemes in specific countries against on the one hand rising and longer-term unemployment throughout the first decade of the 2000s and on the other hand national priorities focused on deficit reduction. Chapters 5 through 9 cover EU nations; chapters 10 through 15, other OECD countries; and chapter 16, Iran.

In chapter 5, Markku Ikkala examines 20 years of political discourse primarily among Finland's politicians during parliamentary elections and to a lesser extent among researchers and societal thinkers. Intermittent political support came primarily from fringe parties, namely the Green Party and the Young Finnish Party, with little political appeal among the population at large despite occasional support from the press. Supportive politicians seemed sensitive to framing issues, indicated by cautiousness when using terms such as "basic income" or "citizens' salary" to promote the idea, but found little traction nonetheless as basic income faded to and from the formal political agenda as mainstream coalition governments were decidedly against any such measure. Ikkala reports some public support for basic income when tied to simplifying Finland's social security system and removing other benefits, but any basic income scheme that provided unconditional support failed or was summarily rejected, in part because so much of welfare-state provisioning had conditionality as a component and because of the strength of the "Lutheran work ethic."

In chapter 6, Sascha Liebermann reports that in Germany, no formal legislation or related legislative initiatives for basic income have ever been proposed, despite academic and public discussions since the 1970s and more concentrated advocacy efforts stressing its unconditional component and greater public exposure since 2005. Liebermann contrasts the concerted efforts to broaden public support for and get basic income on the political agenda in the 1980s with those of the early 2000s. He notes that public intellectuals who have supported efforts for basic income as a social provision in the 1980s, such as Jürgen Habermas, Oskar Negt, or Günter Grass, were notably absent in the grass roots–advocacy efforts since 2005. Liebermann reports that conditionality and reciprocity are viewed as main stumbling blocks to garner a critical mass or tipping point of public support for basic income schemes. In an era when governments are preoccupied with costs, Liebermann contends, advocates for basic income in Germany and by extension elsewhere throughout the EU face an additional challenge to garner sufficient public support that would increase the likelihood of placing basic income on the political agenda.

In chapter 7, activist scholars Seán Healy and Brigid Reynolds update efforts in Ireland to get basic income back on the political agenda despite the drastic downturn in the economy with the mortgage bubble (Kinsella and Leddin 2010; O'Sullivan 2010). After a review of earlier political deliberations, commissioned reports, and activist efforts, all in which they had participated, Healy and Reynolds suggest several concrete pathways that advocates can pursue to increase the likelihood of adopting and implementing an unconditional basic income guarantee for Ireland. They identify three basic strategies, namely an "all-at-once" or comprehensive approach (outright end of current system of social provisioning and immediate replacement with basic income scheme), a "by groups" approach (e.g., children and elderly), and a "gradual" approach that entails a piecemeal dismantling of the current system while concomitantly building up a basic income system. Although Healy and Reynolds prefer the gradual approach, they show that the "by groups" approach that builds upon currently existing social welfare provisioning to children and elderly persons can have both political and popular appeal. The key to political feasibility would be integrating the tax and welfare systems in such a way that refundable tax credits can be granted to low-income individuals and their families. Healy and Reynolds highlight results of a study (Social Justice Ireland 2010) showing how this could be done.

In chapter 8, Michiel van Hasslet notes that in the Netherlands the increased use of conditionality and lower levels of benefits characterize contemporary politics about social welfare provisioning. This is in sharp contrast to a more hopeful optimism for a basic income guarantee that emerged in the 1990s. Van Hasslet contends that Dutch politicians' reluctance or refusal to admit that politics itself cannot initiate or enhance job growth to reach anything near-full employment levels is a main deterrent for adopting basic income legislation. Like Suplicy and Standing in their contributions to this volume, van Hasslet maintains a hopeful optimism that current socioeconomic conditions associated with sustained higher levels of unemployment will compel politicians to think out of the box, so to speak, and take up serious consideration of basic income legislation that the "down-to-earth" Dutch are likely to support.

In chapter 9, Daniel Raventós, Julie Wark, and David Casassas show how in the Kingdom of Spain the present economic crisis (over 20 percent unemployment) and the ensuing economic policy measures introduced by the Spanish government as of May 2010 (deficit reduction) created a two-way shift in the debate on basic income. On the one hand, basic income has virtually disappeared from the official agenda; on the other hand, there is greater interest in it among the activists of quite a wide range of social movements. Raventós, Wark, and Casassas discuss the introduction of basic income legislative in autonomous regions, such as in Catalonia in 2002, and two in the Spanish parliament, one in 2005 and the other in 2007, all to no policy producing avail, but nonetheless, greater public attention and focus on the issue. They highlight the pros (enhancing full citizenship or reducing the likelihood of domination by others with economic means among other "weighty" reasons like poverty reduction and increased consumption) and cons (encourages freeloading, too costly, and attracts too many poor immigrants) of the debates about basic income. Raventós, Wark, and Casassas end their contribution with a discussion of how activists might increase public support to get basic income on the political agenda, especially in economically challenging times.

Other OECD countries in this volume include Australia, Canada, Mexico, Japan, the United Kingdom, and the United States. In chapter 10, John Tomlinson chronicles the development of social welfare provisioning in Australia since the early 1900s and highlights the pendulum-like swings of competing ideologies about universal provision of pensions and targeted, means-tested programs that have accompanied that development. Basic income got on the political agenda in Australia in 1975 when several inquiries and reports highly critical of the categorical, means-tested approach to social welfare provisioning came to public attention. The Australian government changed hands, however, from scandal-beset Gough Whitlam Labor to Malcolm Fraser Liberal-Country Party Coalition, thereby eclipsing concerns of and momentum for basic income schemes. Fiscal restraint characterized government activity throughout most of the 1980s and the 1990s. In addition to cost, the main obstacles against formal political consideration and adoption of basic income include Australia's privatized superannuation-pension system and the "ideological maelstrom" that infuses discussions about social welfare provisioning, migration, the work ethic, age, race, and gender, in general. Tomlinson concludes that universal basic income is no longer a viable policy option in the foreseeable future in Australia.

In chapter 11, James P. Mulvale and Yannick Vanderborght show that in Canada basic income proposals received serious political consideration and sustained public attention not only in the 1970s when as noted above basic income schemes were also on the political agenda in the United States, but also in 2000 and again in 2007, when they received far greater political traction than in the United States. Basic income proposals surfaced in reports of the Senate Sub-Committee on Cities and in a House of Commons Committee. The Green Party is the only federal-level party that explicitly endorses basic income. Nonetheless, one of the most ardent supporters is Senator Hugh Segal from the Conservative Party who proposed a feasibility of a basic income guarantee in 2008. Mulvale and Vanderborght also highlight efforts to adopt basic income legislation at provincial levels in Canada, not only most prominently in Quebec but also to lesser extents in British Columbia and Alberta. They also examine the roles of trade unions and labor, think tanks and academia, and feminists in promoting the idea of basic income. A fear that adoption of a basic income scheme would leave many poor persons, in general, and low-income working persons, in particular, worse off than would be the case under slightly more generous social welfare provisioning has persisted since the mid-1980s and in effect has served to preclude adoption of a full-fledged basic income scheme in the immediate or foreseeable future in Canada. Nonetheless, Mulvale and Vanderborght offer several recommendations to get basic income on the political agenda again, including reintroducing the universal child benefit program that had ended in 1993 and setting an income floor below which no Canadian would be allowed to fall.

In chapter 12, Toru Yamamori highlights social welfare state developments in post–WW II Japan, paying particular attention to the role of interests groups as theorized by political scientist Theodore Lowi (1969). In any meaningful sense, basic income arrives on the scene in Japan only in the early 2000s, with the appearance of publications by academics and the rise of Precariat movements calling for basic income with regulation for labor protection. Standing (2011) provides a more global overview of the rapidly growing number or class of people facing lives of income insecurity moving in and out of jobs he refers to as the Precariat. In Japan, television and Internet media picked up the discussion about basic income. Yamamori highlights several news forums and blogs in which he participated. For the most part, however, formal political interest in basic income has been minimal. A minor or fringe political party, Shinto Nippon adopted basic income in its platform in 2009. Yamamori stresses the need to build public support for basic income in Japan and views the Internet as a viable mechanism to increase public awareness in such a way as to overcome several stumbling blocks, including an entrenched work ethic that distains any proposal perceived as promoting "free riding." In Keynesian fashion, Yamamori recommends tying basic income to increasing demand (consumption) and thereby raising productivity as a way of gaining public support for basic income measures.

In chapter 13, Pablo Yanes shows how deliberations about and specific proposals for a basic income in Mexico City in the early 2000s provided a context or backdrop for national-level initiatives advanced by the Democratic Revolution Party and Elsa Conde, the Social Democrat Alternative Party. Although neither proposal was discussed by Congress, Yanes notes that such proposals at the national level in Mexico signified a symbolic victory of sorts, given the emancipatory rhetoric that accompanies the proposals and broadens the base of public support. Yanes identifies shortcomings of conditional programs targeting children and elderly persons, in particular *Oportunidades* and *Setenta y Más*, and he sees basic income as a viable alternative to them. Yanes stresses the importance of gaining public support and highlights such efforts. Basic income has reached the general public through the media, especially to a radio program that has held related weekly discussions for three years. Significant coverage is also given to *Setenta y Más* that has universal features built into its pensions for senior citizens. Yanes acknowledges that the leap from such pensions for seniors to basic income for all unconditionally faces many challenges in Mexico and that the major battles will be cultural, overcoming the Biblical mandate to the effect that he who does not work does not eat.

In chapter 14, Malcolm Torry recounts the history of Family Allowance / Child Benefit programs in the United Kingdom. Modifications and developments in these programs over several decades nurtured a growing understanding that universal benefits experience high take up, that they are simple, cheap to administer, avoid stigma, ameliorate the poverty, and reduce unemployment traps. Torry sees the political sustainability of the Child Benefit as a model for adoption of a universal income benefit, which in the United Kingdom is considered under proposals for Citizen's Income, even though proposals for an adult-related Tax Credit policy was not adopted in the 1970s. Torry notes that a Citizen's Income has never been the subject of a government green paper (consultation document), but has been discussed by parliamentary select committees, and there are lessons to be gleaned from those discussions. He provides a parallel discussion of guaranteed income schemes from the 1940s, with a 1943 minority report by Lady Juliet Rhys-Williams, secretary of the Women's Liberal Federation, which advanced the idea of a wage subsidy to provide an income floor below which no working adult would fall. Williams' son Sir Brandon Rhys Williams, a Conservative member of Parliament, recommended a personal allowance to several subcommittees for deliberation in the 1980s. Torry notes that the absence of a ministerial champion hampered more extensive parliamentary discussion about adopting a Citizen's Income, since subcommittee reports basically languished there. Despite lack of formal political debates, discussions about the merits of adopting a Citizen's Income continue to occur among academics and in think tanks. Torry highlights activists' efforts aimed at promoting public awareness and support about the merits of universal programs, at the least to retain the Child Benefit and with some measured optimism for adopting a Citizen's Income.

In chapter 15, I discuss how the United States nearly adopted a basic income scheme in the late 1960s and the early 1970s when the Richard Nixon administration sought to nationalize the federal-sponsored, state-administered social welfare program that had provided cash benefits to low-income families, primarily nonworking single mothers with young through adolescent children. I highlight the centrality of reciprocity and priority given to labor-force attachment as contributing to the loss of popular support for the idea of an unconditional basic income guarantee and show how alternative policies such as the Earned Income Tax Credit, were adopted that fit more readily into a cluster of values and a history of social welfare provisioning associated with individual responsibility and with conditionality. The Alaska Permanent Fund, which annually distributes cash income as dividends to all citizens of Alaska who meet basic residency requirements, is briefly discussed, given that it is the subject of another book in the Palgrave Exploring the Basic Income series (Widerquist and Howard 2012). The chapter ends with a discussion of attempts in the early 2000s to get the idea of basic income back on the political agenda and concludes that any such ideas or concrete proposals are political nonstarters in the United States for the foreseeable future.

Finally, in chapter 16, Hamid Tabatabai highlights the cash subsidy program enacted in 2010 in Iran, the only country outside the OECD in this book. He contends that the subsidy program serves as a de facto basic income program for all household heads. Tabatabai suggests that this program can form the basis of an unconditional basic income program for individuals. The cash subsidy program was passed as part of a larger legislative package designed to end price supports and reduce consumption (primarily fuel), despite fears of portended excessive inflation. This raises the prospect of whether a basic income scheme gains greater political traction when tied to solving identifiable social problems rather than by blanket appeals to liberty. Tabatabai also discusses problematic aspects of implementing of the cash subsidy program, which mandated relatively generous cash subsidies not only to household heads, but also to producers and municipal utilities that had also faced the prospect of lost price subsidies. As implemented, it became increasingly clear that the universality of payments, their relatively high level, and overestimation of anticipated revenues strained the financial footing of the program. The mixed consequences of the program (some inflation, some reduced consumption, and the uncertainty of its distributional effects on lower income households) have kept the program in the public eye, so to speak. Whether the universal cash subsidy program will be kept beyond the March 2011–March 2012 budget year is unknown, despite overall popular support as more household heads seem to be taking advantage of the program. Nonetheless, Tabatabai analysis suggests that a transition from cash subsidies based on households to basic incomes to individuals is plausible, especially if tied to resolutions of other social problems such as income inequality.

References

Andersson, Jan-Otto. 2000. "The History of an Idea: Why Did Basic Income Thrill the Finns, but Not the Swedes?" In *Basic Income on the Agenda: Policy Options and Political Feasibility*, edited by Robert J. van der Veen and Loek Groot, 224–237. Amsterdam: Amsterdam University Press.

Bowley, Graham, and Liz Alderman. 2011, September 30. "In European Crisis, Experts See Little Hope for a Quick Fix." *The New York Times*, A1, A8.

Caputo, Richard K. 2006. Review of *The Origins of Universal Grants*, by John Cunliffe and Guido Erreygers. *Basic Income Studies* 1(1): Article 14.

———. 2007. "The Death Knoll of BIG or BIG by Stealth: A Preliminary Assessment of UBIG Viability around the Globe." *USBIG Discussion Paper No. 162*. http://www.usbig.net/papers/162-Caputo-Stealth.pdf.

Central Intelligence Agency. 2011. *World Fact Book: Budget*. https://www.cia.gov/library/publications/the-world-factbook/fields/2056.html.

Christensen, Erik, and Jørn Loftager. 2000. "Ups and Downs of Basic Income in Denmark." In *Basic Income on the Agenda: Policy Options and

Political Feasibility, edited by Robert J. van der Veen and Loek Groot, 257–267. Amsterdam: Amsterdam University Press.
Cunliffe, John, and Guido Erreygers. 2004. *The Origins of Universal Grants.* Basingstoke, UK: Palgrave Macmillan.
Draut, Tamara. 2005. "The Triumph of Market Values and the Denigration of Government." *Boston Review* 30 (5). http://bostonreview.net/BR30.5/draut.php.
Euzéby, Chantal. 2000. "What Reforms are Needed for the Minimum Insertion Income (RMI) in France?" In *Basic Income on the Agenda: Policy Options and Political Feasibility*, edited by Robert J. van der Veen and Loek Groot, 268–275. Amsterdam: Amsterdam University Press.
Gross, Daniel. 2009. *Dumb Money: How Our Greatest Financial Minds Bankrupt the Nation.* New York: Free Press.
Healy, Seán, and Brigid Reynolds. 2000. "From Concept to Green Paper: Putting Basic Income on the Agenda in Ireland." In *Basic Income on the Agenda: Policy Options and Political Feasibility*, edited by Robert J. van der Veen and Loek Groot, 238–246. Amsterdam: Amsterdam University Press.
Hyman, Louis. 2011. *Debtor Nation: The History of America in Red Ink.* Princeton: Princeton University Press.
Jones, Owen. 2011. *CHAVS: The Demonization of the Working Class.* London: Verso Books.
Kinsella, Stephen, and Anthony Leddin. 2010. "Introduction." In *Understanding Ireland's Economic Crisis*, edited by Stephen Kinsella and Anthony Leddin, 1–11. Dublin: Blackhall Publishing.
Lens, V. 2000. "Welfare Reform and the Media: A Content Analysis of Two Newspapers." PhD diss., Yeshiva University. ProQuest (UMI No. 9973140).
Lessenich, Stephan. 2000. "Short Cuts and Wrong Tracks on the Long March to Basic Income: Debating Social Policy Reform in Germany." In *Basic Income on the Agenda: Policy Options and Political Feasibility*, edited by Robert J. van der Veen and Loek Groot, 247–256. Amsterdam: Amsterdam University Press.
Lowi, Theodore J. 1969. *The End of Liberalism: Ideology, Policy, and the Crisis of Public Authority.* New York: Norton.
Marmor, Theodore, and Jerry Mashaw. 2011. "How Do You Say 'Economic Security'?" *New York Times*, September 23, A21.
O'Sullivan, M. 2010. "Ireland's Bubble: The Great Transformation." In *Understanding Ireland's Economic Crisis*, edited by Stephen Kinsella and Anthony Leddin, 12–29. Dublin: Blackhall Publishing.
Social Justice Ireland. 2010. *Building a Fairer Tax System: The Working Poor and the Cost of Refundable Tax Credits.* Dublin: Author.
Standing, Guy. 2011. *The Precariat: The New Dangerous Class.* New York: Bloomsbury USA.
Suplicy, Eduardo Matarazzo. 2005. "The Approval and Sanctioning of the Basic Income in Brazil: How It Will Be Implemented." *USBIG Discussion Paper No. 131.* http://www.usbig.net/papers/131suplicy.pdf.

van der Veen, Robert J., and Loek Groot (eds.). 2000a. *Basic Income on the Agenda: Policy Options and Political Feasibility.* Amsterdam: Amsterdam University Press.

———. 2000b. "Clues and Leads in the Debate on Basic Income in the Netherlands." In *Basic Income on the Agenda: Policy Options and Political Feasibility*, edited by Robert J. van der Veen and Loek Groot, 197–223. Amsterdam: Amsterdam University Press.

Vanderborght, Yannick. 2000. "The VIVANT Experiment in Belgium." In *Basic Income on the Agenda: Policy Options and Political Feasibility*, edited by Robert J. van der Veen and Loek Groot, 276–284. Amsterdam: Amsterdam University Press.

Widerquist, Karl, and Michael Howard. 2012. *Alaska's Permanent Fund Dividend: Examining Its Suitability as a Model (Basic Income Guarantee).* New York: Palgrave Macmillan.

CHAPTER 2

On the Political Feasibility of Universal Basic Income: An Analytic Framework*

Jurgen De Wispelaere and
José Antonio Noguera

For much of the last two decades, debate around the proposal of a universal basic income (BI) centered on arguing the ethical and economic case for instituting a policy that grants each adult citizen a guaranteed income as a right, without a means test or work requirement (Van Parijs 1992, 1995; Dowding et al. 2003; Standing 2005; Widerquist et al. 2005; Ackerman et al. 2006). The question of how to bring about such a policy—the question of political feasibility—has only recently gained traction amongst BI advocates. Leaving aside some notable exceptions, much work remains to be done to further our understanding of the challenges faced by BI advocates and the strategies available to overcome these. In this chapter, we aim to contribute to this enterprise by outlining an analytical framework to think about the political feasibility of BI in a more systematic manner.

We embrace a broad conception of political feasibility according to which a policy is politically feasible when the background conditions are such that there is a reasonable probability of the policy becoming actualized in the foreseeable future. Viewed this way, "feasibility" covers the broad domain where a policy is neither immediately realizable, nor impossible to realize (Brighouse 2004; Gilabert and Lawford-Smith forthcoming). In our view, feasibility is aimed at investigating the factors (e.g., social conditions) that hamper a policy from being actualized, and subsequently, comparing how different policies fare in terms of their probabilities of being actualized given a particular social environment. We adopt a similarly broad notion of "the political" by focusing on those feasibility constraints arising from the human will, as opposed to natural, physical, or technological impediments. The concept of political feasibility embraces the Searlean notion that, not unlike brute natural facts, individual or collective manifestations of the human will are causally relevant in bringing about institutional facts such as BI (Searle 1995, 2010; Brennan and Pettit 2005).

The framework we propose in this chapter is constructed around two key political dimensions that constitute the core of the policy process: agency and constraints. Combined, these dimensions generate a matrix with four types of political feasibility: strategic feasibility, institutional feasibility, psychological feasibility, and behavioral feasibility. Each of these types will be briefly explored in the remainder of this chapter with specific focus on their relevance for BI.

The purpose of the proposed framework is threefold. First, it offers a toolkit to think about political feasibility in a systematic comparative manner, exploring both differences and similarities across types. The proposed typology also allows insight into the dynamic aspects of political feasibility ensuing from the simultaneous or sequential interaction of these different types. Second, when applied to the specific context of BI the insight into these four types of political feasibility offers a better understanding of the many complex challenges faced by those advocating BI schemes. Each type requires a specifically targeted political response, but an appropriate response is complicated considerably by the need to accommodate several types of constraints at the same time, whether simultaneously or sequentially. Third, the typology allows us to assess the current state of knowledge in relation to each type, and identify lacunae (and corresponding research priorities) that need to be addressed in order to better understand the political feasibility of BI. While our aim is to be suggestive rather than exhaustive, this chapter offers a useful tool for exploring [further][1] the political feasibility of BI policies in the concrete cases discussed in the remainder of this volume.

Political Feasibility: A Framework

In this section, we outline our proposed framework for thinking about the political feasibility of BI, graphically represented in table 2.1 below. Let us begin by exploring the two dimensions that construct our typology matrix.

We start from the simple axiom that politics implies agency. In one well-known phrase, politics is the purposeful act of deciding who gets what when (Lasswell 1936). Politics is intimately linked with power, which, in turn, is the ability to produce intentional effects on other people (Dowding 1996). Political power presumes not merely agency in an abstract sense, but concretely at least two agents: those who exert political influence and those who are at its receiving end. On the supply side, different political entrepreneurs—individual, collective, even corporate—employ political resources in an attempt to exert power and influence outcomes. More interesting, however, is the demand side of the equation: those at which political power is addressed and who are the proper subject of specifically designed political strategies. Here, we can distinguish two very different types of agents and agency.

1. *Discrete agency*: Political agency addressed at readily identifiable actors with distinctive interests, roles, capacities, and intentions
2. *Diffuse agency*: Political agency addressed at an amorphous set of actors, a "collective" in the loosest sense of the term, with little or no apparent coordination or collective intention

Discrete agents comprise not only the most visible part of political agents, comprising politicians, policymakers, social movement elites, or bureaucrats, but also clearly identifiable corporate actors such as organizations or distinctive formal institutions (e.g., the executive). By contrast, the typical example of a diffuse agent in the policy process is the general public, which often exhibits the properties of "mass" rather than "collective" behavior. Both types of agencies coexist and interact in a myriad of complex ways to constitute the environment in which political entrepreneurs operate.

The distinction between discrete and diffuse agency is important for understanding the different challenges political entrepreneurs face when exercising political power addressed to each of these groups. Discrete agents are the subject of highly targeted strategies of political power. Strategies aimed at diffuse agents, by contrast, are necessarily less direct and of a broad, "catch-all" format. Where we might think of discrete political agency as similar to a line fisher carefully selecting his bait to capture a particular type of fish, diffuse political agency resembles the trawler fisher who sweeps the ocean floor in the hope to catch as many fish as possible, knowing that much of what he catches may be of little value to him. Nevertheless, even the trawler fisher must carefully select where and when to put out his net to ensure as good a catch as possible. Both approaches require careful strategizing. The main challenge is to simultaneously affect both types of agents.

Moving on to the second dimension, politics takes place between agents in a context that is highly constrained, requiring valuable political resources—time, effort, money, political expertise, and reputation—to be expended in order to achieve intended outcomes. The constraints that make up a particular political environment are again very diverse and can be usefully characterized by adopting a sequential perspective.

1. *Prospective constraints*: Constraints that affect the probability of a policy being instituted
2. *Retrospective constraints*: Constraints that affect both the functioning and resilience of a policy once instituted

Prospective constraints affect the most familiar aspects of the policy process: agenda setting, policy advocacy, coalition building, political negotiation, and legislation. These are the sort of constraints policy advocates face whenever they attempt to move their proposal from the drawing board to its actualization. Retrospective constraints, by contrast, are those background conditions that affect the outcome variables of a particular policy, including whether a particular policy will be vulnerable to internal contradictions or external shocks that may result in it being a very short-lived event. Of course, as with political agency, both sets of constraints coexist in the political environment and typically influence each other in numerous ways.

The distinction between prospective and retrospective constraints bears some interesting similarities with recent work by Erik Olin Wright (2006, 2010) on emancipatory social theory. Wright makes a helpful distinction between the criteria of viability and achievability, both of which can be regarded as a subclass of the concept of political feasibility. Achievability refers to the practical task of realizing a particular policy outcome (or a social transformation), while the criterion of viability "asks of proposals for transforming existing social structures whether, if implemented, they would actually generate in a sustained manner the emancipatory consequences that motivated their proposal" (Wright 2006: 97). Viability enquires into the policy congruence of a particular proposal, the extent to which its outcomes might cohere with or deviate from the stated (or implied) objectives that constitute the reasons for adopting it in the first place. While most theorists debate the value of constructing proposals that may be viable but not achievable (in the short run), equally interesting questions arise when considering proposals that are achievable but perhaps not viable (i.e., they may lead to results that are, all things considered, less than desirable). Mapped onto our framework, we can see that both achievability and viability are necessary conditions and that, in our phrasing, political entrepreneurs must squarely face up to both prospective and retrospective constraints.

Table 2.1 Typology of political feasibility

	Prospective constraints ("achievability")	*Retrospective constraints ("viability")*
Discrete agency	A. Strategic feasibility	B. Institutional feasibility
Diffuse agency	C. Psychological feasibility	D. Behavioral feasibility

The resulting matrix, illustrated in table 2.1, generates the following four types of political feasibility.

A. *Strategic feasibility*: Discrete agency, prospective constraints
B. *Institutional feasibility*: Discrete agency, retrospective constraints
C. *Psychological feasibility*: Diffuse agency, prospective constraints
D. *Behavioral feasibility*: Diffuse agency, retrospective constraints

Strategic and institutional feasibility share a focus on discrete agency. However, where strategic feasibility requires a direct engagement to further a policy, institutional feasibility directs our attention to preexisting sets of rules and regulations that may affect the performance of a policy over time. Similarly, psychological and behavioral feasibility both concentrate on diffuse agency with the general public. The former addresses the psychological processes that *ex-ante* affect popular support of a policy, while the latter is mostly concerned with how behavioral changes *ex-post* affect the performance or continued survival of a policy. In the remainder of this chapter, we examine each of these with a specific focus on BI in mind.

Strategic Feasibility: The Search for a Robust BI Coalition

When thinking about political feasibility, we customarily have some form of strategic feasibility in mind. Political entrepreneurs engaging in all sorts of strategic interventions to build a political coalition enabling the legislation and subsequent implementation of a policy proposal has indeed become one of the hallmarks of modern politics (Sabbatier and Jenkins-Smith 1993). In a very real sense, coalition building constitutes the building block of successful policy advocacy in present-day democracy. Despite this centrality of coalition building, the literature on BI is surprisingly void of systematic discussion of the political strategies required to securing an enduring BI coalition. In this section, we briefly examine a key challenge affecting the strategic feasibility of BI.[2]

When challenged about the political feasibility of BI, its advocates typically refer to numerous instances of individual politicians, political parties, social movements, or interest groups (e.g., trade unions) on record as supportive of BI. This response rapidly takes the form of a simple numbers game, in which the level of support for BI can be read—more or less directly—off the instances of expressed support elicited from such individuals, associations, or organizations. The idea that increased expressed support for BI from a variety of social and political actors is directly conducive to building a sustained political coalition is flawed, however. The reason is that not all instances of expressed support for a policy imply a sustained commitment to promoting this policy. It is one thing for a social or political agent to vocally express a preference in favor of BI, quite a different matter to actively canvass support amongst constituents, party members, or like-minded associations and groups; build a shared platform across political factions; utilize scarce political resources (money, time, and above all political capital) to further the cause; bargain and possibly compromise on other political goals; and so on. Expressed support without either the commitment or the capacity to engage in the necessary political action to build a sustainable coalition around the policy of granting each citizen an unconditional BI is "cheap": it seems of little practical worth to BI advocates.

We may find considerable support for BI in individuals or associations that are often marginally positioned in terms of their ability to influence policy. For instance, Green politicians and parties across Europe typically support BI. However, leaving aside one or two exceptions, European Greens are small protest parties comfortably nested on the side of opposing governing coalitions with little or no direct policy responsibility. Irrespective of the strong links between BI and Green values (Birnbaum 2009; Van Parijs 2009), political support from Green political parties offers BI advocates precious little as a genuine political platform to boost their cause. Or consider support for BI amongst certain trade unions (Vanderborght 2006). Here too, it appears that those unions who support BI are either comparatively small in terms of membership (and thus political leverage) or else operate in a political system in which their policy influence is otherwise constrained; by contrast, larger unions who wield genuine power to engage in policy formation through a variety of corporatist mechanisms appear not to support BI. Counting instances of expressed support might serve a purpose in boosting the morale of those advocating BI, but it remains to be seen whether it produces any further effect.

One might object to this overly pessimistic analysis on the grounds that expressed support from currently marginalized individuals or groups should not be so lightly dismissed. After all, those groups may one day be in a position to genuinely effectuate policy influence, at which point BI support pays off in real terms. However, this argument hinges on the view that political support is sticky, and that political factions who have once expressly supported BI would continue doing so when their power position improves. Unfortunately, there is little reason to think that groups that move up on the political ladder will necessarily sustain their support for BI. For, in the absence of policy responsibility, one's support for BI is cheap in a second relevant sense: there are few political costs associated with supporting BI in an environment in which one is never put in the position of having to defend one's support against a skeptical—at times even hostile—political base, let alone the electorate. This is even more the case when we consider that furthering the case for BI means precious political capital must be spent at the expense of other political objectives. The political opportunity cost of supporting BI once one has achieved a position of policy responsibility may simply prove too high to be politically sustainable. Thus, we likely find the very same parties or politicians who support BI while in opposition suddenly ditching their support when achieving office, typically as part of a governing coalition. In addition, we may plausibly expect a similar scenario in relation to trade unions who become more powerful, in particular given their internal division about BI because of the strong laborist philosophy inherent to most unions.

The fact that cheap political support for BI may not be sufficiently robust to survive a move of its supporters into a position of policy responsibility is not the only problem, however. Worse still, some instances of political support for BI may even be counterproductive as support from one particular faction or group may prevent others from endorsing the same policy. Because political factions generally use identification with policy positions as an instrument to differentiate themselves from their (internal or external) political competitors, support for BI from faction X may prevent faction Y from endorsing a policy that would otherwise naturally fit their political profile. There exists a "first mover disadvantage" to BI being associated with a political faction that is unable to move it up on the policy agenda, when precisely this association prevents more powerful individuals or groups from offering valuable support. In this case, expressed support is not just cheap but represents a real cost in terms of advancing the case for BI. In many countries (e.g., Ireland, Namibia) BI is promoted by groups with a strong religious affiliation, which may well prevent nonconfessional social movements or associations from expressing support. Similarly, BI advocates who adopt a liberal entrepreneurial perspective (e.g., Vivant in Belgium or Götz Werner in Germany) may find it difficult to curry favor with factions endorsing strong socialist values. Initial effects of the identification of BI with one specific faction, combined with the "reactive reluctance" of other factions to support the policy because of such political identification, may produce a form of path dependency that causes BI to be marginalized by association.

The problem of cheap support, as outlined in this section, poses something of an impasse for BI advocates intent on building a robust political coalition. On the one hand, many (if not most) current instances of expressed support may be of little practical use, and in some circumstances could turn "noxious" when support by some factions leads others to oppose rather than support BI. On the other hand, future support of any impact is unlikely in a political environment reluctant to spend political capital on a policy that remains highly divisive, both internally and externally. This makes it difficult to ascertain whose support to seek, and at what price. The underlying concern is that the very reason why political support is relatively easy to come by from marginal political individuals or groups—it is cheap in the sense of expressing such support having few costs attached—is also the reason why such support is relatively worthless to BI advocates. The main challenge to advocates intent on building a robust BI coalition is to find ways to get powerful political agents to express support and simultaneously, to ensure that such support is no longer cheap in either of the two senses canvassed above. Failure to achieve this is one important way in which the strategic feasibility of BI is hampered.

Institutional Feasibility: Implementing the BI Proposal

A second type of political feasibility is of a retrospective nature. Securing a robust enacting coalition of political actors in favor of BI is an important stepping-stone for advancing a BI scheme. However, such a scheme would rapidly prove self-defeating if a BI cannot be implemented in a manner that produces outcomes that are highly congruent with the reasons political actors support a BI in the first place. This brings us squarely to the question of what background institutions must be in place for a BI to produce desired outcomes in terms of combating poverty, unemployment, social exclusion, gender equality, and what not. Institutional feasibility affects both the desirability of BI in a very direct sense, as well as its long-term survival or political resilience. As with strategic feasibility, institutional feasibility is a complex phenomenon capturing a host of different issues, but in this section, we briefly focus on an aspect that is largely ignored in the BI debate, namely the implementation challenges to BI administration.[3]

BI implementation is customarily regarded as unproblematic, in large part, because it is believed a BI fares rather well when compared to more selective forms of social assistance. However, this in no way means the detailed design of a BI is not sensitive to the particulars of the institutional context, as we illustrate in this section. While it avoids many of the complications of selective programs, a BI faces its own set of implementation challenges (De Wispelaere and Stirton 2012a). One important practical challenge arises because BI may be unable to piggyback on existing implementation instruments. The sheer size of the program in practice means that few instruments currently in place have the comprehensive reach that a universal BI requires; moreover, the philosophy underlying BI often proves incompatible with the use of instruments closely associated with a "controlling bureaucracy" (Standing 2002; Offe 2005; Handler and Hasenfeld 2006). The impact of all of this, however, implies a "hard choice" between setting up new institutions from scratch or recombining several administrative instruments in novel ways—in both cases, an administrative challenge fraught with complexity and risk—or, alternatively, compromising on the actual performance of a BI in terms of target efficiency or administrative efficiency, more generally (De Wispelaere and Stirton 2011, 2012a). Let us illustrate the difficulties with several practical examples.

Consider first a variant of BI commonly referred to as PI [Participation Income].[4] A PI comprises an individual entitlement that is not means tested but retains a broad participation requirement going well beyond the conditions of formal employment or full-time education typically associated with entitlement to social assistance (Atkinson 1996). The main argument for adopting a PI instead of a BI has to do with the resistance of the public opinion against giving "something for nothing" (Goodin 2001). Retaining a broad participation requirement looks like a clever strategy for building a coalition between various political factions by combining universal income protection with a commitment to a version of the contribution principle.

Unfortunately, from an implementation perspective, PI rapidly turns into a nightmare scenario (De Wispelaere and Stirton 2007). The notion of a broad participation requirement is difficult to operationalize, leaving us with three main choices. First, introduce a heavy bureaucratic machinery to monitor and control the numerous informal forms of participation that allow citizens to qualify for PI. The administrative apparatus required in this option would exceed anything we witness today in the much-maligned workfare programs.[5] Second, let qualifying conditions for PI mirror existing institutional capacities, effectively reducing PI to little more than entitlement for existing social assistance programs. Third, relax qualifying conditions such that almost any activity is accepted as a valid basis for claiming PI. This solution would turn the participation requirement into a mere formality, and PI would rapidly approximate a genuine BI. While BI advocates naturally favor this third approach (Barry 2001; Van Parijs 2001), other political factions in the coalition may insist on the second or first option. In this scenario, the challenges of institutional feasibility rapidly break down the political coalition around PI (De Wispelaere and Stirton 2007).

Would a genuine unconditional BI escape such worries? Unfortunately, even the fully unconditional model would face important implementation challenges that directly affect the institutional feasibility of BI. Consider three types of bottlenecks that BI implementation needs to address (De Wispelaere and Stirton 2012a, 2012b). First, since BI is meant to cover the whole of the population, we need an updated list (a "cadaster") of every single individual who is entitled to receive the grant: those who do not appear on this list will not receive the BI.[6] Countries vary considerably in their institutional capacity to properly maintain such a list. Some countries have national registers of all citizens, others will have to rely on alternative lists that are typically incomplete (e.g., voting registers or health insurance registers), while others still rely on self-registration. Unsurprisingly, different outcomes result from relying on one solution rather than the other. Second, effective payment tools for disbursing the BI may have difficulties as well. Part of the problem arises in finding a suitable instrument that covers every citizen: although institutional capacity varies considerably, in almost every country a significant part of the population does not have access to a bank account or is too transient to rely on regular postal checks. Here again, BI administrators face hard choices between setting up novel disbursement systems (which incur significant costs and risks of error), combining existing systems without clear indication of how comprehensive the coverage is, or compromising on the target efficiency of BI. Finally, where BI implementation is likely to be imperfect, we still require a monitoring mechanism to ensure that all those entitled to the grant effectively receive it. The emphasis on doing away with bureaucratic interventions means BI advocates customarily underestimate the positive role of monitoring in this sense. As before, institutional capabilities vary extensively across countries, with some almost entirely relying on so-called "police patrol" mechanisms of routine surveillance and others operating primarily with "fire alarm" type of monitoring devices in which those who fail to receive the grant themselves sound the alarm (Lupia and McCubbins 2004; De Wispelaere and Stirton 2012a, 2012b).

The extent to which these three types of bottleneck affect the performance of BI depends crucially on the institutional constellation in which the scheme is implemented. Institutional feasibility can be improved in two main ways. One way is by adjusting the details of the BI proposal to not overreach the capabilities of the implementation system. However, this solution may require BI advocates to compromise on the scope of the proposal, and we can expect understandable reluctance to proceed along this route. The alternative is to boost the institutional capabilities themselves, but this in turn may run into several practical and political problems—not in the least, the cost of upgrading the administrative system. Furthermore, where bureaucratic investments may resolve some of the capability concerns, persistent limits to public administration often defy simple technological upgrades (Hood 2010). In either case, the implementation of BI is an inherently political problem in which institutional limits impose hard choices on decision makers (De Wispelaere and Stirton 2011, 2012a). These choices in turn will affect several individuals or groups differently, and thus also shape the political opportunities for securing a robust coalition in favor of BI. Institutional and strategic feasibility are intricately related: decisions that affect one type will likely affect the other.

Psychological Feasibility: Legitimating the BI Proposal

So far, we have covered two types of discrete agency capturing the notions of strategic and institutional feasibility, respectively. However, even if the proponents of BI successfully meet the challenges of strategic and institutional feasibility, the BI proposal must also withstand the test of psychological feasibility, a prospective form of diffuse agency. Psychological feasibility, as conceptualized here, concerns the legitimation of a policy through securing a broad level of social acceptance among the general public. The legitimation of BI is often called into question (Liebig and Mau 2005; De Wispelaere 2009), and the challenge of psychological feasibility is to convince the public at large that BI is a normatively attractive and practically effective policy.

There are three reasons for taking psychological feasibility seriously. First, in a modern democracy, it would be difficult to defend the imposition of a BI against strong opposition of the public opinion. Persistent substantial disagreement about what constitutes a just policy implies that the legitimate institution of a BI would have to win broad majoritarian support. Second, the importance of securing approval of the public opinion is taken very seriously by political agents and decision makers in democratic societies where taxpayers and voters have access to political mechanisms to demand or resist particular policies. Political entrepreneurs will want to make sure that BI has sufficient public support before committing to promoting its case, which directly impacts on the strategic feasibility of BI as previously discussed. Third, illegitimate policies often fail because those subject to them refuse to play by the rules. Individuals could subvert policy outcomes in numerous ways. The PI proposal, briefly mentioned in the previous section, serves as a perfect example of a scheme that would allow many to claim the grant while only engaging in a "token" form of social participation. Instances of "creative compliance" are likely to increase exponentially where the policy is deemed illegitimate. In the case of an unconditional BI, those who are literally living off their BI face increased social pressure if the scheme itself fails to attract broad social support. This would effectively pervert one of the main reasons why many advocate BI—its capacity to fight social exclusion (Jordan 1996; Van Parijs 1996).

Psychological feasibility entails the capacity to mobilize positive perceptions, emotions, and reasons such that the proposal does not generate strong social opposition. Two types of constraints hamper the psychological feasibility of BI. A familiar type of constraint consists of "contingent" public opinion embedded in a given sociohistorical context. Diverging ideological perspectives on economic distribution, for instance, affect the support for BI or perhaps the particular type of BI supported.[7] A second type of constraint is rooted in the deep structure of human psychology and therefore less fluid, although clever institutional design may be able to manipulate the triggers that activate particular responses. In the remainder of this section, we elaborate a little on the constraints rooted in basic psychological dispositions.

One key disposition that easily conflicts with a BI is the reciprocity norm. Reciprocity is a psychological disposition expressed across different social contexts in the form of the work ethic, the contribution principle, or the deservingness principle. Survey research shows repeatedly that paid work remains a core value among the population in advanced welfare states. This strongly suggests that BI advocates face an uphill battle trying to make the full version of the proposal understood and accepted by the general public. Most people believe work constitutes a central obligation toward society and that social benefits should be restricted to those who really "need" them or "deserve" them (van Oorschot 2000, 2006; Clasen and van Oorschot 2002; Fong et al. 2005; Slothuus 2007). For instance, Liebig and Mau (2005) show that while most people agree that the state should provide a guaranteed minimum income, most nevertheless reject the provision of such an income in the form of a BI independent of level of need or contribution.[8] Interestingly, such attitudes appear to be independent of the objective socioeconomic interests of particular social groups. This poses an intriguing paradox for BI supporters, for precisely those social groups whose support we would like to "strategically" enlist based on their objective interests, turn out to be those who are more likely to "psychologically" reject BI. It is for this reason that many propose that BI proposals increase their political feasibility by recoupling income to work (or social participation) and making BI more sensitive to notions of deservingness and need (Atkinson 1996; Goodin 2003; White 2003).

It would be tempting to think that BI supporters should merely regard the existing dispositional context as an immutable wall. "People don't like free lunches, therefore BI is a non-starter." However, this sort of argument fails to take into account the many ways in which we can purposefully affect public opinion. How should BI supporters go about resolving the apparent conflict between the idea of an unconditional BI and psychological dispositions that favor reciprocity and deservingness? One answer is provided by the extensive literature on the role of framing in the policy process (Chong and Druckman 2007a, 2007b; Jerit 2009). Carefully framing BI proposals to avoid triggering negative perceptions, values, and beliefs and instead trigger positive dispositions may significantly improve the psychological feasibility of BI. For instance, framing BI alternatively as a social heritage, a natural dividend, an antipoverty measure, or a citizenship right might produce different levels of social support, while the distributive outcomes of the policy remain unchanged. Equally, the particular implementation of a BI—for example, BI received integrated in the tax rebate or as a social benefit—might also affect the public perception of the scheme. Furthermore, "sequential implementation" might be easier to frame (Vanderborght 2005): separately instituting a universal child benefit, a universal basic pension, a guaranteed minimum income for those under the poverty line, and a tax credit for low-income workers might be acceptable, where a direct move toward a full BI would be opposed.

Framing effects are only one type of psychological mechanism that affects the psychological feasibility of introducing a BI. Many other mechanisms familiar from the literature on heuristics and cognitive biases are applicable to the psychological feasibility of BI (Kahneman and Tversky 2000).[9] Some of these psychological mechanisms can be expected to work in favor of BI, others to work against it; but in each case, clever design and framing of the BI may ensure the reinforcement of positive triggers and the weakening (or silencing) of negative triggers.

Behavioral Feasibility: BI Effects on Incentives to Work

The fourth and final dimension of political feasibility we term behavioral feasibility. This retrospective form of diffuse feasibility is concerned with anticipating the potentially negative effects of a BI on individuals' behavior after implementation. The general idea is that, for a BI to be behaviorally feasible, it must neither produce perverse or counterproductive effects, nor fail to produce key desired outcomes. Similar to institutional feasibility, either of these failures would negatively affect the viability and political resilience of the BI. Behavioral feasibility is of the utmost importance, for a BI is expected to provoke changes in a vast range of social dimensions: labor-market performance, family composition, education, participation in voluntary work or the shadow economy, tax compliance, and geographical mobility. Behavioral feasibility, as we understand it, is primarily concerned with the incentives affecting the "robustness" of a given policy, where robustness is a form of internal stability in virtue of the capacity to continue functioning when initial conditions change.

Behavioral robustness is achieved when the design of a policy explicitly avoids providing agents with incentives that undermine its existence conditions. In short, behavioral robustness prevents a policy from becoming self-defeating. Self-regulating strategies, such as the indexing of benefit levels or surveillance by external agencies, are examples of mechanisms to increase behavioral robustness in policy design. Unfortunately, a behaviorally robust strategy or policy mechanism may not be attractive in the short term, in spite of its long-term effectiveness or efficiency. Here behavioral feasibility comes into conflict with the dimensions of strategic, institutional, or psychological feasibility, outlined in previous sections. For instance, consider the introduction of a BI with the level of the grant indexed to a macroeconomic performance indicator such as labor-market participation, which effectively operates as a "policy thermostat." This design may enhance behavioral feasibility when a decrease of productivity or labor-market participation is reflected in a subsequent decrease in the BI level, which then induces (some) individuals to take up formal employment again in order to top up their BI with a wage. However, this thermostat design complicates strategic or psychological feasibility, making it more difficult for BI advocates to find political allies or secure public-opinion support for a benefit whose value may fluctuate considerably with aggregate economic performance.

As the preceding example suggests, the most salient behavioral problem pertains to how a BI will affect labor incentives and labor participation. What if the introduction of a BI engenders a significant surfer effect (Van Parijs 1995) such that a large number of individuals decide to "live off their BI" without making a productive contribution to society. If this number were sufficiently high, the strict economic feasibility of a BI funded through a general income tax would be seriously undermined. Indexing the BI as outlined before only partly accommodates this problem, for a high number of "surfers" would likely drive the BI amount down to a level significantly lower than the subsistence level, which may not realize the many positive effects attributed to BI (Groot and Van der Veen 2000; Groot 2004). One avenue of response to such concerns is to deny that the surfer effect will reach such dramatic proportions. Unfortunately, this may offer the BI advocate little solace, for even a tiny minority of surfers has the potential to deal a serious blow to the long-term feasibility of BI.[10] For starters, the perception of surfing may have a snowballing effect causing more to engage in similar behavior: "If they can do it, so can I." More importantly, the perception of surfing will likely foster a public rejection of BI and thus directly affect its psychological feasibility. "There would be no surer way to lose popular and political support...than with a few well-publicized cases of young people blowing their grants on cocaine or wild holidays" (Le Grand and Nissan 2003: 37). It is easy to see, then, that far from BI being neutral between different ways of leading one's life—different conceptions of the good life, as the political philosophers have it—a robust BI is likely to conform to conventions and social norms endorsed by the society.

However, the question remains whether the widespread perception of BI leading to a sustained surfer effect is correct. At this point, both BI advocates and their critics do well to acknowledge upfront significant uncertainty concerning the behavioral effects of a policy proposal that has nowhere been implemented in full.[11] In this context, highly stylized econometric models have serious limitations as macrolevel social dynamics rarely mirror microlevel individual behavior and motivations (Coleman 1990; Hedström 2005; Hedström and Bearman 2009). An interesting alternative is to conduct field experiments like the 1970s and the 1980s Negative Income Tax (NIT) experiments in the United States and Canada (Pechman and Timpane 1975; Robins et al. 1980; Robins 1985). However, the results of these experiments are difficult to interpret and vulnerable to "miscommunication" by politicians and scholars (Widerquist 2005). In addition, the difficulty and costs of replicating the experiments constitutes a major shortcoming of this methodology (Noguera and De Wispelaere 2006). Our preferred method is to explore behavioral feasibility through agent-based social simulations (Axelrod 1997; Hedström 2005; Macy and Flache 2009).[12] Unlike econometric models, agent-based models (ABM) allow us to realistically model the complexity of social interaction and its recursive effects on behavior. Particularly relevant for BI research is that ABM is especially useful for modeling hypothetical situations and answering "what-if" questions.

To illustrate the relevance of ABM for BI research, consider four important behavioral issues. First, the provision of BI funded out of income taxation can be modeled as a social dilemma in which a rational agent with moderate preferences for work (or income) may be interested in "free riding" on a moderate BI, provided the level of BI does not decrease below subsistence following increased free riding by others (González-Bailón, Noguera, and De Wispelaere 2011). In this scenario, rational agents need to pay attention to others' labor decisions when solving their income-leisure trade-off, and the ABM modeling of BI provision produces important insights in the social stability of different types of labor strategies. Second, ABM is also well suited for modeling the importance of social influence and the role of social networks in relation to BI. Research has shown that labor-market behavior is strongly affected by social influence (Aronson et al. 1999; Grodner and Kniesner 2006). ABM research usefully supplements econometric studies focused on "isolated agents" by demonstrating how individuals respond to social influence under particular BI conditions.

Third, ABM takes into account the motivational heterogeneity of agents. Instead of assuming that agents have an artificial similarity across the population, ABM allows us to model different types of agents in terms of attitudes to work attitudes. In addition, ABM models variability in agents' prosocial motivations or attitudes toward distributive justice (Camerer and Fehr 2004; Lindenberg 2006), which interact in complex ways with heterogeneous work inclinations to produce a wide range of labor-market decisions. Even with a substantial BI, it does not automatically follow that a population of heterogeneous agents would produce the disastrous effects on aggregate labor behavior presupposed by the critics. Finally, ABM is a particularly useful tool for evaluating the expected behavioral outcomes of a BI when compared to selective policies such as workfare. Careful modeling of the incentives associated with each type of policy may reveal unexpected findings.[13] In addition, comparing BI with its main competitors through ABM modeling offers important insights that remain obscured by looking at each separately.

The general lesson of this section is that the macrosocial outcomes of BI's behavioral effects cannot be assumed a priori, but should be tested through empirically calibrated and realistic models of social interaction. Behavioral feasibility clearly constitutes a major component of the overall political feasibility of BI, but in this area, we are barely scratching the surface. Much work remains to be done to find out what effects the introduction of a BI would really produce.

Conclusion

In this chapter, we offer an analytical framework that distinguishes four types of political feasibility applied to the politics of BI.

1. Strategic feasibility challenges BI advocates to carefully consider strategies for building robust political coalitions. In particular, concerns about "cheap" expressions of political support strongly suggest more attention should be spent on political strategizing.
2. Institutional feasibility focuses on the necessary background conditions that must be in place for a BI to deliver desirable outcomes. A BI that turns out to be an ill fit for the institutional capabilities

to implement the policy runs the risk of becoming self-defeating and, in the long run, not politically resilient.

3. Psychological feasibility is primarily concerned with the legitimacy of the BI idea with the general public. Careful framing of the BI proposal might counter the uneasy connection between an unconditional BI and strong focus on reciprocity, need, and deservingness rooted in basic human psychology.
4. Behavioral feasibility is strongly affected by individuals' labor-market behavior after a BI is implemented, as small changes in behavior may rapidly unravel the social and political support for BI. However, real questions remain regarding the extent to which introducing a BI will lead to such a collapse. In fact, the most promising methodology to examine these types of questions makes it clear that the answer is likely to be very complex, defying both the simplistic optimism of contemporary BI advocates and the simplistic pessimism of its critics.

This chapter has shown political feasibility to be complex, multifaceted, and highly dynamic, with attempts to affect one type likely interacting with the others. The appropriate response to such complexity is a realization of the big task ahead of us, and perhaps a sense of the urgency with which we should undertake it.

Notes

* We are grateful to Richard Caputo for the invitation to contribute to this volume and for written comments on an earlier draft. We are also grateful to Lindsay Stirton for permission to use the fruits of a long-standing collaborative effort in the institutional feasibility section of this chapter. José A. Noguera also thanks financial support by the National Plan for R&D and the CONSOLIDER-INGENIO Programme of the Spanish Ministry of Science and Innovation (MICINN, Grant Nos. CSO2009–09890, CSD2010–00034-Simulpast).

1. Inserted by editor.
2. This section builds on De Wispelaere (2011).
3. For a more systematic treatment of the "administrative factor" in BI implementation, see De Wispelaere and Stirton (2007, 2011, 2012a, 2012b).
4. Inserted by editor.
5. Take the example of informal care arrangements, which would require regular home visits by program administrators to check that the PI entitlement is justified.
6. Many BI advocates mistake the negative requirement of "not having to satisfy a condition to become eligible for a BI" with the positive requirement of "appearing on a list of all eligible for a BI."

Administratively, the former is only the starting point, while the latter is the one that really matters for the effective implementation of a BI.

7. The differences between so-called progressive and conservative BI models is considerable (compare Van Parijs 1995 with Murray 2006).
8. Relatedly, in a recent survey in Catalonia comparing social support for BI and several cognate policies, only 40.7 percent of the population supports a pure BI. By contrast, 78.2 percent supports a PI; 82.2 percent, a means-tested guaranteed income; 74.1 percent, a negative income tax; and 70.9 percent, a universal basic pension (Noguera et al. 2011).
9. In addition, research shows the institutional background also importantly affects the level of support for particular policies (Albrekt Larsen 2006), suggesting that the institutional and psychological feasibility are linked.
10. A second response of BI advocates—that a BI will likely lead many to contribute to society in numerous informal ways not accounted for in the labor market—does little to alleviate this worry because of the requirement to establish a robust funding source for the BI.
11. The one exception is the Alaska Permanent Fund, which pays every Alaskan resident a little more than $1000 each year. However, for various reasons this model cannot tell us very much about the more ambitious BI schemes proposed by its advocates. On Alaska, see Goldsmith (2005) and Widerquist and Howard (2012).
12. ABM has numerous advantages: modeling a population of heterogeneous agents, emulating the main regulations and circumstances of their environment, and letting them interact autonomously following a set of rules or predispositions; allowing agents to learn and react to social outcomes; identifying social mechanisms that explain how patterns of interaction produce social outcomes at the macro level. One major advantage of ABM is that they can be empirically calibrated to fit a particular case or phenomenon.
13. For instance, Gneezy and Rustichini (2000) show that when incentives are small, work performance declines below the level reached in a zero-incentive situation. Similarly, research on "crowding out" effects suggest that compliance decreases whenever sanctions or controls are perceived as too strict or unfair (Bowles 2008).

References

Ackerman, Bruce A., Anne Alstott, and Philippe Van Parijs, eds. 2006. *Redesigning Distribution: Basic Income and Stakeholder Grants as Cornerstones for an Egalitarian Capitalism*. London: Verso.

Albrekt Larsen, Christian. 2006. *The Institutional Logic of Welfare Attitudes: How Welfare Regimes Influence Public Support*. Aldershot: Ashgate.

Aronson, Thomas, Sören Blomquist, and Hans Sacklén. 1999. "Identifying Interdependent Behaviour in an Empirical Model of Labour Supply." *Journal of Applied Econometrics* 14 (6): 607–626.

Atkinson, Anthony B. 1996. "The Case for a Participation Income." *Political Quarterly* 67 (1): 67–70.

Axelrod, Robert. 1997. *The Complexity of Cooperation*. Princeton, NJ: Princeton University Press.

Barry, Brian. 2001. "UBI and the Work Ethic." 60–69 in *What's Wrong with a Free Lunch?*, edited by Philippe Van Parijs, Joshua Cohen, and Joel Rogers. Boston: Beacon.

Birnbaum, Simon. 2009. "Basic Income, Sustainability and Post-Productivism." *Basic Income Studies* 4 (2): 1–7.

Bowles, Samuel. 2008. "Policies Designed for Self-Interested Citizens May Undermine 'The Moral Sentiments': Evidence from Economic Experiments." *Science* 320: 1605–1609.

Brennan, Geofrey, and Philip Pettit. 2005. "The Feasibility Issue." 258–279 in *The Oxford Handbook of Contemporary Philosophy*, edited by Frank Jackson and Michael Smith. Oxford, UK: Oxford University Press.

Brighouse, Harry. 2004. *Justice*. London: Polity Press.

Camerer, Colin, and Ernst Fehr. 2004. "Measuring Social Norms and Preferences Using Experimental Games: A Guide for Social Scientists." 55–94 in *Foundations of Human Sociality. Economic Experiments and Ethnographic Evidence from Fifteen Small-scale Societies*, edited by J. Henrich et al. Oxford, UK: Oxford University Press.

Chong, Dennis, and James N. Druckman. 2007a. "Framing Public Opinion in Competitive Democracies." *American Political Science Review* 101 (4): 637–655.

———. 2007b. "Framing Theory." *Annual Review of Political Science* 10 (1): 103–126.

Clasen, Jochen, and Wim Van Oorschot. 2002. "Changing Principles in European Social Security." *European Journal of Social Security* 4 (2): 89–115.

Coleman, James S. 1990. *Foundations of Social Theory*. Cambridge, MA: The Belknap Press.

De Wispelaere, Jurgen. 2009. "A Governance Dilemma in Basic Income." Paper presented at the "Income Security for All Canadians" BIEN Canada Congress, Ottawa, October 1–2.

———. 2011. "The Struggle for Strategy: On the Politics of Universal Basic Income." Unpublished paper. Barcelona.

De Wispelaere, Jurgen, and Lindsay Stirton. 2007. "The Public Administration Case against Participation Income." *Social Services Review* 81 (3): 523–549.

———. 2011. "The Administrative Efficiency of Basic Income." *Policy and Politics* 39 (1): 115–132.

———. 2012a. "A Disarmingly Simple Idea? Practical Bottlenecks in Implementing a Universal Basic Income." *International Social Security Review*, 65(2), pp. 103–121.

———. 2012b. "The Politics of Universal Basic Income: Bringing Bureaucracy Back In?" *Political Studies*, forthcoming.

Dowding, Keith. 1996. *Power*. Minneapolis: University of Minnesota Press.

Dowding, Keith, Jurgen De Wispelaere, and Stuart White, eds. 2003. *The Ethics of Stakeholding*. Basingstoke: Palgrave Macmillan.

Fong, Christina, Samuel Bowles, and Herbert Gintis. 2005. "Reciprocity and the Welfare State." 277–302 in *Moral Sentiments and Material Interests: The Foundations of Cooperation in Economic Life*, edited by Herbert Gintis, Samuel Bowles, Robert Boyd, and Ernst Fehr. Cambridge, MA: MIT Press.

Gilabert, Pablo, and Holly Lawford-Smith. 2012. "Political Feasibility. A Conceptual Exploration." *Political Studies*, forthcoming.

Gneezy, U., and A. Rustichini. 2000. "Pay Enough or Don't Pay At All." *Quarterly Journal of Economics* 115 (3): 791–810.

Goldsmith, Scott. 2005. "The Alaska Permanent Fund: An Experiment in Wealth Distribution." 553–566 in *Promoting Income Security as a Right: Europe and North America*, edited by Guy Standing. London: Anthem.

González-Bailón, Sandra, José A. Noguera, and Jurgen De Wispelaere. 2011. "The Provision of a Basic Income as a Social Dilemma: A Simulation Experiment." Unpublished paper. Barcelona.

Goodin, Robert E. 2001. "Something for Nothing." 90–97 in *What's Wrong with a Free Lunch?* edited by Philippe Van Parijs, Joshua Cohen, and Joel Rogers. Boston: Beacon.

———. 2003. "Sneaking Up on Stakeholding." 65–78 in *The Ethics of Stakeholding*, edited by Keith Dowding, Jurgen De Wispelaere, and Stuart White. Basingstoke: Palgrave Macmillan.

Grodner, Andrew, and Thomas J. Kniesner. 2006. "Social Interactions and Labour Supply." *Journal of the European Economic Association* 4 (6): 1226–1248.

Groot, Loek. 2004. *Basic Income, Unemployment and Compensatory Justice*. Dordrecht: Kluwer Academic.

Groot, Loek, and Robert van der Veen. 2000. "How Attractive Is a Basic Income for European Welfare States?" 13–38 in *Basic Income on the Agenda: Policy Objectives and Political Chances*, edited by Robert van der Veen and Loek Groot. Amsterdam: Amsterdam University Press.

Handler, Joel F., and Yeshekel Hasenfeld. 2006. *Blame Welfare, Ignore Poverty and Inequality*. Cambridge, UK: Cambridge University Press.

Hedström, Peter. 2005. *Dissecting the Social. On the Principles of Analytical Sociology*. Cambridge, UK: Cambridge University Press.

Hedström, Peter, and Peter Bearman, eds. 2009. *The Oxford Handbook of Analytical Sociology*. Oxford, UK: Oxford University Press.

Hood, Christopher. 2010. "Can We? Administrative Limits Revisited." *Public Administration Review* 70 (4): 527–534.

Jerit, Jennifer. 2009. "How Predictive Appeals Affect Policy Opinions." *American Journal of Political Science* 53 (2): 411–426.

Jordan, Bill. 1996. *A Theory of Poverty and Social Exclusion*. Cambridge, UK: Polity Press.

Kahneman, Daniel, and Amos Tversky, eds. 2000. *Choices, Values, and Frames*. Cambridge, UK: Cambridge University Press.

Lasswell, Harold D. 1936. *Politics: Who Gets What, When, How*. Cleveland, OH: Meridian Books.

Le Grand, Julian, and David Nissan. 2003. "A Capital Idea: Helping the Young to Help Themselves." 29–41 in *The Ethics of Stakeholding*, edited by Keith Dowding, Jurgen De Wispelaere, and Stuart White. Basingstoke: Palgrave Macmillan.

Liebig, Stefan, and Steffen Mau. 2005. "A Legitimate Guaranteed Minimum Income?" 209–230 in *Promoting Income Security as a Right: Europe and North America*, edited by Guy Standing. London: Anthem.

Lindenberg, Stewart. 2006. "Prosocial Behavior, Solidarity, and Framing Processes." 23–44 in *Solidarity and Prosocial Behavior. An Integration of Sociological and Psychological Perspectives*, edited by Detlef Fetchenhauer, Andreas Flache, Abraham P. Buunk, and Siegwart Lindenberg. New York: Springer.

Lupia, Arthur, and Matthew McCubbins. 2004. "Learning from Oversights: Fire Alarms and Police Patrols Reconstructed." *Journal of Law, Economics and Organization* 10 (1): 96–125.

Macy, Michael, and Andreas Flache. 2009. "Social Dynamics from the Bottom Up: Agent-based Models of Social Interaction." 245–268 in *The Oxford Handbook of Analytical Sociology*, edited by Peter Hedström and Peter Bearman. Oxford, UK: Oxford University Press.

Murray, Charles. 2006. *In Our Hands. A Plan to Replace the Welfare State*. Washington, DC: The American Enterprise Institute Press.

Noguera, José A., and Jurgen De Wispelaere. 2006. "A Plea for the Use of Laboratory Experiments in Basic Income Research." *Basic Income Studies* 1 (2): 1–8.

Noguera, José A., Xavier Guijarro, Francisco J. León, Toni Llacer, Francisco J. Miguel, Eduardo Tapia, Jordi Tena, and Mercé Vinagre. 2011. *Valors i actituds sobre justícia distributiva: prestacions socials i fiscalitat*. Barcelona: Centre d'Estudis d'Opinió.

Offe, Claus. 2005. "Wasteful Welfare Transactions: Why Basic Income Security Is Fundamental." 69–82 in *Promoting Income Security as a Right: Europe and North America*, edited by Guy Standing. London: Anthem.

Pechman, Joseph A., and Michael P. Timpane, eds. 1975. *Work Incentives and Income Guarantees: The New Jersey Negative Income Tax Experiment*. Washington, DC: The Brookings Institution.

Robins, Phillip K. 1985. "A Comparison of the Labor Supply Findings From the Four Negative Income Tax Experiments," *Journal of Human Resources* 20 (4): 567–582.

Robins, Philip K., Robert G. Spiegelman, Samuel Weiner, and Joseph G. Bell, eds. 1980. *A Guaranteed Annual Income. Evidence from a Social Experiment*. New York: Academic Press.

Sabbatier, Paul A., and Hank C. Jenkins-Smith. 1993. *Policy Change and Learning: An Advocacy Coalition Approach*. Boulder, CO: Westview Press.

Searle, John R. 1995. *The Construction of Social Reality*. London: Allen Lane.

———. 2010. *Making the Social World*. Oxford, UK: Oxford University Press.

Slothuus, Rune. 2007. "Framing Deservingness to Win Support for Welfare State Retrenchment." *Scandinavian Political Studies* 30 (3): 323–344.

Standing, Guy. 2002. *Beyond the New Paternalism: Basic Security as Equality*. London: Verso.

———, ed. 2005. *Promoting Income Security as a Right: Europe and North America*. London: Anthem.

Vanderborght, Yannick. 2005. "The Basic Income Guarantee in Europe: The Belgian and Dutch Back Door Strategies." 257–281 in *The Ethics and Economics of the Basic Income Guarantee*, edited by Karl Widerquist, Michael Anthony Lewis, and Steven Pressman. Aldershot: Ashgate.

———. 2006. "Why Trade Unions Oppose Basic Income." *Basic Income Studies* 1 (1): 1–20.

Van Oorschot, Wim. 2000. "Who Should Get What and Why? On Deservingness Criteria and the Conditionality of Solidarity among the Public." *Policy and Politics* 28(1): 33–48.

———. 2006. "Making the Difference in Social Europe: Deservingness Perceptions among Citizens of European Welfare States." *Journal of European Social Policy* 16 (1): 23–42.

Van Parijs, Philippe, ed. 1992. *Arguing for Basic Income: Ethical Foundations for a Radical Reform*. London: Verso.

———. 1995. *Real Freedom for All: What (If Anything) Can Justify Capitalism?* Oxford,UK: Clarendon.

———. 1996. "Basic Income and the Two Dilemmas of the Welfare State." *Political Quarterly* 67 (1): 63–66.

———. 2001. "Reply." 121–127 in *What's Wrong with a Free Lunch?* edited by Philippe Van Parijs, Joshua Cohen, and Joel Rogers. Boston: Beacon.

———. 2004. "Basic Income: A Simple and Powerful Idea for the Twenty-first Century." *Politics and Society* 32 (1): 7–39.

———. 2009. "Political Ecology: From Autonomous Sphere to Basic Income" *Basic Income Studies* 4 (2): 1–9.

White, Stuart. 2003. *The Civic Minimum: On the Rights and Obligations of Economic Citizenship*. Oxford, UK: Clarendon.

Widerquist, Karl. 2005. "A Failure to Communicate: What (If Anything) Can We Learn from the Negative Income Tax Experiments?" *Journal of Socio-Economics* 34 (1): 49–81.

Widerquist, Karl, Michael Anthony Lewis, and Steven Pressman, eds. 2005. *The Ethics and Economics of the Basic Income Guarantee*. Aldershot: Ashgate.

Widerquist, Karl, and Michael Howard, eds. 2012. *Examining the Alaska Model: Is the Permanent Fund Dividend a Model Ready for Export?* New York: Palgrave Macmillan.

Wright, Erik Olin. 2006. "Compass Points: Towards a Socialist Alternative." *New Left Review* 41: 93– 124.

———. 2010. *Envisioning Real Utopias*. London: Verso.

PART 2

Hopes

CHAPTER 3

The Best Income Transfer Program for Modern Economies

*Eduardo Matarazzo Suplicy**

Brazilian entrepreneurs have warned about the increasing lack of competitiveness of national companies that are losing ground to imports. Imports went from 11 percent to 22 percent of GDP from 2003 to 2011. The presidents of Confederação Nacional da Indústria (CNI), Robson Braga de Andrade; of the Federação das Indústrias do Estado de São Paulo (FIESP), Paulo Skaf; of Associação Brasileira de Máquinas e Equipamentos, Abimaq, Luiz Aubert Neto; of Companhia Siderúrgica Nacional, Benjamim Steinbruch; and of Valisère, Ivo Rosset, have warned about the urgent need for the government to take steps to reverse the deindustrialization. On July 8 and August 3, 2011, thousands of metalworkers from CUT (Central Ùnica dos Trabalhadores [Workers' Central Union]) and Força Sindical closed the local track of Via Anchieta, at the ABC Region (Santo André, São Bernardo e São Caetano), and went to the streets of Mogi das Cruzes to protest.[1]

The strong appreciation of real against dollar prompted the minister of finance, Guido Mantega, to take measures to change this trend. A study of FIESP points out that social charges to the payroll in Brazil, about 32.4 percent, also contribute to decrease the competitiveness of industries. Among 34 countries listed by the study of FIESP, Brazil was the one with the highest level of social charges to payroll.

On August 2, 2011, the government of President Dilma announced the Brasil Maior Program (Great Brazil Program). Among the announced measures, we can point out the transfer of social charges from payroll to a proportion of sales in the case of production of some tradable goods, exemption of taxes on imports investments, expansion and simplification of investment and export financing, increased resources for innovation, improvement of the regulatory framework of innovation, stimulating growth of small and micro businesses, strengthening of trade protection, creation of special programs to add value and technology in supply chains, and regulation of government acquisitions to stimulate production and innovation in the country.

When the FIESP research on social charges was published, I asked its vice president, José Ricardo Roriz Coelho, if, in the study, besides social charges, the effects of income transfers existing in developed countries on the competitiveness of our companies had also been considered. He said that it has not been done yet. The Confederação Nacional da Indústria hasn't developed similar work either.

This paper's objective is calling the attention of both entrepreneurs and workers, as well as that of the government, that we Brazilians, Argentineans, and people in the developing countries need to be attentive to the effects of strong income transfers that have become increasingly important in many countries. For example, in the United States, since 1975, there is the Earned Income Tax Credit (EITC), a form of negative income tax that supplements the income of working people who do not reach a level to exit from poverty.

The (US) Earned Income Tax Credit

The EITC has been significantly increased since then. President Bill Clinton who, in his campaign, in 1992, had the slogan "putting people first," increased the value of EITC for the families with one, two, or more children and extended the program to include childless couples. In his book *My Life*, he included 17 quotes about the EITC, which, according to the evidence, contributed to making the US economy more competitive. What was the evidence? Well, when Clinton began his administration in 1993, the unemployment rate was 7.5 percent; when he concluded his government, in 2000, it was 3.9 percent. The economies that interact very much with the American, like United Kingdom, Canada, Mexico, Belgium, Denmark, Finland, France, Ireland, Netherlands, New Zealand, and Sweden, have set similar instruments.

UK's prime minister Tony Blair created the Family Tax Credit in 2000. So, a worker in London who received £800 a month started to receive more payment in the form of 50 percent tax credit, and his payment increased to £1,200. More recently in 2009, President Barack Obama, like Clinton, also increased the value of EITC and extended it to include not only childless families, or those with one, two, or more children, as Clinton did, but also three or more children who now receive a higher amount.[2]

Here is how the EITC works in the United States today. I will give two examples: first, an adult who lives alone, but has a child, and who works for a minimum wage of US$7.25 per hour and is employed throughout the year. Therefore, he receives US$15,080 per year. He is entitled to a tax credit of US$3,121, and his annual income goes up to US$18,201 less related social charges of US$1,154.

In the case of a couple with two children, if the annual income is positive but below the level of US$12,970, this couple has a tax credit equal to 40 percent of every dollar they receive for the work in the range of 0 to US$12,970. Now, if they receive US$10,000, the couple receives tax credit of US$4,000. If they can get, for example, US$18,000 per year, the couple gets a credit of US$5,160 and their income goes up to US$23,160, which means going beyond the official poverty line in the United States, which, for a family of father, mother, and two children is US$23,000 annually. If the labor income of the couple continues to grow and reaches US$21,970, they still have the right to a tax credit up to US$5,160. However, if the couple's annual income continues to rise in the range of US$21,970 until the limit of US$46,471, their tax credit starts to decrease by 21 percent for each additional dollar up to the level of US$46,471. Thus, the income decreases at a rate of 21 percent on the difference between US$46,471 and the income obtained by the couple. Starting at US$46,471, if the income increases, the couple starts to have obligations to pay more income tax.

What have been the effects of EITC or Tax Credit? According to studies by the Center on Budget and Policy Priorities, the EITC has contributed to increased labor and employment levels, has decreased the need for spending on unemployment, has decreased poverty, and has made the tax system fairer. Note that the American society contributes by paying increased taxes to pay the worker. The government, therefore, helps to increase the remuneration of employees in relation to the salary paid by companies. Entrepreneurs have approved this procedure, and the employees, more satisfied and productive, have also agreed.

Besides this program of the federal government—EITC—23 states and the District of Columbia decided to have additional Tax Credits on Earned Income in their respective states.

Brazilian officials have said that the Bolsa Família Program, which currently benefits about 13 million households, equivalent to about 50 or 51 million people, with an estimated annual budget of R$15 billion this year, is the largest income transfer program. However, the EITC in the United States is larger: in 2010, it benefited 26.5 million families, more than 75 million people, with a total of approximately US$59 billion. This meant an average value for each family of US$2,226 per year.

The Alaska Permanent Fund

Hence, the question is whether should we, Brazil, protest with the World Trade Organization because the countries involved are subsidizing their workers? I recommend that we do not! I recommend acting similarly or even better. And what is the best way? Implementing the unconditional Citizen's Basic Income (CBI) for the entire population. How to prove that this is the best way? Through the pioneer and very successful experience existing in a place in the world, where for 28 years, an equal dividend has been paid to all its inhabitants. This has been happening in Alaska, United States, since Governor Jay Hammond, in 1976, led by the great discovery of oil, proposed the separation of 25 percent of the royalties from the exploitation of natural resources to create a fund that belongs to all population, or 300,000 inhabitants. The proposal was approved by referendum: 76,000 to 38,000 voters—two to one. They started to invest those resources in fixed income securities, shares of companies in Alaska, American and international companies, including 30 of the most profitable companies from Brazil, like Banco do Brasil, Petrobras, Itaú, and Bradesco—just look at the site of the Alaska Permanent Fund—besides real estates. The Alaska Permanent Fund was, then, created. Its value rose from US$1 billion in the early eighties to US$40 billion today.

Since 1982, in Alaska, besides EITC, which applies to everyone in the United States, an annual dividend has also been paid to all inhabitants living there for a year or more, which evolved from approximately US$300 up to a maximum of US$3,269 in 2008. As all residents in Alaska have the right to participate in the wealth of that state, in 2008, for a family of five, this meant about US$16,000.[3]

Thanks to equal dividend paid to all its inhabitants, Alaska, today with 700,000 inhabitants, became the most egalitarian of the 50 US states, with a Gini coefficient of inequality, in 2009, of only 0.402. The coefficient in the United States is 0.469. The highest in the United States is in the District of Columbia, where Washington, DC, is located, which is 0.539, similar to Brazil in 2009. Therefore, the system established by Governor Jay Hammond is so popular that, today, proposing the end of the dividend is considered a political suicide for any leader in Alaska. It was precisely during Republican Sarah Palin's last year as governor that the highest dividend to all who lived there for a year or more was paid.

Providing good education opportunities for all boys and girls, young people, and all those adults who did not have opportunities as children is something essential. It is very important that the government, in cooperation with the private sector, ensures this universally to all Brazilians in all age groups. Likewise, in what concerns the universal system of health care, the Sistema Único de Saúde and the family doctor program form a good care that, fortunately, have been developed in Brazil.

I had a dialogue, in 2009, with the winner of Nobel Prize in Economics Paul Krugman during his lecture to the Eastern Association of Economists in the Barack Obama's first year as president of the United States. I asked him how he saw the possibility of the United States sharing the Alaskan experience: a dividend equal to all. He mentioned that he sees the implementation of the CBI as something very positive. However, he also said that first, the public health care should be universalized, like President Barack Obama mentioned. Anyway, he said that the implementation of a citizen's basic income should be in our horizon.

Brazil is ready to follow this way! It is the first nation in the world in which the National Congress approved with consensus of all parties, Law No. 10.835, of 2004, sanctioned by President Luiz Inácio Lula da Silva. Law No. 10.835 established the CBI. It went as far as possible at the time, according to the degree of the development of the country—you cannot make substantive legislative changes overnight—to meet the vital needs of each person. It will be unconditional for all, including foreigners living here for five years or more. It will be established in steps, under the criterion of the Executive Power, starting with the most needy, as the Bolsa Família does.

The Bolsa Família Program

The Bolsa Família Program was created in October 2003 by President Luiz Inácio Lula da Silva when he unified and rationalized the various income transfer programs that were created from the mid-1990s, first locally, from municipalities and the federal district, and later, with increasingly strong support of the federal government to all municipalities that adopted minimum income programs associated with educational opportunities, also called Bolsa Escola. They say that it would be more rational to unify the programs, such as Bolsa Escola, Bolsa Alimentação, Auxílio Gás, which had been created by the Fernando Henrique Cardoso government, and also the Cartão Alimentação (Food Card), created at the beginning of Lula's government, in 2003.

It should be noted that this program, along with other policies, contributed to the reduction of absolute poverty and inequality. The proportion of families with monthly per capita income below R$93.75, in extreme poverty, decreased from 17.5 percent in 2003, to 8.8 percent in 2008, and to 8.5 percent in last year's census. The Gini coefficient of inequality, which had hit 0.599 in 1995, decreased gradually to 0.581 in 2003, and 0.53 in 2009.

President Dilma Rousseff's Administration

Starting June 2, 2011, the Bolsa Família Program gained a new importance as a major instrument to be used by the Dilma Rousseff government to achieve its main goal of the Brazil without Poverty Plan, which aims at eradicating extreme poverty. This will mean that by 2014 there should not be anyone living on less than R$70.00 per month. Considering that the federal government decided to establish partnerships with the state and local governments, and with civil society entities, both corporate and union, to accomplish together the so-called Active Search in order to identify all families and people in extreme poverty and to enroll them in social inclusion programs, it is important to know the clear definition of the Bolsa Família Program and the complementation that it may receive in different states.

The Bolsa Família Program establishes, according to the law and regulations in force since August 2011, that all families in Brazil with per capita income below R$140 per month are entitled to receive an income supplement. If the per capita income is up to R$70 per month, the family is entitled to a basic monthly benefit of R$70. If the family has one, two, three, four, five, or more children up to 15 years and 11 months, the family will have the right to receive an additional benefit of R$32 per month, per child, therefore, R$32, 64, 96, 128, or up to R$160 (in the case of five or more). And if the family has one or two teenagers, in the range from 16 years to 17 years and 11 months, the family will still have an additional benefit of R$38 or R$76 per month, respectively.

There are requirements for the family. If the mother is pregnant, she should have prenatal test in public health units during pregnancy as well as health checks after delivery. Parents should take children from zero to six years of age to have vaccinations in health units in accordance with the timetable of the Ministry of Health. Children from 7 years to 15 years and 11 months must attend at least 85 percent of classes in schools. Teenagers from 16 to 18 years of age must attend at least 75 percent of classes in schools.

The Ministry of Social Development and Fight against Hunger transfers resources to the municipalities to pay the benefits as well as an amount for administration. The municipalities have to forward to the Ministry of Health and Education reports on compliance with the conditionalities.

In order to make the goal of eradicating extreme poverty more efficacious, President Dilma Rousseff has signed agreements with state governments of each of the Brazilian regions. Thus, last August 18, 2011, she signed agreements with the governors of São Paulo, Rio de Janeiro, Minas Gerais, and Espirito Santo to hold operations to locate and register the population with monthly income below R$70 who still does not receive social benefits, professional training and benefit of job generation, access to food produced by family farmers, and family's financial supplement.

Throughout Brazil, with about 191 million inhabitants in 2011, according to the Ministry of Social Development, there are 17,285,646 registered families with monthly per capita income up to R$140. In 2011, of these, 12,999,560, or 75.2 percent, are beneficiaries of Bolsa Família. It should be noted that the number of families who are entitled to the Bolsa Família Program and are not getting the benefit is a little smaller than this difference because families with per capita income between R$70.01 and R$140.00 only have the right if they have children between 0 and 17 years of age, according to Law No. 10.836, of January 9, 2003.

In the state of São Paulo in 2011, there are 1,780,821 registered families with monthly per capita income up to R$140. Out of these, 1,200,499 are beneficiaries of the Bolsa Família Program, or 67.41 percent. In the municipality of São Paulo, the state capital and the largest population in Brazil, 11,300,000 inhabitants, there are 354,793 families with monthly per capita income up to R$140, of which 202,796 are beneficiaries of the Bolsa Família Program, or 57.16 percent.

Additionally, in the state of São Paulo, there is the Programa Renda Cidadã (Citizen's Income Program) that pays R$100 per month to families who do not receive up to half the minimum wage per capita per month, but has a range even lower than that of the Bolsa Família.

Under the agreement signed by President Dilma Rousseff and Governor Geraldo Alckmin, of São Paulo, families whose income per person is less than R$70 even though receiving the Bolsa Família, will be included as beneficiaries of the Renda Cidadã, the state government program. The amount transferred will be the difference between the monthly income per family member including Bolsa Família and the floor of R$70. The minimum benefit will be R$20 and the maximum will still be set by the state. There is a card unifying the two programs for this population.

Let us assume as an example the case of a family of father, mother, three children up to 15 years and 11 months, and two teenagers between 16 and 17 years of age. There are seven people in the family. Let's say the family income is R$420 per month, so it translates to a monthly income of R$ 60 per person. In this case, the family, provided it meets the conditions, is entitled to the benefit of R$70, plus R$96 and R$76, that is, a sum of R$242. Therefore, the family will have a household monthly income of R$420 plus R$242, or R$662, corresponding to R$94.50 per person, which exceeds the limit of R$70. Now, let's consider the example of another family of similar characteristics, seven people, but with a monthly income of only R$200, obtained in the informal market. It will also be entitled to the benefit of the Bolsa Família of R$242 which, added to R$200 corresponds to R$442. Under the established agreement, the São Paulo government will complement this amount with R$58, so that the family gets R$490, or R$70 multiplied by seven persons.

Any sensible person will agree that the calculations above, be it for those who administer the benefit or for the beneficiaries, are of reasonable complexity. It will not be easy for the program administrators to ensure accuracy in calculations about how much each family is entitled to. Moreover, much less accuracy will be achieved by the families that, given their poverty condition, usually tend to have large fluctuations on their monthly income obtained largely in the informal market. It is important that the federal, state, and municipal governments make a fairly accurate estimate of the administrative costs of the unified programs.

According to the minister of social development, Tereza Campello, about 300,000 families will be covered by 2014. In 2012, 100 municipalities in the state of São Paulo with the lowest Human Development Index (HDI-M) will be included, benefiting approximately 21,000 families. In 2013, 458 cities will be benefited, representing 72,000 families. And in 2014, it will benefit the 87 municipalities of the metropolitan regions of São Paulo, Campinas, and Baixada Santista, covering approximately 200,000 families. It is a praiseworthy effort. However, it should be noted that, in fact, the MDS (Ministério do Desenvolvimento Social [Ministry of Social Affairs]) data indicate that this commitment will benefit 300,000 out of the more than 500,000 families that are entitled to receive the Bolsa Família Program in the state of São Paulo. Do those 300,000 families really receive per capita monthly income up to R$70 and actually achieve the goal expressed by the government?

The form of supplementary income now implemented in São Paulo already exists in Rio de Janeiro and Espírito Santo. The government of Rio de Janeiro adds to the Bolsa Família, through Renda Melhor (Better Income), resources ranging from R$30 to R$300 per month per family. The government of Espirito Santo, with the program named Incluir, adds R$50 per month per family to the federal program. In both states, the beneficiaries are also included in programs for education, health, welfare, and work.

Other countries in the Americas have income transfer programs that keep similarity with the Brazilian Bolsa Família. In Argentina, the scheme Jefas e Jefes de Hogar Desocupados (Unemployed Male and Female Heads of Family) was implemented in 2002, and later subject to changes in the governments of Nestor and Cristina Kirschner, becoming, Familias por la Inclusión Social (Families for Social Inclusion) in 2005, and e Asignación Universal por Hijo para Protección Social (Universal Child Allowance for Social Protection), in 2009. In Chile, the Programa Solidário (Solidário Program), also created in 2002, as well as in Mexico the Programa Oportunidades (Opportunities Program), preceeded by Progresa (Progressa), in 1997, had similar developments. These programs, however, do not have an effect like the one provided by the EITC and other similar programs created in developed countries that have a significant effect on the competitiveness of their economies. It should be noted that Mexico, besides Oportunidades, also created Subsidio ao Emprego (Allowance for Emprego), which has similarity with the EITC.

Advantages of Adopting a Basic Income Scheme

It is relevant that we observe the results of the Brazil without Poverty Plan, as well as other similar programs in other countries, especially for those, including myself, who are today more and more convinced that the best solution to effectively eradicate absolute poverty—along with offering good education opportunities for all—is the establishment of a CBI. I believe that countries that adopt the CBI may be at a greater competitive advantage over those who do not. Moreover, if one day we are to move toward full integration of the Americas, with freedom of movement for human beings across the borders, it is interesting to keep in mind the goal of instituting CBI from Alaska to Patagonia.

The CBI, when implemented, will have significant advantages. It will eliminate any bureaucracy involved in having to know how much each one earns in the formal or informal market. It will eliminate any stigma or sense of shame that a person has when she/he must say how much she/he earns, in order to receive an income supplement. It will eliminate the dependency phenomenon that happens when there is a system that says that if the person does not get a certain level of income, she/he is entitled to supplement amount. Moreover, if by chance she/he is to decide whether or not to perform an activity and receive that amount, hence the government takes what she/he was getting, she/he will no longer do the activity, and be caught by poverty or unemployment traps. If all people have the guarantee of a basic income, any work effort will always mean progress.

The biggest advantage will be in regard to dignity and freedom of the human person. For those people who sometimes do not find means of survival but to submit to humiliating or high-risk activities, they would, then, be able to say "no" until the emergence of opportunities in accordance with their vocation and desire. It is true that the basic income will cost more. However, when people understand its effects, the society will embrace it with enthusiasm, including those who have more resources. They will contribute so that they and all the others will receive a basic income, in a way that everyone feels that each one is living in a nation with a greater degree of solidarity, justice, and social peace.[4]

Financing a Basic Income Scheme

From any source of wealth in a community, a municipality, or a nation, we can always set aside a portion to constitute a fund that belongs to all inhabitants to finance the CBI. Similar to the first experiences of minimum income associated with education that began locally and have become the nationwide Bolsa Família Program, it is possible to start the CBI in municipalities, like in Santo Antonio do Pinhal, in the state of São Paulo, which approved a law for this purpose in 2009, and should take steps soon to put it into practice. Proposing that large cities like Buenos Aires, São Paulo, México, Montevideo, and Assumpção become pioneer examples of CBI will be an extraordinary challenge.

A promising way of sustainable development intensively discussed within the academic environment is the financing of the CBI through the establishment of taxes charged on the sources of pollution: those who emit carbon dioxide, and other residues that are harmful to health and weather, which must be preserved for all living beings. Typically, people who have more resources are the ones who use more energy sources that cause pollution. They will be charged more, so that everybody can receive a basic income.[5]

The government of the state of São Paulo informed us a few days ago that in two years it will replace road tolls by chips that will measure the distance traveled by each vehicle. One possible idea is to charge a fee, not only for the conservation of the roads, but also to discourage pollution, improve the climate, and to finance the right of all people to share the wealth of the nation.

By the way, Professor Philippe Van Parijs, one of the founders of the Basic Income Earth Network (BIEN), strongly recommended the divulgation of a reflection expressed in the excellent book of Edward Glaeser, published in 2011, called *The Triumph of the City* (New York, Penguin Press HC), on page 221, where it is written:

> Smart environmentalism needs to embrace incentives...Throughout the world, we can adopt a global emission tax that charges people for the damage done by their carbon emissions...Opponents of big government understandably worry that this type of policy will just turn into an added source of revenue for the government, but this worry can be reduced with a public commitment to rebating the tax to citizens as an energy dividend, much as the state of Alaska pays each of its citizens an annual dividend from oil revenues.

Therefore, besides considering the financing of a basic income for all the Brazilians, through for instance, the revenues generated by presalt and mineral resources in Brazil, we can also consider this proposal, under the name of *Cap and Dividend*, increasingly discussed in international academic circles and now, here in Brazil too.

I received a constructive message from Professor Philippe Van Parijs[6] about the text above, which is worth commenting:

> I read your text with great interest (very instructive about latest developments in Brazil). Quick elliptical remarks:
>
> (1) The case for EITC is persuasive in terms of poverty alleviation and employment boosting, less obvious in terms of competitiveness (need to take the funding side into account).
> (2) Integration of means-tested minimum income schemes of Bolsa Familia type (the more poor people earn, the less they get in benefits) and EITC (the more poor people earn, the more they get in refundable tax credits) is obviously problematic.
> (3) The case for bolsa familia, BI and EITC in terms of competitiveness (and more generally economic efficiency) must be made mainly in terms of their impact on human capital: Do more children go to school? (strongest for conditional BF [Bolsa Família]) Can more parents choose to look after their children when they need it? (strongest for BI) Can more people acquire and retain skills by being at work? (strongest for EITC) Can more people select jobs according to their training content? (strongest for BI).
> (4) A city-level BI is sustainable if protected against the attraction of the poor by time limits; and if protected against the exit of the tax base (wealthy individual and businesses) by the sheer size of the city's territory, the cost in time and money of commuting into the city (for wealthy individuals) and the drawbacks of locating in the periphery (for businesses).

I would like to present some comments on Professor Philippe Van Parijs' message quoted above. It is true that the EITC, as studies reported by the Center on Budget and Policy Priorities, has contributed to poverty alleviation and employment promotion. A deeper review of the form of funding may enhance the arguments relating to economic competitiveness.

It is a fact that the Bolsa Família supplements the income of families earning up to R$140 per capita per month (with an additional R$70 for those who earn up to R$70), with the benefit amount taking into account the number of children and teenagers, going down to zero if that limit is exceeded. In this case, as shown by the analysis above, the phenomenon of dependency and consequent unemployment and poverty traps can occur. In the case of the EITC, it is positive and proportional to income, 40 percent for couples with two children up to certain level. Starting at US$21,970 to US$46,471 annual income, the couple receives a tax credit of US$5,560 less 21 percent of the income that exceeds US$21,970, until it is canceled and the couple of moves to the level to pay positive income tax. By this system, the EITC minimizes the phenomenon of dependency.

The EITC, however, is not an alternative for those who often do not find job opportunities and are not entitled with the advantage provided by the BI to ensure his/her own survival and his/her family's. BI allows one to say "no" to a possible single source of employment that can be humiliating or put his/her life at risk. Above all, the EITC has the same efficiency as the BI to eradicate absolute poverty and to promote greater equity. Again, the evidence that this happens with BI is the fact that Alaska, after having paid, for 28 years, an equal dividend to the entire population residing there for a year or more, has become the most egalitarian of the 50 US states.

Reflections on the effects of the Bolsa Família, BI, and EITC on competitiveness and, above all, its impact with respect to human capital are very relevant and can be object of interesting researches.

The sustainability of the BI within a community, a municipality, a state, a country, or a continent will obviously depend on the rules. For instance, the rule that says that only people who lived there for five years or more or were born there are eligible. Maybe one day we can get the concept of a genuine community of the Americas, with greater uniformity of rights, including free movement of goods and services, capital, and last but not least, of human beings. When there is a BI in all its extensions, this will be feasible and there will be no need to have any more walls that separate our borders.

The further study of these issues will allow President Barack Obama to make a bolder step in his next Employment Incentive Plan. The basic income, unconditional, for all US residents, can combine the achievement of the goals of increased economic activity, employment, equity, eradication of absolute poverty, dignity, and real freedom for all.

Notes

* Paper presented in the following conferences: *Desafíos de la integración latinoamericana*, withing the seminar *El futuro de la integración latinoamericana*, on the 25th and 26th of August, in the Law School of the University of Buenos Aires, Argentina; *XVI Meeting of the Committee of Economic Affairs, Social Debt and Regional Development*, in Aruba on the 22nd and 23rd of September; *International Parliamentary Seminar*, in Santiago, Chile, on the 2nd and 3rd of October.

1. The mentioned news was registered by the newspapers *Folha de S. Paulo* and *O Estado de S. Paulo* in July and August 2011.
2. Information about EITC was collected from studies by "Center on Budget and Policy Priorities," like "A Hand Up: How State Earned

Income Tax Credits Help Working Families Escape Poverty in 2011," by Nicholas Johnson and Erica Willians, April 2011; "Earned Income Tax Credit Overpayment and Error Issues," by John Wancheck and Robert Greenstein, April 2011; Comment on Bruce Meyer; "The Earned Income Tax Credit—A Swedish Perspective" (Economiska Râdets Konferens den 7 maj "From Welfare to Work"), by Ann-Sofie Kolm; and other issues of "Earned Income Tax Credit Archive" from the referred center.

3. Information about the fundaments of the Minimum Income Guarantee and/or the CBI, the evolution of Brazilian social programs that resulted in the Bolsa Família Program, the story of the Alaska Permanent Fund can be found in the book "Renda de Cidadania. A Saída pela Porta," by Eduardo Matarazzo Suplicy, Cortez Editora e Editora Fundação Perseu Abramo, 1st Ed. 2002, 6th Ed. 2010. Regarding the Dividend system of the Alaska Permanent Fund, in the book "Exporting the Alaska Model: How the Permanent Fund Dividend Can Be Adapted as Model for Reform Around the World," that will be released in 2012, edited by Karl Widerquist and Michael W. Howard, by the publishing house Palgrave-MacMillan. The results of a one-day debate about the model of Alaska at the University of Alaska, in Anchorage, on April 22, 2011, are in the editorial of Karl Widerquist in the United States Basic Income Guarantee (USBIG) Newsletter Vol., No. 60, Spring 2011 (www.usbig.net). Data on the Gini coefficients of United States and Alaska are from the US Census Bureau, and of Brazil, from IBGE (Instituto Brasileiro de Geografia e Estatística).
4. The advantages of CBI can be found, among other books, in "Renda Básica de Cidadania. Fundamentos Éticos e Econômicos," by Philippe Van Parijs and Yannick Vanderborght, Civilização Brasileira, 2006, Rio de Janeiro.
5. An example of contribution on how to tax carbon to finance basic income is in the paper presented by Professor Michael Howard, at the XIII International Congress of BIEN, Basic Income Earth Network, "A Cap on Carbon and a Basic Income: A Defensible Combination in the U.S."? (www.basicincome.org).
6. Personal email communications from Philippe Van Parijs to Senator Suplicy dated September 6 and 12, 2011.

CHAPTER 4

An Anniversary Note—BIEN's Twenty-fifth*

Guy Standing

Anniversaries are poignant human moments, points on a journey, never an end in themselves. Twenty-five years ago, on September 4–6, 1986, a small group of us held a workshop on basic income and on September 6 decided to set up a network, BIEN. The memory is blurred; the documentation is scattered. However, this twenty-fifth anniversary is a testament to several aspects of BIEN, and it is perhaps acceptable to reflect on the journey so far.

It is intriguing that a core of the group that set up BIEN has remained active in its cause. Many of the original group, including this writer, had written papers advocating and justifying a basic income before we established BIEN. At the time, and for long afterward, we were regarded by many of our colleagues and friends outside BIEN as quirky, idealistic, stupidly utopian, or naïve. I recall the director of the ILO's [International Labour Organization's] Social Security Department using the expression "bad, mad and dangerous to know." We have always had members who had a talent for giving some credence to that simplistic denigration. However, neither they nor the insults have dimmed the light.

I doubt if any of us would have imagined that BIEN would last more than a couple of years, if that. The longevity is a tribute to many in that group, some of whom moved out after playing important roles, some played leading roles before retiring to the ranks, some moved out and then returned, refreshed. Some of the early figures have died; they are not forgotten. Some of the fresh-faced, long-haired youths who were at the inaugural meeting have shamelessly gone on to become grandfathers and grandmothers. It happens.

In BIEN, it has always been true that the whole is greater than the sum of the parts. It has always had distinguished social thinkers, some of whom have gone on to become distinguished names in their field. Yet, we have always recognized that it is the collective network, not individuals, that makes BIEN special. In a sense, at a personal level, a network such as ours is an exercise in *associational freedom* in that the voluntary unpaid nature of what we have been trying to do together has strengthened each of us, to a greater or lesser degree. Would we have held the line if we had worked individually? I doubt it.

What has also been invigorating is that BIEN has always been ecumenical. Many who have added to its vitality have been profoundly religious and spiritual; many others have been atheists or agnostics. Politically too, we have avoided sectarianism. Some have been on the political right; others have been solidly on the left. It is testament to our charter and the many individuals who have steered the network that BIEN has always been a "broad church." Nobody has been turned away or been subject to insults or disdain because of their personal views. If they have wanted to join the conversation, they have been welcome.

From the outset, there have been at least two lines of thinking that have dominated our conversation, one that is broadly philosophical and libertarian, stressing the appeal of a basic income as a right and as a standalone matter, the other that basic income should be seen as one component of a redistributive political and economic strategy. A third line has always been there as well, but has become increasingly important, the potential of a basic income as a means of enhancing a more [equitably] gendered and ecologically viable future. Perhaps it is this third line that will prove decisive in the next few years.

In sum, a fundamental defining feature of BIEN members is that they have been and will remain inherently *nonconformists*, in the great tradition of thinking that defines humanity. We all believe there is an alternative.

That leads to what has been the primary means by which BIEN has flourished, our national networks and our Congresses. Those networks have tended to fluctuate, sometimes depending on the energies of one or two people, to the extent of making them fragile as their leading lights move through busy lives. It has, however, been particularly invigorating to see how new networks have emerged in recent years.

This has partly been associated with the great change we made to our name, going from BIEN to BIEN in Barcelona in 2004, when after some background wrangling, we opted to formalize reality by changing the "E" from Europe to Earth, recognizing that an increasing proportion of our members were from outside Europe. Looking back, it seems obvious that the name change should be made.

For some in our ranks that was not obvious at the time. Some worried that we would lose our focus; some worried that if, as was felt appropriate, we alternated our Congresses between a European city and one outside Europe that members would only be able to afford to go to one Congress every four years. The former fear has proved unfounded; the latter fear has meant we have a greater responsibility to raise funds to enable as many people as wish to come to be able to do so.

As for the networks, it has been impressive that the second generation have been daring and invigorating. It is invidious to single out particular networks, but besides our wonderful members in Brazil and Argentina, it has been exciting to see the emergence of Basic Income Network Italy (BIN-Italia), Basic Income Korean Network (BIKN) in Korea, Basic Income Japanese Network (BIJN) in Japan, and US Basic Income Guarantee Network (USBIG) in North America. My dream at the moment is to see one in India. In this huge and wonderful country, the debate about income security has suddenly become very topical.

As for our Congresses, I am sure many of us proverbially pinch ourselves from time to time in wondering how we have done them. Every single one has started with a sense of trepidation among the nominated organizers. Who is going to do the work? Where are we going to obtain the money? What should the themes be? Who will be our plenary speakers? Will there be enough quality papers?

Practically every Congress has had its moments of crisis during the organizational phase. Yet, all have taken place, and an assessment of their evolution and contents would make a fascinating topic, perhaps for a PhD. Let me just recall the places where we have held our Congresses since our inauguration in Louvain-la-Neuve in September 1986. In chronological order, they have been held in Antwerp, Florence, London, Paris, Amsterdam, Vienna, Berlin, Geneva, Barcelona, Cape Town, Dublin, and São Paolo. The names trip off the tongue as great cities. In each case, those who did the incredible amount of preparatory work deserve tremendous credit.

In every Congress, there were wonderful contributions, often from newcomers, sometimes from distinguished politicians or personalities. Who could forget the moving speech made by Archbishop Desmond Tutu at the Cape Town Congress? Of course, no BIEN members had anything to do with the content of his speech. It was the delivery and the commitment shown by him that moved us. It is almost unfair to single him out, since over the years there have been numerous fascinating contributions.

At the São Paolo Congress, I recall a private chat with a fellow founder member in which we both remarked how extraordinary it was to find that we learned new ideas and interpretations at every Congress. Only a small fraction of the papers presented over the years have ever been published;

I have a volume from the Geneva Congress in front of me now. However, probably over 600 papers have been presented at the 13 Congresses.

What then of the cause? Twenty-five years is a long time to have been refining our thinking without success. Well, progress has been substantial. In an early paper in the 1980s, I predicted that social policy would drift to workfare before an unconditional universal basic income became part of mainstream thinking, essential for responding to the growing inequalities and insecurities. Regrettably, workfare has been ushered into reality, in the United States, in the United Kingdom and in various ways elsewhere. It runs counter to any legitimate idea of freedom, and is divisive. It may grow uglier before there is a revolt against it. Then, I believe, our time will come.

In that regard, we might reflect on three quotations that have stayed with me during the 25 years. The first is a nice aphorism from Barbara Wootton:

> "It is from the champions of the impossible
> rather than the slaves of the possible
> that evolution draws its creative force."
>
> (*In a World I Never Made*, London: Allen and Unwin, 1967: 279)

We all know the feeling of being told that a basic income is an impossibility. Usually, it is said by people who either presume it is impossible because it has never been done or do not wish it to be possible, because it might mean less for themselves or for their kind.

The second comes from William Morris, one of the early advocates of a basic income in his *News from Nowhere*. It was not from that book that the saying comes, but seems hugely relevant today.

> "I...pondered how men fight and lose the battle, and the thing they fought for comes about in spite of their defeat, and when it comes turns out not to be what they meant, and other men have to fight for what they meant under another name."

Those words were written in 1886. What is in a name? Probably, most of us in BIEN have toyed with terms that might work better than the familiar basic income—"social dividend," "citizen's income," "basic income grant," (BIG), and so on. In the United Kingdom, at the moment, the government's new *universal credit* is not a basic income, but could be seen as a major step in creating a basis for moving toward what we might regard as a basic income.

The third statement is from a stranger fellow traveler. In 1947, a small group of 36 mavericks, led by Friedrich Hayek, convened a meeting in

Montreux and set up the Mont Pelerin Society. Their ideology would not appeal to most BIEN members. However, for the best part of 30 years, they met and wrote and lobbied, mostly ignored or regarded with disdain by conventional circles. In his preface to his 1982 edition of his famous *Capitalism and Freedom* (Chicago, IL: University of Chicago Press), Milton Friedman, who had been a young economist at that 1947 meeting, wrote:

> "Our basic function is to develop alternatives to existing policies, to keep them alive and available until the political impossible becomes the politically inevitable."

Perhaps he was being a little cute, since his thinking had become part of the Washington Consensus by then. None of us thinks we are analogous to the overtly political Mont Pelerin Society, but after decades of neglect, no less than 8 of its 36 founders went on to receive Nobel Prizes in economics. My nominations go in on Monday!

More generally, the view that ideas go from being disregarded to being mainstream only after 30 years has, not surprisingly, appealed to me during the past 25 years. One could say that basic income is one of those ideas that Albert Hirschmann had in mind in saying that whenever a new progressive idea comes up, it is subject to three reactions—the claim of *futility* (that it would be ineffectual), the claim of *jeopardy* (that it would endanger other goals), and the claim of *perversity* (that it would have unintended consequences). We have certainly faced those claims, and still do. However, fewer people are being convinced by them.

As for the 30 years before an idea comes into its own, I feel quietly optimistic that we are ahead of the curve.

Why is that? First, in the so-called rich countries, social policy is in disarray, while insecurity and inequality have become pervasive and threatening to the social stability of society. In this, the precariat has become pivotal, growing angrier and more alienated by the day, and filling the squares of cities in numerous countries.

Second, we have seen a remarkable development in developing countries in the past decade. Here, we have to admit that back in the 1980s we did not anticipate the extraordinary progress the debate on basic income would make in the near future. Yet in the past decade in particular, in Africa, Asia, and Latin America, forms of noncontributory cash transfer have become hugely popular. We have seen the spread of so-called *conditional cash transfers* in Latin America and elsewhere.

These are not basic income schemes, being selective, targeted, and conditional. However, they have legitimized the payment of cash in monthly payments as a vehicle to overcome poverty and insecurity. The task now is simpler—to show conclusively that targeting, selectivity, and conditionality are profoundly wrong. Each day one can find more evidence and each day one can find that prominent policymakers have lost their confidence in one or other of the three. Conditionality is the worst of the challenges before us. It is pervasive and part of the new orthodoxy among politicians and some international financial agencies, notably the World Bank.

While the struggle goes on to show that conditionality is paternalistic, divisive, and contrary to ideas of freedom and equality, a quiet revolution is taking place—basic income has been accepted as a legitimate option in development discourses. And we are seeing several countries where something like it is "on the cards" or being tried. All BIEN members know of the law of 2004 in Brazil committing its government to a basic income. All BIEN members have been thrilled by the Namibian experiment. Now, we are in the middle of a pilot scheme in villages in India and in part of Delhi. Others in Brazil and elsewhere have lifted our spirits.

At national level, what amount to short-term basic income schemes have become integral to relief programs following ecological and social shocks. And we are seeing national moves toward our goal in some unexpected places, including Mongolia and Iran. We should not be carried away by these. However, they may turn out to be harbingers of a breakthrough. The evidence piles up that if the financial constraints are lifted, people everywhere act rationally in the interest of their families and their communities. The essential optimism that lies in the heart of all BIEN members is being supported in wonderful ways.

All of this is for more considered analysis on later occasions. A point on a journey is one for lightness, for reflecting on what drives us. At core, it is a sentiment that goes back thousands of years—a sense of social justice. In that regard, I am reminded of Aristotle's wondrous words about *philia*. As I look back at our modest efforts, I can only think right now that BIEN has been, is, and will remain a tribute to the virtues of friendship. For what has kept it together, is a spirit of philia cemented by a common bond of wanting to make the world of inequality and exploitation a little better for all those who are economically insecure.

La lotta continua!

Notes

* Editor's Note: The attached was sent to the Basic Income European Network (BIEN) membership via email on September 4, 2011. A flurry of complimentary emails followed. I wish to thank Guy Standing for permitting his statement in its entirety to be included in this volume. Bracketed text [] was added by me for informational or clarification purposes only.

PART 3

Realities

European Union Countries

CHAPTER 5

Finland: Institutional Resistance of the Welfare State against a Basic Income

Markku Ikkala[*]

Since the late 1970s, massive and long-lasting unemployment was the primary problem for social economic policy in the welfare states. In Finland, this phenomenon was experienced as a rough time later—at the beginning of the 1990s—when unemployment jumped almost to half a million (about 15.5 percent). Governments tried to relieve the consequences of unemployment and poverty by providing social benefits conditionally and, in so far as in their power, to take employment-promoting measures. Although unemployment is no longer massive, structural and long-term unemployment still exists. It is difficult for governments and political leaders to rethink the changes in the economy and working life. Although the nature of work has changed, almost all benefits are somehow connected with paid work. In addition, the concept of work/labor itself has to be redefined. At least the relation between work and basic livelihood needs a new definition. A major problem is that the social security system in welfare states, for instance in Finland and Nordic countries, is very complicated and leads to poverty and other traps. It also lessens work incentives.

However, there is an alternative available that does not mean too big changes in the social security system of a welfare state; it requires just rethinking of means testing of basic livelihood. This system is known as a basic income (BI) or as a negative income tax (NIT).

The Basic Income European/Earth Networks (BIEN) defines BI as follows:

> A basic income is an income unconditionally granted to all on an individual basis, without means test or work requirement.
>
> (www.basicincome.org)

Other synonymous concepts or models include NIT, civic/citizens' income, universal grant, state bonus, and national/social dividend. Civic/citizens' salary and citizens' wage are also used, and in earlier discussions, these have been generally applied to the same issue. In my opinion, however, although citizens' wage is one of the BI models, it also means something else like connection with traditional paid work. Anyway, BI should be used as a general concept of this issue.

The basic idea of BI is that the society guarantees the citizen's basic livelihood in a simple way and in consideration of human values. In practice, it mostly means integration and reform of the social security and taxation systems.

The core in BI research is the relation between livelihood, work, and working motivation. To examine how the salary/wage affects work incentives would produce relevant information for this purpose. To reform the social security system, BI calls for a change or a new way of thinking in our society. It is useful to ask how social reforms are argued in the Finnish history. Could the state of BI discussion now be compared to important Finnish political and social reforms like a universal right to vote, child benefit, and national pension? The question in my research is: Is BI now possible in Finland in the light of the historical background? In this chapter, I concentrate on the development of the last 20 years and expressions of opinions and actions of political parties. A new kind of legislation, one that removes the principle of means testing on the level of basic livelihood, would require the acceptance of the main political parties and many interest groups, which in the Finnish system have connections with political parties.

About the Political System of Finland

Finland is a parliamentary democracy in which power is divided among the parliament, the government, and the president. The judicial system controls application of laws and action of authorities. Relations of the republic are governed by the principles of European party-based parliamentarianism. Finland has been a member of the European Union since 1995, and it belongs to the Euroarea.

The scene of competition for the political parties is the parliament. During its approximately 100-year history, the Finnish political party system has been relatively stable. The historical background for the party divisions includes the ideal of nationality, the language issue (Swedish is a minority and official language), the socialist versus nonsocialist divide, representation of the rural population, and the two-way division of the political Left. In Finland's multiparty system, support for the parties runs approximately along the following lines: the three or four biggest parties each have around 20 percent of popular support and about ten smaller parties compete for the remainder—and half of them succeed in getting seats in the parliament. See table 5.1.

In the type of party-based and consensus-oriented parliamentarianism practiced in Finland, political coalitions may be large and unconventional in composition. Interparty relationships may overshadow formal institutional ones. Decision-making requires the formation of coalitions and the acceptance of compromises. Nowadays, Finnish politics is characterized by pragmatism and a strong penchant toward consensus. In

Table 5.1 Political parties in Finland 2011 (2007)

Name of the party	*Seats in the Finnish Parliament*	*Group in the EU Parliament/Finnish delegates 2010 (2005)*	*About ideologies of the Finnish parties*
National Coalition Party (KOK)	44 (50)	EPP-ED/Christian Democrats/3 (4)	Conservative-liberal
Centre Party (KESK)	35 (51)	Group of the Alliance of Liberals and Democrats for Europe/3 (4)	Former agrarian party, now liberal-conservative
Swedish People's Party (RKP/SFP)	9 + 1 (9+1)	Group of the Alliance of Liberals and Democrats for Europe/1 (1)	Liberal, represents Swedish speaking Finns
Finnish Christian Democrats (KD/KRIST)	6 (7)	Christian Democrats/1 (0)	Religious party
True Finns (PER)	39 (5)	Independence/Demo-cracy Group/1 (0)	Populist
Green League (VIHR)	10 (15)	Group of Greens/European Free Alliance/2 (1)	Green ideology
Finnish Social Democratic Party (SDP)	42 (45)	PSE Socialist Group/2 (3)	Social democracy
Left Alliance (VAS)	14 (17)	Confederal Group of the European United Left/0 (1)	Socialism (former Communists)
Total	200	13 (14)	

June 2011, Finland got a new government, which consists of six parties, from political Right to Left.

Typical of Finland has been that interest groups, trade unions, and industrial organizations negotiate income's policy agreements. These agreements include many other issues of working life such as working hours, taxation, health care, and so forth. Traditionally, trade unions and left-wing parties have had close relations. If there are difficulties in reaching agreement between trade unions and industrial organizations, the government has come to help and made proposals for legislation. Due to this tripartite treaty system, our interest groups, trade unions, and industrial organizations have affected politics very strongly during the past 60 years. Social policy has been developed simultaneously like in other Nordic countries, toward the welfare state in which interest groups can almost dictate labor legislation in the parliament. It is sometimes difficult to develop social political systems without an approval by trade unions.

Empirical Research Material

This chapter is based on extensive material about Finnish BI discussion from magazines, newspapers, pamphlets, discussions on television, in the radio, and research reports. There are a few master thesis (*pro gradu*) papers, one licentiate work, and one doctoral work available about BI in Finland.

This chapter focuses mainly on discussions of politicians during the parliamentary elections covering the last 20 years and on some expressions of researchers and societal thinkers. The chapter does not include very many journalistic opinions or views of the public at large.

Previous Discussion

In Finland, the idea of a "BI" was probably first presented in 1970 by an author, Samuli Paronen. He wrote about "an independent person's money," which in his opinion should be granted just "for being a human being." The terms "civic salary," "citizens' salary," or "citizens' wage" were introduced in a Finnish discussion in a book called *Suomi 1980-luvulla* (Finland in the 1980s) written by Osmo Soininvaara and Osmo Lampinen in 1980. This was an initial step of the Green movement in Finnish politics. Later, Osmo Soininvaara became a leading ideologist of the Green movement and the Green Party in Finland. There were also many researchers like Jan-Otto Andersson, Simo Aho, Markku Ruohonen, Matti Virtanen, Osmo Kuusi, and Pekka Korpinen from various scientific fields who wrote about a BI or citizens' salary. In the 1980s, there was no thorough presentation about BI written in Finnish. The researchers and societal thinkers can be regarded as pioneers of BI discussions.

In 1986, the National Board of Social Welfare first published a report on "Basic livelihood" and later, another report on "Poverty in households." In these reports, the term "income guarantee" was used with meaning something in between BI and "subsistence subsidy." This subsistence subsidy is guaranteed for all citizens in Finland, if he/she has no other income, but it is very carefully means tested and controlled. Politicians joined the BI discussion before the parliamentary election in March 1987 but they did not use the term "basic income" or "citizens' salary." In this discussion about "basic livelihood guarantee" / "basic security," different concepts on BI were used. The right-wing parties spoke about "negative income" and the leftist party (the communists) about citizens' income. The Greens were already very strongly in favor of BI then, but they did not have any systematic presentation about it yet. At the same time, the Social Democrats were already doubtful about BI. The election brought a new government into power consisting of right-wing parties and the Social Democrats. The economic boom interrupted the discussion even about problems of poverty and basic security. In the following election of 1991, BI was not brought up in political discussions; basic security talk still continued.

Young people became gradually interested in BI. In 1988, the social political secretary of the National Union of University Students in Finland (SYL), Ilpo Lahtinen, compiled a book out of many articles called *Kansalaispalkka. Ken elää sen syömänkin pitää.* (Citizens' Salary. Who Lives Must Also Eat). Simultaneously two young politicians, a Green Party member David Pemperton and centrist Olli Rehn, later a member of the Finnish Parliament and the EU Parliament, and now also a member of the European Commission, pointed out that "something has to be done because a citizens' salary is a good idea." In January 1989, a Finnish Basic Income Group with members from all important Finnish parties was founded. Among others were the Green Osmo Soininvaara, also a member of parliament, and a Social Democrat Pentti Arajärvi, who has later been one of the leading specialists in social political questions and BI of the Social Democratic Party. This team asked Ilpo Lahtinen to become a secretary. He made university research (licentiate work) later and published a book in 1992 called *Perustulo. Kansalaisen palkka.* (Basic Income. Citizens' Salary). This was the first thorough presentation and initiative about BI in Finland but it got very little publicity.

Political Debate in the 1990s and at the Beginning of the Twenty-first Century

During the last 15 years, the political BI debate has mostly been of interest to the Greens and their supporters. The Greens' leader figure, Osmo Soininvaara, has been in many roles in this debate. As a societal thinker he has published several pamphlets presenting BI during the last 25 years; as a researcher, he together with some others drew up a report called "Outline of a BI model" for the Ministry of Social Affairs and Health in 1994; and as a Green politician and even as minister of health and social services (minister of "Basic Services") 2000–2001, he tried to keep BI in the press. Osmo Soininvaara used material about BI model also in his book *Hyvinvointivaltion eloonjäämisoppi* (A Survival Doctrine for the Welfare State), which was published in 1994 and then rewarded as the "Economics Book of the Year."

Starting 1992, Finland experienced perhaps its biggest economic depression ever, and Finnish unemployment jumped almost to half a million (about 15.5 percent). In addition, the Finnish banking sector and the social security system were in crisis. During the parliamentary election of 1995, BI did not have a very important role; the discussion focused more on livelihood, incentive traps, and poverty traps caused by the complicated social security system and the economic depression. The new government, led by the Social Democrats, was a "rainbow government" because it was formed by the right-wing parties, left-wing parties, and the Greens. Only the Centre Party and some smaller groups stayed outside the government. The new government founded an "incentive trap" working group in which also Osmo Soininvaara was a member. The results of this working group were rather meager, although negative income was also discussed. The final report included an interesting detail; the working group members were "afraid that the development would lead to a negative income or BI system if the existing social security system was ruined." Thus, this work did not provide the government with any new tools; employment and incentive politics were carried out and the poorest people became even poorer.

Something, however, needed to be done about our complicated social security system. For this reason, Pentti Arajärvi was in 1996 commissioned by the Ministry of Social Affairs and Health to make an administrator's memo "Towards Clearer Livelihood," which was published in 1998 under a title *Toimeentuloturvaa koskevan lainsäädännön selkeyttäminen*. (How to clear the legislation of livelihood, basic livelihood). Arajärvi also wrote an article in the *Talous ja yhteiskunta* (Economy and society) magazine 1/1998, in which he estimated the BI systems to be too expensive. In the same magazine, there was an article by Matti Tuomala, professor of economics, on incentive and encouraging welfare state, in which he gave a strong support to the existing insurance and means-tested social security system. For this reason, this government had no further interest in BI.

In the parliamentary election of 1999, the issue of BI was brought up again. The Greens had internal discussions in their party 1997–1998 about a suitable BI model, and Soininvaara wrote a column about "Time of Basic Income?" in the *Suomen Kuvalehti* magazine March 27, 1998. This magazine has also later supported BI in its leading articles. In April 1998, the Greens organized a public panel discussion with Centre Party, Leftist League, and Young Finnish Party (a new small liberal group of two parliament members). They all supported BI. Two of these parties were in opposition and two were sitting in the government. The main opposition party, the Centre Party, developed a program called "Work reform" for the election. On the one hand, this was an attempt to weaken the generally binding agreement in the labor market made with the Finnish trade unions and to support local labor agreements. On the other hand, it was about BI. Further, the social political program of the Young Finnish Party, led by Risto E. J. Penttilä, was based on BI. In the election campaign, the Social Democrats, with a support of the trade union, saw "work reform" as a danger to workers' rights, and the Centre Party lost the election. This work reform was so difficult an issue to the Centre Party that in the following election of 2003 their chairman had to swear never to carry out the concerned reform. The point, however, is that the Social Democrats together with the Centre Party did carry it out afterward in 2003–2007. Finally, BI played a role in the election of 1999, albeit a minor one. The Centre Party got a bad image due to their "work reform" program and the party had to continue in opposition. The Young Finnish Party disappeared from the parliament. This party was labeled as a group supporting extreme market liberation and their program, based on BI, seemed to be too radical for Finnish voters. In the election campaign, the Greens did not keep BI very much in the press, and the party won two seats in the parliament. The "rainbow government," now also including the Greens, continued in power.

In this government, the Green Osmo Soininvaara was minister of health and social services (minister of "Basic Services") 2000–2001. His intention was to advance BI but he was very careful about the term "basic income" or "citizens' salary" because in the government particularly the Social Democrats were against it. However, all parties in the government agreed that something has to be done about structural unemployment, poverty, complicated social security system, and low salary work. Soininvaara's intention was to show that BI would have been the answer to all these problems or at least a way in the right direction. However, Soininvaara had to concentrate on other projects of his ministry and he did not have enough time for "his BI project." The main government parties, which were the Social Democrats and the conservative Coalition Party, somehow faded out the whole idea of BI both in the government and in its social political working group. In the winter of 2002, at the end of Soininvaara's minister period, the parliament had to decide about permission for the fifth nuclear power plant. The Greens were very much against it and decided to leave the government because the parliament voted for the nuclear power plant. A BI discussion was very quiet also during the next parliamentary election of 2003. The Centre Party won the election and formed a new "red-soil" government with the Social Democrats. The rightist Coalition Party and the Green Party stayed in opposition. Previously, this kind of government combination ruled the country in 1987. Instead of BI, political questions connected with power played the main role in a political debate.

In the spring of 2001, there was a short but an interesting episode in the BI discussion. According to Björn Wahlroos, bank manager and doctor of economics, the problem of poverty in Finland could be solved by a simple recipe, a citizens' salary. According to his calculations the citizens' salary should be about €850–1000 a month. His arguments were mainly the same as those presented by Soininvaara and other BI supporters. He suggested traditional ways to finance the system, including reductions in expenses in the social security systems by cutting down bureaucracy and by encouraging low-salary workers to work spurred by lower taxes. He stated that most national economists would agree with him. However, he was not the right person to propose any kind of BI system because he was one of the richest men in Finland and one of the leading market liberals in the Finnish economic discussion and politics. Trade unions, Social Democrats, Leftist League, and the tiny Communist Party doomed Wahlroos' proposal. The Social Democratic ministers considered the proposal unrealistic and claimed that Wahlroos did not understand normal citizens' everyday life. The tiny Communist Party called Wahlroos' proposal a joke of May 1, and the Leftist League regarded it as a plot of extreme capitalists. Obviously, the Leftist League, which had proposed some BI models every now and then, kept away from all BI discussion and spoke only about basic security. In the press, Wahlroos got much support for his citizens' salary/BI proposal. However, inside the parties there was hardly any BI discussion on the political agenda in the following years.

Researchers and Societal Thinkers in Discussion

Many researchers participated in the societal debate on BI, and many of them have even supported BI during the last 15 years. The essays published in various books and magazines in the 1990s were philosophical and ideological speculations. A few master's thesis (pro gradu) papers on BI were written in universities. Osmo Soininvaara's works, books, and reports for the Ministry of Social Affairs and Health were important documents. However, a few articles and "counter memos" written by Pentti Arajärvi and some others made it difficult to find financial resources for a proper research.

In the 1990s after the publication of Ilpo Lahtinen's work, there was no thorough research until Anita Mattila's dissertation *Tarvitaanko perustuloa? Suomalaisen kansalaistulo-, kansalaispalkka ja perustulomallien teoreettinen analyysi.* (Is Basic Income needed? Theoretical Analysis of Finnish Civic Income, Civic Salary and Basic Income Models), December 2001, at the University of Kuopio. Mattila's work was an important theoretical analysis of a Finnish BI model and BI discussion. She first developed two microsimulation models for experiments and then carried out experiments in some limited geographical/municipal areas. However, this work got very little attention among researchers and hardly any publicity. When Mattila stated that further BI research was needed, she mentioned an opinion analysis of the political parties (that is what in part I am doing in this chapter), and development and use of microsimulation models.

These simulation models were gradually introduced by the Ministry of Social Affairs and Health to be used for the evaluation of BI models. In 2000, two leading Finnish poverty researchers, Matti Heikkilä and Jouko Karjalainen, edited and published a book *Poverty and Rupture of Welfare State* that included Seppo Sallila's chapter "Evaluation of a BI model." Sallila evaluated Soininvaara's models presented in 1994 using the simulation model developed in the ministry to simulate combined influences of social security benefits and taxation on the livelihood of individual citizens. In this Soma-model, statistical data of the whole population was used to find the population groups of "losers and winners." Most people, especially very poor, would be winners but average-income employees would lose some. Sallila also studied influences of equal tax in this model. According to his evaluation, Soininvaara's BI model combined with equal tax would work well and reduce poverty. However, it seems the result of this study could not exclude different conclusions and was contradictory. No trade unionist would tolerate a discussion about a BI model that could decrease wageworkers' income. It seemed as if the BI system did not change the living standard of the Finns very much, which in my opinion was the most important result. However, the interest of politicians and publicity was not awakened.

During the last few years, a new simulation model of BI was introduced. The Social Insurance Institution of Finland (Kela) developed a model called JUTTA, which appears to be an upgrade from a previous model called Soma. In 2004, a researcher, Pertti Honkanen, made calculations using the JUTTA model. His duty was to estimate a taxation percentage feasible in Finland assuming that the BI was €400 a month and replaced social benefits up to that sum. This would have been a partial BI and neutral for public financing. According to the calculation, the income tax percentage for those who earned more than €60,000 a year would be 55 percent and for the rest of the citizens 48 percent. However, if a citizens' BI was €400 the percentage would be smaller in lower income classes. In this sense, BI is a "negative progressive tax" for lower income classes. In this model, reductions in expenses due to decreasing bureaucracy and behavior of citizens were not taken into account. These issues would be worth a new research in different scientific fields. Anyway, the Greens used these results in their election program in the parliamentary election of 2007.

In 2005 and 2006, at least two surveys about BI/citizens' salary were carried out. In 2006, all political parties ordered a study from TNS Gallup Oy containing questions about the citizens' salary. The question presented was: "Should citizens' salary be paid to all citizens in our country?" The results were very detailed and sorted out according to different age groups, professional status, areas, parties, and so on. According to the final result, 29 percent of all the citizens said, "Yes"; 47 percent, "No;" whereas 25 percent could not say anything. In this inquiry, also the Greens were split up: 36 percent said, "Yes" and 44 percent, "No." In the parliamentary election of the following year, however, BI was one of the main issues of the Greens. In 2005, the rightist Coalition Party began to prepare their new program for the party and carried out a survey asking about BI: "Do you support a citizens salary or a basic income if it simplifies the existing social security system and removes other benefits simultaneously?" The answering percentage of this inquiry (response rate) was 58 percent; 64 percent of those who answered supported BI, 31.1 percent were against BI. This raises a question about the reason for this kind of different results in different studies. I assume the Finns generally understand that pay and work belong together. In the second survey, when more information was available, people thought that BI and citizens' salary meant different things. BI was accepted only if it helped to simplify our social security system.

Parliamentary Election 2007 and BI

When the Greens began to prepare themselves for the parliamentary election in 2007, they decided to include BI again as one of the main issues in their election program. This time the matter was better prepared than previously. For a good start Osmo Soininvaara and Ville Niinistö, who was a new leader of the BI working group of the Greens and now in 2011, the minister of environment, wrote a column about possibilities of combining work and social security in *Helsingin Sanomat*, which is the biggest newspaper in Finland. This inspired a lively discussion in this paper for and against BI.

One of those who participated in the discussion in the press was Seppo Lindblom, an experienced economist and a Social Democrat, whose party has generally opposed BI. He headed his column "Pari piirua pienen ihmisen suuntaan" (A couple of points toward humanity). The main message was:

> Basic income represents wider societal thinking in which an old-fashioned and conservative antithesis between the right-wing and the left-wing is not valid anymore and in which equality and solidarity are enriched by new conceptual and target oriented thinking.

The Greens' BI project continued when they, in September 2006, together with the Centre oriented research union organized a working seminar for BI experts. In this seminar, Osmo Soininvaara held a leading speech, which was succeeded by introductions presenting views of many leading economic and societal research institutes. In the audience, there were many university professors, researchers, and politicians from different parties. Discussion was lively, but according to many representatives of the research institutes, there was still no exact information on BI available sufficiently. Later in November, the Green Party organized a BI Seminar at which Professor Philippe van Parijs from Belgium lectured on BI. He is the founder of BIEN (Basic Income Earth Network) and one of the leading specialists of BI. The Greens developed a BI model, which was accepted in the party council in December 2006 and finally published with exact calculations in February 2007. These calculations were based on the JUTTA simulation model program. The Greens' BI proposal, called "Model 2008," was €440 a month partial BI, to be introduced step by step during 10–12 years. The Greens also underlined that this was just a proposal that needed further research. At the end of April, after the election the Greens published their study on BI written by Pertti Honkanen, Osmo Soninvaara, and Ville Ylikahri under a title *Perustulo—kohti toimivaa perusturvaa* (Basic Income—Toward Practical Basic Security).

In the winter of 2007 before the parliamentary election, it seemed that BI would be an important subject. *Suomen Kuvalehti*, the leading magazine in the Finnish political debate, published some articles about BI and the leading article in March 2007 was very positive toward BI. The article was headed "New bases" with the following idea: "Basic income would be the most remarkable societal reform of this time. It would free energy for work and help men shake off the yoke. After the election it will be in front of us." Many parties had "Think Tank" projects that also dealt with BI. The Social Democratic Kalevi Sorsa Foundation released a publication *Perustulo. Kova vai pehmeä paketti?* (Basic Income. A Hard or Soft Solution?) It was written by a trade union researcher Ville Kopra who was very critical toward BI. In a press conference at the end of February 2007, before the parliamentary election, there were Social Democrats like Tuula Haatainen, minister of social affairs and health at that time, and Professor Pentti Arajärvi, the president's spouse, who supported Kopra's critical view on BI. In addition, another big party, the rightist Coalition Party had a "Think Tank" project of their own. In connection with this project, a BI seminar was organized at the end of February before the election. One of the speakers was Osmo Soininvaara. The audience with many entrepreneurs was very much for BI, but a representative of the Confederation of Finnish Industries and one member of parliament were against it. In the summer of 2007, this "Think Tank" also published a book *Sisällä vai ulkona—kohti perustuloa?* (In or out—Toward Basic Income?) edited by Sari Hintikka-Varis in which all articles dealt with BI in one way or another (this chapter is partly based on one chapter in the book concerned).

However, despite many BI projects the issue did not play a very important role in the debates during the parliamentary election (the election was March 18, 2007). All the leaders of the parliament parties participated in a TV discussion where the TV editors asked the party leaders about their opinions on the existing social security system and about BI as a solution to solve problems involved in the system. They all agreed that the existing system needed a reform but none, except the Green Tarja Cronberg, saw BI as a solution. Social democratic Eero Heinäluoma had learned his lessons from Kopra's book. As soon as he had spoken out his arguments about BI, nobody had anything to add. He stated, "Basic income encourages inactivity, is too expensive, means just an additional system among the others and does not support Lutheran work ethics." In this quick and short discussion, it was difficult for the Green Cronberg to catch up and express her views.

In the parliamentary election of 2007, the Social Democrats lost eight seats and the Centre four. The rightist Coalition Party from the opposition was the greatest winner with ten new seats. The Greens won one seat. The Centre Party maintained its position as the greatest party with 51 seats against the Coalition Party, which got 50 members to the parliament. As the biggest party, the Centre had the prime minister's post and the new government was formed together with Coalition Party,

Green Party, and Swedish People's Party. The Social Democrats, the Left League, and some smaller parties had to stay in opposition. This new "blue-green" government included a statement in their program, according to which a reform of the social security system would be started to improve incentives of work, to reduce poverty, and to guarantee a sufficient level of basic security in all life phases. The government founded a "Committee for reforming social protection" (the SATA Committee) and a subordinate committee called "Basic security sub-committee" with Osmo Soininvaara as the chairman. Many believed in Osmo Soininvaara's capabilities to further the development of BI.

Committee Work for Reforming Social Protection (the SATA Committee)

The SATA Committee was set up in June 2007, and it was assigned to prepare a total reform of social protection by drawing up a proposal for adequate basic protection/security, earnings-related security with focus on active alternatives, improving incentives (for work), clarification of social security, and ensuring the sustainability of social protection.

The committee consisted of the representatives of the government parties, of the Ministry of Social Affairs and Health as well as of the Ministry of Finance, and of many interest groups. Trade unions and industrial organizations had a substantial representation among the 19 committee members. The Social Democrats, as an opposition party, were excluded from the committee. However, their "voice" was heard through the trade union representatives. The chairman of the committee was Markku Lehto, former permanent secretary of state at the Ministry of Social Affairs and Health, and vice chairman was Martti Hetemäki, permanent undersecretary of state at the Ministry of Finance. In the four subcommittees, there were almost 50 members and one of them was Osmo Soininvaara, chairman of the basic security subcommittee. After the committee work, he wrote a book *SATA-komitea—Miksi asioista päättäminen on niin vaikeaa* (SATA Committee. What Makes the Decision-Making So Difficult?).

J. P. Roos, professor of social policy, who has criticized the Finnish basic livelihood protection system, was very skeptical of the SATA Committee. Although Roos appreciated the goals and the members of the committee, he regarded the Finnish committee practice to include "all possible organizations" as a problem, which makes it almost impossible to achieve a good comprehensive reform and makes the Finnish social security system and legislation too complicated. Osmo Soininvaara agreed with him, and, as a member of the committee, he realized that most of the committee members simply watched the interests of their own groups. Especially, the representatives of the trade unions and the industrial organizations considered the whole committee as a threat to their interests; they wanted a subcommittee for earnings-related security of their own. The fact that the Finnish social security system is divided into two parts—in basic security and earnings-related security—made the issue the most difficult one in the committee.

Because trade unions and industrial organizations have traditionally been against BI, their representatives nearly always tended to start their speeches by pointing out that the social security system has to be based on conditional benefits. They were always suspicious of Soininvaara's proposals because, as a supporter of BI, Soininvaara might hide "BI germs" in everything. Therefore, Soininvaara could not use the term "basic income" but naturally, he tried to use BI elements in his proposals. In addition to BI, Soininvaara has a wide command of the Finnish social security systems. For this reason, he is able to make constructive proposals for many committee issues.

The first report and the basic lines for the comprehensive reform of social protection were published in January 2009, although by the autumn of 2008 many concrete proposals for legislation had existed. However, in the autumn of 2008, interest groups started their own negotiations of general agreement about social politics. In January 2009, the interest groups made a social incomes policy agreement, which improved earnings-related security considerably. They also agreed that basic security cannot be raised more than earnings-related security. Thus, if basic security will be raised, the earnings-related security also has to be raised equally, and this becomes very expensive for the society. Professor Roos described the situation: "By tying this improvement to the improvement of earnings-related security in the social incomes policy agreement the trade union knowingly prevented the improvement of the economic situation of people getting basic benefit and of those who would have needed the improvement most." This was a shock to most of the committee members, and Chairman Markku Lehto considered leaving the committee.

However, Markku Lehto led the committee until the end, and the final report was ready at the end of the year 2009. Although the comprehensive reform of social protection was not realized, the committee collected a lot of important information and put forward 31 recommendations. The effort also resulted in many good principles to follow if there would be further interest toward realization in the future. The most important achievement was a guarantee pension, which was also included in legislation. This improved the situation of about one hundred thousand poor pensioners. At least in this case, it was possible to improve basic security without any linkage to earnings-related security. This is also a small step toward BI. Other improvements, which can be seen as progress toward BI, are an extended index protection and a higher basic deduction.

This committee work was characterized by institutional resistance of a Nordic welfare state with strong interest groups and social democratic ideology against BI, which Raija Julkunen, an experienced researcher of social policy, has described in her articles (2009). Julkunen cannot see any reason why the successful middle class would support BI because they believe that everybody must earn his/her living, and benefits must be strictly controlled. Many practical social workers understand that this massive control takes too much of their time that could be used for "real social work." However, their own interest organization is still very skeptical of BI.

Parliamentary Election in 2011

Before the parliamentary election in 2011, BI was rarely mentioned in discussions by the name. It was not forgotten, however. The Greens have it in their social political programs, and there are supporters in many other parties too. An interesting example is the conservative-liberal National Coalition Party. During the party meetings in 2008 and in 2010 member initiatives for BI (or NIT) were presented. In the meeting of 2008, the idea was approved but in the meeting of 2010, it was rejected. The leading politicians were not ready to support it. However, it was discussed in every party and many politicians talked about it as a feasible way to raise basic security of the poorest people.

In the European parliamentary election of 2009, the candidates were asked to answer the questions presented by newspapers in election machines on the Internet, and to give their opinions for instance about a European-wide BI. Almost all candidates were against BI. In the parliamentary election of 2011, newspapers were not interested in inquiring about the matter. In election campaigns, other themes became more important. Immigration and economic problems of the EU were the issues that the populist True Finns Party brought up for discussion and won 34 additional seats, now holding 39 seats in all in the new parliament. The Greens, campaigning for BI, lost 5 seats out of 15 and now have 10 seats in all. In addition, other parties lost seats; some more, some less. The economic problems of the EU are waiting to be solved. As the True Finns Party did not agree on Finnish EU policy, the party decided to stay in opposition. The leader of the biggest party, National Coalition Party (44 seats), Jyrki Katainen formed a new cabinet in June 2011 with five other pro-EU parties like the Social Democrats and some small parties, the Greens included. The new government wants to improve basic security but the concept of BI is not mentioned in the government program. The Greens are now in cabinet, the new party leader Ville Niinistö is the minister of the environment, and Osmo Soininvaara has become a member of parliament once more. The years to come will show if they can find new ways to further the development of BI.

Summary of the Debates

The Greens and Osmo Soininvaara have been very much in the public eye in the debate. During the last few years also, other Green politicians like Ville Niinistö, now as a new minister, have presented opinions in favor of BI. More researchers and societal thinkers have joined the discussion. However, the funds for bigger research projects dealing with BI are still missing. New and better microsimulation programs are available for the evaluation of the consequences of different BI models and levels.

Institutional resistance is also still very strong in many parties and interest organizations. The work of the SATA Committee is one example of how interest groups keep the positions and structures of the social security systems unchanged. The main argument against BI in Finland, like in other Nordic welfare states, is that "free money" lessens work motivation and therefore the benefits of social security need to be strictly controlled and need/means tested. It is ironical that BI is resisted because of the problems of the present system, which allows "free money" but the control of which requires huge bureaucratic organizations. The trade unions and industrial organizations are inclined to think that BI would weaken their power.

Within a political party, there are supporters as well as opponents. The division, however, also goes by the parties; the Greens belong to the supporters and the Social Democrats to the opponents. Further, different BI models have supporters of their own regardless of their political stands. This makes it very difficult to achieve a general agreement on BI. If a "wrong" party or group proposes a BI model it is not very easily acceptable. According to right-wing supporters (mostly pro–negative income model) BI frees you of the "chains of the state" and reduces public control, for example, by means-tested social security. Left-wing supporters regard BI as a way to root out the "slavery to bad capitalists" from the market, especially from the labor market. Many researchers and societal thinkers doubt whether BI is feasible in our society as criteria vary considerably. Nevertheless, behind this practical thinking, there are different ideas of how we see human nature; are we trustworthy or do we need to be controlled? Is BI just another practical method to distribute material wealth or is it also a new citizen right like a universal right to vote, child benefit, and national pension?

Notes

* This chapter was based on a paper presented at the BIEN Congress 2008, in Parallel Session 4c, "The Debate in Europe." Updated in June 2011.

Bibliography

Allén, Tuovi et al. 1993. *Täyskäännös? Taloutemme valintojen edessä.* Helsinki: Kirjapaino-Osakeyhtiö Like.

Arajärvi, Pentti. 1997. *Selkeämpään toimeentuloon: selvitysmiesmuistio toimeentuloturvalainsäädännön selkeyttämisestä.* Helsinki: STM.

———. 1998. *Toimeentuloturvaa koskevan lainsäädännön selkeyttäminen.* Helsinki: STM.

———. 1998. "Tomeentulo ja perustulo." *Talous ja yhteiskunta* 1/1998.

Basic Income. 1993. *Newsletter of BIEN* No. 15. January. Brussels.

Hakkarainen, Outi, Jaana Airaksinen, and Tove Selin (eds.). 2005. "Talous ja demokratia." *Ratkaisuja Suomesta ja muualta maailmalta.* Keuruu: Otavan Kirjapaino Oy.

Heinonen, Jari. 1993. *Kattotarinasta monikärkiseen pohdintaan.* Tampere: Tammer-Paino Oy.

Hintikka-Varis, Sari (ed.). 2007. *Sisällä vai ulkona—kohti perustuloa?* Helsinki: Kansallinen Sivistysliitto ry.

Honkanen, Pertti, Soininvaara, Osmo and Ylikahri, Ville. 2007. *Perustulo—Kohti toimivaa perusturvaa* (*Basic Income—Toward Practical Basic Security*). Vaasa: Oy Arkmedia Ab.

Ikkala, Markku. 1978. "Ihmisarvo ja työ." *Luotain nro 2.* Helsinki: Suomalaisen Kirjallisuuden Kirjapaino Oy.

Julkunen, Raija. 2009. "Perustulo—Kuinka sama idea toistuvasti kohtaa sosiaalidemokraattisen ajattelun?" *Ajatuksen voima: ideat hyvinvointivaltion uudistamisessa.* Edited by Johannes Kananen and Juho Saari. Jyväskylä: Minerva.

Juuti, Pauli. 1983. *Työkäyttäytymisen teoreettinen tausta.* Helsinki: Kirjapaino R. Lunkka Ky.

———. 1988. *Työilmapiiri ja työolot.* JTO: n tutkimuksia. Sarja 2. Kokemäki: JTO.

———. 1991. *Työ ja elämän laatu.* JTO: n tutkimuksia. Sarja 6. MyCo Oy / Kirjapaino R. Lunkka.

———. 1996. *Suomalainen elämänlaatu.* JTO: n tutkimuksia. Sarja 10. Tampere: Tammer-Paino Oy.

Kasvio, Antti. 1985. "Duaalitalous ja huomispäivän yhteiskuntamallit." *Talouden kahtiajako. Mykät pakot ja vapauden visio.* Edited by Timo Kyntäjä. Jyväskylä: Gummerus Oy.

———. 1994. *Uusi työn yhteiskunta.* Jyväskylä: Gummerus Oy.

Kopra, Ville. 2007. *Perustulo. Kova vai pehmeä paketti?* Helsinki: Kalevi Sorsa Fund, Yliopistopaino.

Lahtinen, Ilpo (ed.). 1988. *Kansalaispalkka. Ken elää sen syömänkin pitää.* Ylioppilaspalvelu ry: n julkaisusarja 2/88. Helsinki: Ylioppilaspalvelu ry.
———. 1992. *Perustulo. Kansalaisen palkka.* Tampere: Tammer-Paino Oy.
Mattila, Anita. 2001. *Tarvitaanko perustuloa? Suomalaisten kansalaistulo-, kansalaispalkka- ja perustulomallien teoreettinen analyysi.* Kuopio: Savon Kopiokeskus Oy, Yliopiston painatuskeskus.
Offe, Claus. 1994. *Vollbeschäftigung.* Unpublished introduction in BIEN conference in London Sebtember 8–10, 1994.
Ojapelto, Ari. 1989. *Lisääkö automaatio kilpailukykyä vai työttömyyttä?* Jyväskylä: Gummerus.
———. 2006. *Ahneuden aika.* Saarijärvi: Saarijärven Offset Oy.
Parker, Hermione. 1989. *Instead of the Dole. An Enquiry into Integration of the Tax and Benefit Systems.* London: Routledge.
Peltola, Kati. 1997. *Hyvinvointivaltion peruskorjaus.* Jyväskylä: Gummerus Kirjapaino Oy.
Penttilä, Risto E. J. 1994. *Ultimatum isänmaalle. Nuorsuomalainen näkemys Suomen mahdollisuuksista.* Keuruu: Otava.
Peränen, Hanna-Leena. 1990. *Kansalaispalkka—tutkimus 1980-luvulla Suomessa käydystä kansalaispalkkakeskustelusta.* University of Jyväskylä. Department of social policy. Pro gradu study.
Perheentupa, Antti-Veikko. 1993. *Oikeudenmukaisuutta toisin tavoin. Haasteita 90-luvun sosiaalipolitiikalle.* Juva: WSOY.
Perustoimeentulotyöryhmän mietintö. 1986. Työryhmämuistio 1986: 2. Helsinki: STM.
Pursiainen, Terho. 1995. "Nousukauden etiikka." *Suomen Kuvalehti magazine 16/95.*
Sailas, Raija. 1986. *Köyhät keskuudessamme?—Pienituloisten kotitaloudet vuoden 1981 kotitaloustiedustelussa.* Helsinki: Sosiaalihallituksen toimeentuloprojekti.
SAK ry. 1994. "Mikä ihmeen perustulo?" *Taloustietoa 28.10.94.*
Sallila, Seppo. 2000. "Erään perustulomallin arviointi." *Köyhyys ja hyvinvointivaltion murros.* Edited by Matti Heikkilä and Jouko Karjalainen. Helsinki: Gaudeamus.
Särkelä, Riitta, and Anne Eronen (eds.). 2007. *Perusturvan pulmat ja uudistamisen vaihtoehdot.* Sosiaali- ja terveysturvan keskusliitto ry. Helsinki: Hakapaino Oy.
Soininvaara, Osmo. 1992. "Minun perustulomallini." *Perustulo. Kansalaisen palkka.* Edited by Ilpo Lahtinen. Tampere: Tammer-Paino Oy.
———. 1994. *Hahmotelma perustulomallista.* STM: n monisteita 2/04. Helsinki: STM.
———. 1994. *Hyvinvointivaltion eloonjäämisoppi.* Juva: WSOY: n graafiset laitokset.
———. 1998. "Time of Basic Income?" *Suomen Kuvalehti* March 27: 73.
———. 2002. *Ministerikyyti.* Helsinki: WSOY.
———. 2010. *SATA-komitea—Miksi asioista päättäminen on niin vaikeaa.* Helsinki: Kustannusosakeyhtiö Teos.

Soininvaara, Osmo, and Osmo Lampinen. 1980. *Suomi 1980-luvulla* (Finland in the 1980s). Juva: WSOY: n graafiset laitokset.

Sosiaaliturvan uudistamiskomitean (SATA-komitean) ehdotukset sosiaaliturvan uudistamiseksi. Sosiaali- ja terveysministeriön selvityksiä 2009: 62. Helsinki: STM.

Teollisuuden ja Työnantajien Keskusliitto. 1995. *Työtä vai kansalaispalkkaa*. Maaliskuu. Helsinki: TTK.

Vartia, Pentti, and Pekka Ylä-Anttila. 2005. *Kansantalous 2008*. Taloustieto. 2. painos. Helsinki: ETLA.

Ylä-Liedenpohja, Jouko. 1994. *Taloustiede tänään*. Keuruu: Kustannusosakeyhtiö Otava.

———. 1995. *Kansalaislisä—ja työtä!* Unpublished introduction in the University of Jyväskylä. Taloustutkijoiden XII kesäpäivät in Jyväskylä June 19–20, 1995.

CHAPTER 6

Germany: Far, though Close—Problems and Prospects of BI in Germany*

Sascha Liebermann

Basic income (BI) in a very general sense has been discussed at intervals in Germany since the 1970s, with emphasis being placed on its unconditional dimension since 2003. Despite the stunning attention it has gained due to intense debate, BI has not made it into legislation or legislative initiatives. When I talk about BI, I follow more or less the criteria proposed by the Basic Income Earth Network (BIEN): (1) it is paid to individuals rather than households; (2) it is paid irrespective of any income from other sources; (3) it is paid without requiring performance of any work or the willingness to accept a job if offered. Limitations and constraints of these three criteria are pointed out in the section "Arguments and Debates." It is because of these criteria that I do not consider *Bürgergeld* (Citizen's Money, see Mitschke 2000) in my chapter.

Mostly confined to academic circles or at best featured in few articles by magazines, BI has nonetheless made it into the public. Broader attention has been paid to BI since 2005. I will begin by tracing a very brief history of the current debate. Then, I will turn to precursors in the 1980s and give hints to why BI might have been off the agenda in the 1990s following German reunification. After this, instead of presenting several contested concepts of BI, I will give a general idea of main arguments and objections to BI that allow drawing the lines in the German debate. Finally, I will turn to prospects of BI in Germany and deal with the question whether it is just a pipedream or likely to be introduced.

A Very Brief History of the Current Debate

In Germany in the 2000s, as in other countries like the United Kingdom or, much earlier, in the United States and Switzerland, employment became the utmost goal of social policy, tightening measures against unemployed persons and focusing more than ever on the willingness to work. Workfare was widely celebrated as the best way out of unemployment.

In 2002, former chancellor Gerhard Schröder launched the *Hartz-Commission*—named after the chair Peter Hartz, former member of the board of Volkswagen AG—an advisory board in charge of designing welfare reform. In 2003, the Schröder government set up the *Agenda 2010* (Bundesregierung 2003) reinforcing workfare policies as a remedy for high unemployment. Schröder did not invent workfare ideas; he picked up what had been around already even before the turn of the century (Fleckenstein 2008). The trade unions were involved in the *Hartz-Commission* and signed the report as well. Following *Hartz* legislation in 2004, unemployed persons came under the control of the *Bundesagentur für Arbeit* (National Department of Work, Bundesagentur für Arbeit 2011). In a cynical or euphemistic use of the term, the agency refers to unemployed persons as its "customers," even though these "customers" cannot choose whether to turn to this agency at all. To receive benefits, they have to register.

In an early stage of the current BI debate, public response largely followed a poster campaign in Frankfurt in December 2003 initiated by the group *Freiheit statt Vollbeschäftigung* (Freedom, not Full Employment).[1] We—the author is one of its founding and still active members—rented advertising space and put up 50 posters in several subway stations so that people waiting on the platform and passengers in the coaches were able to see them.[2] Surprisingly quickly, within the first two weeks of campaigning, we received a large number of emails and within a few weeks, more interview requests arrived. Journalists saw the posters in subway stations and contacted us.

TV-journalist Henning Burk, who was working (2003–2004) on the subject of German unemployment legislation, produced a five-part feature called *Hartzreise* (Hartz-Journey) alluding to the "Hartz-Commission." Part five entitled *Freiheit statt Vollbeschäftigung* (Freedom, not Full Employment) included very short interviews with Robert Kurz, Claus Offe, and me. It was broadcasted on German public TV program *3Sat* in March 2004 (and an invitation to a radio interview and a talk show followed in May). *Frankfurter Allgemeine Zeitung* was the first one to print an article by Thomas Loer, also an activist of *Freiheit statt Vollbeschäftigung* in May 2004 (Loer 2004). In September, we were interviewed by the German newspaper *tageszeitung* and the *Frankfurter Rundschau* printed an article entitled *Freiheit der Bürger statt Arbeitszwang* (Freedom of Citizens instead of Coercion to Work) (Liebermann 2004). As far as I know, no other groups or individuals were advocating BI in public at that time to initiate a debate among fellow citizens. There were people in favor of BI or at least amenable to it who discussed pros and cons among themselves. A group consisting of unemployed and precariously employed people supported *Existenzgeld* (Subsistence allowance, see Bundesarbeitsgemeinschaft der Erwerbslosen- und Sozialhilfeinitiativen e. V.2008) and a subdivision of *attac,* which is called *Genug für alle* (Enough for all, founded in October 2003; see Attac AG "Genug für alle" 2010), argued for BI as well. There were also a few social or political scientists such as Ulrich Oevermann (2001), Claus Offe (2005, a founding member of the BIEN), and Michael Opielka (2000) who were discussing BI.

Surprisingly at the time, none of the well-known public intellectuals such as Jürgen Habermas, Oskar Negt, or Günter Grass were supporting BI activities. Habermas had been arguing for BI in the 1980s (Habermas 1985), but has not picked it up again yet; Negt, first, in 2004, argued for a rather low *Grundgehalt* (Basic Salary, Negt 2004) that should be linked to the obligation to vote. In 2010, he seemed to abandon the obligation to vote, but was still unclear whether BI should be rather low or sufficient; Grass, however, by signing a newspaper advertisement in support of *Agenda 2010* by chancellor Schröder entitled "Auch wir sind das Volk" ("We, too, are the people," Jürgs 2004) showed that he regarded workfare policies the right way. Later, in 2009, Grass seemed to have changed his mind slightly. He supported an appeal to a moratorium of sanctions against welfare recipients (Sanktionsmoratorium 2009). Following Hartz legislation, Job-Centers (Arbeitsagenturen or Arbeitsgemeinschaften) were allowed to use sanctions (e.g., reduce benefits) against those recipients who were not willing to cooperate.

In July 2004, the German *Netzwerk Grundeinkommen* (Network BI) was founded. It has been trying to serve as a platform for activists with some success, organizing conferences and talks, but it has also attracted much criticism of its policies. Much of the criticism was directed toward the way the Network has acted in the public as if it were the national speaker of the BI activists. Recently, it attracted criticism for the way it dealt with the petition submitted to the German Parliament by Susanne Wiest in 2008 (Wiest 2008). The German Network BI brings together people from different backgrounds, many of them without any affiliation, and is open to different concepts of BI. Most active groups are registered and displayed on a map now provided by the German BI

Network,[3] several of them members of the Network. The Network itself, affiliated with the international BIEN, has continuously increased its members from 700 in June 2006 to 3,166 in August 2011, of which 96 were organizations.[4]

Using media attention as a relative measure of success, 2005 was a turning point in the debate. From well-known daily newspapers like *Frankfurter Allgemeine Zeitung*, *Süddeutsche Zeitung*, *Die Welt* to smaller ones like *Frankfurter Rundschau, Tagesspiegel* and *tageszeitung* to weekly newspapers like *Rheinischer Merkur* and *Die Zeit* to monthly magazines like *brandeins*—BI was widely recognized as an important issue. Articles, features, and interviews on television and radio programs dealt to an enormous extent with BI.

It was, largely, Götz W. Werner, founder and former CEO of the drugstore chain dm-drogerie markt (DM), who got the ball rolling. He has published three books since 2006 of which more than one hundred thousand copies were sold. In March 2005, he gave an interview to the magazine *b* with the headline "Wir leben in paradiesischen Zuständen" (We live under paradisiac circumstances) (Werner 2005). He emphasized the enormous wealth in Western European countries and their ability to produce a large surplus of goods and services. *brandeins* picked up on BI again in its August 2005 (brandeins 2005) issue with the title "*Arbeit. Nie wieder Vollbeschäftigung. Wir haben Besseres zu tun*" (Work. Never full employment again. We've got better things to do). In November 2005, Werner initiated a newspaper campaign by taking out a half-page advertisement entitled *Ein Grund für die Zukunft: das Grundeinkommen* (A reason for the future: Basic Income). In the advertisement's text, he pointed out why BI would help solve problems and foster initiative. Later, in an interview with the magazine *stern* in April 2006, he blamed social policy following *Hartz IV*[5] as being *offener Strafvollzug* (for treating welfare recipients as inmates of an open penal system).

Media response increased in 2006. In early summer, the former prime minister of the Free State of Thuringia, Dieter Althaus, member of the *Christlich Demokratische Union* (CDU, Christian Democratic Party), released his concept of *Solidarisches Bürgergeld* (Citizen's Solidarity Allowance, Borchard 2007; Althaus and Binkert 2010), apparently inspired by the ongoing debate.[6] His proposal, not as far-reaching as BI and recently renamed *partial* BI, suggested that he realized it was the time to turn to alternatives and no longer stick to the full employment idea. The amount of minimum income he proposed though was too low to live on, and was based in a certain sense on the Negative Income Tax (NIT). However, for the public debate, it was an important step to have a politician taking it seriously, emphasizing the decoupling of "willingness to work" and eligibility to benefits.

Since 2006, the debate has become more realistic and considerate. Still, objections are elaborated from all sides. For example, former federal minister of labor (from 1982–1998) Norbert Blüm (Blüm 2007), member of the CDU and a persistent critic of welfare retrenchment under the Schröder Government, attacked BI in the weekly newspaper *Die Zeit.* In his article titled "*Wahnsinn mit Methode*" (Madness with Method), he characterized the idea of BI as being unjust and against solidarity, as a means to abolish the *Sozialstaat* (welfare state) (Butterwegge 2007) or as unrealistic, a means to take people's mind of urging problems (Müller 2010). Some pundits—market liberal economists as well as their critics—argue BI makes achievement obsolete and rewards laziness (for the former, see Siebert 2007; for the latter, Busch 2005, Schlecht 2006). Advocates and critics are to be found on each side of previously established ideological standpoints.

In November 2007, the German Council of Economic Experts (2007) published its annual report 2007–2008 dealing with Althaus' proposal. The experts concluded:

> A completely misguided idea . . . is the endeavor to replace the social welfare state in its traditional form by a guaranteed basic income scheme (*Grundeinkommenssicherung*) by largely abolishing the participative equivalent (*teilhabeäquivalent*) statutory unemployment and pension insurance schemes and, in contrast to the present basic allowance concepts that are geared to neediness . . . would entitle everyone to an unconditional claim to a government transfer in the amount of the socio-cultural subsistence minimum level of existence.
>
> (German Council 2007, 17)

BI has also been the subject of documentaries, which helped to spread the idea. In 2006, Daniel Häni and Enno Schmidt (in Basle, Switzerland) started filming interviews with people on the street about BI. They made the videos available online and later included parts of these in a BI documentary called *Kulturimpuls Grundeinkommen. Ein Essay* (Cultural Impulse Basic Income. A Film Essay; see *Movies and Videos,* Häni and Schmidt 2008). Released in September 2008, this film became the most popular documentary on BI in Germany, shown at many places all over the country. It is available online, and in a dubbed version, too. In 2007, Christoph Schlee produced and directed the documentary *Götz W. Werner—Grundeinkommen für alle* (Basic Income for all, see *Movies and Videos,* Schlee 2007a) and another one gathering statements by known advocates *Sechs Positionen zum Grundeinkommen* (Six Positions toward Basic Income, Schlee 2007b). Jördis Heizmann together with Andreas Zgraja (see *Movies and Videos* Heizmann and Zgraja 2007) released a documentary in the same year called *Designing*

Society. This movie combines interviews with advocates and critics. The way it was assembled evokes striking insights into the resistance BI faces. Especially statements by people who would directly benefit—a woman who, as she says, works off the books not just to improve her pension but to meet people, or a man who was ill for a long time and not able to work—provide a whole range of arguments for BI. However, they do not support BI. Almost rudely, the man declares that he who does not work shall not eat, while the woman fears a collective stultification and decline of civilization.

Since 2008, the *Woche des Grundeinkommens* (Week of BI) is held around mid September. Throughout Germany, local activists organize panel discussions, talks, and movie screenings to spread the idea and to get fellow citizen's attention.[7]

In December 2008, Susanne Wiest, referred to by the media as *Tagesmutter aus Greifswald* (independent child day care professional from Greifswald), submitted an online petition to the German Bundestag proposing to introduce an Unconditional Basic Income (Wiest 2008). In her substantiation to the petition, she suggests an amount of fifteen hundred Euros for adults and a thousand for children per month, nearly doubling the currently defined minimum income for single households with no children—in-kind- and in-cash benefits altogether (Federal Ministry of Finance 2008). Nearly fifty-three thousand (52,973) people signed the petition within six weeks. The hearing by the *Petitionsausschuss* (commission that treats petitions) took place on November 8, 2010.[8] Again, media response since she submitted the petition until the hearing and after was stunning. Susanne Wiest has given many interviews and talks since then. Features about her were published in well-known daily newspapers like *Frankfurter Allgemeine Zeitung.*

In the same year, a campaign by the *Bürgerinitiative bedingungsloses Grundeinkommen Berlin* (Citizens' Group BI Berlin) draw enormous media attention. On April 1, they launched a website that looked like the one of the National Department of Work, but they renamed it "National Department of Income."[9] The website also provided a form almost identical to the one that has to be used to apply for *Arbeitslosengeld II*, a very rigid workfare-oriented assistance program. The National Department of Work threatened to sue the group if they would not change the layout of the website. To avoid this, the group changed it.

It took only three years, from winter 2003 to winter 2006, until almost all established political parties—*Sozialdemokratische Partei Deutschlands* (SPD, Social Democratic Party), CDU, *Bündnis 90/ Die Grünen* (the Green Party),[10] *Die Linke* (the Left)[11]—associations of employers as well as employees, think tanks, and churches responded.

The number of video- and audio recordings of talks and panel discussions of BI now available on the net, for example, via YouTube, as well as articles in newspapers and magazines, and an increasing number of academic works, confirm and record the level of intense and lively discussion, although it has not made its way into the daily news. By different means such as poster campaigns, talks, and panel discussions addressing fellow citizens, Internet sites, and weblogs, activists have been very successful in spreading the idea.

Precursors—Similarities and Differences

BI did not appear in Germany from nowhere; the idea has been around since the late 1970s, although mostly confined to certain milieus around the ecology movement (out of which the Green Party emerged), groups of unemployed, precariously employed (Bundesarbeitsgemeinschaft der Erwerbslosen- und Sozialhilfeinitiativen e. V. 2008), and academic circles. Those involved, however, rarely considered how a BI could reinforce citizenship and so strengthen the political community. The idea of citizenship as constituent of political community remains underestimated. Social scientist Ralf Dahrendorf (1986) was one of the few who pointed out that BI should not be seen from the point of view of the tax system. First, citizen rights have to be defined, he contended, and then, means must be found to provide the income that these rights should guarantee.

In the early 1980s, congresses were held picking up the idea of Guaranteed Income, or at least an income irrespective of work obligation. The number of publications was increasing. A well-known article by Ralf Dahrendorf *Im, Entschwinden der Arbeitsgesellschaft* (Disappearing Employment Society, Dahrendorf 1980) was published in the German monthly magazine *Merkur*. Later in the 1980s, two books became particularly popular. The first, *Befreiung von falscher Arbeit* (Liberation from false work, Schmid 1986 [1984]) was published in two editions (the second completely revised). The second book *Garantiertes Grundeinkommen* (Guaranteed Income, Opielka and Vobruba 1986) has become a classic when referring to the eighties.

In 1982, it was, in particular, associations of unemployed and receivers of *Sozialhilfe*[12] (social assistance, see Erster Bundeskongress der Arbeitslosen 1983) at a conference in Frankfurt who demanded a "right to income," which was picked up later (in 1992) and turned into *Existenzgeld* (Subsistence Allowance; see Bundesarbeitsgemeinschaft der Erwerbslosen- und Sozialhilfeinitiativen e. V. 2008). The same year, 1982, the biannual congress of the German Sociological Association focused on "The Crisis of the Employment Society," a congress often referred to when talking about the BI debate. Within the Green movement and then within the Green Party (founded in the early eighties), BI gained some support, often related to ideas of social ecology or ecological libertarianism. Nonetheless, it never entered official statements and where BI is mentioned in Green Party programs—for example, the program *Umbau der Industriegesellschaft* (Reorganizing Industrial Society) adopted at a meeting of national delegates in 1986 (Die Grünen 1986)—it is much closer to a means-tested, but less bureaucratic cash benefit that NIT provides.

Reading articles published in 1986 reminds one of arguments outlined today, as if times have not changed at all. In *Die Zeit*, for instance, Wolf-Dieter Hasenclever's[13] (1986) "Ein Weg ins Schlaraffenland? Das Grundeinkommen für jeden Bürger könnte ein Schritt zur sozialen Freiheit sein" (A way to the land of milk and honey? A basic income for every citizen could be a step toward social freedom) elaborates the pros and cons of BI. Some of his arguments could easily be transferred to the present. Although BI was a hot issue, publications were numerous, and media response, especially among newspapers, was noteworthy, it disappeared in the late eighties to the early nineties, lingering on only in rather small circles. It is difficult to be confident about the reasons for the decline, but several influences can be suggested. Advocates did not address fellow citizens directly in the public sphere to try to gain followers. In addition, aspects of BI were discussed in more theoretical than in practical terms. Those who intended to gain people's attention had it in mind to organize a "different" or "alternative" public (Opielka 2000), in fact, a public besides the public, and consequently, only reached certain milieus. Little or no attention was paid to what is now one of the most prominent arguments: BI as means to reinforce citizenship as fundamental to democracy. Rather, the state was considered as an adversary that, first and foremost, one has to be protected from by recourse to rights. Demanding the "right to income" stressed the freedom from obligation without taking into consideration that BI would not last without citizens' willingness to contribute whatever they can or wish to. Furthermore, German reunification in 1990 dominated political debates and entailed many challenges. Meanwhile, due to generational transformations of gender identity, the growing labor participation of women was seen as running counter to BI arguments and amplified the idea that paid work was an ultimate goal—which is now reinterpreted as gender equality. By the end of the 1990s, BI seemed to have dissipated even though articles in magazines like *brandeins* in 2001 "Wege in die Zukunft—Grundeinkommen" (Paths to the Future—Basic Income) (Spielkamp 2001), or in *Die Zeit* indicated that the idea was still known. BI, however, needed a few more years to return and find a public response.

Arguments and Debates

I now want to give a general idea of main arguments for and objections to BI in the current debate. I hope to clarify obstacles that BI faces due to prevailing ideas of autonomy, individual capacities, social justice, democracy, and equality.

Unconditionality

In current debates in Germany, the adjective "unconditional" has a prominent position. Why is "unconditionality" so important and what does it mean? The German welfare state provides an assortment of different insurance benefits (e.g., Unemployment Benefit I, Pension), assistances, and allowances managed by independent funds. All are conditional; they either require willingness to work (Unemployment Benefit, wage related), acquired entitlements or claims to benefits through contributions (Unemployment Benefit and Pension), a certain age (child benefits),[14] or means testing (social assistance) (Fleckenstein 2008). Stressing unconditionality,[15] however, as it is expressed in the goal, to provide BI from cradle-to-grave, counters an even stronger regime of workhouse policies that arose with the Schröder government. The term unconditional in the German debate clearly refers to the "achievement" conditions a beneficiary must meet to receive benefits today. So, that a beneficiary of BI must meet "status" conditions, either citizenship or a permanent residency, does not—as some pundits mock—contradict the idea of unconditionality.

Education: Prerequisite to BI or Goal in Itself?

The more the debate has broadened the easier it becomes to advocate conditions, while still calling it BI. Sneaking in the back door, one finds conditionality in terms of educational obligations BI beneficiaries must meet. Wolfgang Engler (Engler 2007) regards education as a prerequisite for leading a self-determined life, and his fellow citizens largely agree.[16] Education, they argue, is necessary in a world of alienated individuals not capable of coping with freedom and so accustomed to life guidelines of the "employment society" or "consumer society." Thomas Poreski and Manuel Emmler (Poreski and Emmler 2006) restrict conditions to children, who must go to kindergarten or school for parents to be eligible for BI.

Educational obligations would undermine the citizen's status as the building block of a political community. Instead of necessitating education as a condition for receiving BI, a guaranteed income from cradle-to-grave could help to transform the educational misery we are facing following labor-centered policies in past years. Education today serves as a means to successful employment, the "master" way to prepare people for the labor market. Starting with early childhood education, the groundwork for occupational skills is laid, improved at school, and optimized at university. Educational success equals employability these days. BI would foster a debate whether education should be a goal in itself, taking the individual's interests and inclinations into consideration. Consequently, idleness, that is, doing something for its own sake, would be recognized more positively as the basis of exploring the unknown. BI would support inquisitiveness, a capacity fundamental to innovation in all aspects of community life.

Citizenship? Political Community, Internationalism, and Human Rights

Unconditionality would turn the German welfare system upside down. The higher BI is, the more conditional benefits it eliminates, and the further it gets in recognizing wage labor as only one among other important activities within a political community of citizens. The status of wage labor would decrease; that of child care, volunteering, and other activities would increase. BI would not have this equalizing effect immediately; it is rather a result of recognizing people as citizens and not as contributors through wage labor. By being provided without obligation, BI tells "beneficiaries" that they receive it for their own sake. As citizen rights are bestowed without obligation, so is BI.[17] Does such a status, as some argue, pervert the idea of unconditionality?

Indeed, it is sometimes argued that BI should be provided to everybody. Various proposals advocate BI as a global necessity. The *attac* subdivision *Genug für alle* (Attac AG "Genug für alle" 2010) argues that BI is not a national goal, it is universal and global, and it is a right for all people to have a decent life. Members of the party *Die Linke* (The Left, BAG Grundeinkommen 2010) also advocate a human rights approach. From this point of view, citizenship is not a necessary condition to be eligible; instead, the criterion is permanent or principal residency. The fundamental question, though, is who decides and provides BI for whom and why?

If there is no international government, some infer, the only recourse to achieve a global BI may come through human rights. Consequently, some derive BI from human rights—rights supposed to be valid everywhere. Article 23 of the Universal Declaration refers to a right to work[18] (i.e., consequently the right to a workplace). By agreeing on the right to work instead of a right to income, plurality of life conduct is constrained and paid work as normative ideal is upheld.

As long as there is no international democratic government and no corresponding body politic, the nation-state is the ultimate institution to provide a BI. Contrary to notions of the nation-state being an obstacle to universalism, it has been the main driving force in bringing it about. It took particular communities and their political organizations to survive and prosper and so reinforce universalistic ideals and guidelines. For all practical purposes, neither universalism would exist without national political communities and nor would human rights. Moreover, rights as such do not create a community; rights are only as strong as the citizens who are willing to abide by them. In fact, rights need to be rooted in everyday life—in a given community's perception that it exists, that it has a particular culture, and that its members "belong," and are at home in it.

While citizens have rights and responsibilities, permanent residents have rights, but not necessarily responsibilities. Does this imply that BI should not be provided to permanent residents? Not at all, but to provide it to permanent residents derives from the constitutive meaning of citizenship for a political community.

Redistribution of Working Hours, a Minimum Wage and Automation Technology

The more detail we go into, the more it becomes apparent how contested some aspects of BI's impact are. Therefore, different proposals highlight different aspects and combine different means to attain the kind of freedom they seek.

There is a strong consensus that through a BI, high enough to secure a livelihood, employees would gain bargaining power. Being independent of wage labor implies the ability to say "No" (Offe 2008), an ability trade union functionaries deny or they are at least skeptical whether people would use it (Neuendorff et al. 2009).[19] On the one hand, companies could rely on motivated employees who work voluntarily and, on the other hand, companies would have to offer attractive working conditions and an attractive working environment. Both would help to create an innovative atmosphere in companies and organizations. The community could get rid of legal restrictions necessary to protect the employee's status today; for example, restrictions on laying off and hiring employees. To hire individuals for only a short time in order to work on a project would become common (if employees agree) and not a threat to the individual.

Some argue (e.g., Opielka and Vobruba 1986; Neuendorff et al. 2009; Blaschke et al. 2010) that BI must be combined with a reduction of working hours to redistribute work. Additionally, they contend, a minimum wage is indispensable to protect employees against a race to the bottom where wages are concerned. Why reduce working hours in general? If BI were sufficient to say "No," neither working hours nor wages could be imposed on employees. Because of bargaining power, it would be up to them to define acceptable working hours. Each individual would be in a much better position to find an appropriate answer in accordance with his or her life, inclinations, capacities, and so forth. The amount of time someone is willing to spend in an occupation depends on what he or she regards as reasonable. Reducing working hours would ignore individuals' decisions and desires. Furthermore, the normative status of wage labor would be upheld; to generally distribute working hours declares labor to be a scarce and desirable good that people should have the opportunity to share.

To reduce working hours ignores that creative and innovative work cannot be measured in hours—such work is too closely connected to the individual's dedication to a set of problems or questions. Applying a formal scheme, not measured by the content of work, instead of leaving it up to employees to bargain, deprives them of a responsibility that BI would enable them to carry out. The same holds true for minimum wages. Why protect people double—the aim of a minimum wage—who are able to refuse unattractive working conditions? Both measures, reduction of working hours and minimum wage, stick to the idea that wage labor is more desirable and meaningful than other occupations or activities.

A relatively low wage under circumstances of BI does not necessarily mean low income. While today wages fulfill two functions: (1) to secure a minimum, and (2) to provide a share in the company's success, with BI the situation is altered. BI would secure a steadily available minimum income; a wage would be additional and separate. Consequently, if BI were relatively high, a lower wage than today would not imply a lower income (BI plus wage).[20] BI is the grounding that every wage would be additional.

A further consequence of reducing working hours and introducing minimum wages might be to restrain severely the process of rationalization. There is evidence that the present insistence on paid labor is an obstacle to the active implementation of technology, which allows for the substitution of human labor. Managers feel loyal to their political community (against all prejudices) and try to avoid laying off staff for as long as they can (Liebermann 2002). Thus, companies do not make use of the full potential for efficient production. Once the technology is available, a job loses its economic raison d'être to technological progress and this inevitably alters its meaning. Because it is dispensable, an employee cannot be proud of such a job. He is not contributing to innovation or even a meaningful activity but competing with machines that could easily do his job. For example, checkout operators operate a cash register and ring up items, usually with a bar code scanner. Why not leave the checkout operation to the customers as some supermarket chains have begun to do? By using automation technology where reasonable, people with a BI would regain leisure time. Any limitation on such rationalization should be taken away since the community as a whole would stand to gain.

To Live at the Costs of Others and Plurality

One objection often made against BI—from more conservative to left-wing parties—is that such a grant allows some "to live at the cost of others without any contribution" (Busch 2005; SPD 2009; for the Free Democratic Party [FDP], see Atmiks 2009). At first sight, it appears to be a plausible objection. Those who engage in wage labor contribute to the production of goods and services and their income is taxed and, thus, public infrastructure is made available. However, taxed income is not the only contributor to the general tax revenue. Consumers in general contribute where a value added tax is levied. Moreover, volunteers also provide services and produce goods without being paid, as do all people serving in unpaid work, for example, in churches, charity organizations, and even in political parties. In Germany, the amount of unpaid work exceeds that of paid work. Data by the Federal Bureau of Statistics (Statistisches Bundesamt 2003) says that 96 billion hours per year are unpaid work, while only 56 billion hours are paid work.[21] Are these activities unimportant to a community because they are unpaid?

What does the phrase "to live at the cost of others" account for? In a community, every individual lives "at the cost of others," because each and every person depends on the contribution of others in the sense that each and every person relies on his or her fellow citizens to lead a self-determined life following his or her capacities and loyalty toward the community. Living at the cost of others is a mere fact today that a BI would not change at all. Rather, it is unavoidable. BI would make this transparent.

From this point of view, the term "contribution" underlying this objection implies the same normative assumptions as the term "unemployment."[22] It is all about the contested definition of what society regards as a "contribution." As long as we insist on defining it, we constrain autonomy by defining what is accepted as an autonomous life.

Advocates largely agree that activities "outside" of the labor market would, under a BI, gain an independent status. They would lose the stigma of being "second choices" because there would no longer be an obligation to earn an income by doing paid work. Activities and occupations would have equal moral worth. Citizens would gain the freedom to choose between paid work and other activities such as volunteering. On the one hand, BI would give citizens the possibility to make choices and, on the other hand, would give them more responsibilities.

Plurality would be encouraged. Neither growth nor labor is a goal in itself. With a BI, different ways of living a self-determined life are respected. Instead of financing employment programs and educational trainings to "bring" people back into the labor market—both of which are more or less compulsory for the unemployed—education could be a goal in itself, following the individual's interests and inclinations. By providing a BI, the community signals that it trusts in the citizens' will to contribute to the well-being of the polity and, thus, fosters solidarity.

Families, Child Care, and Emancipation

Mothers and fathers who stay at home for their children—are they not contributing to the common welfare, are they "unemployed?" In the common use of the term, stay-at-home parents are unemployed because they do not work in the paid-labor market. Of course, they contribute to the common welfare—without families, the political community has no future. Nevertheless, their contribution neither helps to acquire entitlements to benefits, nor is it recognized as central in the same way as having a full time occupation.[23] Instead, public debates following activation policies and the ideal of wage labor as the most important contribution to the common welfare devalue nonwage activities such as family care.

A debate about extending child-care institutions to support working parents accompanies current activation policies. What seems to be progressive and emancipatory turns out to be the opposite. Parents are put under increasing pressure by public debates and political decisions. They have to decide whether they should take care of their children, or whether they should pursue their professional career to fulfill the community's normative expectations. By enhancing child-care institutions without providing means such as BI to opt out of the labor market, the normative ideal of doing paid work is reinforced. Therefore, what is considered to be a step into the future by praising, for example, Scandinavian child-care policies, is a step backward. We can call this phenomenon the "employment trap." BI, however, would open up the opportunity for staying at home, without stigmatizing it. BI would leave the decision up to parents, without directing them toward any normative goal.

Some pundits in Germany argue that a BI is regressive for women; it would send them back to the cooker (Nida-Rümelin 2008) and, furthermore, would "shut those persons down" without any chance to earn more than BI provides (Schlecht 2006; SPD 2009). To me, this is a very pessimistic view of women, as if they were not strong enough to defend and follow their interests (Fischer 2006). If they decide to go back to their households, why not, it is up to them. Those incapable of attaining more than a BI are at least able to live a dignified life. What seems to be a thoughtful objection shows the same mistrust in people's capabilities as those against BI in general.

Note on Taxation and Social Justice

To sum up, let me add a very brief note concerning taxation and social justice—another contested issue in the German debate.[24] Most proposals to finance BI combine taxes on income and consumption. Götz W. Werner (Werner 2007) and Benediktus Hardorp (Hardorp 2008), however, argue for totally rebuilding the taxation system by eliminating income taxation and concentrate on taxing consumption.[25] The objection is often made that this proposal is unjust because it burdens the poor. Werner and Hardorp point out that all costs a company has—wages, social insurance, taxes, infrastructure—are more or less contained in prices for goods and services, so it is the consumer who pays everything. To contain costs in prices is indispensable because selling goods and services is the only way to meet the costs and make profits. Accordingly, to tax consumption is the only way out of the dilemma. But what about the rich, one might say? Werner's and Hardorp's proposals challenge prevailing ideas of social justice by simply hinting at the fact that things are not as they seem to be, and by raising the question whether it is appropriate to build a taxation system which concentrates on income, that is, on having money, instead of what it is used for either consumption or investment. They are also discussing ways of how the use of resources could be taxed to support sustainable production (e.g., by applying carbon footprint).

BI—Close, though Far?

As we have seen support for BI comes from all sides, but conceptions differ widely in what they are aiming at. From those suggesting a BI below or at the poverty line to abolish the *Sozialstaat* to others arguing for a high and sustainable BI to allow for a self-determined life to those combining BI with an educational obligation, a minimum wage, and a distribution of working hours—under the notion of BI a wide range of conceptions have been put forward. For some to foster democratization by linking BI to citizenship is crucial, because by doing so political communities as such would be strengthened; others regard BI simply as human right and rather, fear citizenship as condition for being eligible. They blame its supposedly excluding and nationalistic character.

BI support is found within all political parties, churches—catholic and protestant—trade unions, and welfare organizations. Even though support does rarely come from top-level representatives, discussions within parties might accelerate depending on pressure coming from public opinion. While in the beginning of the BI debate political parties rather avoided contact with BI activists, it has become common for activists to receive invitations to talks or panel discussions. Although the financial crisis could have put BI on the agenda more than ever, it has not pushed the debate significantly. Germany—as other European countries—predominantly tries to solve problems by saving "costs."

Being a member of the European Union, fellow citizens wonder whether BI could be implemented in Germany only or if an EU-wide implementation is inevitable. Of course, EU legislation is complex and a BI implementation on a national level has to tackle certain challenges. According to Jürgen Erdmenger, who gave a talk about BI and the European Union in Berlin in 2008 (Erdmenger 2008: 11; see also, Brenner 2011: 224), a national implementation must be coordinated with EU legislation even more, as he told me, since the Lisbon treaty has come into effect in 2009; a national implementation, thus, is possible.

EU legislation is not the main obstacle to the introduction of a BI in Germany. It is rather found in a contradictory phenomenon; on the one hand, there is a discrepancy between the fundamental meaning of citizenship and political community already incorporated in democratic institutions; on the other hand, there are differences in how it is interpreted in the self-conception of the people. Especially, the ongoing public debate about BI has helped to make this contradiction apparent and, thus, set interpretive patterns going.

To my mind, any likelihood that a party might support BI totally depends on how the public debate develops and how much support BI gains. It was public debate that put BI on the agenda in 2005; it will be public debate that decides whether BI moves forward and whether it will become more than a pipedream. When an issue gains more and more attention, political parties will deal with it, that is what the debate has taught us.

Notes

* I am grateful to Richard Caputo and Ian Copestake for their support in writing this paper. This paper is an abridged and revised version of a more comprehensive one, see Liebermann (2012). Translations of German publications displayed in brackets are mine.

1. Even earlier, in August 2003, we—Ute Fischer, Axel Jansen, Stefan Heckel, Sascha Liebermann, and Thomas Loer—published our website (see http://www.freiheitstattvollbeschaeftigung.de) to inform

about us and to provide short papers in which BI was explained and its various effects were outlined.

2. Poster campaigns were carried out in Berlin (2004, 2005), and again in Frankfurt (2004), Dortmund, Cologne, and Hamburg (2005). Sticker campaigns followed in Cologne, Bonn, and Berlin (2009) and in Cologne and Hamburg (2010). Photos and activities can be found at http://www.freiheitstattvollbeschaeftigung.de, menu item *Aktionen*.
3. See the map at http://www.grundeinkommen.de/karte and for events, the BI calendar http://www.grundeinkommen.de/termine.
4. To become a member you register, for example, online; membership fees are voluntary (August 2010); and membership does not involve any obligation except adhering to the idea defined by the network. Only 43 members attended the latest general meeting in October 2010. http://www.grundeinkommen.de/mitglieder-netzwerk-grundeinkommen-deutschland.
5. *Hartz IV* is an abbreviation, which refers to the fourth law of the legislation by which the German welfare state was rebuilt, see Fleckenstein (2008).
6. A CDU commission's report on the impact of Althaus' proposal was expected in November 2010, but was cancelled. Instead, at a hearing held on November 1, 2010 experts involved in the commission presented findings, which Althaus and colleagues took up to revise the concept, see Althaus and Binkert (2010).
7. Austrian and Swiss activists got involved as well. For Austria, see *Netzwerk Grundeinkommen und sozialer Zusammenhalt* (B. I. E. N. Austria, http://www.ksoe.at/ksoe/index.php) and *attac Austria* (http://www.attac.at/bge.html); for Switzerland, see *Initiative Grundeinkommen Basel* (a group in Basle, http://www.initiative-grundeinkommen.ch/) and *B.I.E.N Switzerland* (http://bien-ch.ch/).
8. The hearing was broadcast by *Parlamentsfernsehen*, the TV channel of the German parliament via internet and is still available as videocast, see http://www.bundestag.de/bundestag/parlamentsfernsehen/index.jsp.
9. See http://www.bundesagentur-fuer-einkommen.de/.
10. A variety of conceptions circulated by members of the Green Party that came close to a BI, but on a low-income level not sufficient for a livelihood and sometimes conditional by linking BI to an obligation to send children to Kindergarten (Poreski and Emmler 2006; for further information, see Grünes Netzwerk Grundeinkommen 2011). A national assembly was held in November 2007 and the majority of delegates voted against BI. Since then, BI in the Green Party is off the national agenda, though there still are advocates among party members.
11. A small group called *BAG Grundeinkommen* (2010) within the party advocates BI as well. Katja Kipping, member of the German parliament, is the most outstanding advocate. She was a founding member

and one of the spokespersons of the German Network BI in 2004. She has been very active in spreading the idea since then.

12. *Sozialhilfe* is one of the existing means-tested social assistances serving to provide a minimum income and support. It consists of several different forms of payment some directed to the beneficiary and some to the institution that provides aid to men and women. Legislation was comprehensively reformed in 2003 (see Federal Ministry of Labour and Social Affairs 2010).
13. Hasenclever was member of the Green Party and also member of the parliament of the state of Baden-Württemberg from 1980–1983. He left the Green Party in 2001 and became member of the Free Democratic Party (FDP).
14. Generally, children are entitled to child benefit from birth until the age of 18. Under certain circumstances child benefits can be paid for a longer period. Child benefits are defined as a tax refund, primarily to meet the constitutional rule that income is untaxable up to a child's subsistence level (see, Federal Ministry of Labour and Social Affairs 2010).
15. The German BI Network is quite unclear on that point, because it regards NIT as BI as well. See frequently asked questions, paragraph 22, http://www.grundeinkommen.de/die-idee/fragen-und-antworten.
16. In this context, Hannah Arendt and Erich Fromm are quoted quite often. Pundits refer to Arendt's culturally pessimistic judgment put forth in *The Human Condition*: "What we are confronted with is the prospect of a society of laborers without labor, that is, without the only activity left to them. Surely, nothing could be worse" (Arendt 1958: 5). Erich Fromm in "The Psychological Aspects of the Guaranteed Income" (Fromm 1967 [1966]: 191) is slightly less pessimistic but also skeptical about citizen's capacity to cope with the end of employment society or the freedom from work obligation.
17. It must be said that some countries do have obligations, such as the one to vote. However, as far as I know, people who do not vote, do not loose their rights. We can call this a constitutive asymmetry between citizen rights and obligation, which is fundamental to political communities.
18. See, Universal Declaration of Human Rights (http://www.un.org/Overview/rights.html), Article 23, Section 1: "Everyone has the right to work, to free choice of employment, to just and favourable conditions of work and to protection against unemployment."
19. This book gathers papers by trade unionists, traditional and critical, and BI advocates presented at a workshop. It provides an insight into trade union arguments against BI.
20. Götz W. Werner (Werner 2007: 100; Werner 2010) sometimes argues that BI has a substitutive effect on wages. Some BI advocates (for example, Blaschke et al. 2010; Wagner 2007) use this argument to blame him for presenting BI as a means to reduce wages without employees being asked and brand this argument for being neoliberal. Although Werner is not always clear in this respect, he himself

mostly hints to the fact that wages result from bargaining (Werner 2007: 100) and BI only substitutes benefits to the level of BI, but not beyond (ibid.: 99).

21. I am totally aware how little insight these data allow into the motivation of those doing unpaid work and how much the amount of time spent differs according to definitions applied.
22. The term "unemployment" goes back to what is regarded as employment or meaningful activity and, thus, defined by legislation. BI allows a totally different understanding of occupation, whereby people could be fully occupied with whatever they wish to do, without being employed at all.
23. The German statutory pension insurance scheme, which defines minimum conditions for being entitled to benefits, takes periods of child care (up to three years per child) into account. Certainly, this contribution is not enough to receive a decent pension. In 2007, the government introduced *Elterngeld* (federal parental benefit; see Federal Ministry of Labor and Social Affairs 2010) for the first 14 months of a child's life. Parents are divided into two categories. Those, who worked can claim an earnings-related benefit, whereas others who did not work can claim a lump sum.
24. Several attempts were made to calculate prospected costs of different Guaranteed Income proposals in Germany not all of which are a real BI (see, e.g., Poreski and Emmler 2006; Opielka and Strengmann-Kuhn 2007; Pelzer and Fischer 2009).
25. This includes the idea to measure the carbon footprint of goods and services and include it in the tax rate.

References

The following is a very selective collection of available information. More details can be found on the website of the German BI Network (http://www.grundeinkommen.de/die-idee/literatur).

Althaus, Dieter, and Hermann Binkert, eds. 2010. *Solidarisches Buergergeld. Den Menschen trauen—Freiheit nachhaltig und ganzheitlich sichern*. Erfurt: Institut für neue soziale Antworten, November.

Arendt, Hannah. 1958. *The Human Condition*. Chicago: The University of Chicago Press.

Atmiks, Peter. 2009. "Liberales Buergergeld kontra bedingungsloses Grundeinkommen." *Friedrich-Naumann-Stiftung für die Freiheit*. http://www.freiheit.org/.

Attac AG "Genug für alle." 2010. http://www.grundeinkommen-attac.de/.

BAG Grundeinkommen. 2010. "Konzept der BAG Grundeinkommen in und bei der Partei DIE LINKE für ein Bedingungsloses Grundeinkommen (BGE) in Existenz und Teilhabe sichernder Höhe." http://www.die-linke-grundeinkommen.de/WordPress/wp-content/uploads/2010/04/10_-_04_-_08_BGE-Konzept2010_Endfassung.pdf.

BIEN, Basic Income Earth Network. http://www.basicincome.org/bien/.

Blaschke, Ronald, Adeline Otto, and Norbert Schepers, eds. 2010. *Grundeinkommen. Geschichte–Modelle–Debatten.* Rosa-Luxemburg-Stiftung Texte 67. Berlin: Karl Dietz Verlag. http://www.rosalux.de/fileadmin/rls_uploads/pdfs/Publ-Texte/Texte_67.pdf.

Blüm, Norbert. 2007. "Wahnsinn mit Methode. Ein Grundeinkommen für alle ist ungerecht und bläht den Staat auf." *Die Zeit* April 19: 17.

Borchard, Michael, ed. 2007. *Das Solidarische Bürgergeld. Analysen einer Reformidee.* Stuttgart: Lucius & Lucius.

brandeins. 2005. *Nie wieder Vollbeschäftigung. Wir haben Besseres zu tun.* 7. http://www.brandeins.de/archiv/magazin/nie-wieder-vollbeschaeftigung.html.

Brenner, Michael. 2011. *Solidarisches Bürgergeld und Grundgesetz.* Baden-Baden: Nomos-Verlag.

Bundesarbeitsgemeinschaft der Erwerbslosen- und Sozialhilfeinitiativen e. V. (BAG-SHI), eds. 2008. *Existenzgeld Reloaded,* edited by Bundesarbeitsgemeinschaft der Sozialhilfe-Initiativen. Neu-Ulm: *AG SPAK Bücher.*

Bundesregierung. 2003. *Agenda 2010. Deutschland bewegt sich* (Germany is moving). http://archiv.bundesregierung.de/artikel/81/557981/attachment/557980_0.pdf.

Busch, Ulrich. 2005. "Falscher Traum vom Schlaraffenland. Ist das bedingungslose Grundeinkommen wirklich ein linkes Konzept? Ein Ökonom sagt nein." *Neues Deutschland,* October 15.

Butterwegge, Christoph. 2007. "Grundeinkommen und soziale Gerechtigkeit." *Aus Politik und Zeitgeschichte* (51–52): 25–30.

Dahrendorf, Ralf. 1980. "Im Entschwinden der Arbeitsgesellschaft." *Merkur* 34 (8): 749–760.

———. 1986. "Ein garantiertes Mindesteinkommen als konstitutionelles Anrecht." 131–136 in *Befreiung von falscher Arbeit,* edited by Thomas Schmid, see Schmid 1986.

Die Grünen. 1986. *Umbau der Industriegesellschaft. Schritte zur Überwindung von Erwerbslosigkeit, Armut und Umweltzerstörung.* Bonn: Selbstverlag. http://www.boell.de/downloads/stiftung/1986_Umbauprogramm(1).pdf.

Engler, Wolfgang. 2007. *Unerhörte Freiheit. Arbeit und Bildung in Zukunft.* Berlin: Aufbau-Verlag.

Erdmenger, Jürgen. 2008. "Das Grundeinkommen und die Europäische Union. Ein Diskussionsbeitrag," paper presented in Berlin. http://www.geistesschulung.de/bbg/erdmenger.pdf.

Erster Bundeskongress der Arbeitslosen, eds. 1983. *Arbeitsloseninitiativen der BRD und Westberlin.* Frankfurt: Fachhochschulverlag.

Federal Ministry of Finance. 2008. *Bericht über die Höhe des Existenzminimums von Erwachsenen und Kindern für das Jahr 2010 (Siebenter Existenzminimumbericht).*

Federal Ministry of Labor and Social Affairs. 2010. *Social Security at a glance.* http://www.bmas.de/portal/10116/social__security__at__a__glance.html.

Fischer, Ute Luise. 2006. "Entkopplung von Arbeit und Einkommen—Emanzipierende Konsequenzen eines bedingungslosen Grundeinkommens," *Beiträge zur feministischen Theorie und Praxis: Frauen, denkt ökonomisch!?* 68: 71–81.

Fleckenstein, Timo. 2008. "Restructuring welfare for the unemployed: the Hartz legislation in Germany." *Journal of European Social Policy* 18 (2): 177–188.

Fromm, Erich.1967 [1966]. "The Psychological Aspects of the Guaranteed Income." 183–93 in *The Guaranteed Income: Next Step in Economic Evolution?* edited by Robert Theobald. Garden City: Anchor Books.

German Council of Economic Experts. 2007. *The Gains Must not be Squandered*. Annual Report 2007/08. http://www.sachverstaendigen-rat-wirtschaft.de/50.html.

Grünes Netzwerk Grundeinkommen. 2011. http://gruene-berlin.de/grundsicherungswiki/index.php/Das_Gr%C3%BCne_Netzwerk_Grundeinkommen.

Habermas, Jürgen. 1985. "Die Krise des Wohlfahrtsstaates und die Erschöpfung utopischer Energien." 141–163 in *Die Neue Unübersichtlichkeit*, Kleine Politische Schriften V, by Jürgen Habermas. Frankfurt: Suhrkamp.

Hardorp, Benediktus. 2008. *Arbeit und Kapital als schöpferische Kraefte. Einkommen und Besteuerung als gesellschaftliches Teilungsverfahren*. Karlsruhe: KIT Scientific Publishing.

Hasenclever, Wolf-Dieter. 1986. "Ein Weg ins Schlaraffenland? Das Grundeinkommen für jeden Bürger könnte ein Schritt zur sozialen Freiheit sein." *Die Zeit* 19, May 2: 40.

Jürgs, Michael. 2004. "Auch wir sind das Volk." *Süddeutsche Zeitung*, October 2.

Liebermann, Sascha. 2002. *Die Krise der Arbeitsgesellschaft im Bewusstsein deutscher Unternehmensführer. Eine Deutungsmusteranalyse*. Frankfurt: Humanities Online.

———. 2004. "Freiheit der Bürger statt Arbeitszwang." *Frankfurter Rundschau*, September 2.

———. 2012. "Manifold Possibilities and Peculiar Obstacles—Basic Income in the German Debate" in *Horizons of Reform—Basic Income Solutions around the World*, edited by Carole Pateman und Matthew Murray. International Political Economy Series, Palgrave Macmillan.

Loer, Thomas. 2004. "Freiheit statt Vollbeschäftigung." *Frankfurter Allgemeine Zeitung*, May 26: 9.

Mitschke, Joachim. 2000. *Grundsicherungsmodelle—Ziele, Gestaltung, Wirkungen und Finanzbedarf. Eine Fundamentalanalyse mit besonderem Bezug auf die Steuer- und Sozialordnung sowie den Arbeitsmarkt der Republik Österreich*. Nomos: Baden-Baden.

Müller, Albrecht. 2010. "Macht es Sinn, eine Idee zum Dauerthema zu machen, wenn sie nie realisiert werden wird?" http://www.nachdenkseiten.de/?p=7849.

Negt, Oskar. 2004. "Grundgehalt." *Frankfurter Rundschau*, July 30.

Netzwerk Grundeinkommen. 2004. *Presseerklärung* 1. http://www.grundeinkommen.de/ueber-uns.

Neuendorff, Hartmut, Gerd Peter, and Frieder O. Wolf, eds. 2009. *Arbeit und Freiheit im Widerspruch? Bedingungsloses Grundeinkommen—ein Modell im Meinungsstreit*. Hamburg: VSA.

Nida-Rümelin, Julian. 2008. "Integration statt Ausstieg. Ein bedingungsloses Grundeinkommen würde unsere Gesellschaft noch weiter spalten." *Frankfurter Rundschau*, June 5. http://www.fr-online.de/kultur/integration-statt-ausstieg/-/1472786/3325866/-/index.html.

Oevermann, Ulrich. 2001. "Die Krise der Arbeitsgesellschaft und das Bewährungsproblem des modernen Subjekts." 19–39 in *Eigeninteresse und Gemeinwohlbindung. Kulturspezifische Ausformungen in den USA und Deutschland*, edited by Roland Becker, Andreas Franzmann, Axel Jansen, and Sascha Liebermann. Konstanz: UVK.

Offe, Claus. 2005. "Nachwort" (Afterword) in *Ein Grundeinkommen für alle? Geschichte und Zukunft eines radikalen Vorschlags*, edited by Philippe Van Parijs and Yannick Vanderborght. Frankfurt: Campus.

———. 2008. "Basic Income and the Labor Contract." *Basic Income Studies* 3 (1), Article 4.

Opielka, Michael. 2000. "Gespräch mit Opielka. Arbeitet man wirklich für sich selbst?" 187–205 in Hans-Peter Krebs, and Harald Rein, eds. 2000. *Existenzgeld—Kontroversen und Positionen*. 1. print, Münster: Westfaelisches Dampfboot.

Opielka, Michael, and Georg Vobruba. 1986. *Das Garantierte Grundeinkommen*. Frankfurt: Fischer Taschenbuch Verlag.

Opielka, Michael, and Wolfgang Strengmann-Kuhn. 2007. "Das Solidarische Bürgergeld—Finanz- und sozialpolitische Analyse eines Reformkonzepts." 13–143 in *Das Solidarische Bürgergeld. Analysen einer Reformidee*, edited by Michael Borchard. Stuttgart: Lucius & Lucius.

Pelzer, Helmut, and Ute Fischer. 2009. "Ein bedingungsloses Grundeinkommen ist bezahlbar und wirtschaftspolitisch sinnvoll—Die Finanzierung über das Transfergrenzen-Modell." 114–134 in *Arbeit und Freiheit im Widerspruch? Bedingungsloses Grundeinkommen—ein Modell im Meinungsstreit*, edited by Hartmut Neuendorff, Gerd Peter, and Frieder O. Wolf. Hamburg: VSA.

Poreski, Thomas, and Manuel Emmler. 2006. "Die Grüne Grundsicherung. Ein Diskussionspapier für den Zukunftskongress von Bündnis 90/ Die Gruenen Version 1.0." http://www.grundsicherung.org/.

Sanktionsmoratorium. 2009. http://www.sanktionsmoratorium.de/.

Schlecht, Michael. 2006. "Solidaritätsprinzip aufrechterhalten. Die Forderung nach einem bedingungslosen Grundeinkommen ergibt sich aus einem schiefen Blick auf den realexistierenden Kapitalismus und ist deshalb nicht umsetzbar." *Junge Welt*, September 15: 10.

Schmid, Thomas. 1986 [1984]. *Befreiung von falscher Arbeit*. Berlin: Verlag Klaus Wagenbach (The second edition in 1986 was completely revised).

Siebert, Horst. 2007. "Gegen ein bedingungsloses Grundeinkommen. Eine abstruse Idee mit massiven Fehlanreizen." *Frankfurter Allgemeine Zeitung*, June 27.

SPD, Grundwertekommission beim Parteivorstand der SPD. 2009. *Bedingungsloses Grundeinkommen? Geld allein genügt nicht! Sozialstaatliche Verantwortung für gesellschaftliche Inklusion.* http://alt.spd.de/de/pdf/2008_GWK_Grundeinkommen.pdf.

Spielkamp, Matthias. 2001. "Wege in die Zukunft—Grundeinkommen." *brandeins* 10: 68–69. http://www.brandeins.de/archiv/magazin/mach-was-draus/artikel/wege-in-die-zukunft-1-grundeinkommen.html.

Statistisches Bundesamt. 2003. *Wo bleibt die Zeit? Die Zeitverwendung der Bevölkerung in Deutschland 2001/02*, edited by Bundesministerium für Familie, Senioren, Frauen und Jugend. Wiesbaden: Statistisches Bundesamt.

Wagner, Björn. 2007. *Das Grundeinkommen in der deutschen Debatte. Motive, Leitbilder, Interessen.* http://library.fes.de/pdf-files/wiso/06194.pdf.

Werner, Götz W. 2005. "Wir leben in paradiesischen Zuständen." *brandeins* 3: 72. http://www.brandeins.de/archiv/magazin/was-bleibt/artikel/wir-leben-in-paradiesischen-zustaenden.html.

———. 2007. *Einkommen für alle.* Köln: Kiepenheuer & Witsch.

———. 2010. "1000 Euro für jeden machen die Menschen frei." *Frankfurter Allgemeine Sonntagszeitung*, August 15. http://www.faz.net/-01r7af.

Wiest, Susanne. 2008. "Petition: Reformvorschläge in der Sozialversicherung—Bedingungsloses Grundeinkommen vom 10.12.2008." https://epetitionen.bundestag.de/index.php?action=petition%3Bsa=details%3Bpetition=1422.

Websites

Archiv Grundeinkommen (Basic Income Archive), the most comprehensive privately run BI archive in Germany. http://www.archiv-grundeinkommen.de/.

Die Glücklichen Arbeitslosen (The Happy Unemployed). http://www.dieglueecklichenarbeitslosen.de/dieseite/seite/glueck.htm.

Existenzgeld (Subsistence Allowance). http://www.bag-shi.de.

Freiheit statt Vollbeschäftigung (Freedom, not Full Employment). http://www.freiheitstattvollbeschaeftigung.de.

Netzwerk Grundeinkommen (German Network BI, affiliated to BIEN). Here you find a comprehensive list of weblinks including local groups. http://www.grundeinkommen.de.

Werner, Götz W., and Unternimm die Zukunft. http://www.unternimm-die-zukunft.de/.

Wiest, Susanne, Grundeinkommen im Bundestag (BI to German Parliament). http://grundeinkommenimbundestag.blogspot.com/.

Movies and Videos

Häni, Daniel, and Enno Schmidt. 2008. *Kulturimpuls Grundeinkommen. Ein Filmessay.* http://www.kultkino.ch/kultkino/besonderes/grundeinkommen. Available in english at dotsub: http://dotsub.com/view/26520150–1acc-4fd0–9acd-169d95c9abe1.

Heizmann, Jördis, and Andreas Zgraja. 2007. *Designing Society.* http://www.designing-society.de/index.swf.

Schlee, Christoph. 2007a. *Grundeinkommen für alle* (Basic Income for all). http://www.youtube.com/user/allmende.

———. 2007b. *Sechs Positionen zum Grundeinkommen* (Six Positions toward Basic Income). http://www.youtube.com/user/allmende.

YouTube, keyword "grundeinkommen."

TV Documentaries

3SAT. 2004. *Jobs, Würde, Werte. Eine Hartz-Reise in fünf Teilen* (Jobs, Dignity, Values. A Hartz-Journey in five parts; part 5 dealing with BI). http://www.3sat.de/page/?source=/kulturzeit/themen/63528/index.html.

3SAT. 2011. *Bedingungslos glücklich. Freiheit und Grundeinkommen* (Unconditionally Happy. Freedom and Basic Income). http://www.3sat.de/page/?source=/dokumentationen/152534/index.html.

CHAPTER 7

Ireland: Pathways to a Basic Income in Ireland

Seán Healy and Brigid Reynolds

This chapter is divided into two sections. In section one, we outline in a summary manner the discussions and studies of Basic Income in Ireland since the first such study in 1977. In section two, we focus on possible pathways toward introducing a Basic Income in Ireland. In this section, we outline various pathways that have been studied and assessed in recent decades and set out a further option that we believe could lead, over time, to the introduction of a full Basic Income system in Ireland.

Section One: The Story to Date

Basic Income has been examined in various degrees of intensity in the 1970s, 1980s, 1990s, and 2000s. It is now coming back onto the agenda again in the 2010s. In 1977, Ireland's National Economic and Social Council (NESC) published a report on how personal income tax and welfare transfers might be integrated (Dowling 1977). Basic Income was one of the three options included in that study. NESC is Ireland's major "think tank." It is organized and supported by government. Its members are drawn from the various pillars of social partners (i.e., employers, trade unions, farming organizations, community and voluntary sector, and environmental organizations), and also includes senior government officials and independent nominees drawn from a variety of backgrounds who are chosen by government. This body's purpose is to assist government to review economic and social policy and the options that are available in these areas. (In late 2011, government stated that it intended to add sustainability and environmental policy to the areas being addressed by NESC.) The analysis of Basic Income conducted by NESC in this report had no impact of substance; in reality, policymakers were preoccupied at that time with reform of the taxation system, and this aspect of the report was the only one subsequently taken forward into the policymaking arena.

In the 1980s, government commissions produced two major reports. The first analyzed taxation (Commission on Taxation 1982); the second analyzed the social welfare system (Commission on Social Welfare 1986). Both looked at Basic Income but rejected it without any serious analysis of its cost or impact. The Commission on Taxation claimed it was too costly despite doing no analysis of any consequence on what that cost might be. Its conclusions were simply wrong, and studies conducted during the following decade (discussed later in this chapter) showed this to be the case. Their cavalier approach caused even further damage when the Commission on Social Welfare report simply cited the Commission on Taxation's conclusion as sufficient evidence for rejecting the idea of a Basic Income.

The failures of both these commissions to analyze Basic Income in a fair manner did not put an end to its consideration. Since the late 1980s, two approaches to introducing a Basic Income were developed in Ireland. The first of these approaches worked on the assumption that much of the current structure would be maintained. The second saw the current system being replaced by a Basic Income system. We now provide a summary of both of these approaches in turn.

In 1987, Patrick Honohan published a study on Basic Income (Honohan 1987).[1] In 1994, Tim Callan and his team in Ireland's Economic and Social Research Institute (ESRI)[2] also produced a study on this issue (Callan et al. 1994). Both these studies preserved much of the existing tax and spending systems. Their models were very similar: each adult of working age would receive an untaxed basic payment equivalent to the welfare payment paid to people who were long-term unemployed. The payments for older people were a little higher and for children they were lower. These payments would be a Basic Income. All social welfare payments would be discontinued but "discretionary" tax breaks would remain and all government spending programs would stay in place.

Both of these studies found that income tax rates in excess of 65 percent would be required on all personal income. And both studies concluded that such rates would be a disincentive to people taking up paid employment and, consequently, that this approach to introducing a Basic Income should be rejected. The ESRI team also concluded that the income distribution effect of the proposal did not benefit many low-income households. In the years that followed, there were a number of official reports produced by government departments, agencies, and working groups that endorsed Callan's conclusion that a Basic Income system was not viable in Ireland.[3]

The second approach, mentioned earlier, saw Basic Income replacing the present system. This approach was developed and pursued by CORI Justice. CORI Justice was an arm of the Conference of Religious of Ireland. It analyzed and critiqued public policy from a social justice perspective with a strong focus on issues such as poverty, inequality, social exclusion, and sustainability. Its work, including that on Basic Income, was taken over by Social Justice Ireland in 2009.

The first costed set of proposals emerged in a study by Ward (1994), which focused on introducing a Basic Income system at a level that could be funded by an acceptable income tax rate. Ward's approach retained the main benefits of Basic Income but kept the income tax rate below 50 percent. Every person would receive the Basic Income and would continue to receive it after taking up a job. Having taken up a job a person would be liable to pay tax from the first penny they earned while retaining their untaxed Basic Income. This study looked very closely at Ireland's budgetary situation and outlined a set of proposals aimed at reducing public expenditure. The main components of the system proposed by Ward included the following:

- A full Basic Income for older people and children
- A partial Basic Income for people of working age
- A "top-up" payment for people who were unemployed
- Abolition of all discretionary tax reliefs
- Elimination of a range of public expenditures that would no longer be needed
- Abolition of employers' social insurance
- Reduction of government support for industry

This study found that an approach along these lines would:

- benefit many low- and middle-income households in terms of net income and work incentives;
- provide more equity both horizontal and vertical;[4]
- improve incentives to recruit labor and to seek work;
- provide greater simplicity and certainty;
- be better than the current tax and welfare systems in tackling problems of poverty, work incentives, and exclusion;
- reduce poverty; and
- reduce unemployment traps for people who want to take up employment but would find themselves worse off if they did so. (There would also be no situation in which a person would lose out by taking up a job in these circumstances. In practice, there would always be a gain for the employee in taking up a job and for each additional hour worked.)

Ward's analysis was developed and expanded in a study done by Charles Clark and John Healy.[5] This study looked at the CORI Justice plan for a partial Basic Income contained in Planning for Progress (CORI Justice Commission 1997). It looked at the financing as proposed in that plan and had this checked by the Irish tax authorities (Revenue Commissioners). The study found that the plan for a Basic Income outlined by Ward had been substantially underestimating the income that would be available for the funding of a Basic Income. In fact, a full Basic Income could be implemented in Ireland within a three-year time frame.

Following on from this point, government became directly involved in discussion and study of Basic Income. In the negotiations that produced the national agreement entitled *Partnership 2000* (1996), CORI Justice succeeded in getting agreement from the other social partners to include a section on Basic Income which reads as follows:

> Further independent appraisal of the concept of introducing a Basic Income for all citizens will be undertaken, taking into account the work of the ESRI, CORI and the Expert Group on the Integration of Tax and Social Welfare and international research. A broadly based steering group will oversee the study.
>
> (*Partnership 2000 for Inclusion, Employment and Competitiveness* 1996, section 4.35, 23)

A working group established to implement this commitment included one of the authors (Seán Healy). The work was divided into two phases:

- Phase one examined the tax rate needed to fund Basic Income and the distributional implications of introducing Basic Income with this tax rate.
- Phase two looked at the dynamic effects of the proposal, including its effects on employment, effects on economic growth, short- and long-term budgetary implications, and the gender dimensions of all of these.

Three studies were completed and published (Clark 1999; Callan et al. 2000a, 2000b). These studies found that a Basic Income system would have a substantial impact on the distribution of income in Ireland in that, compared with the present tax and welfare system it would

- increase the income of 70 percent of households in the bottom four deciles (i.e., the four-tenths of the population with lowest incomes);

- raise half of the individuals who would be below the 40 percent poverty line under "conventional options"; and
- provide options above this poverty line.[6]

According to the studies, these outcomes would be achieved without any additional resources beyond those available to "conventional" options. These conclusions vindicated CORI Justice's claims that a Basic Income system would have a more positive impact on reducing poverty than the current tax and welfare systems. It would reduce the number of people in poverty while requiring no further public expenditure. It would also target resources on the poorest two-fifths of the population, that is, those with the lowest incomes. While the tax and welfare system could reduce poverty, these studies found that a Basic Income system would reduce poverty even further without any additional resources being allocated. It was a more effective and targeted approach than any other being proposed at the time.

Following on from the Partnership 2000 Working Group on Basic Income, government moved to prepare and publish a green paper on Basic Income. The publication of a green paper in Ireland sets out options for consideration on a particular topic. Following on from this discussion, government publishes a white paper outlining what it proposes to do. This forms the basis of a bill that goes before Parliament, or it leads to the introduction of a series of government initiatives if a new law is not required.

This green paper was published in the autumn of 2002 (Department of the Taoiseach 2002). It was a very welcome development after all the work that had been done to get such a paper published. The green paper's most welcome conclusion from the perspective of supporters of Basic Income was that it would have a far more positive impact on reducing poverty than the present tax and welfare systems. The green paper also concluded, as did the Working Group's study, that a Basic Income system would have a substantial positive impact on the distribution of income in Ireland and would result in a significant reduction in poverty. The green paper also concluded that this would be achieved without any resources additional to those available to "conventional" options. The green paper showed that a Basic Income system was far more effective at tackling poverty than the present tax/welfare system.

On the issue of employment, the green paper concluded that the positive and negative effects put forward reflect,

> the impact of financial incentives to work, with some improvement in the financial incentive to work for the unemployed, as measured by replacement rates. But the incidence of high replacement rates rises for those

> in employment and women engaged in "home duties." These findings are not particularly sensitive to the tax rate required to finance the Basic Income. The marginal direct tax rate for those in employment is roughly constant for top rate taxpayers, but rises by about 20 percentage points for the majority of those in employment. Combining these findings with the available evidence on labour supply, we can conclude that a fall in labour supply is more likely than an increase.
>
> (Green Paper, 46)

The green paper also analyzed the impact on migration, on economic growth, on innovation and entrepreneurship, and on greater participation in adult education. This analysis showed that little negative impact would ensue.

Section Two: Pathways toward a Basic Income

Discussion on Basic Income in Ireland has focused on two key questions: its affordability and how it might be implemented. While many have argued that it is not affordable, section one of this chapter and the studies to which it refers have shown that the proposal is affordable although there is some disagreement on the level at which a Basic Income payment should be set. The second question concerns possible pathways toward implementing a Basic Income. While there is general agreement that the present tax and welfare regimes are not what would be designed today if one were to develop such systems from the beginning, there is no agreement on whether or not a Basic Income system should be the accepted alternative if the present systems are to be redesigned. Some have argued genuinely that no pathways can be found toward the implementation of a Basic Income. Others have agreed with this because it would block the development of a Basic Income system to which they are ideologically opposed. To address this issue the Clark and Healy (1997) study on *Pathways to a Basic Income* referred to earlier in this chapter was commissioned by CORI Justice. This study paid particular attention to implementation and analyzed three different implementation options that would lead to the implementation of a full Basic Income system along the lines proposed by CORI Justice. These pathways were

- an "all-at-once" approach entailing a sudden removal of the current system and the implementation of a Basic Income plan;
- a "by groups" approach involving introducing Basic Income payments to certain groups in society one after the other (children, older people, etc.); and

- a "gradual" approach that involves dismantling the current system while building up the Basic Income system.

These three approaches are spelled out in detail in chapter 3 of the study (Clark and Healy 1997: 24–35), and remain valid for consideration even today.

The "all-at-once" approach would see the complete elimination of the current income tax and welfare benefit system and the installation of the Basic Income system in its place. On the last day of the tax year, taxes and benefits would be collected and paid based on the existing system. Then, during the first week of the new tax year, taxes would be collected and basic income payments would be made according to the Basic Income system. Clark and Healy concluded,

> The "all-at-once" approach has the advantages of quickly realising the benefits of the Basic Income plan . . . and of quickly eliminating the current tax and benefit system . . . The disadvantage is that it might be too much of a change. People would not be able to become gradually accustomed to receiving Basic Income payments. This is particularly true for people who have purchased a home with a mortgage and have included the tax advantages as part of the economic rationale for making such an investment. This is not as important as it might have been in the past, as the tax benefits of a mortgage have decreased for high income families over the past few years.
>
> (Clark and Healy 1997: 25)

A decade and a half later as we write this chapter, mortgages are again an issue in Ireland following the collapse of the property "bubble" in 2008. However, the implications of mortgages for implementation of a Basic Income system are the same now as they were when Clark and Healy wrote their assessment in 1997. Choices would have to be made concerning tax "breaks." Should the "break" for mortgages be retained or removed? If it were removed then the implications for those in negative equity situations or those struggling to meet their mortgage repayments would have to be addressed. These choices have to be made even if the present system continues to be in place. The government's Commission on Taxation has made proposals for reform in this area (Commission on Taxation 2009).

The second approach identified above is a "by groups" approach that would involve the introduction of Basic Income payments to certain groups in society one after the other. This could be done, according to Clark and Healy, over a four-year period (Clark and Healy 1997: 26). There are several ways in which this could be done. To illustrate how it might work, the Clark and Healy analysis suggested that one way of proceeding would be to introduce a partial Basic Income for adults in the 21–64 age group in year one. In year two, most of the children's Basic Income would be introduced. In year three, the full payment for older people would be introduced. In year four, the outstanding parts of the children's and adult's payments would be introduced. The financing of these changes over the four years were spelled out in the study, which showed the tax changes that would be introduced and the other adjustments that would be made to the public finances. The destination would be the same as that achieved by the other two approaches but the pathway would be different.

Clark and Healy were quite negative on their assessment of this particular pathway. They comment:

> The "by-groups" approach has many unattractive features. First, if a Basic Income is introduced by groups then the winners and losers will be to a certain extent arbitrarily set, and can be quite different from those at the eventual full implementation of the Basic Income plan. This is necessarily the case. As some groups go first, others will have to wait…Certain sections of society are given priority and given basic income payments first. This could cause resentment especially amongst those that would be subject to increase tax rates. Even if taxpayers are first to receive Basic Income payments, they may be reluctant in subsequent years to experience dramatically increased tax rates as others are given Basic Income payments.
>
> Another limitation of the "by groups" approach is that we are less confident of the estimates of the tax-take with this approach than we are with the "gradual" or "all-at-once" approaches.
>
> (Clark and Healy 1997: 29–30)

The latter limitation was based on the lack of detail on the tax base in 1997 when the study was conducted by Clark and Healy.

The third approach is a "gradual" one that involves dismantling the current system while simultaneously building up the Basic Income system. One of the more difficult issues to be addressed in any move from the current tax and welfare system to a Basic Income system concerns the reform of the existing tax and welfare system. It could well be argued that this is especially the case for Ireland where the tax and welfare systems are extremely complex and include many allowances, reliefs and exemptions, as well as various tax bands and rates many of which were designed for specific purposes, some of which have long since passed their "sell-by" date. Some of these were originally put in place to counter already-existing anomalies. However, there is a range of tax breaks for which the Department of Finance or the Revenue has no estimate of cost to the Exchequer.

The "gradual" implementation approach identified by Clark and Healy addresses these problems in a very simple way. This approach would establish the Basic Income system separately from the current tax and welfare systems. It would see the gradual phasing in of the Basic Income system while the current tax and welfare systems would be gradually phased out. This can be done over whatever phase-in period one chooses. Clark and Healy proposed a three-year phase-in period. They state that

> the "gradual" implementation approach is very simple. We introduce the Basic Income plan over a three-year period by implementing one third in year one, two thirds in year two and full implementation in year three. We also do the reverse for the current tax and benefit system, reducing it by one third in year one, by two thirds in year two, and finally eliminating it in year three...
>
> This approach is gradual and equitably distributes the gains and costs of introducing the Basic Income plan. This approach avoids the disruption caused by the "all-at-once" approach. Everyone gets the initial benefits of the Basic Income payments and the labour force does not suffer dramatic rises in the tax rates at certain stages in order to fund payments to other groups in society, as is the case in the 'by groups' approach.
>
> (Clark and Healy, 1997: 31, 35)

The authors of this chapter are convinced that the Clark and Healy conclusions remain valid today and that a "gradual" implementation strategy would be the smoothest pathway to a full Basic Income in Ireland.

We now wish to add a further dimension to the discussion of pathways toward a Basic Income by presenting another version of the "by groups" approach that eliminates many of the problems correctly identified by Clark and Healy in their 1997 analysis. We believe that the current tax and welfare systems can be adjusted to provide a Basic Income *structure,* which can then be developed toward becoming a full Basic Income *system*. The key steps in this approach would be as follows:

1. Protect the present Child Benefit system and do not tax this payment
2. Make the State Pension a universal payment for all adults 66 years of age and above
3. Make the two major tax credits refundable

Once these three steps are put in place, every person in society would have access to a payment of some sort by right, that is, a Basic Income *structure*. This structure can then be developed into a full Basic Income *system* over time, that is, set at a reasonable income level (with variations depending on age—child, working age, and older person) and paid to all without any work requirement. We know from previous studies on Ireland that a Basic Income system can be financed with a fair tax system and a reasonable tax rate. The challenge is to deal with the objections and arguments presented by serious commentators as well as those ideologically opposed to such a development.

Is our proposal viable in Ireland today? We believe that it has major attractions as a pathway that can be progressed even in difficult times.

With reference to step 1 identified above, Ireland has a Child Benefit payment that is universal and is, in effect, a Basic Income payment that goes to all children. In 2011, these payments were worth €140 a month for the first and second child; €167 a month for the third child; and €177 a month for the fourth and subsequent children. Therefore, in effect there is a Basic Income system in place for children. This means that as long as government does not tax or means-test this payment step 1 identified above has already been achieved in Ireland.

Step 2 would see the State Contributory Pension becoming a universal payment for all adults 66 years of age and above. In 2011, the State Contributory Pension was €230.30 a week for those under 80 years with an additional €240.30 a week for those aged 80 or over. It is not means tested. This pension is taxable but those who receive this payment are unlikely to pay tax if it is their only income. However, this payment is not universal as can be seen in the following:

- There are about 46,000 women who do not have an entitlement to a State Pension for a number of historical reasons and government continues to ignore the claims of this group of women. A universal system would see all of these women receiving a State Pension.
- A State Contributory Pension is paid only to people from the age of 66 who have *enough Irish social insurance contributions.* The social insurance conditions are very complex and there are many who do not qualify under this provision.
- The State Pension (Noncontributory) may be paid from age 66 to people in Ireland who do not qualify for a State (Contributory) Pension. This is a means-tested payment.

Therefore, not everyone aged 66 and over receives a State Contributory Pension. To move to this situation, it would require additional expenditure from the Exchequer. A study currently being conducted by Social Justice Ireland will determine how much such a move would cost and how it could be funded over the next half century. This study will be published in 2012. It is clear from the work already completed as we write this chapter that such a move would not be difficult to achieve or to fund on a sustainable basis.

This brings us to step 3 identified above: making the two major tax credits refundable. In recent years, many advocates of Basic Income in

Ireland have suggested a policy that sees it being developed initially through making tax credits refundable. Such an innovation would see everyone in Ireland having an entitlement to a payment of some sort (e.g., child benefit for all children, state pensions for all older people, social welfare payments, and/or refundable tax credits for all people in between). However, the proposal to make tax credits refundable has also met with much resistance. Remarkably, much of this resistance has come from officials in the Department of Finance rather than from political parties or others involved in discussion of these issues.

Ireland has had a tax credit system in Budget 2001. In practice a tax credit system means that a person's tax is calculated from the first penny they earn, the tax credit is subtracted from this and they pay the balance to the government as their actual tax bill. If the person's tax bill is lower than the value of their tax credit then the tax bill is zero. This means that people at all income levels could benefit to the same extent from these credits, which was not the situation with the tax allowance system. A person is entitled to tax credits depending on their personal circumstances, for example, married person's tax credit, employee Pay As You Earn (PAYE) tax credit, and so on. These tax credits are used to reduce tax on a person's gross pay. The tax credit is subtracted to determine tax payable (gross tax less tax credits = tax payable).

One group, however, does not benefit as much as others from the tax credits system, that is, low-income people who do not have a high enough tax bill to benefit from the full value of the tax credit. If a person does not earn enough income to use up his or her full tax credit then he or she will not benefit from any tax reductions introduced by government in its annual budget. This is how this happens: In a normal situation, the Irish government's annual budget reduces people's income tax and increases social welfare rates. This ensures that people's incomes do not fall in real terms when inflation is rising. Those with high enough incomes benefit because an increase in the value of tax credits means people's tax bill goes down and they keep more of their income for themselves. Social welfare recipients also benefit as they gain from increases in social welfare rates. However, one group gains nothing. A person whose income tax liabilities are zero when his/her tax credit is subtracted from their tax bill before the budget will still have a zero-tax bill but will have got no increase in income after the budget. In effect, this means that those with the lowest pay, many of whom are among the working poor, would be the only group not to benefit in any way at budget time.

To rectify this problem, a person could receive a payment from the government, (i.e., a refund) equivalent to the value of the portion of the tax credit they have lost. This is known as a refundable tax credit system or a negative income tax system. In Ireland, it is referred to as the former for the most part. This would mean that the part of the tax credit not needed to meet an employee's tax liability would be "refunded" to him/her by the state.

If tax credits were refundable then all those employed would have a right to this minimum level of income. All those of working age receiving welfare payments (i.e., those who are unemployed, ill, have a disability carers, etc.) would be receiving those payments to which they are entitled. In practice, all adults of working age would have an entitlement to some payment, that is, a Basic Income. However, the level of the payment would vary.

Social Justice Ireland has commissioned and published a peer-reviewed study on making tax credits refundable (Social Justice Ireland 2010). The results of this study were published in 2010 in a report entitled *Building a Fairer Tax System: The Working Poor and the Cost of Refundable Tax Credits.* This study addressed two key issues in Irish social and economic policy:

- The need to reform and develop Ireland's taxation system so that it becomes fairer.
- The need to address the issue of the "working poor." Many people with jobs receive an income that is below the poverty line—one in every three households at risk of poverty is headed by a person with a job.

This study showed that

- making tax credits refundable would benefit 113,000 low-income individuals in an efficient and cost-effective manner;
- when children and other adults in the household are taken into account, the total number of beneficiaries would be 240,000;
- the cost of making this change would be €140 million; and
- this costing is in stark contrast to the estimate provided by the Department of Finance to the Oireachtas Committee on Social and Family Affairs in 2009, which claimed the cost would be €3,000 million (i.e., €3 billion).

Two issues arose from these conclusions:

- Concerning tax credits: The government should make tax credits refundable. Making tax credits refundable would:
  - Make Ireland's tax system fairer (e.g., by ensuring that people employed in low-income jobs would not lose out in the annual budget)

- Address part of the working poor problem (by ensuring that all of those working poor people who benefited previously from only a part of the value of their tax credit would benefit from its full value once tax credits were refundable, and thus would have a higher income)
- Improve the living standards of a substantial number of people in Ireland (as there would be more than 240,000 beneficiaries who would benefit from higher incomes).

- Concerning costs: The study raised serious concerns regarding the Department of Finance's calculations. Evidence-based policy making should be based on solid evidence. The costings supplied by the department were over 95 percent incorrect. The proposal has been very badly served by poor "evidence" from a source on whom we should otherwise be able to rely.

This work continues. Progress on it can be tracked on Social Justice Ireland's website www.socialjustice.ie. For the purposes of this chapter, we have simply included the basic conclusions and foreseeable issues.

In practice, making tax credits refundable would secure a Basic Income structure, that is, everyone would be in receipt of a basic payment. However, there would still be some distance to travel before the conditions on which some of these payments were made could be deemed to be a full Basic Income system, that is, a system in which an income is granted to every person on an unconditional basis without any means test or work requirement. A Basic Income system recognizes the right of every person to a share of the resources in society and that everyone has the right to meaningful work and to have sufficient income to live life with dignity. However, in Ireland in the second decade of the twenty-first century, it may be that the pathway to a Basic Income that most likely reaches the destination of a full Basic Income is the one outlined here.

Of the three stages listed above the most difficult stage to achieve is likely to be the final one, that is, making tax credits refundable. It may, however, not be too difficult to get allies in this process. The major advantage of making tax credits refundable would lie in addressing the disincentives currently associated with low-paid employment. The main beneficiaries of refundable tax credits would be low-paid employees (full-time and part-time). All of the benefits from introducing this policy would go directly to those with the lowest incomes. Following the introduction of refundable tax credits, all subsequent increases in the level of the tax credit would be of equal value to all employees. There would be real equity in using this tax-credit instrument to distribute the benefits and burdens of budgetary taxation changes. The benefit to all categories of income earners, whether claimed by a single person or a couple would be the same. Consequently, in relative terms, those earners at the bottom of the distribution do best. These outcomes seem to the authors to provide a solid basis around which to build a coalition large enough to deliver on this initiative. There would still be work to be done but much of the road toward a Basic Income system would have been traveled. The fundamental building blocks would be in place.

The authors have argued since the early 1980s that the present tax and social welfare systems should be integrated and reformed to make them more appropriate to the changing world of the twenty-first century. To this end, we have argued for the introduction of a Basic Income system. This proposal is especially relevant at the present moment of economic upheaval.

Basic income is a form of minimum income guarantee that avoids many of the negative side effects inherent in social welfare payments. A basic income differs from other forms of income support in that

- it is paid to individuals rather than households;
- it is paid irrespective of any income from other sources;
- it is paid without conditions (it does not require the performance of any work or the willingness to accept a job if offered one); and
- it is always tax free.

There is real danger that the plight of a large number of people excluded from the benefits of the modern economy will be ignored. Governments and other policymakers and commentators assure society that prosperity for all is just around the corner. Likewise, the claim is often made that a job is the best poverty fighter and consequently, all priority must be given to getting everyone a paid job. While jobs are important the sheer scale of the "working poor" problem shows that jobs alone will not eliminate poverty. Concrete policies are required to ensure that all are included. Twenty-first-century society needs a radical approach to ensure the inclusion of all people in the benefits of sustainable development. Basic income is such an approach.

As we have designed it, a basic income system would replace social welfare and income tax credits. It would guarantee an income above the poverty line for everyone. It would not be means tested. There would be no "signing on" for those who are unemployed as well as no restrictions or conditions. In practice, a basic income recognizes the right of every person to a share of the resources of society.

The Basic Income system ensures that looking for a paid job and earning an income, or increasing one's income while in employment, is always worth pursuing, because for every euro or dollar earned the person will retain a large part. It thus removes the poverty traps and unemployment traps in the present system. Furthermore, women and men get equal payments in a Basic Income system. Consequently, the Basic Income system promotes gender equality because it treats every person equally.

It is a system that is altogether more guaranteed, rewarding, simple, and transparent than the present tax and welfare systems. It is far more employment friendly than the present system. It also respects other forms of work besides paid employment. This is crucial in a world where other forms of work need to be recognized and respected. It is also very important in a world where paid employment cannot be permanently guaranteed for everyone seeking it. There is growing pressure and need in Irish society to ensure recognition and monetary reward for such work. Basic Income is a transparent, efficient, and affordable mechanism for ensuring such recognition and reward.

Basic income also lifts people out of poverty and the dreadful dependency mode of survival. In doing this, it also restores their self-esteem and broadens their horizons. Poor people, however, are not the only ones who should welcome a basic income system. Employers, for example, should welcome it because its introduction would mean they would not be in competition with the social welfare system. Since employees would not lose their basic income when taking a job, there would always be an incentive to take up employment.

A basic income system would create a platform for meaningful work. It would benefit paid employment as well as other forms of work. It would also have a substantial impact on reducing income poverty. The present tax and welfare systems were designed for a different era. They have done well in addressing major problems of the second half of the twentieth century. The world, however, is changing radically. A new system is required for the twenty-first century. Basic income is such a system.

For the authors there are ten reasons to introduce a Basic Income system:

i. It is work and employment friendly.
ii. It eliminates poverty traps and unemployment traps.
iii. It promotes equity and ensures that everyone receives at least the poverty level of income.
iv. It spreads the burden of taxation more equitably.
v. It treats men and women equally.
vi. It is simple and transparent.
vii. It is efficient in labor-market terms.
viii. It rewards types of work in the social economy that the market economy often ignores, for example, home duties, caring, and so on.
ix. It facilitates further education and training in the labor force.
x. It faces up to the changes in the global economy.

Ireland is in a very difficult situation at present. It faces decades of challenging economic pressures and stringent fiscal parameters as it seeks to repay debts caused by banks and financial institutions but which are now being repaid to a great degree by the Irish taxpayer. This whole series of crises gives pause for thought. As Ireland reflects on the crises of recent years it will seek pathways to a future where these failures will not be repeated. In this search, Basic Income has a lot to offer and in due course, the logic of its position may come to be acknowledged and acted upon.

In the meantime, making tax credits refundable would go quite some way toward that ultimate destination. If tax credits were refundable then every person in the society would have an entitlement to some payment; older people would be entitled to a State Pension; younger people would be entitled to Child Benefit; and people in between would be entitled to a refundable tax credit or a social welfare payment. The levels of these payments, of course, would vary. However, everyone would be entitled to some payment. Making tax credits refundable would also mean that a structure was in place for dispensing these payments. The structure could be simplified and integrated over time to maximize its efficiency and effectiveness. All of which would bring Ireland much closer to a Basic Income system.

As the world continues its search for viable options in these precarious times, it is clear that traditional approaches to work, to income distribution, to poverty alleviation, to social inclusion, to sustainability, and to so much more will be seen to be inadequate, providing old and inadequate answers to new questions. The authors believe Basic Income will be recognized for what it is—society's best option currently available for producing a more sustainable, humane, and fairer world where every woman, man, and child will have the income and resources required to live life with dignity.

Notes

1. He became governor of Ireland's Central Bank in 2010.
2. The ESRI is an independent think tank although much of its funding comes from government.
3. These were produced by the Department of Enterprise, Trade and Employment (1996), Forfás (a subdivision of the Department for Enterprise, Trade and Development also in 1996), and the Expert Group on the Integration of the Tax and Social Welfare Systems (1996). None of these reports, however, conducted any further analysis of the proposal.
4. More horizontal equity would ensure people on the same levels of income or in very similar situations would be treated in a more equal

manner than was currently the case. More equity at a vertical level would ensure people with higher incomes would not be favoured as they are in the already existing system.

5. Clark and Healy, 1997.
6. The 40 percent poverty line was calculated as 40 percent of the median income in the society. Other poverty lines were set at 50 percent and 60 percent of the median.

References

Callan, Tim, C. O'Donoghue, and C. O'Neill. 1994. *Analysis of Basic Income Schemes for Ireland*. Dublin: ESRI.

Callan, Tim, B. Nolan, J. Walsh, J. McBride, and R. Nestor. 2000a. *Basic Income in Ireland: A Study for the Working Group on Basic Income*. Dublin: Department of the Taoiseach.

Callan, Tim, G. Boyle, T. McCarthy, B. Nolan, J. Walsh, R. Nestor, and D. van de Gaer. 2000b. *Dynamic Effects of a Basic Income: Phase 2 of a Study for the Working Group on Basic Income*. Dublin: Department of the Taoiseach.

Clark, Charles M. A. 1999. *Report for Working Group on Basic Income*. Dublin: Department of the Taoiseach.

Clark, Charles M. A., and J. Healy. 1997. *Pathways to a Basic Income*. Dublin: CORI.

Commission on Social Welfare. 1986. *Report of the Commission on Social Welfare*. Dublin: Stationery Office.

Commission on Taxation. 1982. *First Report of the Commission on Taxation*. Dublin: Stationery Office.

Commission on Taxation. 2009. *Commission on Taxation Report 2009*. Dublin: Stationery Office.

CORI Justice Commission. 1997. *Planning for Progress*. Dublin: CORI.

Department of the Taoiseach. 2002. *Basic Income: A Green Paper*. Dublin: Department of the Taoiseach.

Dowling, Brendan. 1977. *Integrated Approaches to Personal Income Taxes and Transfers*. Dublin: NESC.

Enterprise, Trade and Employment. 1996. *Growing and Sharing Our Employment: Strategy Paper on the Labour Market*. Dublin: Stationery Office.

Expert Group on the Integration of the Tax and Social Welfare Systems. 1996. *Report of the Expert Group on the Integration of Tax and Social Welfare*. Dublin: Stationery Office.

Forfás. 1996. *Shaping Our Future*. Dublin: Forfás.

Honohan, Patrick. 1987. "A Radical Reform of Social Welfare and Income Tax Evaluated." *Administration* 35 (1): 69–87.

Partnership 2000 for Inclusion, Employment and Competitiveness. 1996. Dublin: Stationery Office.

Report of the Working Group on the Integration of the Tax and Social Welfare Systems. 1996. Dublin: Stationery Office.

Revenue Commissioners (various). *Statistical Report (various years)*. Dublin: Stationery Office.
Ward, Seán. 1994. "A Basic Income System for Ireland." In *Towards an Adequate Income for All*, edited by Brigid Reynolds and Seán Healy, 74–136. Dublin: CORI.

CHAPTER 8

The Netherlands: Final Piece of the Welfare State Is Still to Come

Michiel van Hasslet

In December 1994, the idea of a (modest) basic income was publicly supported by two members of the Dutch cabinet, both liberals (Holland[1] has two liberal parties: D66* and VVD*). However, the socialist members of the same cabinet dismissed the idea. Therefore, basic income did not become a policy item of the cabinet. Politicians of both sides nonetheless generated headlines in newspapers and attention on television. The basic income at that time was closer than ever to being accepted as an item on the political agenda in the Netherlands, even closer than in 1985, when the advisory body for the government WRR* proposed a partial basic income—and found no support whatsoever in the main political parties.

A Dutch book, *The Basic Income: Final Piece of the Welfare State?* by R. J. van der Veen and seven other eminent social scientists was published in 1995.[2] The authors assumed that in about two decades the then existing social security at the minimum level would be replaced by a basic income. The suggested level of this personal basic income was 50 percent of the household amount that the existing social security granted to couples entitled to social benefits. (In 2011, this meant an unconditional basic income of about €650 a month per person.) The level of the basic income would be adjusted to changes in the average income.

In the Dutch welfare state as of the time of this writing, the unconditional basic income is still to come. The portended arrival of BIG (basic income guarantee) in the Netherlands before 2015 is highly improbable. Politics are not moving in the direction of a basic income; on the contrary actual policy tightens the conditionality of social benefits, tending to lower the levels.

What happened in Holland between 1995 and 2011? Why did the basic income in this period fail to come about? What happened in Dutch politics making it so improbable that basic income legislation would be considered in the near future?

BIG-Favorable and -Unfavorable Developments

During the decade 1995–2005, Dutch politics showed mixed tendencies toward facilitating the future introduction of basic income. Four BIG-favorable developments were as follows:

1. The basic income became more affordable for the Dutch welfare state, thanks to the rise of the GNP and the tax yield.
2. When some political parties put the 65+ pension scheme AOW* into question, the popular support for this scheme remained very strong. (AOW was the opening piece of the Dutch welfare state in 1957: a basic income for the elderly. Conditional only as to age.)
3. "Algemene heffingskorting," a new tax credit for partners of taxpayers, has been given to the referred partners, without means testing. It is conditional only as to the fiscal partnership. In the experience of nonworking partners, this tax credit feels like a partial basic income.
4. Population grew faster than employment. Between 1970 and 2010, the number of paid worked hours in the Netherlands increased from 10 billion to 12 billion: 20 percent. During these four decades, the working age group (20–65) increased from 7 million to 10 million: 43 percent. So the political aim to provide incomes to all people by employing them becomes increasingly unrealistic. Therefore, the alternative—an unconditional basic income—ought to be thought of as more realistic.

Four other related developments were not favorable:

1. Social security became increasingly conditional. Social benefits without means testing (WW*, WAO*) were reduced in favor of a "means-tested" scheme on a lower level (WWB*). This WWB also tests the "absence of a wage-earning partner" in the household. "Job seeking" became an obligation too, not only in the WWB, but also in other social benefit schemes for Dutch citizens below 65 years of age. Existing exceptions to this obligation—mothers of children, jobless people above the age of 57, and the partial disabled—were abolished: now they all must be job seeking. In

2020, those aged above 65 will be reduced in their pension rights under AOW—in order to extend their participation in jobs or in job seeking tested social benefits. And in 2025, the same recipe will be measured out to the aged above 66. This is what politicians and the representatives of employers and workers are talking about in 2011.

2. Politics became overoptimistic as to future full employment, thereby downplaying the risk of unemployment. This overoptimism has much to do with dominant economic thinking, the belief that "demand" and "supply" always move toward each other—toward parity of quantities. In this economic thinking, more supply of labor (more job seeking) will lead to more demand (more jobs) sooner or later. The demographic reality of a shrinking supply of labor also supports the overoptimism, at least when combined with the fictionality that demand for labor is not shrinking. The overoptimism as to the labor market also has to do with a certain unpoliteness in existing politics: the political class does not have the decency to acknowledge responsibility to the people for the fact that the quantity of available jobs falls short as compared to the quantity of job-seeking people. The political class rather pretends that joblessness is due to the jobless themselves.
3. Politics—in Holland and elsewhere—became less directed to creating good policy results and more directed to creating the impression of good policy results. Spinning and framing, instead of really helping job-seeking people, the political class creates the impression of really helping job-seeking people—suppressing the fact that there are never enough jobs for all possible job seekers. As a (researched) matter of fact, the reemployment business—which recently took €2 billon Dutch public expenditure a year—did not really help its clients into jobs. Clients who found a job would have done so too without the reemployment business ("deadweight loss"). And more clients did not find jobs at all.[3] But the reemployment business was still helpful: to spread the impression that failure to find jobs was due, not to the shortage of jobs, but to the shortcomings of job seekers. The politicians swept the failure of the reemployment business under the carpet, in order to hide their own misrepresentation (misunderstanding) of the real labor market in the preceding years. At the time when they decided to engage this business—the late nineties—the overoptimism regarding the labor market already dominated the political decision-making. This overoptimism did not lessen, not even in 2002 when employment started going down. Politics even now sticks to the widespread impression that by and large

the reemployment business in the Netherlands may be helpful to job seekers and job growth.

4. A broad discussion in Dutch society about revising the social security system—announced by the cabinet in 1996—was not held and was cancelled in 1998 by that same government, a coalition of socialists and liberals. This coalition was hopelessly divided over revising the social security system, the conditions, the level, and duration of the benefits. Socialists wanted to maintain the welfare state and opposed the liberal strive to minimize both benefits and bureaucracy. A compromise between the coalition partners to reform the system was not possible (or, at least, not found). So they did not change the system but changed only the executive structure of the system. This diversion to reforming the executive structure, rearranging the responsibilities of the concerned actors, degenerated into what researchers of the consecutive changes have called "the reform swamp of the Dutch welfare state."[4]

These researches discovered (among other things) that during the consecutive reshufflings of the executive structure, in the period 1980–2008, the average transaction costs of granting one unemployment (WW) or disablement (WAO) benefit rose, while the profits in terms of reemployment did not rise. Their main finding was that the reshufflings were ill-considered. So their main recommendation to Dutch politics was that if you want to reshuffle again make sure that the new reshuffling will be well considered in advance. This late call for the broad discussion was not heard. The new government in 2011 started at once to again reshuffle the social security system and its executive structure, without any broad discussion or good consideration in advance, whatsoever.

Favorable Turned into Unfavorable

After 1995, basic income became increasingly a nondiscussable item in Dutch politics. This may be illustrated by the typical political reception since 2005 of the four mentioned BIG-favorable developments.

First, the more favorable financial situation has been reframed to suggest that basic income in the Netherlands is unaffordable, especially in an aging society where a growing proportion of the population will be unemployed.[5] This reframing got momentum after the 2008 crisis and the bail out with billions taxpayers money to remedy the crisis, resulting in a disturbingly high level of national debt.

Second, the support for maintaining the pension scheme AOW 65 decreased when the influential economic planning agency CPB* stated that the costs of the scheme in the future would be too high. Then, the political parties took this for granted and started to change their positions on the issue. In 2006, D66 proposed to extend the pension age from 65 to 67. In 2010, all main parties—liberal, christian, and socialist—proposed more or less the same, presuming that otherwise the future numbers of elder people would make the AOW "impayable." They passed the fact, in silence, that in 1997 they all had supported the creation of a new state fund to save up billions in order to be able to pay the AOW to 65+ aged people in the future. Already in 1997, Dutch politicians were fully aware of the future financial problem that the numbers of AOW recipients would rise steadily (as a consequence of demographic factors). Nevertheless, in the years to follow they omitted to fill the new fund with the promised billions. Their actual silence with regard to a fund that turned out to be only a virtual fund is understandable. Yet it should be said that failing to fill the fund clearly is the main reason for a new policy aimed at changing the pension age from 65 into 67. Politics rashly followed the CPB in its overoptimistic prognosis that a higher pension age will lead to higher labor participation and higher tax yield.

The third mentioned favorable development "*algemene heffingskorting*," a partial basic income to the partners of taxpayers, was also recently reframed by Dutch politics into a "stay-in-the-kitchen subsidy" to suggest that many housewives *because of this tax credit* do not participate in the labor market. Though, there is no evidence that this causality is the case, but in Dutch politics, the mere suggestion sufficed to revise the tax credit policy; step-by-step this partial basic income will disappear in the years to come.

As to the fourth development, Dutch politicians refuse to face the fact that the population grew faster than the participation in paid labor. Politicians prefer to believe in the feasibility of full employment.

Political Misrepresentation of Labor Market and Basic Income

The aforementioned vicissitudes of the four BIG-favorable developments all point to one explanation why most politicians in Holland still do not recognize the merits and the viability of a basic income: they do not admit that Dutch politics itself cannot initiate or enhance job growth—do not admit that the modern economy cannot come close to full employment.

Basic income will not arrive in Holland unless this misrepresentation of the labor market stops. Is this stop to happen in the near future?? In all probability: yes!! For the Dutch are a down-to-earth people, who don't like to deny the facts.

Increasingly Undeniable Facts of the Labor Market Will Ask for a Basic Income

Facts increasingly show that full employment in the Netherlands is not feasible at all. Participation in paid labor (> 12 hours a week) reached its highest point in 2008: 68 percent of the potential occupational population, the age group 16 to 65. Since then, the quantity of jobs and the participation in paid labor has gone down. A realistic prognosis says that in 2012, the percentage will be the same as in 2000 and 2006: again 65 percent. Compared with other countries—and with Holland's own past—this is a high percentage. Almost 7.5 million persons (aged 16–65), out of a potential of 11 million, have jobs (paid for at least 12 hours a week). The official optimism that employment will recover soon is not trustworthy. When one looks into the jobs that have been cut recently, it is highly improbable that many of these jobs will return when the economy recovers. Yes, some sectors grow. In the Dutch economy, however, most sectors shrink. The actual overall recovery in 2010–2015 is anticipated to average below 2 percent GNP growth. This is not enough to enable overall job growth. To make things worse, the government has started cutting expenses, which means retrenchment—directly and indirectly cutting many jobs.

In this context, the last thing to expect is new politics opting for new expenses in order to create a basic income for all adults. But surprise, surprise: all the same, there is still a real probability that the very retrenchment policy resolve will generate a new propensity toward the basic income. The ongoing economic crisis compels us to go on thinking out of the box and finding new solutions never been practiced before, such as the unconditional basic income.

Basic Income to Overcome the Resistance to Retrenchment

Some actual plans to cut public expenditure meet much resistance because they threaten lower-income groups with poverty. For example, the cabinet's plan to cut not only benefits for disabled youngsters but also to cut a state subsidy for relief work is a typical case that meets much resistance. As a consequence, the parliament may reject main parts of the contested plan. And there is more to come. The government needs many more retrenchment plans to realize the promised total expense cutting of €18 billion in 2014. However, conceivable plans are not being conceived, because of the foreseeable resistance of the people. Voters fear the financial consequences to their incomes—including voters of all parties, the governing ones included: the VVD liberals, the CDA* Christian democrats, and also the PVV* populists of Wilders, who are by special contract the special partner of the government (that otherwise would lack a majority in parliament). The cabinet could, for instance, conceive a several billions saving retrenchment plan by a new policy to heal the ill-functioning housing market, repealing the existing tax credits for house owners and tenants. However, without a basic income such a plan will not be accepted by the parliament. Basic income is a provision against poverty that otherwise would be the consequence of such conceivable retrenchment policies.

Basic Income Solves the Puzzle of Integrating Social Security in the EU

Although the EU does not yet have substantial authority on social security, which is still the sovereign competence of the individual member states (such as the Netherlands), inevitably, the ongoing process of integration will increase the likelihood in the near future of asking for improving European coordination of the social security systems. Present national systems are all very complex but not in the same aspects. The patchworks differ in many aspects, which may be understandable in the light of national histories but not in the light of what European citizens need nowadays. The increased labor migration between the member states already leads to more problems and increasing coordination for social security. It becomes increasingly clear that the problems experienced in coordination will ask for further integration. Patching or pasting the existing complexities together will not suffice. European policy for social security needs an overall concept and must go back to basics in order to avoid unworkable complexities with high transaction costs and low transparency for the European citizens. In the context of social security, the word "basics" refers to basic income.

The Dutch Association for Basic Income in the Years to Come: A Tough Proposition

The described political situation is a BIG problem for the headstrong people who recognize the desirability and possible viability of the basic income nowadays in the Netherlands and elsewhere. More than a hundred of these people participate in the Dutch Association for Basic Income (VBi*), which is a member of the Basic Income Earth Network (BIEN). In the past decade, the association had to realize how much Dutch politics and public opinion have turned away from the basic income as an optional perspective for a better future in the Netherlands. In 2006, when the association held its fifteenth birthday, Paul de Beer, one of the authors of the 1995 book, said that basic income has been locked up in the fridge of Dutch politics. These frozen Dutch politics induced the association to divert its attention to other countries with more open attitude toward basic income. For example, in Africa, Namibia was willing to start partial basic income experiments in a region with extremely poor people (Otjivero). The Dutch contribution to this could be organized based on a "micropartnership," a contract between Dutch individual contributors and an intermediate organization that guarantees an unconditional partial basic income to the inhabitants of the concerned region. Unfortunately, the Dutch government at the time (2008) did not cooperate to allow the start of the intermediate organization, misunderstanding its very innovative concept. After that, the association for basic income paid more attention to countries nearby, namely: Belgium, Germany, and Switzerland, as can be seen on www.basicincome.nl. In these countries nowadays, more than tens of thousands adherents of the basic income idea are active, inspired by the philosophical and practical ideas of Rudolph Steiner, Philippe van Parijs, Götz Werner, and many others.

In October 2011, the association will have its twentieth birthday with a special conference in the University of Utrecht, a new attempt to attract Dutch political attention to an old genial idea. Basic income diminishes poverty, liberates people, limits bureaucracy, and modernizes the labor market.[6]

The final piece of the Dutch welfare state is still to come.

* Abbrevations (and translations)

AOW Algemene Ouderdoms Wet 1956, law on state pension for the aged

BIEN Basic Income Earth Network

CDA Christelijk Democratisch Appel. A Christian political party

CPB Centraal Planbureau, the influential economic planning agency

D66 Dutch democrats who started a liberal political party in 1966

PVV Partij van de Vrijheid. Political party of the freedom; the new populists of Wilders

SEO Stichting voor Economisch Onderzoek. Foundation for economic research (related to Amsterdam university)

VBi Vereniging Basisinkomen. The Dutch Association for Basic Income (member of BIEN); www.basisinkomen.nl

VVD Volkspartij voor Vrijheid en Democratie, people's party for freedom and democracy, a (right wing) liberal political party, bigger than D66.

WAO Wet op de Arbeidsongeschiktheid. Old law on disability benefits
WRR Wetenschappelijke Raad voor het Regeringsbeleid, scientific council for the government policy
WW Wet werkeloosheid. Law on (conditional) benefits for the unemployed
WWB Wet Werk en Bijstand (Wet Water and Bread)

Notes

1. "Holland" is synonymous with "The Netherlands." The adjective is "Dutch." Language is wonderful. Abbrevations marked * will be explained at the end of this article.
2. Robert J. van der Veen en Dick Pels, red. *Het basisinkomen (Sluitstuk van de verzorgingsstaat?)'* Van Gennep, Amsterdam 1995.
3. Out of the WW and WWB clients of the reemployment business, 41 percent and 29 percent, respectively, found jobs within a year. The minister of social affairs in 2010 who presented these percentages to the parliament (letter dated July 12, 2010) rightly says that research to establish the amount of deadweight loss in these percentages is difficult. His best guess in an earlier letter was that the deadweight loss was so high that only a very low percentage—3 to 5 percent—may be the real result of the reemployment business. He used evidence from evaluation research on clients in 2005, when the reemployment business did not yet cover the total population of WW and WWB. At that time researchers were able to compare the clients of the reemployment business with a constructed control group of people who were not helped by the business to find jobs. Between both groups there appeared to be very little difference in the extent of job finding, according to the Rekenkamer (Accounting Board), Amsterdam, who researched their WWB population. The SEO (Stichting voor Economisch Onderzoek. Foundation for economic research [related to Amsterdam university]) too found very little difference, as to both WW- and WWB populations. SEO (2006) nonetheless constructed a financial success story, asserting that in ten years few in the reemployment business really helped job finders make money in their jobs, enough to compensate the costs of the reemployment business. This assesment (of what the reemployment business yields to our society) is too high, first, because within two years many of these job finders appear to lose their job, and second, because the costs of displacement have been left out; in other words, SEO did not research the effect that the job finders prohibit other job seekers to find the same jobs. Because of this displacement effect the other job seekers must wait longer for their opportunity to make money in the economy. This means less gains and more benefit costs for society, which ought to be discounted against the gains. The spurious gains of the reemployment business get a more detailed discussion in my self-published

book *Politiek in verzorgingssaat Nederland: misrepresentatie en civiele reconstruction* (Politics in the Dutch welfare state: misrepresentation and civil reconstruction), Utrecht, The Netherlands: CIVES, 2011 (Contact me at cives@ziggo.nl for copies). As to the reemployment business in the US, see Barbara Ehrenreich, *Bait and Switch. The (Futile) Pursuit of the American Dream,* London: Granta Books, 2006.

4. Nicolette van Gestel, Paul de Beer en Marc van der Meer, *Het hervormingsmoeras van de verzorgingsstaat* Amsterdam University Press, 2009.
5. The proportion decreases not only because of the increasing number of elderly-retired people with prolonged life expectance, but also because of the number of job decreases since 2009. In 2008, almost 68 percent, a historic high percentage, of the age group 16–65 participated in paid labor for at least 12 hours a week; in 2011, this percentage will be less than 67 percent; and in 2012, further decrease is expected, probably to 65 percent.
6. Modernization of the labor market in the ongoing political discourse in the Netherlands means something quite different: reduction of the duration of the benefits of the unemployed and less protection of the employed against dismissal. Proponents pretend that participation in paid labor will rise as a consequence of this "modernization." However, Dutch history has already displayed that this kind of modernization showed no consequential increase in labor participation. Decrease is more expectable not only for historical empirical reasons but also for the following theoretical reason. If employers are allowed to dismiss their employees more easily, on the one hand there will be more dismissals and on the other hand there will be more appointments. There is no reason beforehand to expect more appointments than dismissals. The only expectable effect is more job change. This enables employers to consider more often what to do with the vacancies: filling, reorganizing, or striking out jobs. So we may expect after all that the so called modernization—actually a reactionary policy—leads to a modest decrease of labor participation.

CHAPTER 9

Kingdom of Spain: Basic Income from Social Movements to Parliament and Back Again*

Daniel Raventós, Julie Wark, and David Casassas

With the present economic crisis and the ensuing economic policy measures introduced by the Spanish government as of May 2010, a curious two-way shift has occurred in the debate on basic income. On the one hand, basic income has virtually disappeared from the official agenda, even in the form of piecemeal discussion among the political parties whereas, on the other hand, there is greater interest in it among the activists of quite a wide range of social movements. A short history of basic income in the Kingdom of Spain[1] is essential here if one is to comprehend and contextualize what this means in political terms. Before providing this, however, we shall give a brief outline of the present situation in Spain as a result of the economic crisis and, more important, an account of the economic policies adopted since May 2010. Otherwise, it is difficult to understand the recent two-way shift regarding basic income, at the level of government in the political parties represented in the Spanish parliament and at the grassroots level among the social movements.

The Crisis and Economic Policy Proposals in Spain

Until well into 2009, the Spanish Socialist Party (PSOE [Partido Socialista Obrero Español]) government headed by José Luis Rodríguez Zapatero denied that Spain was gravely affected by the downturn in the global economy. This was almost two years after the onset of the crisis that is rightly described as one of the worst of the last 80 years.

One of its most devastating effects in the Spanish economy has been a much greater rise in unemployment than in other economies. The most recent official data, published at the end of April 2011, give a figure of 4,910,200 unemployed, a rate of 21.29 percent and, more importantly, the unemployment rate among the under-25s is almost 50 percent. Both the general and youth rates are the highest in the European Union. Moreover, according to data from the end of 2009, 63 percent of the working population, which is to say 18.3 million people, are paid less than €1,000 or less per month, hence acquiring the name *mileuristas* or, to give an idea of the extent of the problem, the *mileurista* generation.

On May 12, 2010, Prime Minister Zapatero appeared before the parliament to announce that, as a result of massive speculative attacks of the previous week against the public debt of the member states of the European Union, and the recent Economic and Financial Affairs Council (ECOFIN) agreements, he was going to embark on severe austerity measures in an attempt to rein in the public deficit and allay fears of a Greek-style bailout. Notable among the measures that were approved a few days later are a 5 percent cut to public sector salaries, a pension freeze, slashing public infrastructure investment by €6,000 million, and cutting public expenditure for the administration of the autonomous regions and municipalities.

Zapatero also mentioned three sweeping structural reforms envisaged and demanded by the Bank of Spain, the European Central Bank, and the International Monetary Fund, these hitting the job market and pensions and entailing a restructuring of savings banks. All these "reforms" ("counterreforms" would be closer to the reality), which have been applied since May 2010, are described by many people as the biggest offensive against the social and economic rights of the working class since the end of the Franco regime or in almost four decades. This is the position of the trade unions, which organized a general strike against the measures on September 29, 2010. In this situation, a first impression might be to suppose that basic income should have had greater prominence in the social debate. Indeed, this has been the case with some grassroots organizations but it has completely disappeared from the parliamentary arena where it had once got as far as the legislative bill stage.

Basic Income Beginnings in Spain

The first legal steps were taken in February 2001 to create the Red Renta Básica (Basic Income Network—RRB) association. Prior to this, there was scant knowledge among Spanish politicians, unions, social movements, and citizens in general about the proposal. A few articles had been published, along with a book or two, and basic income was propounded only by a few academics and activists. In sum, its presence was quite insubstantial.

If we are to put a date on the turning point in the process of divulging basic income in Spain, it would be June 2001, when the first symposium on basic income was held in Barcelona. It is true that, in 2000, some of the more widely read newspapers (*El País*, *El Mundo*, *La Vanguardia*, *El Periódico*, *Gara*, *La Gaceta de los Negocios*, and the now nonexistent *Egunkaria*) and a few prestigious reviews (*Claves de Razón Práctica*, *El Viejo Topo*) had published some articles describing the essential principles of basic income as well as interviews with several of its advocates. Moreover, quite a lot of radio and, to a lesser extent, television programs ran interviews with basic income supporters. However, the qualitative and quantitative leap in knowledge about, and interest in basic income came with the first Basic Income Symposium of June 8, 2001. Participating in this Symposium were academics, representatives from the main trade unions, members of social movements together with three members of the Catalan and Spanish parliaments (José Luis López Bulla, Carme Porta, and Jordi Sevilla), all from left-wing parties—the eco-socialist Iniciativa per Catalunya-Verds (ICV [Initiative for Catalonia Greens]), the proindependence Esquerra Republicana de Catalunya (ERC [Republican Left of Catalonia]), and PSOE, respectively. López Bulla and Porta presented some of the content of the draft law that their two parties were working on for presentation to the Catalan parliament. We shall give more details of this below.

Since this first symposium on basic income, nine more have been held on an annual basis, the last venue being Gijón in 2010. The second symposium was held in Vitoria-Gasteiz with the collaboration of the Basque government. The third was in Barcelona and so was the fourth, which took place as part of the tenth Basic Income Earth Network (BIEN) Congress organized by RRB that year after its recognition as an official section of BIEN in its Geneva congress of 2002. The fifth Spanish symposium took place in Valencia, the sixth in Santiago de Compostela, the seventh in Barcelona once again, the eighth in Madrid, and the ninth in Bilbao. Each one of these symposia has, to a greater or lesser extent, resulted in wider knowledge of basic income, especially in the venues themselves, thanks to the impetus and enthusiasm of local organizers and the usually accurate coverage in the different branches of the media.

Legislative Bills

Over the last decade, several basic income bills have been presented in different autonomous regions of Spain and two in the Spanish parliament. We shall refer to these two and the pioneering bill that was debated in the Catalan parliament in May 2002. In fact, the bill presented in Catalonia by ICV and ERC was used as the reference for the two subsequent bills that were presented in the Spanish parliament.

The explanatory preamble[2] to the former states:

> The introduction of a Basic Income of Citizenship is proposed, this being defined as an income paid by the state to each member or accredited member of society, regardless of whether he or she wishes to engage in remunerated employment, independently of other sources of income the individual may possess and irrespective of cohabitation arrangements in the domestic sphere. The quantity of the Basic Income of Citizenship proposed in this Bill should always exceed the poverty threshold and it will be based on the principles of: ending poverty, preventing stigmatization of those members of the population that are obliged to demonstrate their inability to earn an income in order to obtain certain benefit payments, and increasing the degree of real autonomy and freedom of a considerable part of the population in their choices concerning participation in the job market.

In its articles, the bill continues:

> ARTICLE 2. *LEVELS OF PROTECTION*
>
> 1. The Basic Income will be provided, as a lifelong measure from the moment of birth, to each and every citizen that accredits his or her permanent residence in State territory, in a quantity that is never inferior to the poverty threshold, although different endowments may be established in strict accordance with the age of the beneficiary.
>
> ...
>
> 3. The Basic Income will be paid on a monthly basis over the twelve months of the year.
>
> ARTICLE 3. *PROTECTED PERSONS*
>
> The right to receive the Basic Income of Citizenship is inherent to the condition of full citizen in accordance with Article 11.1 of the Spanish Constitution.

As for its aims, the bill declares:

> ARTICLE 5. *ON THE ENDS PURSUED*
>
> The following ends are pursued by means of introducing the Basic Income:
>
> a) To end the situation of poverty of citizens;
> b) To prevent stigmatization of those members of the population that are presently obliged to demonstrate their inability to earn an income in order to obtain certain benefit payments;

c) To increase the degree of real autonomy and freedom of a considerable part of the population in their choices concerning participation in the job market;
d) To rationalize the system of conditional benefit payments of the present welfare state;
e) To avoid the perverse effects shown in the present system with certain cases of fraud and the existence of a submerged economy.

The first basic income bill was presented to the Spanish parliament in April 2005. Its Article 1 reads:

ARTICLE 1. *AIM OF THE GRANT*

The present Basic Income Draft Law aims to introduce an economic endowment, a Basic Income of Citizenship that is to become effective for every full citizen who can accredit his or her permanent residence in Spanish territory, independently of his or past, present or future situation of remunerated work, regardless of his or her other possible sources of income, and irrespective of arrangements in the domestic sphere.

The draft law is very clear as to the onset of the grant and its duration:

ARTICLE 7. *COMMENCEMENT OF THE RIGHT*

The right to receive the economic grant of a Basic Income commences with birth or upon obtaining full citizenship.

ARTICLE 8. *DURATION OF THE RIGHT*

The right to a Basic Income is lifelong.

The characteristics of the Basic Income proposed are also stated without the slightest ambiguity.

ARTICLE 5. *ON THE GENERAL GUIDING PRINCIPLES*

The essential principles of the Basic Income will be:

a) The universal character of the economic grant;
b) Its individual nature;
c) Its unconditional nature with respect to the individual's having engaged in remunerated employment or being willing or not to do so;
d) Its unconditional nature with respect to the sources of income an individual may have, whether they are family or personal in origin and independently of whether or not they are subject to taxation according to the prevailing regulations.

The second basic income bill was debated on October 2, 2007, in the plenary session of the Spanish parliament. The bill was drafted in very similar terms to those of its predecessor two years earlier, and the interesting debate is detailed in the *Diario de sesiones del Congreso de los Diputados* (Parliamentary Gazette).[3] The robust defense of the proposal by the Catalan parliamentarian Joan Tardà of the ERC includes such statements as:

> Permit me to mention yet another beneficial result for those of us who aspire to a society that is very different from what we have at present. I refer to the increased degree of autonomy and freedom of the population when it comes to choosing employment. In broad terms, I should say that our Bill aims to recognize a new right of citizenship. All citizens will receive a tax-free quantity that is not inferior to that established as the poverty threshold, although this may differ in accordance with the age of the beneficiary.

A little later he says,

> We shall speak, then, of the universal Basic Income as a constitutive element of the right of citizenship. Basic Income is the political realization of republican values that our democracy should aspire to enact, in other words liberty, equality and fraternity. It grants fraternity in the sense that society shares a part of the wealth it generates among the citizens as a way of guaranteeing their right of existence, of life itself. It respects equality because it is bestowed on each and every citizen independently of any other socioeconomic condition. It endows liberty in guaranteeing the minimum conditions of life that would allow individuals to make real decisions pertaining to their personal development and their conditions of access to the job market without having to jeopardize their rights in response to permanent blackmail of the possessors of wealth who use it as a tool of subjugation.

One of the consequences of the two debates in the Spanish parliament on basic income was a triggering of considerable public interest in the proposal. The coverage of the debate in the country's newspaper of largest circulation, *El País*, was followed up with an opinion piece in defense of basic income titled "*El sueldo del mendigo y del banquero*" (A Wage for Banker and Beggar) on October 3, 2007, which, in turn, was discussed in a range of electronic forums.[4] Later, another outcome was the establishment of a parliamentary subcommittee to study the viability of introducing a basic income in Spain as a whole. Joan Herrera, one of the members of parliament in favor of basic income argued:

> I hope that, besides today's debate, the arguments previously expressed against basic income will not reappear in the subcommittee. One can

> express measured and nuanced arguments against it or be radically in favor but the proposal must not be dispatched in the contemptuous way it was in the plenary session of October 2007, and neither should such arguments be heard again in Spain, or anywhere else on the planet. This is not about a payment made so that people don't have to work, which was what was claimed then, but a modest sum that would give greater freedom to people in choosing what kind of work they will do. I want to make it clear that what we are talking about today is, first of all, setting up a subcommittee to study basic income and, second, that the final aim of the discussion is even more important in a situation of crisis because today, precisely, there is an even greater risk of social exclusion.

Now, more than two years later, the subcommittee has not yet begun work. Given the short time remaining for the present legislature, it is reasonable to think that it never will. At the time it was approved—and it must be said that the vote of all the parties in parliament was unanimous—the economic crisis had already hit the Spanish economy, and very brutally at that.

Basic Income as an Emerging Human Right

As far back as the first Basic Income Symposium in 2001, one of the speakers, the philosophy lecturer Miguel Candel, not only went directly to the heart of the matter but also anticipated what was to come three years later at the Universal Forum of Cultures:

> I see basic income as a necessary corollary to the Universal Declaration of Human Rights. There is no need to appeal to "natural law", a concept that is quite difficult to grasp. Rather, there are rights that emerge from social consensus and are accordingly accepted by everyone, at least since 1948. These rights imply that the human species has decided that life is sacred or, in lay terms, that all members of the human species have an inalienable right to life. If that is the case, then the sociopolitical structures must guarantee this right because every right generates its corresponding duties. And in order to guarantee this right, it would seem clear that, if it is an unconditional right, no conditions pertaining to any kind of action, initiative or contribution by the individual should be imposed on the assignation of a certain quantity of resources necessary for life.

With the first Universal Forum of Cultures, which was held in Barcelona in 2004 and included the tenth BIEN Congress, several organizations concerned with human rights came together to produce a draft of what was to become the Universal Declaration of Emerging Human Rights.

This first version was debated and amended at the second Universal Forum of Cultures in Monterrey in 2007. Its Article 1.3 upholds:

> The right to a basic income or universal citizens' income that guarantees to every human being, independently of age, gender, sexual orientation, civil or employment status, the right to live in material conditions of dignity. To this end, a regular cash payment, financed by tax reforms and covered by the state budget, and sufficient to cover his or her basic needs, is recognized as a right of citizenship of every member-resident of the society, whatever his or her other sources of income may be.

The importance of this article of the Monterrey declaration resides not so much in the fact that it enshrines the right of material existence, of having the guarantee of certain minimum vital resources, but that it explicitly speaks of the "right to a basic income or universal citizen's income." The great significance of this crystal-clear specification of a new emerging right in the form of a basic income might be summed up in the words of Philippe Van Parijs, an eminent figure in BIEN, in an interview he gave to Benedetta Giovanola at the end of 2005:[5]

> Invoking a human right when speaking of minimal subsistence would not be sufficient *per se* to justify a proposal, since this right could be fulfilled through conventional social service welfare mechanisms that focus on the poor and require from them a willingness to work. An adequate justification would require calling on a conception of justice anchored in the aspiration of endowing each and every person not only the possibility of consuming but of choosing his or her way of life.

In the view of Philippe Van Parijs, in normative terms, some approximation to a conception of justice is required. As noted above, the Monterrey declaration, appeals directly to the human right of a basic income or universal citizens' income. This particular point has been greatly appreciated as support for the arguments of some politicians who advocate basic income.

Financing Basic Income in Spain

The matter of financing a basic income is one of the areas of research where most progress has been made in the last 15 years or more.[6] In 2005, a Barcelona-based team produced a detailed report[7] that enquires into in-depth reform of the Spanish Personal Income Tax (IRPF) system as a way of financing basic income. A study of this type of tax proved to be especially helpful in showing the resulting distribution of income and other changes that would occur if a basic income were introduced. The research is based on a microsimulation program, especially designed for the study, and applied to 110,474 income tax declarations in Catalonia, with the aim of evaluating a range of policy options for tax-benefit integration, which would include a basic income. The study shows that the proposal is viable in economic terms and that the impact of the distribution would be highly progressive. The most interesting option among those studied was a basic income equivalent to the Spanish Minimum Wage of 2003 (when the research began), in 12 annual payments of €451 per month or €5,414 per year, a sum which is close to the poverty line for an individual living alone. This model showed a saving in social spending of an estimated €9,249.1 million while the cost of a basic income for that part of the population that does not pay personal income tax was €8,756.4 million. The main results were that there was no net deficit, so the reform proved to be self-financing and the redistributive impact was progressive with the figure for net winners after the reform being 63.3 percent (including the dependent members of the taxpayer's household). The study aroused considerable interest in Catalonia and Spain and, since IRPF is a common form of taxation, with some variations among the states of the European Union and other geographic zones, it is a model that can easily be adapted to other taxation systems.

The Most Debated Aspects of Basic Income in Spain

Most of the discussion over the last 10 or 11 years has mainly arisen in the wake of the basic income bills in parliament and the annual RRB symposia. In addition, several seminars and public lectures have been organized by political parties, trade unions, or university-based groups. The debate at this more official level might best be described by means of a summary of the arguments presented by those in favor of basic income and those against it.

Among the dissenters, the most frequently heard arguments begin with the claim that a basic income would encourage "scroungers," "freeloaders," with the variations that "nobody would want to work for a wage" or "it would encourage parasitism," a view generally expressed by right-wing opponents. Second, many people mostly from the right but also from the left say that a basic income is too costly and impossible to finance. Third, and not so often proffered, is the view, coming in almost equal proportion from both right and left, that a basic income would encourage more poor immigrants. These arguments are not so different from the ones that are heard in other parts of the world.

Among basic income supporters in Spain, however, there are two more or less explicit debates, as well as one contribution unique to this country. The first debate revolves around the most appropriate strategy for introducing a basic income and essentially focuses on the effectiveness or otherwise of bringing it in through the back door. The second is concerned with different types of financing it. The contribution we mention is a normative justification of basic income. We believe that the first discussion is not of major interest and at times, it simply boils down to the different general political views of the participants in the debate. If the debate were further advanced in the first domain, it would have to take in issues of institutional design, which would depend on the political constellation at any point. However, matters are not yet so advanced. The discussion over how to go about financing a basic income in Spain (and in Catalonia in some cases), in contrast, has produced some very useful results. These funding proposals go back some ten years and some were presented in the Catalan parliament by members of the left-wing parties of the tripartite government of the time: ICV, ERC, and Partido Socialista de Catalunya (Catalan Socialist Party—PSC).

The specifically Catalan—rather than Spanish—contribution to basic income is that of furnishing a political-philosophical grounding for the proposal on the basis of historical republicanism.[8] In order to avoid confusion, we should give a brief account here of the philosophical distinctiveness of this normative framework. Proponents of academic neorepublicanism including Quentin Skinner, J. G. A. Pocock, and, in particular, Philip Pettit are well known for their distinction between interference in general and arbitrary interference when they set about defending the republican conception of freedom based on an absence of arbitrary interference. The predominant theoretical focus in Spain, however, is the historical republican concept of freedom (or what has been dubbed "the Catalan contribution" to the political-philosophical grounding of basic income), which takes the position that the neorepublican account glosses over the relationship between property and republican freedom while also understating the essential connection between democracy and property. Pettit theorizes republican freedom as a dispositional concept, contrasting it with the purely negative liberal freedom based on noninterference. This version of republican freedom would entail absence of domination and of arbitrary interference from other individuals of groups, including the state. Herein lies a crucial difference, since, for historical republicanism, the essential source of vulnerability and arbitrary interference is the absence of material independence owing to lack of property. The set of opportunities of any individual is clearly delimited by the material resources that do or do not enable him or her to lead an autonomous social existence. This is not any old set of opportunities. Full citizenship is not possible without material independence or without some "control" over the set of possibilities we have just specified. If the essential material roots of the historic role of property and the capacity of property owners to dominate are overlooked, then the notion of "domination" is diluted and stripped of its institutional nature. Moreover, other more personal aspects of human relations that have never been deemed politically pertinent by historical republicanism, such as cheating or swindling, which arbitrarily interfere in the life of the person so deceived, then come under the heading of "domination."

The Crisis and Basic Income

In May 2010, the Spanish Basic Income Network published a manifesto in several languages and titled "A Basic Income in the Current Situation of Economic Crisis." It noted, or perhaps foreboded that:

> In a situation of economic crisis, attacks on both jobs and salaries abound: the International Monetary Fund, the Spanish Central Bank, the Banco de Bilbao Vizcaya Argentaria (BBVA), and the Spanish Employers' Organisation (CEOE [Confederación Española de Organizaciones Empresariales]), amongst other organizations, have made explicit their agreement with salary moderation and redundancies, with cutting costs of the "work factor" and reducing pensions and social protection. We are witnessing constant announcements of wage settlements and staff regulation, and we are also seeing the closure of innumerable small businesses.[9]

Again, with the crisis, it is clear that, while the reasons for introducing a basic income are ever weightier, the political stumbling blocks are ever greater. All the arguments in favor of introducing a basic income have been made more than explicit in this manifesto and in articles published both before and after it appeared.[10]

In sum, there are five main reasons presented as to why a basic income would be an effective—in more ways than one—measure in the present crisis. First, involuntary job loss causes extreme economic and personal insecurity. Losing one's job while being able to count on the cushion of a basic income would alleviate the distress and better equip people to confront the situation. In a situation of crisis when the unemployment figures are much higher and persist much longer, and especially in the extreme situation of Spain with half its youth jobless and the increasing fragility or out-and-out nonexistence of unemployment benefits, a basic income acquires even greater social significance.

Second, a basic income could play a major role in bolstering the collective interests of the working class and their struggles, both for workers who have trade union backing and those who have no such institutional support and are left to fend for themselves. One can see clearly in this crisis that a basic income would neither be an alternative to a working wage and nor would it undermine the workers' defense of their interests but, rather, it would be an instrument that strengthens the position of the entire workforce, both in the workplace and in the search for a job. In strikes, it would represent a form of unconditional resistance fund that would clearly give workers greater bargaining power. Having a basic income would mean being able to deal with bosses and conflict in the workplace on a much less vulnerable and insecure basis when, in present conditions and depending on how long the strike lasts, wages can be cut to intolerably unsustainable levels if, as is the case with the great majority of workers, no other resources are available.

Third, a basic income would reduce the risks taken by people who opt for self-employment. Not only would it facilitate the different tasks involved but it could also foster cooperative organization among people wishing to start a business together. In the case of failure of a small business, it would offer a kind of safety net and could even make it possible to try again.

Fourth, one of the great advantages of basic income is general alleviation of poverty and it even holds out the possibility of its total eradication. Not only would it bring millions of people out of poverty but it would also offer protection against it in future. In Spain, some 20 percent of the population is defined as poor and, with the crisis, the numbers are fast rising.

Fifth, one much-discussed issue in the context of the crisis is the need to sustain family consumption. In fact, in the boom years, many families were consuming above their means thanks to the inflated prices of financial assets and easy credit, not only for mortgages but also for other kinds of consumption. This debt-based consumerism by families in general does not favor the poorer segments of the population. With the crisis measures, moreover, any extra income has been cut off and reduced wages tend to be used, at least in part, to pay the accumulated debt. Basic income could stabilize basic consumption in order to sustain demand in times of crisis, especially among the more disadvantaged groups.

Despite all these weighty reasons in favor of a basic income in a situation of economic crisis, the political parties in parliament are under increasing pressure to tailor their economic policy to reducing the public deficit along the lines imposed by neoliberal institutions. This essentially amounts to drastic cuts in social spending, which only give more grounds for arguments in favor of basic income. It is a truly vicious circle.

Increasing Interest in Basic Income at the Grassroots Level

The creation in April 28, 2009, of the parliamentary subcommittee to study the viability of basic income turned out to be a lost opportunity.

The majority parties, the right-wing Partido Popular (PP [People's Party]) and the PSOE, which is presently in power and dropping fast in the opinion poll ratings, are either totally against basic income or not interested. The minority parties where the proposal has hitherto found support have very few members of parliament, and those they have are engaged on many fronts. There can be no doubt that since the onset of the crisis there has been a steadily growing interest in basic income among social movements in Spain. Hence, there are a lot more initiatives of organizing lectures on the basic income proposal by human rights groups, associations advocating mortgage forgiveness in the case of foreclosure, teachers, and activists in the sphere of public health, student groups, and so on. It can only be expected that this interest will keep growing, especially among young people who are so hard hit by unemployment and with very few prospects of finding work and therefore of being independent. One might say that, for the moment, the fate of basic income lies more in the hands of activists than with the political parties in parliament. In the protests of the *indignados* involving thousands of campers occupying squares in Madrid, Barcelona, and many other Spanish, Catalan, and Basque cities throughout May 2011, basic income has been one of the subjects discussed.[11] The present lack of interest of the political parties (excepting the aforementioned ERC and IU-ICV [Izquierda Unida-Iniciativa per Catalunya Verds: United Left-Initiative for Catalonia Greens]) could well change in the future and the account we have given is by no means evaluative but strictly descriptive of the way things are now. It is heartening, for example, to see that the new Basque party Bildu, second in the vote count of the municipal elections in May 2011 and the party with most town councilors in the Basque Country, has included support for basic income in its program.[12]

As with any other serious social policy, the future of basic income in Spain will depend, in the end on the quality of its analysis, both in terms or normative principles and financial feasibility and, in particular, on the number of people who decide to support it. At present, its destiny seems to lie with the social movements.

Notes

* This paper was written under the auspices of the European Research Council's Seventh Framework Program (FP7/2007–2013 / ERC / Agreement No 249438—TRAMOD) (Casassas) and the Spanish Ministry of Science and Innovation Research Project FFI2009–10941 (Raventós).

1. Let us not gloss over the fact that Spain is a monarchy. The official name of the country is *Reino de España* (Kingdom of Spain). However, it would be cumbersome to try to reflect the reality by

referring to "a set of nations including Catalonia and the Basque Country," for example, and the term *Estado Español* ("Spanish State") is not satisfactory either. We use the official denomination here to make our point and henceforth, in keeping with common usage in English, "Spain" will suffice.

2. The original passages quoted in our translation from the Catalan may be found in *Butlletí oficial del Parlament de Catalunya*, February 18, which can be accessed at http://www.nodo50.org/redrentabasica/descargas/RenBaERC.pdf.
3. This may be accessed at http://www.nodo50.org/redrentabasica/descargas/debatparlamentari.pdf.
4. For example, the weekly publication *Sin permiso* (www.sinpermiso.info), which is widely read in both Spain and Latin America, frequently publishes articles on basic income.
5. Philippe van Parijs (2005: 205–210).
6. See Arcarons et al. (2005), Arcarons and Raventós (2010), Pinilla (2006), and Sanzo (2005).
7. Arcarons et al. (2005). Raventós (2007, Chapter 8) offers a detailed account in English of the Catalan microsimulation study.
8. There is a wide range of written material available in Spanish. For some English versions see Casassas (2007), Domènech and Raventós (2007), and Raventós (2007).
9. This is a slightly (grammatically) modified version of the Manifesto in English at http://www.nodo50.org/redrentabasica/descargas/Manenglish.pdf (translation by RRB). The Spanish version may be accessed at http://www.attacmadrid.org/d/10/090508130644.php.
10. See Lo Vuolo and Raventós (2009) and Lo Vuolo, Raventós, and Yanes (2010).
11. Two of the authors took part in the open forum organized by the *indignados* camping in the Plaça de Catalunya of Barcelona on May 25, 2011.
12. The program states as follows:

    We advocate holding a social and political debate with the aim of drawing up a proposal for a Basic Income of Citizenship that is to be universal, on an individual basis and unconditional.

    This Basic Income of Citizenship would, *inter alia*, have the following effects:

    - It would eradicate poverty and the stigmatization it entails.
    - It would guarantee a more equable distribution of wealth.
    - It would eliminate humiliating bureaucratic checks and save on administrative costs.
    - People would have more possibilities than they do at present for choosing the combination they wish of the three types of work identified as wage work, domestic work and voluntary work.
    - It would favour self-employment and initiative.
    - It would bring about higher wages in unappealing and unfulfilling types of work.

- By making it possible for citizens to work fewer hours, it would give rise to a spontaneous redistribution of work.
- It would afford greater autonomy for women living in cohabitation.
- It would reduce fraud and eliminate the "poverty trap."
- It would guarantee the material conditions of freedom.

Bibliography

Arcarons, Jordi, Àlex Boso, José Noguera, and Daniel Raventós. 2005. "Viabilitat i impacte d'una Renda Bàsica de Ciutadania per a Catalunya" (Viability and Impact of a Basic Income of Citizenship in Catalonia). Barcelona: Mediterrània-Fundació Jaume Bofill.

Arcarons, Jordi, and Daniel Raventós. 2010. "Al voltant de la Renda Básica" (Concerning Basic Income). Lleida: Universitat de Lleida.

Casassas, David. 2007. "Basic Income and the Republican Ideal: Rethinking Material Independence in Contemporary Societies." *Basic Income Studies* 2 (2, Article 9).

Domènech, Antoni, and Daniel Raventós. 2007. "Property and Republican Freedom: An Institutional Approach to Basic Income." *Basic Income Studies* 2 (2, Article 11).

Lo Vuolo, Rubén, and Daniel Raventós. 2009. "Basic Income: Good in the Boom, Essential in the Crisis." Online opinion. http://www.onlineopinion.com.au/view.asp?article=9172&page=0.

Lo Vuolo, Rubén, Daniel Raventós, and Pablo Yanes. 2010. "The War on Social and Working Rights. Basic Income in Times of Economic Crisis." Counterpunch. http://www.counterpunch.org/vuolo11052010.html.

Parijs, Philippe Van. 2005. "Reditto di base I diritti humani," in an interview by Benedetta Giovanola in Stefano Semplici (ed.), 2005, Il mercato giusto e l'etica della Società Civile, 205–206. Milan: Vita a Pensiero.

Pinilla, Rafael. 2006. "Más allá del bienestar. La renta básica de ciudadanía como innovación social basada en la evidencia" (Beyond Welfare: The Basic Income of Citizenship as Social Innovation According to the Evidence). Barcelona: Icaria.

Raventós, Daniel. 2007. "Basic Income: The Material Conditions of Freedom." London: Pluto Press.

Sanzo, Luis. 2005. "La introducción de la Renta Básica en España" (The Introduction of Basic Income in Spain). *Cuadernos de Relaciones Laborales, Rentas básicas y Protección Social*, 23 (2): 123–149. Madrid: Universidad Complutense.

Other OECD Countries

CHAPTER 10

Australia: Will Basic Income Have a Second Coming?

John Tomlinson

Australia has had a federal social security system since the inception of the 1908 age and disability pensions legislation in 1910. From then until the late 1980s, the system became more comprehensive and generous. It was and still is a categorical and means-tested system paid from the Commonwealth government's general tax revenue. It provides assistance to older Australians; to families with children; to people when they are sick, unemployed, experiencing a disability or illness; and to those enrolled in some education programs. The Commonwealth system runs alongside private superannuation, commercial unemployed and sickness insurance, and a war veteran's benefit system.

In 1975, in its first main report, the Poverty Inquiry, headed by Professor Ronald Henderson, recommended the introduction of a system of guaranteed minimum income that had the potential to ensure that no Australian permanent resident would be left without some form of financial assistance. Since the late 1980s, in response to economic fundamentalist and neoconservative attacks upon welfare assistance and social security recipients, Australian governments have tightened conditionality and imposed increased obligations upon those needing to rely on social security.

The seesawing between a universal philosophical approach and an individualized categorical means-tested charity approach to the provision of social security assistance has been part and parcel of the income-maintenance debate in Australia for well over a century. This chapter will describe that debate, particularly some of its most recent manifestations, and attempt to predict the direction in which it is heading.

The Decade Following Federation

Australia began as a series of British colonies, which by the end of the nineteenth century had become states and subsequently federated in 1901. There was never an established poor law system as in England—rather welfare provision was provided by church-based charities and state or local governments. Despite the absence of poor law administrators, the attitudes with which much of the delivery of welfare assistance was imbued shared a great similarity with that of the British poor law system. Given that the overwhelming majority of migrants had arrived from Britain, this is hardly surprising.

By the turn of the twentieth century, there were other influences at work, deriving in part from the tradition of Bismarck's Germany and other continental European traditions and emerging political movements. Indigenous Australians, once subdued, were controlled on government reserves and church missions. Race was a predominant consideration in the young Australian nation. The immigration act was the first piece of legislation passed by the Australian Parliament. Permanent Asian residents were not provided with social security until the 1940s. From 1945, some Indigenous Australians who could establish that they had previously maintained full-time work for considerable periods of time were paid unemployment or sickness benefit in the event of unemployment or illness. Although in 1959 Commonwealth social security legislation was amended to place Aborigines on the same footing as other Australians (Kewley 1980: 122, n. 7), city dwelling Aboriginal people were not properly incorporated in the social security system until the mid-1960s, and their rural and remote cousins had a further decade's wait before they were assisted.

In 1907, the Industrial Arbitration Commission in the Harvester Judgment set a minimum wage sufficient for a male worker to support a wife and three children. Women's wages were subsequently set at between 60 and 75 percent of the male wage until 1967 when an equal-pay judgment was handed down. However, because of the gender segregation of much of Australian industry, women still do not have full wage equality with men. Aboriginal workers were also accorded formal wage equality with other Australians in the late 1960s but because of continuing discrimination in employment and education and because of the remote localities in which many Indigenous people live, there is still a huge gap in wage, health, and educational outcomes between them and other Australians.

In 1908, legislation was passed in both houses of the federal parliament introducing pensions for citizens in the event of permanent injury or reaching the age of 60 for women and 65 for men. These pensions began to be paid in 1910 to aged citizens who could establish that they were of good moral character and who had previously adequately supported their families. Invalid pensioners needed to establish that they had resided in Australia for five years but were not required to pass a character test (Kewley 1973: 91). Means and asset tests applied to pensions and, in addition, applicants for an invalid pension had to establish their relatives could not maintain them. So, by the end of the first decade of the twentieth century, the full-time white-male workers (in unionized work) and their families had a minimum wage and social security cover in the event of permanent injury or old age.

Gradual Increments in Social Security Provision

In 1912, the social security legislation in relation to applicants who were legally blind was amended to allow for the payment of a blind pension without the requirement to establish that they were permanently incapacitated. All other invalid pensioners had to establish that they could not work. In relation to blind pensioners, "the desire was to provide them with every inducement to earn" (Kewley 1973: 93). This eventually led to subsequent changes that provided legally blind citizens with a means and asset test-free pension. Such a provision has particular relevance in relation to "Basic Income."

The Commonwealth Treasury Department administered social security until 1927, after which time a new department was set up. In this early period, clear eligibility categories were established in order to facilitate accountable, bureaucratic decision-making. Yet even then, discretion was widely used to determine who was/was not of good moral character. It seems that blind musicians playing in the street caused consternation to the treasury officials who were uncertain as to whether they should be classed as working or begging and usually, decided that they were beggars who should not be paid a blind pension (Jordan 1984).

Also in 1912, legislation was enacted that provided for maternity allowance to be paid to non-Asian and non-Aboriginal mothers. When the 1929 Depression hit Australia, a third of the workforce was left without a job. There was no federal unemployment benefit. Various state and local governments provided dole/rations in return for work and, often, forced men to move on after short periods allegedly to encourage them to find work. Pension payments were reduced and increased effort was put into making relatives support pensioners in the early 1930s. Any pension paid was held as a debt against the estate. This practice was abolished in 1936.

The Depression and the Second World War made a major impact on the Australian mindset and this subsequently led to increased solidarity and support for an expansion of the social security system. In 1941, a universal child endowment was paid for each child after the first, was paid to migrants with children a year after they entered Australia, was paid in respect to adopted children, and could be paid to Aboriginal mothers provided they were not nomadic or wholly dependent upon the Commonwealth or state governments. In 1950, child endowment was paid in respect to the first or only child. This child payment was granted without a means test and was disregarded as income for taxation purposes (Kewley 1973 Chapter 10).

The early 1940s saw legislation providing widows with a pension provided the child was under the age of 16 or under the age of 18 if in full-time education and not employed. A pension was also paid to widows over the age of 50 whose youngest child was over 16 years of age. A woman who had lived in "a bona fide domestic relationship" with a man for a period of three years immediately prior to his death could be paid a pension provided she had custody of a child under the age of 16 years. A widow without children in "necessitous circumstances" could be paid a pension for up to 26 weeks following her husband's death. Widows needed to have lived continuously in Australia immediately prior to her husband's death. In 1960, a woman whose husband was in jail for longer than six months could, if she had a child, be paid a widow's pension.

Unemployment and sickness benefits were provided for in the 1944 legislation that came into effect in July the following year. Aboriginal Australians who worked for award wages in the towns qualified for benefit in times of unemployment or sickness. This 1944 legislation created a "special benefit" that was to be paid to those in financial need who did not meet the totality of eligibility requirements for other social security payments. The special benefit was paid at the discretion of the director-general to a person who "by reason of age, physical or mental disability or domestic circumstances, or any other reason . . . is unable to earn sufficient livelihood" (Kewley 1973: 269). This benefit was to be paid at the same rate as the unemployment and sickness benefit. The special benefit was paid to a relative who was required to care for a sick or incapacitated child or parent. It was paid to people who could not meet the residency requirement for other payments. It is clear from the documents at the time that the special benefit was designed as a catchall benefit capable of providing anyone in financial need with sufficient income to sustain them when they were unable to establish eligibility for other benefits or pensions. The requirement that the director-general use his discretion in granting the benefit meant that the benefit was not conceived of as being the equivalent of the French Minimum Insertion Income. Even so, when I worked in the department in the mid-1960s, the special benefit was a widely used benefit paid to people who were in the process of establishing their eligibility for another benefit or pension. This benefit could have easily been extended to become something similar to the French Minimum Insertion Income.

The Consolidation Act of 1947 brought all the federal social security legislation together in one place and made the administration of a range of benefits and pensions much easier to manage. From then until the mid-1980s, the generosity and the range of benefits gradually increased. Some of these extensions to welfare provision will be elaborated upon later in this chapter following a discussion of universal income guarantees.

Competing Ideologies

Throughout the entire period since federation, no single ideological force has held total sway over the motivations of politicians controlling the social welfare system. There have been differing ideological positions taken by the public at large when particular pieces of social welfare legislation have been discussed. There have been times when support for universal provision of pensions and benefits has commanded greater approval in the parliament and the public generally. At other times, the general mood has turned away from universal provision toward support for more targeting and means testing of social security (Mays 2012).

The major political parties have generally tended to have candidates with a wide range of views. The major parties on the right attract conservative, agrarian socialist, neoliberal (economic fundamentalist) and small "l" liberals. On the left, the Labor Party has combined neoliberal, small "l" liberals, laborist, social democrat, socialist, and the occasional (undeclared) communist as candidates. Currently, the Greens candidates are nature conservationists and further to the left on most social issues than the Labor Party. In the first half of the twentieth century, the Communist Party attracted a significant following.

In relation to social welfare policies, a number of competing ideas are likely to emerge in a parliament with such a range of political positions represented. It is not surprising that conservatives with their beliefs in traditional values, established order, the sanctity of private property, and small government should champion the targeting of welfare benefits to those in most "need" and refusing those whom they believe should fend for themselves. This sieving out the "needy" from the "greedy" is a distinction harking back to the days of the poor laws and the concept of "less eligibility." Conservatives, because of their belief in the imperfection of humans and their desire to enforce traditional values, want governments to impose obligations upon recipients in return for providing assistance.

Neoliberals join with their conservative colleagues in such targeting of assistance and the imposition of onerous obligations upon recipients of social welfare because they know that such mechanisms decrease the number of people applying and thereby the amount of taxpayer's funds needed. The conservative attachment to the sanctity of private property leads them to insist that welfare services should encourage thrift. Neoliberals support such views because they can't see further than the government's economic bottom line.

Mainstream liberals are philosophically attached to the idea of individualism, freedom, self-help, property, progress, rule of law, and the free play of market forces. Neoliberals join them in their belief in self-help and progress, which in turn leads them to the old "rising tides lifts all boats" cliché without taking into account the need to ensure that everyone's hull is in a sound condition prior to the turn of the tide. There seems little understanding that insufficient social security creates for many doubts that they will escape poverty even in prosperous times. Both mainstream and neoliberals interpret the combination of freedom and the free play of market forces to insist that recipients take any available job, irrespective of how suitable it is for the individual. This leads them to limit the amount of assistance provided so as to ensure recipients are not tempted to stay on welfare indefinitely.

Some small "l" liberals have an attachment to equity whereas social democrats and socialists see themselves as striving for equality, albeit for social democrats the attainment of equality is something to strive toward. Socialists and Marxists see equality as a prime and immediate goal. The socialist belief that treating unequals equally is as unfair as treating equals unequally confounds their desire for absolute equality yet leads them in the general direction of universal provision of welfare assistance. In this, they are joined by social democrats.

The hallmark of the social democratic position is equality, government intervention, representative government, and the peaceful transition to socialism. The last flowering of this tradition in Australian social welfare was in 1973–1975 during the Whitlam Labor government. The widow's pension was extended to lone mothers, the necessity to pass a character test before an applicant was "deemed worthy" to receive a pension was abolished, and the government set in train a number of inquiries designed to recommend ways to improve worker compensation and social welfare services generally. I worked in the department at the time and the mood changed for many from being there to ensure that nobody got more than they were entitled, to a feeling that it was necessary to ensure that all people obtained the totality of benefits to which they were entitled.

It is not only conservatives and liberals who rely upon "the need for welfare assistance" as the prime justification for the supply of benefits. Marxists also rely on "need," exemplified in their maxim "From each according to ability, to each according to need" (Wikipedia 2011). In this statement, Marxists are attempting to come to terms with their desire for both equity and equality.

Beyond the political ideological struggle described above, there are other ideological tussles in the society, generally and the welfare arena, in particular. Feminists argue that discrimination on the basis of gender is not peripheral to an understanding of power in Australia but is a core feature that structures social interaction. The individual is the main unit utilized in relation to taxation but the social security system insists that the family is the appropriate unit to be used for determining means and assets when assessing benefit applications. Many people who might otherwise qualify for a benefit are refused payment because of the income of their partner. Conservatives see the family as the main vehicle for controlling reproduction and transferring property between generations. Marxists are divided between those who see the nuclear family as a major bulwark against ruling class oppression and those who envisage the family as the way the ruling classes ensure the reproduction of the next generation of exploitable workers.

In addition to gender, the main organizing features of Australian society are class, age, race, and locality. Australia is a huge country but most people live in the capital cities or along the Eastern seaboard. Those living in the major urban conglomerations have better access to health, education, and other services and live longer than their rural counterparts. Teenagers and young adults who were unemployed have been singled out for the imposition of the most repressive obligations through programs such as "work for the dole" and compulsory training by Labor and Conservative governments in the last decade and a half. Older unemployed workers frequently encounter employer resistance to employing them. Teenage social security recipients are paid considerably lower rates of benefit than are adult recipients. Class is an accurate determinant of lifespan. Racism is a daily experience for Aboriginal people whether they live in towns, cities, or remote communities. Despite these ideological features, people with significant impediments find that they are regularly discriminated against in relation to employment, education, and access to buildings. Recent governments have argued that many disability support pensioners do not have disabling conditions sufficient to warrant their being paid a pension and have shifted many to less generous unemployment benefits with onerous work search obligations (Mays 2012; Galvin 2004).

Income Guarantees in Australia

The conservative Menzies government initiated the child endowment legislation. The widow's pension legislation was put forward in 1942 by the incoming Labor government but had bipartisan support. Labor enacted unemployment and sickness benefit provisions and spearheaded the improvements in the Consolidated Act in 1947. Labor lost office in 1949 and Menzies returned to the prime ministership and stayed there until 1966. The conservatives continued in power for a further six years.

By the time conservatives relinquished office, despite Menzies' efforts to gradually extend social welfare resources and programs, poverty, particularly poverty amongst the aged, was starting to emerge as an issue. Writers like John Stubbs (1966) and Professor Ronald Henderson with his colleagues Alison Harcourt and John Harper (1970) played important roles in raising the issue of poverty. Church-run charities like the Brotherhood of St. Laurence took leading advocacy roles. The McMahon conservative government, which was to lose office in 1972, set up the Henderson Poverty Inquiry. The incoming Whitlam Labor government massively expanded the scope of the Poverty Inquiry.

In 1975, in the first main report of the Poverty Inquiry, Henderson set out (at Chapter 6 of Vol. 1 and Appendix 6 of Vol. 2) a detailed suggestion for the introduction of a guaranteed minimum income in Australia. The income guarantee that Henderson proposed was intended to simplify and move toward unifying the social security and taxation systems and to treat those with stable and those with fluctuating income equitably. He wanted to reduce the emphasis on the various categories of pensions and benefits and make the withdrawal rate on earned income more transparent and hence, understandable. Under the proposal, the population was divided between those who qualified for a social security benefit or pension whom he called "Categorical" and those who were not able to establish eligibility for an existing payment. He foreshadowed subsequently broadening the eligibility provisions in order that "no person at risk of poverty will henceforth be denied an income" (Henderson 1975 Vol. 1: 67, see also 30–32). For those whom he called categorical, Henderson proposed a rate of payment at 106 percent of the poverty line, but he suggested paying the noncategorical groups as little as 50 percent of the poverty line. He considered abolishing all categories within the system of income support but decided against it on the grounds that a simple guarantee at the poverty line for all would result in a taxation rate of 50 percent that he considered politically unsalable (Henderson 1975 Vol. 1: 74).

The Henderson proposals were compatible with the existing social security system in that they were in the form of a demogrant, expressed as a social right, flat rate, and noncontributory. He considered the guaranteed minimum income would make the income-maintenance system in Australia more humane, less categorical, and more comprehensive. It would have done all this; however, the basic weakness of the proposal was that it failed to dismantle the existing system and restructure it in a way that would facilitate the complete integration of the income-maintenance and taxation systems. The Henderson proposal would have reduced but not abolished the advantages accruing to people with fluctuating incomes compared with those in stable employment. His proposal to abolish the existing progressive taxation system and replace it with a proportional tax would on the face of it appear to advantage the more affluent. He did, however, propose a 5 percent tax surcharge for incomes over A$240 per week as at August 1973 (Henderson 1975 Vol. 1: 78).

The major problem with the Henderson proposal was that dividing the population between the categorical and noncategorical and providing the categorical group with a guaranteed income equal to or better than the poverty line but only guaranteeing others an income of between 50 and 71 percent of the poverty line would not decrease the desire of the noncategorical group to be considered as categorical. Because it does not guarantee the noncategorical group an income above the poverty line, it cannot ensure that some Australians would not remain in poverty. Another disappointing aspect of the Poverty Inquiry's guaranteed minimum income scheme was that it used the family as the basis of calculating the appropriate rate of benefit. It did envisage older children living in the family home being paid in their own right.

Also in 1975, a group of senior public servants predominantly from the Treasury and calling themselves the Priorities Review Staff proposed introducing a negative income tax or a tax credit scheme. Like the Henderson proposal, they proposed a two-tiered scheme that treated more favorably those qualifying for pensions and benefits than those who could not establish their eligibility for assistance. The categorical group would receive 100 percent of the Henderson poverty line (nonworking) and the noncategorical group would receive 55 percent of the poverty line (working). They suggested a proportional tax rate of 43 percent for prime earners and a 33 percent tax rate for a second earner in a family. They recommended a tax surcharge of 5 percent for those with an income of A$17,000–A$20,000, rising to 25 percent for those over A$58,000 (Priorities Review Staff 1975: 34). They too adopted the family as the unit of income for assessing their income guarantee.

The Priorities Review Staff had a similar desire as Henderson in wanting to mesh the tax and social security systems, provide assistance to those poor people who were not assisted by existing categorical schemes, and generally simplify the social welfare system. Whereas the Poverty Inquiry wanted to put in place an increased range of services, the Priorities Review Staff wanted to limit or abolish as many supplementary services as possible. The Priorities Review Staff set out a way to mesh their proposal with the recommendations of the Woodhouse National Compensation Scheme (1974).

The Woodhouse injury compensation scheme has continuing relevance because, in 2011, the Productivity Commission has made similar recommendations (Productivity Commission 2011). The Woodhouse Commission was charged with designing a comprehensive income support system for injured, disabled, and sick people. Woodhouse recommended that people who were sick or disabled would be paid a benefit at 85 percent of their previous wage up to an amount of A$425 per week. Nonearners were to receive A$42.50 per week. Low-income earners would be paid at 100 percent of the minimum wage. His scheme was designed to replace the expensive worker and road accident legal jungle in which many wait an inordinate time before settlement and then, some get windfall settlements whilst others receive nothing. It was intended to fund the scheme via a 2 percent levy on wages and 10¢ per gallon petrol tax. In addition, the government would provide A$370 million annually (the amount it was then spending on invalid pensions and sickness benefits [Woodhouse 1974: 260]).

Another contemporaneous inquiry was asked to design a national superannuation scheme to replace the means-tested age pension. This Hancock Committee failed to come to a unanimous conclusion and brought down a majority and minority report in 1976 (Hancock 1976). The majority report recommended a pension of 25 percent of the average weekly earnings, with a means-tested supplement raising the income to 30 percent of the average weekly earnings for those without other income. The more affluent would receive the base 25 percent without a means test plus a purchased pension dependent upon contributions. The proposal was to be funded by an extra 5 percent income tax levy on income over 30 percent of average weekly earnings. The minority report thought Hancock's proposal placed too high a burden on low-income earners and recommended a pension without a means test for all over 65 years of age and supplementary means-tested benefits.

A common feature of all these inquiries was that they were all critical of the existing categorical means-tested social welfare system. Even so, none of these proposals could entirely wrench themselves away from the categorical targeting of particular groups of people. Both the majority and minority Hancock proposals would have guaranteed an income to the elderly—but the age pension already provided most poor older people with an income guarantee. The Woodhouse scheme would have rationalized workers and road accident compensation as well as unifying sickness benefit and invalid pension provisions but would have still left many who did not fit into the existing categorical welfare system without assistance. The Woodhouse and Hancock majority reports both extended the inequalities of the employment situation into the postwork phase of peoples' lives.

Henderson (1977: 103 and 108) rejects the recommendations of both the Woodhouse Inquiry and the Hancock majority report on equity grounds. He quotes the words of the minority report of the Hancock Inquiry to help establish his case: "Benefits payable under the scheme (Hancock) in 1977 would require an estimated 5.1 percent of Gross Domestic Product. This may be contrasted with the 2 percent required to finance the age pension system."

Only the Henderson and Priorities Review Staff suggestions had the potential to ensure that every Australian received an income. Neither would have resulted in equal or equitable distribution but either of them would have rationalized and modernized the social security system, simplified the tax and social security combined withdrawal rates, and watered down the excessive targeting that is the hallmark of the Australian welfare system.

The Outcome of the Inquiries

As mentioned earlier, the period of the Whitlam Labor government saw the last flowering of the social democratic philosophical position in Australia. There was a real concern that poverty should be addressed, that the social security system should be equitable, that people should obtain the totality of benefits to which they were entitled, and that Aboriginal people should be granted land rights to traditional lands, which had not, by then, been alienated to white interests.

The abolition of the character test and the expansion of the widow's pension scheme by the addition of a separate but reasonably similar payment to single mothers with a child in their care exemplified the difference between the Labor government and the 23 years of unbroken conservative rule that had preceded Whitlam's 1972 electoral victory. Bill Hayden, the minister for social security, described himself as a socialist and worked hard to promote equal treatment of recipients. A prime example of this was the considerable increases in the benefit rate that occurred on his watch.

Pensions, which had both income- and asset-means tests, were paid substantially higher amounts than were unemployment, sickness, and special benefits, which had only an income-means test applicable to them. Traditionally, there were three benefit rates for those aged 16–18 years of age, those aged between 18 and 21, and an adult rate. In February 1973, the Whitlam government introduced legislation providing "for a common rate of benefit, irrespective of the age of the beneficiary, and brought the rates to parity with those for pensions" (Kewley 1978: 125).

This action was repeated four more times by the Whitlam government although on the last occasion in November 1975 and just before being dismissed from office, the benefit rate for unmarried unemployed recipients under the age of 18 years was not raised in line with the other increases.

Perhaps, the litmus test of generosity in Australian social welfare is the degree of robust enforcement of the "work test provisions" applying to applicants for unemployment benefit. In May 1973, Hayden believed that the overwhelming majority of unemployment beneficiaries wanted work and instructed that there should be a less strict enforcement of the work test saying it was preferable that a few people took advantage of the system "than that people genuinely seeking work should be unfairly penalized" (Kewley 1980: 134). Hayden and other ministers declared themselves in support of generalized income guarantees as a way of rationalizing the hodgepodge of benefits, pensions, and allowances (ACOSS 1975).

Whether the Whitlam government would have accepted the recommendations of the Poverty Inquiry in relation to the introduction of a guaranteed minimum income or the negative income tax proposals of the Priorities Review Staff, or adopted some of the suggestions of the Woodhouse or Hancock Inquiries cannot be known. Wider political events overtook the Whitlam government, in particular ill discipline amongst several members of the cabinet, the Khemlani overseas loans affair (Whitlam dismissal 2011), and losing its majority in the Senate led to the governor general dismissing Gough Whitlam and installing the conservative Malcolm Fraser as leader of a caretaker government. The Fraser government won the subsequent general election. What can be asserted with confidence is that the Australian Council of Social Service produced two monographs supporting the introduction of a guaranteed minimum income.

Many social welfare academics and practitioners supported such a change in income-maintenance policy whilst others were critical of such a change. Many of the papers written about Basic Income at the time and since then have been placed on the Basic Income Guarantee Australia web site. It is my belief that had the Whitlam government been able to retain office, some form of generalized income guarantee would have eventuated. The general thrust of the rationalization of rates of benefit aimed at developing equity between beneficiaries and pensioners signals the direction in which the Labor Party was heading.

The unemployed and the young unemployed, in particular, were to experience far stricter work and other eligibility tests under the Fraser government. In March 1976, the Fraser government announced that as of the end of that school year, school leavers would not be paid unemployment benefit until the start of the new school year. The agrarian socialist philosophical position of the conservative side of the parliament was revealed later that year when it was announced that farmers who had previously been denied unemployment would henceforth be assisted when experiencing financial hardship.

Fast Forward to the Mid-1980s and the Early 1990s

The Fraser government did not raise the benefit rates for teenage beneficiaries in its entire three terms of office. By the time Labor regained office, a considerable gap between pension and benefit levels had again emerged, and the young were most severely affected by this change in thinking. In 1977, the conservative government did extend the supporting mothers payment to include lone fathers who had custody of one or more children. Fraser slightly amended the Northern Territory Land Rights draft prepared by the Whitlam government and pushed it through the parliament. Apart from these changes, the period of the Fraser government was one of general continuity on the social welfare front.

Whitlam had abolished the means test for age pensioners over 75 years of age in 1973 and for those between 70 and 74 years in 1975. In 1976, Fraser removed the asset test for those over 70 years of age but retained an income test. In 1983, the Hawke Labor government was elected. In November of that year, Hawke reintroduced a slightly more generous income test for those over 70 years of age, as compared with that of younger pensioners. In 1985, he reintroduced an asset test.

The mid-1980s to the early 1990s was a period of fiscal restraint in social welfare spending. Hawke had come to an accord with the trade unions to limit wage demands in return for tax, Medicare, and superannuation benefits. The Labor Party had traditionally opposed privatized superannuation because they feared it would undermine support for the age and invalid pension but times had changed, as will be seen when superannuation is discussed in detail below.

The Fraser government changed the child allowance system to a family allowance system. Like the child endowment, it was not subject to any income or asset test, nor was it taxable. Subsequent Labor governments basically retained the family allowance system but gradually applied mechanisms to limit payment when families had other income. In 2000, the conservative Howard government replaced the existing family allowance system with a family tax benefit that assists families, with incomes of up to A$150,000 per annum, raise their children. This benefit is paid through the tax system and the amount received is in inverse proportion to other income.

The recession in the late 1980s and the early 1990s led to a substantial rise in unemployment as well as a rise in interest rates. Brian Howe, who had been minister for social security since 1984 was deputy leader of the Keating Labor government from 1991–1995. Prior to entering parliament, he had studied theology in Chicago 1967–1969 before returning to Australia and serving as a Methodist minister in various parts of Victoria. He had been preoccupied by the idea of intergenerational welfare dependency at least since 1987. He took every opportunity to save funds in his portfolio. In the 1988 minibudget, the most miserly reduction was the imposition of a stricter income test on (short-term) special beneficiaries who received payment for less than 13 weeks. The majority of those who received the payment were single women immediately prior to and just following the birth of their baby. In order to receive the payment, mothers had to establish that they were not working, not living in a bona fide domestic relationship, and had no other substantial income. This income test imposed a 100 percent withdrawal rate on all earned income in excess of A$20 per week. At the time of this action, I suggested that Howe was behaving like a Victorian parson doling monies out of the parish poor box.

Economic fundamentalists had a considerable influence in the Hawke and Keating governments. The social welfare emphasis had shifted from assisting applicants in need to delivering occupational benefit and generalized assistance to families. Following the Mabo High Court Judgment, Keating pushed through the Native Title Act that provided an opportunity for Indigenous traditional owners to lay claim to unalienated land.

Unemployment became a considerable problem for the Keating government and, in 1994, the prime minister issued a white paper entitled "Working Nation" in which he set out his prescription to solve it (Keating 1994). The plan included guaranteeing employment to every unemployed person out of work for 18 months. However, in return for this employment guarantee plus other assistance, the unemployed were required to accept their "reciprocal obligation" to do all that was possible to find work or make themselves "job ready."

Superannuation

Contributory superannuation schemes had been promoted by the conservative side of politics in Australia and several attempts had been made to introduce them. The Labor Party had opposed them on the grounds that they would undermine support for social security programs. During the Hawke/Keating period in office, Labor changed its approach and introduced a compulsory privatized contributory form of superannuation, quite unlike the social insurance model of superannuation prevalent in Europe.

The change came about in part as a result of the accord and the amalgamation of craft unions into super unions whose leaders saw an opportunity to bolster their power by setting up industry superannuation funds to safeguard their members' contributions and tie the workers more intimately to the union. The banking and insurance industries offered private superannuation schemes and welcomed the opportunity for a massive expansion. Prior to compulsory superannuation, some firms had set up superannuation schemes for their workers and permanent government employees were provided with defined benefit superannuation as part of their salary package. Most defined benefit schemes have now closed their books to new members and the system of superannuation that has evolved in Australia means that the superannuation that people receive is roughly proportional to what they paid in, the wisdom of fund investors, the choice that individuals make about investment strategies, and just plain luck. Those in seasonal, part-time, or casual employment find that many employers either don't deduct superannuation contributions or if they do, the contributions are not passed on to superannuation funds.

The banking and insurance industry controlled funds usually charge larger fees than industry superannuation funds, so, this too affects the amount of money people receive when they retire. Social insurance superannuation generally results in superannuation payouts roughly in line with the contributions and a country's capacity to pay. Privatized superannuation is often less equitable and tends to advantage those with greater financial resources (Hughes 2008).

Howard Government

John Howard swept Paul Keating from office in March 1996. Howard (1999) described himself as a social conservative but an economic liberal. Many of the policies he pursued certainly placed him in the camp of the neoliberal economic fundamentalists. His deputy, Peter Costello, had made his name as a relentless employers' advocate. Their first target focused on young-employed people whom Costello described as "job snobs." The solution was the imposition of compulsory literacy training, compulsory "work for the dole," and other "mutual obligations."

Howard's next target was the Native Title Act. He set out to win what became known as the "culture wars." He described the position taken by many pro-Aboriginal historians and anthropologists as representing a "black arm band" view of the early days of white expansion of the continent. In turn, Howard was regarded as having a "white blindfolded" view of the early Aboriginal/white interaction. Howard amended the Native Title Act to increase the difficulty that Aborigines had establishing their claim. The amendments included a clause insisting that Aboriginal applicants had to establish a continuous and unbroken connection with any land claimed. This made it impossible for many traditional owners, who had been forcibly removed from their traditional land and herded onto missions or settlements, often at gunpoint, to launch a successful claim.

The main weapon in the Howard government's industrial arsenal was the Work Choices legislation that created extensive penalties for both workers and unions taking unauthorized industrial action. In the early years, this legislation was not as strongly proemployer as the government wanted because their zeal was held in check by the fact they did not have an absolute majority in the Senate. In their last term, they obtained control of the Senate and were able to pass more repressive industrial provisions. This eventually led to a backlash. The trade unions successfully mobilized substantial opposition.

The Howard government persevered with the policy of mandatory detention begun by Labor and imposed harsher internment conditions upon asylum seekers, who arrived by boat. The government set up detention centers on Nauru and on Manus Island in New Guinea. This offshore processing of asylum seekers was termed the "Pacific Solution." Refugee advocates waged a determined and prolonged campaign and toward the end of Howard's term, five of his senior backbenchers forced the government to release children from detention.

Howard expanded family benefits, boosted careers benefits, significantly increased the pharmaceutical benefits for pensioners and self-funded retirees, and allowed people to make huge contributions to private superannuation schemes. This conservative government became alarmed by large increases in the number of people receiving the disability support pension and set out to reduce that number by one-third (Galvin 2004; Mays 2012).

In June 2007, the Howard government announced the Northern Territory Intervention into 73 Aboriginal communities. This intervention was supposedly instigated in response to "The little children are sacred" report coauthored by Rex Wild and Pat Anderson (2007). The intervention was justified on the grounds that it would protect Indigenous children from neglect and pedophilia and would protect women and vulnerable people from being assaulted or stood over for money. In order to facilitate the intervention, the Howard government suspended the Racial Discrimination Act, quarantined half of people's social security, and placed this money on a "Basics" card that could only be used for approved purposes (Altman and Hinkson 2007). It imposed compulsory town leases and health checks.

Labor in the Twenty-first Century

Kevin Rudd led the Labor party to victory in 2007. The unions' massive mobilization around the excesses of Howard's Work Choices legislation played no small part in that victory but the Labor Party needed a leader who would not frighten the horses. Rudd declared that he was a fiscal conservative, a church going Christian, someone who would continue the Northern Territory Intervention for at least another year and his wife was a wealthy businesswoman. He looked and sounded like a safe pair of hands. Rudd promised to end the offshore processing of refugees, to restore a balance in industrial relations, and bring a new humanity to the administration. Howard on the other hand looked old, tired, and mean.

The Rudd government removed the most draconian aspects of the Work Choices legislation, through Keynesian countercyclical pump priming managed to avoid the recession that enveloped other developed countries, abolished the Pacific Solution, and tried to cope with the increased boat arrivals. An inquiry was held into the effects of the Northern Territory Intervention. This Inquiry recommended ending the suspension of the Racial Discrimination Act, restricting the compulsory quarantining of half of peoples' welfare payments to those people who wanted it or who were actually neglecting their children, and ending other repressive aspects of the intervention. Rudd insisted tha the intervention continue. Rudd championed significant increases in taxes to be paid by multinational mining conglomerates and the imposition of a carbon pollution reduction scheme. The multinational companies launched a massive media campaign opposing the tax increases and caught Rudd on the hop. He decided after two failed attempts to get his carbon emission through the hostile senate to shelve it at least until 2013.

Rudd's deputy, Julia Gillard, in June 2010 with overwhelming cross-factional support (within the parliamentary Labor Party) toppled her leader and became Australia's first female prime minister. She quickly struck a deal with the mining companies. When the Gillard government faced the electors, in August 2010, Labor failed to get a majority of seats in the lower house and has been forced to rely upon cross-bench support in order to govern.

The Gillard government continued the crackdown on disability support pensioners and the unemployed that Howard had started and Rudd had continued. In February 2011, Gillard appeared on the ABC Four Corners program (Four Corners 2011) arguing that it was her ambition to get as many people off welfare as possible by getting them a job "for the simple dignity that work brings."

The Gillard government took a harsher attitude to asylum seekers arriving by boat. By the middle of 2011, the Gillard government claimed to have struck a deal to return asylum seekers arriving by boat to Malaysia for processing. Malaysia is not a signatory to the Refugee Convention and regularly canes asylum seekers entering its territory. The government claimed that it intended returning unaccompanied minors and pregnant women to Malaysia (ABC News June 4, 2011).

In 2007, most progressives assumed that, after a year, the Northern Territory Intervention would be replaced by a community development approach that would include consulting appropriately with Indigenous communities, ensuring the Racial Discrimination Act was reinstated, an end to quarantining of social security, and expanding health, housing, and education programs (Tomlinson 2011). What progressives had not understood was that though Howard had won the "culture wars," Rudd and Gillard either were not interested in the ideological battle, shared many of the same values as Howard, or were just incapable of mounting a sufficiently sustained ideological defense of social democratic values.

A Universal Basic Income

In Australia, a full universal Basic Income, if it were to abolish poverty, would need to be paid to every permanent resident at or above the existing single rate of age pension (that is pegged at 25 percent of the average wage and is slightly above the Henderson poverty line). It would be paid to individuals irrespective of their marital status, whether they lived alone or with others, irrespective of their race, age, gender, or other social status.

In the short term, partly because of attitudes surrounding the nuclear family and partly because of the history of family payments, it would probably be necessary to pay parents of children who are under the age of 16 years and who live in the family home at a rate of half the adult rate. It would be paid to rich and poor, whether or not they were employed or in education. No work or other obligations could be attached to the receipt of the Basic Income and governments or other bodies could not garnishee it (see Tomlinson 2003).

Basic Income: Obstacles and What Is Going for It?

The major obstacles to the introduction of a Basic Income in Australia are questions surrounding affordability, the presence of a privatized superannuation system, and the ideological maelstrom that envelops discussions of social welfare, migration, the work ethic, race, age, gender, and disability. Several of these issues have been discussed above and there will be further discussion of some of them here.

Governments and oppositions in Australia have demonstrated a capacity to bamboozle the public about the capacity of the nation to afford to introduce improvements in the social wage, protect the environment, lift wages, and increase or decrease other expenditures. Political parties talk about lowering carbon dioxide levels, yet allow the Defense Department unlimited access to petrocarbon guzzling planes, tanks, trucks, and ships.

Every Australian Broadcasting Commission's news and current affairs program has several items dealing with the economic implications of this or that aspect of our economy. Yet, the public is not sufficiently economically literate to understand the implications of a lot of the discussion. They tend to get swayed by the cleverest 10 second grab. To be fair to them, the old adage "Give me 10 economists and I'll supply you with 15 different answers" applies in this country.

There is obviously sufficient money available to pay every individual an income at 25 percent of the average wage. It is not a question of affordability—it is a question of whether the public is prepared for such an egalitarian redistribution. In 1975, Australia went within a stone's throw of introducing an income guarantee for all residents. The economists of the Poverty Inquiry and the Priorities Review Staff believed it was affordable then. Australia is a far more wealthy country today than then—we could more easily afford to introduce a Basic Income now. The question is whether as a nation we desire a universal Basic Income.

The privatized compulsory superannuation scheme delivers considerable benefits to the better-off sections of Australian society. The one-third of Australians who earn more than the average wage are the prime beneficiaries. Many of the two-thirds who earn less than the average wage see whatever superannuation they receive as their entitlement: unlike social security or the family tax benefit, which they view as complicated, hedged around with conditionality, and given grudgingly. Most of the two-thirds aspire to climb the income ladder and are prepared to allow the perks of the rich to remain whilst they still dream of joining them. Most of the two-thirds have little idea of just how inequitable the privatized superannuation system is—few understand that thousands of the very rich get more government assistance (in the form of foregone tax on their superannuation) than age pensioners get from the government.

Superannuation contributions are taxed at a rate of 15 percent. As Ben Eltham (2011: 4) notes, those earning less than A$37,000 get no concessions (because they pay a tax rate of 15 percent on their salary). People paid a salary of million dollars a year pay 45 percent on their salary but only 15 percent on any contributions they make to superannuation. He also points out that the forgone capital gains tax exemption on the sale of the family house will cost A$23.5 billion in 2011–2012, the same amount as the total outlay for unemployment benefits and the disability support pension combined.

The Howard government managed, in 1996, to poach many blue-collar workers from the Labor Party by suggesting that Keating was wasting government monies pandering to Aborigines, asylum seekers, single mothers, and dole bludgers. This group, mainly from the outer suburbs of cities, became known as "Howard's battlers." Downward envy drove them to criticize social security payments to low-income single parents, disability support pensioners, the unemployed, refugees, and Aborigines on the grounds that they did not receive such payments. The "battlers" seemed oblivious to the fact that they were not a single parent living below the poverty line, did not have a disability, and were not unemployed or sick. This fracturing of working class solidarity allowed the rich to continue to enjoy their benefits and the government to tighten conditionality and targeting of social security benefits.

The current situation is one where such downward envy is still bubbling below the surface but has an additional component, namely the suggestion that middle-income earners do not need help to raise their children. In other words, a lot of the family tax benefit is being wasted on "middle class welfare." Eltham (2011: 3) suggests that the expression middle class welfare is misleading because the Australian welfare state is "among the most targeted in the western world, with steep cut-offs for many entitlements. It's a measure of the 'downward envy' of voters that the issue is even a live one." Whilst the two-thirds of the population who earn less than the average wage can be distracted from the real income-distributional debate and kept struggling amongst themselves, the perquisites of the rich and very rich are safe from scrutiny.

The government wants to reduce the number of disability support pensioners because it has observed a rise in the number of such pensioners caused by a crackdown on recipients of other benefits such as unemployment and raising women's qualifying age for the age pension. People under 35 years of age will be required to develop a contract setting out their work-participation plan with the disability support pension-paying agency. Howard and Rudd tried to cut the numbers by threats; now the Gillard government is trying to ease people into work by allowing them to work up to 30 hours a week for up to two years and still remain eligible for a part pension (Karvelas 2011). This returns disability support pensioners to roughly the same position they were in before Howard tightened the eligibility requirements in 2005.

The public is of two minds when it comes to the question of disability. Some are positively disposed toward disability support pensioners but others see them as bludgers as the headline in the populist *Sydney*

Daily Telegraph reflects when it proclaims, "We're an army of shirkers in NSW—disability pensions are a losing battle (Jones 2011)."

Despite the fact that Australia is now wealthier than ever, it is unlikely that a universal Basic Income paid to all permanent residents at a rate above the Henderson poverty line will be enacted in the foreseeable future. It would appear that if there is going to be any substantial social welfare advance, it is most probably going to be to specific categories of people considered to be "worthy of extra assistance."

One such indication of this is that in February 2011, the Productivity Commission recommended the establishment of a no-fault National Injury Insurance scheme and a separate dedicated agency with the task of ensuring that all permanent residents with significant disabilities receive appropriate services. Were such a proposal accepted, then all permanent residents who can establish that they have a significant disability will be guaranteed an above the poverty line income. This would be brought about either by the National Injury Insurance scheme or via the blind or disability support pension or some combination of all of these. The nonaffluent aged already have such a guarantee, as do families with children.

Other permanent residents, provided they meet categorical eligibility requirements and fulfill the associated "obligations," are provided with some income. However, the levels of benefits paid to full-time students, unemployed, and temporarily sick people are not sufficient to lift them out of poverty. Young beneficiaries can receive as little as 40 percent of the poverty line.

However, both the Howard and Rudd governments looked seriously at introducing a single rate of benefit for all working-age people, one that would have simplified the current system immensely. Ken Henry the recently retired head of the Treasury, in 2010, recommended introducing a far more egalitarian superannuation system through increasing the amounts low-income earners would receive.

Still, there are no apparent signs on the horizon that a universal Basic Income is about to be introduced. Despite the Rudd government using Keynesian countercyclical pump priming to escape the recession, neofundamentalist economists maintain a stronghold in government and business in Australia. It took 23 years of conservative rule before the last truly social democratic Labor Party came to power with a progressive social welfare agenda.

Neofundamentalists have held sway for 25 years; the mining boom looks like continuing for at least another 20 years and hopefully, some time soon the "Big wheel will turn;" and Australians will again realize that we can afford an income guarantee for all permanent residents (paid above the poverty line) without compromising the economic prosperity of the nation.

References

ABC News. 2011. Radio National News. *Australian Broadcasting Commission* June 4, 7.00 a.m.

Altman, Jon, and Melinda Hinkson (eds.). 2007. *Coersive Reconciliation: Stabilise, Normalise, Exit Aboriginal Australia.* North Carlton: Arena.

Australian Council of Social Service (ACOSS). 1975. Seminar on Guaranteed Minimum Income. Sydney: ACOSS.

Eltham, Ben. 2011. "Middle Class Welfare and Other Furphies." *New Matilda* May 4. http://newmatilda.com/2011/05/04/budget-preview-middle-class-welfare.

Four Corners. 2011. "The Real Julia." *Australian Broadcasting Commission* February 7.

Galvin, Rose. 2004. "Can Welfare Reform Make Disability Disappear." *Australian Journal of Social Issues* 39 (3): 343–355.

Hancock, Keith. 1976. *A National Superannuation Scheme for Australia.* Canberra: Australian Government.

Henderson, Ronald. 1975. *Poverty in Australia: First Main Report.* Vols. 1 & 2. Canberra: Australian Government.

———. 1977. "Criteria for Welfare: Needs or Earnings?" *Australian Journal of Social Issues* 12 (2): 100–110.

Henderson, Ronald, Alison Harcourt, and John Harper. 1970. *People in Poverty: A Melbourne Survey.* Melbourne: Cheshire.

Howard, John. 1999. "Building a Stronger and Fairer Australia: Liberalisation in Economic Policy and Modern Conservatism in Social Policy." Roundtable Speech. May 4. http://home.vicnet.net.au/~victorp/21st_century/johnhoward.htm.

Hughes, Gerard. 2008. "The Case for a Universal State Pension." In *Making Choices—Choosing Futures*, edited by Brigid Reynolds and Seán Healey, 104–147. Dublin: Cori.

Jones, Gemma. 2011. "We're an Army of Shirkers in NSW—Disability Pensions Are a Losing Battle." *The Daily Telegraph* June 2. http://www.dailytelegraph.com.au/news/sydney-nsw/were-an-army-of-shirkers-in-nsw-disability-pensions-are-a-losing-battle/story-e6freuzi-1226067497524.

Jordan, Allan. 1984. *Permanent Incapacity: Invalid Pension in Australia.* Canberra: Department of Social Security.

Karvelas, Patricia. 2011. "'Incentives' to Cut Welfare Dependency." *The Australian* May 10. http://www.theaustralian.com.au/national-affairs/incentives-intended-to-cut-welfare-dependency/story-fn59niix-1226053605849.

Keating, Paul. 1994. *Working Nation.* Canberra: Australian Government Publishing Service.

Kewley, Thomas H. 1973. *Social Security in Australia.* Sydney: Sydney University Press.

———. 1980. *Australian Social Security Today.* Sydney: Sydney University Press.

Mays, Jennifer. 2012. "Australia's Disabling Income Support System: Tracing the History of the Australian Disability Income Support System 1908 to 2007—Disablism, Citizenship and the Basic Income Proposal." PhD thesis Queensland University of Technology, Brisbane.

Priorities Review Staff. 1975. *Possibilities for Social Welfare in Australia.* Canberra: Australian Government.

Productivity Commission. 2011. "Disability Care and Support." (Draft Report). Canberra: Australian Government.

Stubbs, John. 1966. *The Hidden People—Poverty in Australia.* Melbourne: Cheshire.

Tomlinson, John. 2003. *Income Insecurity: The Basic Income Alternative.* BIGA, Brisbane. http://www.basicincome.qut.edu.au/interest/e-books.jsp.

———. 2011. "Needs Must When the Devil Drives." Online opinion. http://www.onlineopinion.com.au/view.asp?article=11494.

Whitlam dismissal. 2011. http://whitlamdismissal.com/loans/.

Wikipedia. 2011. "From each according to his ability, to each according to his need." http://en.wikipedia.org/wiki/From_each_according_to_his_ability,_to_each_according_to_his_need#References.

Wild, Rex, and Anderson Pat. 2007. "The Little Children Are Sacred." http://www.inquirysaac.nt.gov.au/pdf/bipacsa_final_report.pdf.

Woodhouse, Owen. 1974. *Compensation and Rehabilitation in Australia.* Canberra: Australian Government.

CHAPTER 11

Canada: A Guaranteed Income Framework to Address Poverty and Inequality?

James P. Mulvale and Yannick Vanderborght[*]

Like other economically advanced democracies, Canada has had recurring discussions on how to provide more effective income security measures as a key component of the welfare state. This discussion has arisen on a regular basis, particularly since the period of rapid growth in Canadian social programs in the 1960s. Not only through numerous reports and academic publications, but also through the action of several groups ranging from trade unions to small associations, innovative proposals have been made and debated. Among these proposals, the most controversial might be the idea of giving all Canadians the right to an unconditional and universal "basic income" (BI)—frequently referred to in English-speaking Canada as Guaranteed Annual Income (GAI).[1]

Since the late 1960s, this idea has surfaced regularly in official publications at the federal and provincial levels (especially in the French-speaking province of Quebec). In the 1970s, both levels of government experimented with a Negative Income Tax (NIT) version of GAI in Manitoba. The idea of a guaranteed income once again resurfaced in 2000, when some media sources indicated that federal prime minister (PM) Jean Chrétien wanted to "leave his mark with cradle-to-grave program of guaranteed annual income."[2] Under catchy headlines, the press reported that the PM had decided to set up an expert group to study the feasibility of a federal GAI. Because of harsh criticism from the Conservatives, Chrétien denied his part in suggesting the idea, and the trial balloon was quickly shot down.[3]

More recently, federal senator Hugh Segal has been championing a NIT version of GAI (Segal 2011), and the idea has come up in parliamentary committee reports. In the 2011 federal election campaign, a significant issue that arose was the need to provide better pensions for the elderly, including an improved Guaranteed Income Supplement (GIS) that works like a NIT for very low-income seniors. This election also resulted in the Green Party of Canada gaining its first ever seat at the federal parliament, which is now occupied by party leader Elizabeth May. The Greens are committed in principle to a "guaranteed liveable income," and May has already raised this idea in her early days in the House of Commons.[4]

In this chapter, we will examine the challenges and provisions of the Canadian income security system, some historical background and the current status of the BI debate in Canada, and the likelihood of some form of guaranteed income as a politically viable proposition in the foreseeable future. Today, the idea of GAI is neither absent from the political landscape, nor is it highly prominent in the minds and hearts of most politicians and social justice advocates. Still, in comparative perspective it remains clear that Canada is one of the OECD countries where the public debate about BI has been liveliest since the 1960s.

The Canadian Welfare State: Its Challenges and Provisions

Canada is often described as being very close to the ideal type of the so-called "liberal" welfare regime. In his famous *Three Worlds of Welfare Capitalism*, Gøsta Esping-Andersen even argues that Canada is, along with the United States and Australia, an "archetypical" example of the liberal welfare state, characterized by a low-level decommodification.[5] However, a detailed examination of the Canadian welfare programs would suggest a slightly more balanced picture. For instance, in the field of health care and pensions, Canada has a long tradition of *universal* provision, which is said to be so typical of the "social democratic" regime (i.e., Scandinavia). Also, one should insist on the fact that speaking of a single "Canadian welfare model" is highly problematic, given the complex mix of federal and provincial competences in social policy. If some provinces (e.g., Alberta) are closer to the liberal tradition, others (e.g., Quebec) have clearly followed a social democratic path. These reservations notwithstanding, it remains true that Canada, along with the other so-called "English-speaking" nations, is characterized by high levels of inequality and poverty.

It is beyond the scope of this chapter to give an exhaustive description and analysis of Canada's welfare state. We limit ourselves to provide the reader with a brief general overview. Against this background, we then turn to the BI debate itself.[6]

Income Inequality and Poverty

Canada is a wealthy, industrially developed, and resource-rich country, but it has relatively high rates of poverty and income inequality. According to the OECD (2011), the percentage of persons in Canada living with less than 50 percent of median-equalized household income in the late 2000s was 11.4 percent. This figure is close to the OECD average of 11.1 percent, and much lower than that of Canada's southern neighbor, the United States, which stands at 17.3 percent. It is, however, considerably higher than other OECD countries such as the Czech Republic (5.4 percent, the lowest rate), the Netherlands (7.2 percent), France (7.2 percent), Germany (8.9 percent), or the Scandinavian countries. At the end of the 2000s, 14.8 percent of Canadian children were living in a poor household, against an OECD average of 12.3 percent. Similar trends can be observed in terms of income inequality, Canada being one of the most unequal countries within the OECD, with a Gini Coefficient of 0.32, above the OECD average of 0.31.[7]

Canada has no *official* poverty line, but the measure most frequently used is the Low Income Cut-Off (LICO).[8] Using this metric, Statistics Canada (2011) points out that after taxes and transfers "almost 3.2 million Canadians lived in low income in 2009, virtually unchanged from 2008. This accounts for 9.6 percent of the population." Hidden within Canada's overall poverty rate are constituencies that experience much higher and deeper rates of poverty including "women (particularly young mothers and unattached seniors), recent immigrants, people with disabilities, and Aboriginal people" (Hay 2009: 5). The rate of poverty among Aboriginal children is much higher than the rate among all children in Canada. In one study using 2006 data, the Aboriginal child poverty rate was double the general figure, specifically 36 percent compared to 18 percent (Campaign 2000, 2010: 5 [Chart 3]).

Social Assistance

Canada's income support program of last resort is social assistance, often referred to as "welfare." It is means tested, as applicants for benefits must justify their need for financial help to caseworkers or civil servants. There is no federal minimum-income scheme or federal standard, since social assistance is the sole responsibility of the provincial/territorial governments, although its costs are shared with the federal government through the Canada Social Transfer (CST).

Canada's relatively high levels of economic inequality and vulnerability are due in part to social assistance rates that are very low. The National Council of Welfare (2011) studied benefit levels for 4 family types across all ten provinces and three territories, for a total of 52 profiles. The Council concluded that "regardless of the measure used, welfare incomes were consistently far below most socially accepted measures of adequacy." In only 3 of 52 cases across the country, did benefit levels reach or come close to the poverty line (LICO), namely the rates paid to lone parents in the provinces of Quebec, Newfoundland and Labrador, and Saskatchewan.

Since the mid-1980s, Canadian provinces and territories have adopted various versions of welfare-to-work programs, often referred to as "workfare."[9] This shift from "passive" to "active" provision of social assistance was intended to "to improve the attitudes and motivation of the unemployed," and to this end "benefits were increasingly conditional upon job search and/or a demonstrated willingness to improve employability, with an overall goal of rapid labor market entry" (Lightman et al. 2010: 523).

This shift was hastened and facilitated by an important change in the way the federal money flowed to the provinces to help fund social assistance. In 1995, the Canada Assistance Plan (CAP, originally adopted in 1966) was replaced by the Canada Health and Social Transfer (CHST). At that time, and in a panic to eliminate the federal deficit, the Liberal government totally abandoned CAP standards for federal cost sharing of provincially delivered income security and social support programs. Day and Brodsky (2006: 7) point out that CAP "standards were significantly incomplete," but that they did approximate a guarantee of economic assistance to the poor. These standards included accessibility (granting financial aid or other assistance to any person in need), adequacy (providing an amount that is consistent with a person's basic requirements), universality (waiving any residency requirements), the right to appeal decisions of welfare agencies, and restraints on the imposition of work requirements upon those receiving social assistance. Lightman et al. (2010: 524) argue that CAP was "perhaps the most progressive social assistance legislation in Canadian history." Under CAP, those in financial need (or at risk of being in need) were entitled to benefits; government officials could not impose qualifications or conditions.

As CAP's successor, the CHST emphasized "compulsion rather than voluntarism, sanctions rather than incentives and individualized obligations rather than collective rights." This change "formalized over a decade of incremental change during which time the foundations of Canada's welfare state settlement had been gradually eroded" (ibid.).

The Canadian versions of welfare-to-work programs were somewhat less draconian than their US counterparts. Snyder (2006: 315) points out that "while Canadian legislation now permits workfare, U.S. legislation requires it." However, this may be a moot point. Despite political rhetoric about workfare giving social assistance recipients a "hand up," "empirical evidence reveals that, while social assistance caseloads have decreased, the economic well-being of many former recipients has worsened" (Snyder 2006: 325). Gorlick and Brethour (1998a and 1998b) collected extensive data on provincial- and territorial-workfare programs in 1997–1998. Their studies led the Canadian Council on Social Development (CCSD) to conclude that "recent welfare reforms appear to be contributing to worsening poverty in Canada by lowering benefits and forcing some people off assistance and into uncertain employment" (CCSD 1999).

In 2004, the CHST was split into the Canada Health Transfer (CHT) and the CST. The CST is now the mechanism by which the federal government transfers to provinces and territories its share of funding for social assistance and social services, services for preschool children (early childhood development and learning and child care), and postsecondary education.[10] The amount of cash allocations from the federal government to the provincial/territorial governments under these categories has been determined until fiscal year 2013–2014. Before that time, the federal–provincial transfer arrangement has to be renegotiated. The outcome of these negotiations will be very significant for the future of social assistance as the income-security safety net of last resort. Key matters to be determined include the amounts that the federal government is willing to transfer to the provinces and territories; the division of resources among the three envelopes; and what degree and kind of conditions are to be attached to distributing social assistance benefits.

Social Insurance

Canada's major contributory programs at the federal level are Employment Insurance (EI) and the Canada / Quebec Pension Plan (C/QPP). Despite its contradictory name, EI pays benefits to those who have lost their job "through no fault of their own." C/QPP is the national contributory seniors' pension scheme, and also pays disability and spousal/child survivor benefits. Employers as well as employees contribute to EI and C/QPP. Workers' Compensation (WC) that pays benefits for injury, illness, and death on the job is also in place across the country. The various WC programs are administered by the provinces, with funding coming from employers.

Of course, these social insurance programs do not follow the BI model, since benefits are limited to those who have contributed and are subject to complex sets of rules governing eligibility, the level, and duration of benefits. However, these benefits are nonetheless very important sources of income security for many Canadians.

Other Cash Benefits

Canada has one benefit that is still paid out as a "demogrant" (i.e., on a universal basis) to all persons in a particular category—in this case individuals 65 years of age and over. The Old Age Security (OAS) is available universally, but since 1989, it is taxable for higher income earners. The basic OAS benefit was set at Can$534 per month in mid 2011. Seniors lacking other sources of income can also apply for a means-tested GIS.

Canada has a multilayered set of income-tested benefits for children. These benefits have superseded the Family Allowance program, a universal "demogrant" that was eliminated by the federal government (after many years of attrition) in 1993.[11] The current range of benefits mainly include the Canada Child Tax Benefit (CCTB), "a tax-free monthly payment made to eligible families to help them with the cost of raising children under age 18," and the Universal Child Care Benefit (UCCB) program, which "issues a taxable Can$100 monthly payment to families for each child under the age of six." The federal and provincial/territorial governments and First Nations also jointly offer the National Child Benefit (NCB) program targeted at low-income families. The NCB is a complex mixture (varying from one province/territory to the next) of cash benefits, incentives for parental attachment to the paid-labor force, and intervention services for low-income parents.[12]

Other cash benefits include the Working Income Tax Benefit (WITB), a small refundable tax credit for low-paid workers, and the Goods and Services Tax/Harmonized Sales Tax (GST/HST) Credit, a program designed to lessen the financial burden on low-income people of regressive sales taxes levied by the provincial and federal governments. Even if the amount of the yearly benefit is very modest, the GST/HST Credit could be seen as the seed of a guaranteed income program for Canada, based on a negative income mechanism, *if* there were the public support and political will to increase the level of benefits and breadth of coverage.

BI and Canadian Politics

Official Reports

BI had already been briefly on the agenda in the 1930s, thanks to the rise of the Social Credit Party that came to power in Alberta in 1935.[13] The real public discussion, however, started in the 1960s, under the impulse of a few social scientists who were inspired by the American debates on "demogrants" and the NIT.[14] Between the early 1970s and the mid-1980s, an impressive number of official reports were published on the issue of a GAI, both at federal and provincial level. Even if most of them were cautious on the idea of implementing such a reform in the short term, some concrete proposals were made to engage Canada (or a given province) into this direction.[15] For instance, the Castonguay-Nepveu report in Quebec (1971) suggested the introduction of a NIT-like "General Social Benefits Regime" that was partly inspired by US president Nixon's Family Assistance Plan [elaborated by Caputo's chapter on the United States in this volume].[16] The same year and in a similar vein, the influential Croll report (1971) issued by the federal senate was advocating a NIT scheme with a maximal benefit at 70 percent of the poverty threshold.[17]

Perhaps the most widely discussed publication was the report by the Royal Commission on the Economic Union and Developments Prospects—the "Macdonald Commission" (1985).[18] Among its most important recommendations to the then federal PM Mulroney were the idea of a free-trade agreement with the United States, and the introduction of a Universal Income Security Program (UISP). The UISP would have replaced most existing transfers by a single guaranteed income for all Canadians, under the form of a NIT or even a modest "demogrant."[19] The report was criticized by some on the left (see the discussions on trade unions, *infra*) on the grounds that it paid too much attention to economic efficiency, and that its UISP was close to a Friedman-like scenario that amounted to dismantling the welfare state. On the right of the political spectrum, some were afraid that such a GAI scheme would amount to paying the "undeserving poor." As one columnist of the *Toronto Star* commented on the report, they believed that BI would "spawn idleness" (Jones 1985).

Interestingly, in a later interview, the head of the commission, Donald Stovel Macdonald from the Liberal Party argued that the main issue, during the discussions on economic security within the commission, was precisely the question of the deserving working poor, "the number of people who wanted to work but who were punished by the structure of the support system." According to Macdonald, the UISP was "representing a way for enabling the working poor...to work their way out to get something from a job."[20]

Aside from the 1986 Forget report, which was focused on the unemployment insurance and argued for a UISP-like scenario, BI did not resurface in official publications at federal level until very recently. Exceptional political circumstances in the Parliament of 2008–2011 offered new opportunities to the supporters of income security reform. During this Parliament, the Conservatives had a minority of seats in the elected House of Commons and (at the beginning of the parliamentary sessions) also in the appointed Senate. This resulted in a minority Conservative Party government, led by Stephen Harper, which was opposed by the Liberal Party as the official opposition, as well as the New Democratic Party (NDP [with a social democratic orientation]) and the Bloc Québécois (dedicated to the sovereignty of Quebec). This composition of the parliamentary chambers ensured a majority of opposition members on committees of both the House and the Senate. As a result, there was the ability to not only discuss but also make recommendations concerning creative ideas, even though the Conservative government was not likely to support them or ensure their passage into legislation.

In this political context, the idea of guaranteed income or BI resurfaced in at least two significant forums. The Senate Sub-Committee on Cities published a report entitled *In from the Margins* on a wide range of measures to address poverty, housing, and homelessness (Senate of Canada 2009). The report makes two recommendations specifically on guaranteed income:

> The federal government publish a Green Paper by 31 December 2010, to include the costs and benefits of current practices with respect to income supports and of options to reduce and eliminate poverty, including a basic annual income based on a negative income tax, and to include a detailed assessment of completed pilot projects on a basic income in New Brunswick and Manitoba.
>
> (Recommendation 5)

> The federal government develop and implement a basic income guarantee at or above LICO for people with severe disabilities.
>
> (Recommendation 53)

On the one hand, a House of Commons Committee also made a recommendation to the Conservative government that it should "create a federal basic income program for persons with disabilities and support a disability-related supports program to be delivered by the provinces and territories" (House of Commons 2010: 143). On the other hand, this committee "decided not to make a recommendation regarding a universal GAI, considering it preferable to take one step at a time and begin with a program benefitting only persons with a disability" (ibid.: 194). Although the Commons Committee was less supportive of a GAI than the Senate Committee, the former did not dismiss the goal of a universal guaranteed income out of hand. Rather, the MP's who sat on the committee recommended an incremental approach that would first of all extend GAI benefits to persons with disabilities.

At Federal Level: Discussed in All Parties, Supported by a Few Individuals

Despite the criticisms (see *supra*), the BI scenario that was at the core of Macdonald's social policy recommendations in 1985 also received some support from both left and right. During the debates around the UISP proposal, the *Winnipeg Free Press* even ran as headline "guaranteed income gets support from all sides."[21] This seems to be a permanent feature of the GAI discussion in Canada (see for instance the current situation in Quebec, *infra*): advocates and opponents of a guaranteed income can be found across the whole political spectrum. The major parties themselves, however, never incorporate GAI into their electoral platform. In the 1960s, the NDP and the Liberal Party did adopt vague motions in favor of a GAI (Bryden 1969; Head 1969), but it was a short-lived move. Overall, in political circles support for BI was and remains the matter of a few committed individuals.

Significantly, one of the most prominent BI advocates today is a so-called "Red Tory" Senator Hugh Segal from the Conservative Party. In recent years, he has publicly and repeatedly defended the introduction of a federal GAI, arguing that Canada has the money to ensure that every citizen can live with dignity: "when we look at the billions we now spend on social policy, it's clear we have the capacity," he says.[22] In February 2008, he introduced a notice of motion in the federal Senate calling for "a fulsome study on the feasibility of a Guaranteed Annual Income . . . or Negative Income Tax as a means of reducing poverty and providing a real solution to those currently living below what is considered the Canadian poverty line."[23]

In the final months of the minority Parliament in 2011 (see *supra*), the NDP poverty critic Tony Martin—interestingly, with support from colleagues in the Liberal Party and the Bloc Québécois—introduced a private member's Bill C-233, *An Act to Eliminate Poverty in Canada*.[24] This Act did not specifically propose guaranteed income, but outlined a number of measures that would "impose on the federal government the obligation to eliminate poverty and promote social inclusion." This bill was not adopted, but was intended to send a political message on the need to act politically at the national level and in a concerted manner on the problem of poverty in Canada. Tony Martin himself took part in a debate on BI with Hugh Segal at the 2011 North American BI conference in New York City.

Today, the only federal party that explicitly supports a guaranteed income is the small Green Party of Canada, which has one seat at the House of Commons in Ottawa. It proposes a NIT, or Guaranteed Livable Income (GLI), for all. This Green Party version of BI would see "various 'poverty-industry' programs of welfare, disability pensions, seniors' benefits, unemployment insurance...collapsed within one simple single payment system, administered through taxes." It would go to everyone, regardless of income, but would be clawed back completely from the well off. According to the Greens, their GLI proposal could yield significant savings through "policy coherence" between the federal, provincial, and municipal levels of government, while "simultaneously reversing the negatives of a shame-based system that perpetuates poverty" (Green Party 2011: 91–92).

At Provincial Level: The Special Case of Quebec

BI has not only been discussed at federal level. Across Canada, several proposals have also been made to introduce a GAI at provincial level, but with the noticeable exception of Quebec—they never attracted much public attention.

In September 2010, for instance, the leader of the NDP in Yukon (one of Canada's three federal territories), Steve Cardiff, had put forward a notice of motion for the Yukon government to introduce a "Guaranteed Minimum Annual Income Allowance." According to the official report from Yukon's legislative assembly, he urged "the Yukon government to implement a guaranteed minimum annual income allowance for all eligible Yukon citizens," referring to the work of federal senator Hugh Segal and the report of the Macdonald Commission (see *supra*).[25]

In November 2010, the Green Party of British Columbia (one of Canada's most populated provinces) released a statement advocating a BI plan under the form of a GLI. According to the statement, such a GLI would "reserve people's dignity and assume people want to do what is best for themselves and their families." Significantly, it also expresses the view that there will be no move into this direction from the current conservative federal government. Hence, the Greens argue, one has to "consider how British Columbia could finance such a change on its own."[26]

One province has even implemented a small BI under the form of an oil dividend, be it for a short period of time. At the end of 2005, the government of Alberta led by Progressive-Conservative PM Ralph Klein announced that residents of the province would start seeing Can$400 per person "Alberta Resource Rebate" checks in their mailboxes in January 2006.[27] At the time, Finance Minister Shirley McClellan said, "Albertans work hard and contribute to the strength of the province. Alberta has eliminated the accumulated debt, invested in priority programs, and sustained the lowest overall tax burden in Canada. This is money Albertans can use for themselves, to spend or save as they see fit."[28] However, no dividend was paid in subsequent years, and this controversial prosperity bonus remained a one-shot operation.

The BI discussion, however, has nowhere been more intense than in the French-speaking province of Quebec, where several political actors and movements have expressed favorable views toward a provincial GAI. As was mentioned above, in the 1970s official publications from the government of Quebec—such as the Castonguay-Nepveu report (1971) and the Fréchette report (1978)—did explicitly consider the implementation of some sort of guaranteed income for all residents of the province. In the 1990s, partly under the influence of the ongoing discussions in French-speaking Europe (esp. France and francophone Belgium), BI regularly resurfaced in the media. These developments led to the drafting of an unpublished report by a directorate within the Ministry of Employment, which was entirely devoted to the examination of the BI debate in Quebec and Europe. The conclusion was cautious: in the short term, the authors argued, its implementation seems "highly unlikely."[29]

In October 2005, an informal group of prominent intellectuals that included the former PM of Quebec Lucien Bouchard published a widely discussed manifesto on the future of *la nation québécoise*. In "*Pour un Québec lucide*" ("A clear-eyed vision of Quebec"), the group suggested a few paths for change, including massive investments in education and innovation, and a substantial tax reform. They also strongly argued for a BI: "Quebec could also consider creating a guaranteed minimum income plan. This plan would make direct transfers to each citizen and would replace several existing income transfer programs...Such a system would have the advantage of reducing the cumbersome bureaucracy required to administer multiple, complex programs. The Quebec model is founded on the ideal of social solidarity that we espouse with conviction" (Bouchard et al. 2005: 9).

Within the Parti Québécois (PQ) itself—of which Lucien Bouchard was a former leader—BI was officially endorsed by two of the candidates for the leadership of the party in 2005, Pauline Marois and, in a more vigorous way, Gilbert Paquette. In a short but detailed document, Paquette argued for a "citizen's income," which he saw as a major reform to be implemented in an independent Quebec.[30] Marois became leader of the party in 2007, but did never reaffirm her support to BI.

Again, as was the case for federal parties (see *supra*), one should stress the fact that this individual support did not translate into an official party line of the PQ. More than that, other prominent figures of the party have openly expressed their skepticism toward a provincial GAI. For instance, when in 2001 the newly created small left-wing party Rassemblement pour l'alternative progressiste (RAP) stated its support for an "unconditional citizen's income,"[31] Bernard Landry—the then

PQ leader and PM of Quebec—clearly expressed his rejection of GAI: "it has been carefully examined in all western democracies, including ours. One has always stumbled over the exorbitant cost of such a universal measure."[32] Since then, RAP has merged with other parties to form Québec Solidaire (QS), a larger left-wing political movement that has won one seat at the 2008 provincial election. Even if BI has been widely discussed within the party, QS did not incorporate it into its 2008 electoral platform (Douville 2010).

Somewhat surprisingly, however, new developments in the political discussion of a GAI in Quebec might come from the right side of the political spectrum. A new political party, Coalition pour l'avenir du Québec (Coalition for the future of Quebec, CAQ) was about to be launched in the Autumn of 2011. One of its two cofounders, businessman Charles Sirois, is a long-standing advocate of BI (Sirois 1999). Opinion polls suggest that if it took part in the next provincial elections, CAQ would gain a significant portion of the vote, and might even become Quebec's first political force.[33]

Basic Income and Civil Society

Trade Unions and Grassroots Movements

In 2008, the OECD measured Canadian union density at 27.2 percent, a rate that has shown very little fluctuation over the last decade.[34] Canada's union density is much lower than in several European countries (although it is much higher than the US figure of 11.2 percent). Aside from being a numerically weak constituency, Canadian unions have been marginalized in social policy debates due to the liberal character of the Canadian welfare system (see *supra*). Nevertheless, unions are a more important social force in Quebec, where coverage extends to almost 40 percent of total employees (Statistics Canada 2009).

According to Haddow (1994), the Canadian union movement did not always take coherent positions on the issue of BI. In fact, Haddow argues, "organized labor's early response to the GAI was muted and confused . . . it was slow to form a coherent assessment of the implications of a negative income tax for its program" (1994: 353). Overall, negative feelings were clearly dominant, as Canadian unions have "always treated the GAI with considerable caution and viewed it as potentially antithetical to [their] social policy goals" (1994: 350). The publication in 1985 of the bulky and influential report by the Macdonald Commission (see *supra*) triggered harsh reactions. In 1986, the convention of the Canadian Labour Congress (CLC), Canada's largest union confederation, expressed serious doubts about the desirability of such a reform and denounced its "neoliberal" character. A GAI, the CLC argued, was going to undermine the minimum wage legislation, and more generally the whole welfare state (Haddow 1993). These views have remained widespread within Canada's union movement. According to Jim Stanford, a highly regarded economist working for the Canadian Auto Workers (CAW) union, "if a BI ever were to be enacted, its benefits would turn out to be significantly lower than the rates envisioned by these well-meaning advocates" (as quoted in Canadian Centre for Policy Alternatives 2000: 10).

Once again, the story is quite different in Quebec. In a reaction to the Macdonald report in 1985, labor leader Louis Laberge (Federation of Labour [FTQ]) declared that "the labor movement has long favored the idea of a guaranteed income."[35] His colleague Michel Chartrand, a colorful and tremendously popular figure of Quebec's trade union movement, publicly supported BI for many years before his death in 2010.[36] In 1999, Chartrand's union CSN (Confederation of National Trade Unions)—Quebec's main union in terms of membership—published a detailed and balanced study on BI in order to foster a reasoned discussion of the proposal (Aubry 1999). Even if other unions (FTQ and the Trade Union of Quebec [CSQ]) did not undertake similar initiatives, they never expressed any hostility toward the idea of an unconditional minimum income. It does not mean, however, that they would support any move into that direction.

Indeed, interviews with Quebecois union officials have shown that they have mixed feelings about the possible introduction of a BI in Canada or in Quebec (Wernerus 2004). Most of them do actually endorse the proposal on ethical grounds, but reject it for pragmatic reasons. They see themselves as lacking the power resources needed to impose a truly *progressive* package of reform. At present, they fear, a discussion of the introduction of a BI might degenerate into a Friedman-like scenario as advocated by the Macdonald commission in 1985. In other words, Quebecois unions are clearly on the defensive: "we should defend what we already have," a FTQ official says (Wernerus 2004: 113). "We should keep fighting for higher wages" and "progressively improve the current welfare system," a CSN representative argues (Wernerus 2004: 114; Vanderborght 2006).

Within the civil society, other groups have been more active in advocating BI, at least since the 1980s. In particular, the National Anti Poverty Organization (NAPO) was directly involved in the hearings of the Macdonald Commission (see *supra*). It urged the commission to include GAI into its reflections on the future of Canada's social policies. The executive director of NAPO at the time, Patrick Johnson, wrote in a letter to Donald S. Macdonald, "I would like to suggest that the Commission itself initiate or contract with a third party to undertake research on a guaranteed annual income."[37] Already in the 1970s,

NAPO had published several documents in order to explain the differences between a NIT and a "demogrant." More recently, it launched a nationwide campaign in favor of a "guaranteed adequate income."[38] In 2009, it changed its name into *Canada without Poverty*, and continues to support the idea.

Think Tanks and Academics

In the framework of the Macdonald commission hearings (see *supra*), the most vigorous plea for a federal GAI came from the Vanier Institute of the Family, an independent think tank committed to the defense of the interests of Canadian families. "It is recommended," it argued in 1983, "that a basic living (money) income be available to the Canadian population, universally, through a form of flat-rate-tax-related demogrants or a negative income tax variation... Such a universal program could probably be funded at sufficient levels of adequacy if all basic and many subsidiary income transfer programs in Canada were blended."[39] In a somewhat radical fashion, the Vanier Institute considered that this GAI program could be a good way to value unpaid activities, those activities "where the work is more varied, self-defined, self-scheduled, self-managed." (Dyson et al. 1983:15).

By contrast, however, most social policy think tanks have not been enthusiastic about BI. The very influential Caledon Institute of Social Policy, for instance, has consistently argued for targeted, income-tested benefits for segments of the population such as children, seniors, and persons with disabilities. In 2000, as federal PM Jean Chrétien was told to be in favor of a federal GAI (see *supra*), it released a short and illustrative commentary: "While its simplicity is appealing, a 'one-size-fits-all' GAI would fit no one, because income security needs are so varied and diverse... A big bang, one-size-for-all guaranteed income plan is not the way to go... there is no single magic bullet to achieve the goal of a guaranteed adequate income" (Battle and Torjman 2000: 2).

Significantly, in one of its more recent publications, it applies, somewhat misleadingly, the term "BI" to a proposed set of benefits for a very specific category of individuals, persons with severe disabilities (Mendelson et al. 2010). In fact, Caledon argues for the need for "a high fence around the Basic Income program in respect of determining eligibility"—that is, one must be judged to have a "severe disability." However, "once a person is over the fence, there will be relatively generous treatment and many fewer rules" (Mendelson et al. 2010: 18). Interestingly, the authors also express a "vision for the longer term" that "the Basic Income program should become a mainstream measure not just for people with severe disabilities, but available to anyone who cannot reasonably be expected to earn an adequate income from employment" (Mendelson et al. 2010: 18).

The leading left-of-center public-policy think tank in Canada is the Canadian Centre on Policy Alternatives (CCPA). It has published one study on guaranteed income (Young and Mulvale 2009) in which arguments for and against this model are presented, reflecting the fact the one of the authors (Young) is skeptical, and the other (Mulvale) is favorably inclined toward the BI approach.

Given the partly neoliberal genealogy of BI in the work of Friedman (1962), it is notable that the most well resourced and visible right-wing think tank in Canada, the Fraser Institute, does not focus on guaranteed income. The major preoccupation of the Fraser Institute in regard to poverty and welfare is the need to lower poverty lines, and to focus on absolute rather than relative measurement of poverty (e.g., Sarlo 2008). In this way, there would be a large decrease in the number of people in Canada judged to be poor, and there presumably would be even less need for income-support programs.

Aside from "grey papers" produced by policy think tanks, there has been a significant production of scientific work on BI (see for instance Lerner et al. 1999; Blais 2002; Araar et al. 2005; Mulvale 2008). One important piece of recent academic analysis focuses on the guaranteed income experiment called Mincome that took place in the town of Dauphin, Manitoba in the 1970s. Evelyn Forget has analyzed health and educational data from this community for the period of time when Mincome was providing guaranteed income supplements to those with low incomes. Forget found that hospitalizations, accidents, injuries, and mental health problems declined, and that the high school completion rate increased, during the Mincome experiment. It is possible, she argues, to demonstrate linkage between these undesirable health outcomes and failure to complete school on the one hand, and income inequality and poverty on the other hand. Therefore, it appears that Mincome had demonstrably beneficial effects for the community, while at the same time having very little negative impact on labor-market participation (Forget 2011).

Much more academic research needs to be done on Mincome and various other topics related to BI in Canada. Whether or not findings from such research will inform future political debates will depend, no doubt, on politicians' willingness to be guided by evidence rather than their own preexisting (and perhaps stereotypical) views and those of their constituents. In order to foster an informed debate on the topic, several academics and BI activists launched the Canadian BI network, which was officially recognized by Basic Income Earth Network (BIEN) in 2008. Since 2010, BIEN Canada holds its annual conference together with the United States Basic Income Guarantee Network (USBIG).

Feminists' Faint Support for Guaranteed Income

BI has both opponents and proponents among feminist writers and researchers (Robeyns 2008). Feminist calls for a form of guaranteed income that would benefit women have been heard, but only to a limited extent, in Canada.[40] Until 1998, the National Action Committee on the Status of Women (NAC) was the leading feminist umbrella group in English-speaking Canada and represented a broad range of organizations and constituencies. NAC favored guaranteed income as a step toward justice and equality for women (Mulvale 2001: 103). However, NAC is no longer active, due in large measure to its loss of federal funding after many years of success in advancing feminist positions with politicians and in the media. With the waning of NAC's influence, a major organizational proponent in Canada that took a feminist position for guaranteed income has fallen silent.

NAC's francophone counterpart is *La Féderation des femmes du Québec* (FFQ). FFQ (2008a) points out that the right to a decent standard of living is part of the *la Charte des droits et libertés du Québec*, but it is contained in a Charter section that is not justiciable and therefore does not provide an effective legal guarantee against poverty. FFQ actively participates in campaigns against poverty and for women's economic autonomy. It also staunchly defends collective public measures for women's equality. In 2008, when the opposition leader Mario Dumont called for a Can$100 weekly payment to families in Quebec with children under five years old who are not enrolled in the public child-care system, FFQ strongly opposed this proposal. The FFQ (2008b) argued that such a policy would impede labor market entry for women—thereby increasing women's poverty—and would undermine the highly developed child-care system that is a source of pride for Quebec.

While both the FFQ and NAC (in its day) have supported the principle of guaranteed income, this new model of economic security has not been a key priority in the social campaigning of either organization. Both groups have been much more focused on improving existing income-support programs such as the GIS for seniors, which benefits mostly women as they are much less likely than men to have substantial income from a corporate pension or C/QPP. These leading feminist groups have also made a priority of services such as child care, and policies such as pay and employment equity, that are likely to advance gender equality in ways other than paying cash benefits.

The Canadian Feminist Alliance for International Action (FAFIA) seeks to "further women's equality in Canada through domestic implementation of its international human rights commitments."[41] FAFIA examines how Canadian social programs could more closely approximate expectations set out in international documents such as the United Nations Convention of the Elimination of All Forms of Discrimination against Women, and the International Covenant on Economic, Social and Cultural Rights. FAFIA addresses various issues of importance to women, including federal and provincial cost sharing of social programs, pay equity, child care, housing, and family violence prevention. FAFIA has called for the adoption of a new Canada Social Programs Act to govern federal transfer payments to provinces for income support. Such legislation would "set out funding formulas and standards, specify the programs and services that the CST is intended to support, and establish monitoring and accountability" (Day and Brodsky 2006: 16). Such measures would fill in the gap left by the federal government's repeal of the CAP in 1995 (see *supra*).

Articulating, adopting, and implementing such a new set of standards for federal cost sharing of income-security programs, and doing so in cooperation with the 13 provincial and territorial governments who deliver these programs, would be a very complex and politically challenging undertaking. The inherent difficulty of attaining national standards for income security as advocated by FAFIA begs the question. Perhaps, a better feminist strategy for economic security for Canadian women would be to press for an unconditional and universal guarantee of adequate income as one of our first premises in social policy. Should feminists—as well as other progressives in think tanks, the labor movement, and other organizations who seek better economic security for all—adopt a more radical commitment to guaranteed income? Such a clearer and conceptually simpler model might, at least in the longer run, offer greater hope of achieving positive practical outcomes.

Conclusion: What Political Prospects for BI?

Canada is undoubtedly one of the few western democracies where the BI debate has been noticeable and ongoing over the past decades. The idea has been promoted by numerous social and political actors, and it has even attracted sporadic but significant media attention. However, as its advocates are spread across the political spectrum, its political viability remains relatively low. No doubt, making progress toward some sort of guaranteed income for Canada will depend upon building and connecting these points of interest and support. This is far from being an easy task, since not everyone has the same vision of what they want to achieve and how they want to get there. Even in progressive circles and on the political left in Canada, fear persists that certain versions of GAI would leave working people and the poor worse off than they are now. As we have shown, this was at the core of the controversy in the aftermath of the Macdonald commission's report in 1985.

There are certainly no glimmerings on the horizon that Canada will implement a full-fledged BI anytime soon, and if ever introduced, it will inevitably be the result of a compromise. The Canadian way in past social policy development has been to move forward in incremental, pragmatic, and fiscally prudent steps. In this framework, the most promising avenue for BI advocates might consist in taking advantage of political windows of opportunity for fostering the development of a tapestry of programs that would approximate a guaranteed income *framework*. Such a framework could include a modest unconditional income support, improved labor-market access and mobility, and robust public services.

A first feasible step should be the reintroduction of a true universal child benefit, a program that existed in Canada until 1993. The current child benefit system is nothing if not complicated (see *supra*); one could even argue that the array of benefits is almost the *antithesis* of the BI model in regard to design and delivery. The BI model is often touted as relatively simple to understand, uncomplicated to administer, and transparent in its costs and benefits (De Wispelaere and Stirton 2011).[42] These features are of crucial importance in the case of needy families, which are too often lost in the labyrinthine complexity of targeted schemes. Another, complementary step is the establishment of a federal legislative guarantee that would set an income floor below which no one is to fall across Canada. Both steps would reinforce the historical role of the federal level as responsible for income security, while maintaining provincial and territorial responsibility for social services.

As always, practical progress toward such a framework would have to navigate the labyrinth of constitutional jurisdiction and division of powers between the federal government and the provincial and territorial governments in regard to who does what and who pays. Part of this challenge would be to accommodate Quebec's distinctiveness, perhaps in an asymmetrically federalist or cofederalist model of governance.

Furthermore, at first sight the political context looks rather gloomy. Like other countries, Canada's welfare state has sustained ideological attacks by the political right in recent years. Neoconservative forces have delegitimized social programs designed to redistribute wealth and to promote equality and justice for women, racial minorities, and others. Neoliberal forces have supported deep tax cuts, thereby diminishing public revenue streams and making social programs less affordable. The conservative government elected in May 2011 cuts spending in order to tackle the federal deficit that results from heavy spending to stave off the feared negative economic effects of the global financial crisis. It is extremely unlikely that there will be any bold new spending initiatives in such a fiscal environment. This will lead many to believe that something like a guaranteed income framework is ill-advised or unattainable.

However, there are also signs that the ideological ground is currently shifting. There is evidence of increasing concern about the persistence of poverty and the growing levels of inequality, and about the fact that the federal government needs to take steps to address these problems (CCPA 2007). This partly explains the electoral success of the left-of-center NDP at the May 2011 federal elections. The NDP, which is the current official opposition, promised a broad array of improvements and extensions to existing in-cash and -kind programs.

Time will tell if the idea of BI takes hold in Canada, and if practical progress is made toward implementing some sort of guaranteed income framework. A careful look at the recent history of the Canadian discussion about BI shows that one should not be overly optimistic about its political chances. However, it is also remarkable that—contrary to what happens in many other OECD countries—in Canada BI is not simply dismissed as a somewhat eccentric idea. Turning this proposal into reality will, obviously, require that proponents of more universal and unconditional approaches to economic security continue to mobilize, do critical analysis and careful research, and develop and execute effective forms of political advocacy. The launch in 2008 of the Basic Income Canada Network/Réseau Canadien pour le Revenu Garanti (an affiliate of the BIEN) can be considered as a helpful step in fostering such mobilization, research, and advocacy.

Notes

* We would like to thank François Blais for useful suggestions.

1. In French-speaking Canada, one often refers to a "Revenu minimum garanti" or a "Revenu annuel garanti." In recent years, however, the expression "Allocation universelle" (universal grant, see Vanderborght and Van Parijs 2005), which is widely used in French-speaking European countries (France, Belgium, Switzerland), has gained increasing visibility.
2. See "Chrétien Wants to Leave Mark with Cradle-to-Grave Program of Guaranteed Annual Income," *Ottawa Citizen*, December 9, 2000.
3. "Foes Decry 'Socialism' by Stealth," *National Post* December 11, 2000; "Harris Wary of Chrétien's Income Plan," *Ottawa Citizen* December 12, 2000.
4. *Hansard*, June 20, 2011.

5. See Esping-Andersen (1990: 27). In a more recent attempt to measure the degree of decommodification in 18 OECD countries, Scruggs and Allan (2006) conclude that Canada has a higher decommodification score (25.0) than in Esping-Andersen's seminal essay (22.0). Among the countries they have reexamined, Canada is "perhaps the most confounding case," they argue. Whereas, "most of the literature has grouped [Canada] with the United States as a case of unadulterated liberalism," it has "more decommodifying programme scores than all other liberal countries, especially for pensions" (2006: 62).
6. For further information on the Canadian welfare state, see for instance Rice and Prince (2000); Fortin, Noël, and St. Hilaire (2003); Lightman (2003).
7. These data are from OECD (2011).
8. LICO is a relative measurement of poverty that takes into account average expenditures on the essential items of food, shelter, and clothing.
9. In his *Workfare States*, Jamie Peck focuses on the Canadian case, see Peck (2001: 213–260).
10. In the 2011–2012 fiscal year, the amount of the CST totalled Can$11.5 billion, of which Can$6.8 billion was allocated to social assistance and related services, Can$1.2 billion to early childhood programs, and Can$3.5 billion to postsecondary education.
11. A clawback on family allowances of upper-income families had already been introduced in 1989 (Battle 1999: 3).
12. There is also a Child Disability Benefit (CDB), "a tax-free benefit for families who care for a child under age 18 with a severe and prolonged impairment in mental or physical functions." Information in this paragraph is drawn from multiple pages of the website of the Canada Revenue Agency: http://www.cra-arc.gc.ca/menu-eng.html.
13. See Van Trier (1995: 146).
14. For a significant example, see Cutt (1968).
15. For further details, see Young and Mulvale (2009).
16. Bracketed information inserted by editor.
17. The Croll report was said to be "as important a social document in Canadian social history as the *Beveridge report* was for postwar Britain" (McCormack 1972: 366).
18. On the Macdonald report, see the special supplement of *Canadian Public Policy*, vol.12, Feb. 1986.
19. See Hum (1986); Tanguy (2001).
20. The interview was conducted by Patrick Tanguy in Toronto on January 11, 2001 (see Tanguy 2001).
21. *Winnipeg Free Press*, September 11, 1985.
22. According to the *Toronto Star*, March 5, 2007.
23. Quoted from a "Communique" and "Notice of Motion" released by the Office of Senator Hugh Segal (2008), Senate of Canada, February 6, 2008.
24. See http://parl.gc.ca/HousePublications/Publication.aspx?Docid=5100295&file=4, retrieved on August 12, 2011.

25. BIEN NewsFlash 63, November 2010. Steve Cardiff was killed in a car accident in early July 2011. The Yukon NDP has formed the territorial government in the past, but currently holds 1 / 18 seats.
26. http://www.greenparty.bc.ca/news/green-party-bc-calls-basic-income-plan, retrieved on August 12, 2011. Note that the Green Party holds no seats in the current British Columbia legislative assembly. In the 2009 provincial election, it received 8.1 percent of the vote.
27. Alberta Legislative Assembly 2005.
28. *Canadian Press*, October 11, 2005.
29. Québec 2000. A similar report had been published by Ministry of Income Security in the mid-1990s (see Bernier and Lévesque 1995).
30. The document was published on his website http://www.gilbertpaquette.org/ (retrieved on August 9, 2011).
31. "Le RAP dit oui à l'union de la gauche," *Le Devoir*, June 11, 2001.
32. "Landry fait une mise en garde au RAP," *Le Devoir*, June 12, 2001.
33. *Le Devoir*, June 11, 2011. In the 2000s, another right-wing political party, the *Action démocratique du Québec* (ADQ), had incorporated its own version of the NIT into its electoral platform. The ADQ could possibly merge with the CAQ in the near future.
34. See http://stats.oecd.org/Index.aspx?DataSetCode=UN_DEN, retrieved on August 12, 2011.
35. "Quebec reaction to report 'muted,'" *The Financial Post* September 1985.
36. Cf. Bernard and Chartrand (1999). Chartrand was a leader of the CSN.
37. October 31, 1983.
38. See *NAPO News* Spring 2007, or visit http://www.napo-onap.ca/.
39. *The Toronto Star*, December 4, 1983.
40. Brossard and Morel (2002) offers an overview of Quebec's academic debate on basic income from a feminist perspective.
41. See http://www.fafia-afai.org/en/about/who-we-are, retrieved on August 12, 2011.
42. However, De Wispelaere and Stirton (2011) caution against underestimating the administrative complexity of basic income.

References

Alberta Legislative Assembly. 2005. *Alberta Resource Rebate Statutes Amendment Act*, bill 43, 26th legislature, 1st session.

Araar, Abdelkrim, Jean-Yves Duclos, and François Blais. 2005. "Effets redistributifs d'un régime d'allocation universelle: une simulation pour le Québec." *L'Actualité économique* 81 (3): 422–484.

Aubry, François. 1999. *L'Allocation universelle, fondements et enjeux*. Montréal: Confédération des syndicats nationaux.

Battle, Ken. 1999. "Child Benefit Reform: A Case Study in Tax/Transfer Integration." Paper presented at the Canadian Tax Foundation Tax Policy Conference, April 9–10, 1999.

Battle, Ken, and Sherri Torjman. 2000. "Yes, Virginia, There is a Guaranteed Annual Income." *Caledon Commentary*, Ottawa: Caledon Institute of Social Policy, December 2000.

Bernard, Michel, and Michel Chartrand. 1999. *Manifeste pour un revenu de citoyenneté*. Montréal: Editions du renouveau québécois.

Bernier, Jean, and Suzanne Lévesque. 1995. *Le revenu minimum garanti: formes et modalités possibles*. Québec: Direction de la recherche, de l'évaluation et de la statistique, Ministère de la sécurité du revenu, February 1995.

Blais, François. 2002. Ending Poverty. A Basic Income for All Canadians. Toronto: Lorimer.

Bouchard, Lucien et al. 2005. *For a clear-eyed vision of Quebec*. Online manifesto, October 19, 2005, available at, http://www.pourunquebeclucide.info/ (retrieved March 20, 2012).

Brossard, Louise and Sylvie Morel. 2003. L'allocation d'existence: quelques propositions québécoises. Montréal: Institut de recherches et d'études féministes—UQAM.

Bryden, Marion. 1969. "A Guaranteed Annual Income." *NDP/NPD Discussion Papers* Winnipeg Convention, October 28–31, 1969.

Campaign 2000. 2010. "2010 Report Card on Child and Family Poverty in Canada: Reduced Poverty = Better Health for All." Toronto: Campaign 2000.

Canadian Centre for Policy Alternatives. 2000. "Debate: Should Canadians be Guaranteed a Basic Income?" *The Monitor* (November): 8–11. Ottawa: CCPA.

Canadian Centre for Policy Alternatives. 2007. What Can Governments Do about Canada's Growing Gap? Canadian Attitudes toward Income Inequality. Toronto: CCPA.

Canadian Council on Social Development (CCSD). 1999. "Communiqué: Welfare-to-Work Programs Cause for Concern." Ottawa: CCSD, March 3, 1999.

Cutt, James. 1968. *A Guaranteed Income for Canadians*. Toronto: The Ontario Woodsworth Memorial Foundation.

Day, Shelagh, and Gwen Brodsky. 2006. "Strengthening the Canada Social Transfer: A Call to Account." Ottawa: FAFIA, available at http://www.google.com/search?hl=en&q=Strengthening%20%20the%20Canada%20Social%20Transfer.

De Wispelaere, Jurgen, and Lindsay Stirton. 2011. "The Administrative Efficiency of Basic Income." *Policy and Politics* 39 (1): 115–132.

Douville, Luc. 2010. "Qu'est devenu le revenu de citoyenneté?" *Vigile* 27 (January 2010).

Dyson, William A., and Associates. 1983. *Briefing Materials. The Vanier Institute of the Family*. Edmonton: Hearings of the Macdonald Commission, November 15, 1983.

Féderation des femmes du Québec. 2008a. Projet de loi 63 – Loi modifiant la Charte des droits et libertés de la personne: la fédération des femmes du Québec somme le gouvernement de mettre en œuvre les moyens pour une égalité réelle. Québec: FFQ.

———. 2008b. 100 $ par semaine: une recette pour la pauvreté des femmes (lettre ouverte). Québec: FFQ.

Forget, Evelyn. 2011. "The Town with No Poverty: The Health Effects of a Canadian Guaranteed Annual Income Field Experiment." *Canadian Public Policy* 37(3), 283–305.

Fortin, Sarah, Alain Noël, and France St-Hilaire (eds.). 2003. *Forging the Canadian Social Union: SUFA and Beyond.* Montreal: Institute for Research on Public Policy.

Friedman, Milton. 1962. *Capitalism and Freedom.* Chicago: University of Chicago Press.

Gorlick, Carolyne, and Guy Brethour. 1998a. *Welfare-to-Work Programs in Canada: A Discussion Papery.* Ottawa: Canadian Council on Social Development.

———. 1998b. *Welfare-to-Work: A National Inventory.* Ottawa: Canadian Council on Social Development.

Green Party of Canada. 2011. *Vision Green.* Ottawa: Green Party of Canada, April 2011.

Haddow, Rodney S. 1993. *Poverty Reform in Canada, 1958–1978. State and Class Influences on Policy Making.* Montréal and Kingston: McGill-Queen's University Press.

———. 1994. "Canadian Organized Labour and the Guaranteed Annual Income." 350–366 in *Continuities and Discontinuities: The Political Economy of Social Welfare and Labour Market Policy in Canada*, edited by A. F. Johnson, Stephen McBride, and Patrick J. Smith. Toronto: University of Toronto Press.

Hay, David I. 2009. *Poverty Reduction Policies and Programs in Canada.* Ottawa: Canadian Council on Social Development.

Head, Wilson A. 1969. "Poverty—A Major Issue Confronting Canadians." Paper presented at the Harrison Liberal Conference, Harrison Hot Springs (BC), November 21–23, 1969.

House of Commons, Canada. 2010. Federal Poverty Reduction Plan: Working in Partnership Towards Reducing Poverty in Canada. Report of the Standing Committee on Human Resources, Skills and Social Development and the Status of Persons with Disabilities. Ottawa: 40th Parliament, 3rd Session, November 2010.

Hum, Derek. 1986. "USIP and the Macdonald Commission: Reform and Restraint." *Canadian Public Policy* 12 (supplement): 92–100.

Jones, Frank. 1985. "Basic Income Will Spawn Idleness." *The Toronto Star* September 9, 1985.

Lerner, Sally, Charles M. A. Clark, and W. Robert Needham. 1999. *Basic Income. Economic Security for All Canadians.* Toronto: Between the Lines.

Lightman, Ernie. 2003. *Social Policy in Canada.* Don Mills, ON: Oxford University Press.

Lightman, Ernie, Andy Mitchell, and Dean Herd. 2010. "Cycling Off and On Welfare in Canada." *Journal of Social Policy* 39: 523–542.

McCormack, Theresa. 1972. "Poverty in Canada: The Croll Report and Its Critics." *Canadian Review of Sociology* 9 (4): 366–372.

Mendelson, Michael, Ken Battle, Sherri Torjman, and Ernie Lightman. 2010. *A Basic Income Plan for Canadians with Severe Disabilities.* Ottawa: Caledon Institute of Social Policy.

Mulvale, James P. 2001. Reimagining Social Welfare: Beyond the Keynesian Welfare State. Aurora, ON: Garamond Press.

———. 2008. "Basic Income and the Canadian Welfare State: Exploring the Realms of Possibility." *Basic Income Studies* 3 (1): Article 6.

National Council of Welfare. 2011. "Welfare Incomes: Key Patterns and Trends." Ottawa: National Council of Welfare.

Organisation for Economic Development and Cooperation (OECD). 2011. *Society at a Glance 2011: OECD Social Indicators.* Luxembourg: OECD Publishing.

Peck, Jamie. 2001. *Workfare States.* New-York and London: The Guilford Press.

Rice, James J., and Michael J. Prince. 2000. *Changing Politics of Canadian Social Policy.* Toronto: University of Toronto Press.

Robeyns, Ingrid. 2008. "Introduction: Revisiting the Feminism and Basic Income Debate." *Basic Income Studies* 3 (3): Article 3.

Sarlo, Chris. 2008. "Measuring Poverty in Canada: What Happened to the Copenhagen Agreement?" *Fraser Forum* February 2008: 11–12.

Scruggs, Lyle, and James Allan. 2006. "Welfare-state Decommodification in 18 OECD Countries : A Replication and Revision." *Journal of European Social Policy* 16 (1): 55–72.

Segal, Hugh. 2008. "Guaranteed Annual Income: Why Milton Friedman and Bob Stanfield Were Right." *Policy Options* 29 (4): 46–51.

———. 2011. "Let's Refocus on a Guaranteed Annual Income." *The Globe and Mail* January 19, 2011.

Senate of Canada. 2009. In from the Margins: A Call to Action on Poverty, Housing and Homelessness. Ottawa: Senate of Canada.

Sirois, Charles. 1999. *Passagé obligé. De la gestion mécanique à la gestion organique.* Montréal: Editions de l'Homme.

Snyder, Linda. 2006. "Workfare: Ten Years of Pickin' on the Poor." In *Canadian Social Policy: Issues and Perspectives (4th edition)*, edited by Anne Westhues, 309–330. Waterloo, ON: Wilfred Laurier University Press.

Statistics Canada. 2009. *Labour Force Historical Review.* Ottawa: Statistics Canada.

———. 2011. *Income in Canada 2009.* Ottawa: Statistics Canada.

Tanguy, Patrick. 2001. Le Régime universel de sécurité de revenu de la Commission Macdonald: une analyse de son origine et de son échec. Sainte-Foy: Université Laval (Master Thesis).

Van Trier, Walter. 1995. Everyone a King. An Investigation into the Meaning and Significance of the Debate on Basic Incomes with Special Reference to Three Episodes from the British Inter-War Experience. Leuven: Katholieke Universiteit Leuven (PhD Thesis).

Vanderborght, Yannick. 2006. "Why Trade-Unions Oppose Basic Income." *Basic Income Studies* 1 (1): Article 5.

Vanderborght, Yannick, and Philippe Van Parijs. 2005. *L'allocation universelle.* Paris: La Découverte.

Wernerus, Sabine. 2004. Les syndicats contre l'allocation universelle ? Mise en perspective des points de vue belges et québecois, Louvain-la-Neuve: FOPES/Université catholique de Louvain.

Young, Margot, and James P. Mulvale. 2009 (November). *Possibilities and Prospects: The Debate Over a Guaranteed Income.* Vancouver: Canadian Centre for Policy Alternatives (BC Office).

CHAPTER 12

Japan: Political Change after the Economic Crisis Introduces Universalist Benefit

*Toru Yamamori**

Employment insecurity after the financial crisis of 2007 finally destroyed the "We are all middle class" myth. Another result of the crisis was the defeat of the Liberal Democratic Party (LDP). After over half a century as the majority party in the Diet, the LDP lost the 2009 election to the Democratic Party of Japan (DPJ). A prominent economist made the statement, "The logic of the income security and household subsidies indicated in the DPJ's manifesto ultimately lead to the Basic Income discussed in Western Europe" (Ito 2009). In this vein, the DPJ's Tax Policy Investigation Committee organized seminars on the topic of Basic Income (BI) in which I and two other experts gave presentations.

However the DPJ has never officially endorsed the BI policy. Media treatment of BI is extremely rare, and, even among people knowledgeable of the policy, the majority is of the view that the guarantee is not in accordance with the traditional ethics of Japanese society.

The goal of this chapter is to show the role that we see is starting to be played by the debate over BI during the past few years of economic crisis and political change.

The first section will provide an overview of Japan's system of income security over the past half century and show the various causes of the current system's dysfunction. In the second section, I will cover economic policy and political reality while analyzing the vocabulary used to describe the situation. I will point out the lack of a vocabulary of use for describing the new direction gradually being taken under the DPJ. After briefly outlining the debate surrounding BI in the third section, I will use the fourth section to propose using the vocabulary accumulated in the BI debate to fill the explanatory gap in discussions of current economic and social policies.

The Myth, the Reality, and the Collapse of the "Japanese Welfare Society"

After World War II, Japan built up an income security system using the Beveridge Report as a blueprint. The social insurance pillars were pensions, unemployment insurance, and health insurance. Social assistance policies were built in as supplementary additions. Pensions and health insurance systems for employed people preceded the establishment, in 1961, of the National Pension and National Health Insurance to cover the self-employed and the unemployed to achieve universal coverage for citizens.

In the second half of the 1960s, Socialist and Communist party candidates were elected to head local municipalities spawning many "progressive" administrations. This led to 1973 becoming known as "The Year of Welfare" as the LDP, fearing for its survival, passed large increases in the social welfare budget. As seen from the inclusion of "to insure the completion of a welfare states" as a goal in the party's founding declaration of 1955, the LDP was not openly against the welfare state. From the 1950s to the beginning of the 1970s, at least as a slogan, the welfare state enjoyed a broad majority of support among citizens.

This support broke down with economic restructuring after the oil shock of 1973. The "Japanese Style Welfare Society" policy paper put out by the LDP in 1979 can be taken as an ideological blueprint for the social security policies of the 1980s. The paper severely criticizes the welfare state that the party had intended to "ensure the completion" of in its founding declaration. The document saw the experiences of the United Kingdom and Sweden as total failures. Ever since the United Kingdom had "pursued equality and social security expansion" the diagnosis was that the United Kingdom had caught an "English Disease," a kind of "economic diabetes."

> Swedish life for the elderly is lonely, isolated and cold, resulting from a society based on extreme individualism... The Swedish philosophy of all-round welfare coverage that provides full benefits rather than regulation and control has brought about a tendency to shift the costs of personal troubles onto society... If an unwed mother gives birth to a child, the costs are shifted to society as the mother and child are on welfare benefits. Once this system is put in place people become "complacent" and behave with the knowledge that society will bear the costs of their troubles. They

> become a type of parasite, accustomed to exploiting the system. Suppose our country made a similar system with "divorce insurance" and made insurance payments to divorced women, or implemented generous protections and subsidies for unmarried mothers and their children, perhaps even establishing institutions for their care. This would give rise to "free love," or from a man's point of view "free sex," and we would certainly see lower rates of marriage, higher rates of divorce and more illegitimate children, all of which is seen in Sweden. Is this the kind of civilized progress of which we can be proud? No, this is nothing but foolishness showing an extreme lack of civilization and wisdom (LDP 1979).

The principles of a "National Minimum" and "Equality of Outcome" were dismissed as harming civilization to no benefit. Families and corporations were put first and individual welfare became a matter of personal responsibility.

The characteristics of two social security reforms from 1985 represent policies based on the principle of subsidizing the family as opposed to the individual. Payments to single mothers for their dependent children were attacked and decreased. This "reform" is usually explained away as the result of a financial need to cut budgets in a slowed economy. However, we cannot accept this explanation upon considering another reform of the same year: Newly implemented exemption of the national pension insurance premium for full-time housewives of regularly employed men (Tax exemption for those regularly employed men with full-time housewives was also enlarged two years later).

Japan was often seen as a society with a "traditional" division of labor between the sexes, where men worked outside the home while women became housewives. This view of "traditional" society is not accurate. In 1970, Japan's rate of employment for women was second highest among OECD nations.[1] The employment rate for women in Japan has been losing ground to other OECD countries ever since. Japan's characteristic high number of full-time homemakers is not "tradition" but the intended consequence of policies adopted after the oil shock of 1973. The manifesto for this system change is the LDP's 1979 policy paper and the reforms of 1985 were the culmination of the policymakers' intentions.

Was the sexist content of social security severely criticized? Unfortunately, other than criticism by a handful of feminists, the majority of Japanese society seemed to have taken for granted the sexist nature of the system. These views remain unchanged today. Of course, the social movements of single mothers and other minorities criticized and struggled against the "reforms" at the time (Yamamamori 2010.[2]

"The Japanese welfare society" depends on the family, and at the same time, upon corporations. This dependence on corporations has brought about inequalities between the employees (and their families) in large corporations and the less fortunate people excluded from such employment. This gap has met relatively strong criticism from scholars. However, this criticism has remained limited to academics and a small minority in the labor movement while the media inundates viewers with the myth that "All Japanese are Middle Class." The reality is that only workers in large corporations and their families were able to attain middle class lifestyles. The Japanese welfare society actually opened up a gap between these workers with their families and the rest of Japanese society. How have the myths that "everyone is middle class" and about the existence of "Japanese welfare society" survived for so long in this unequal society? Perhaps the myths didn't die because many male college graduates had the opportunity to secure employment in large (and midsized) corporations. This avenue was open to some male high school graduates also, and to women as well; whether women continued working or not, it was assumed that they would marry a man.[3]

The myths survived until the mid-1990s. Let us look at the data for the "welfare society" at this point in time. We'll start with an international comparison of social expenditures. The 1995 OECD data showed that as a percentage of GDP, Japan (14.3 percent) looked to be more of a "small government" society than the United States (15.4 percent); after besting the United States in the field of "small government" with regard to welfare it is needless to say that Japan also surpasses other OECD countries such as the United Kingdom (19.9 percent), France (28.5 percent), or Sweden (32.0 percent) in its neglect of welfare.[4] Looking at just social assistance expenditures as a percentage of GDP makes Japan, at 0.3 percent, stand out even more for its form of "small government" when compared with other countries' social expenditures seen as a percentage of GDP, with the United States at 3.7 percent, the United Kingdom at 4.1 percent, France at 2.0 percent, and Sweden at 1.5 percent.[5]

Does this "small government" budget match a similarly small problem with poverty? Unfortunately, this is not the case when considering relative poverty, or even absolute poverty. In 1994, OECD calculates Japan's rate of relative poverty at 13.7 percent. This rate is higher than the OECD average of 10 percent and even higher than England after the desolation of Thatcherism. By comparison, Sweden's rate is 3.7 percent.[6] It is difficult to pin down absolute poverty with statistics but let us use social assistance criteria. In 1995, 7.45 percent of households lived beneath the income threshold line for meeting social assistance requirements. Among these households, the percentage actually receiving assistance, the take-up rate, was only 19.7 percent (Tachibanaki and Urakawa 2006). There was an actual need for a budget five times as big as the current expenditures.

At any rate, until this period, the myth that Japan, being an equal society, was different than Western societies with their economic classes went unchallenged. However, looking at the Japanese welfare society while considering poverty exposes this myth as a lie and "welfare society" as just another name for a "dual society" of the secure middle class and the impoverished.

The Japanese welfare society was based on the possibility of entering the middle class if you graduated from college for men, and for women, if you married one of those men. This state of affairs ended in the 1990s with the collapse of the bubble and the "lost 20 years" that bring us to the present day.

The corporate manifesto for dismantling the welfare state was put out by the Japanese Business Federation (Nikkeiren) in 1995. The document is titled "Japanese-style Management for a New Era: the direction we should strive for and the concrete measures entailed." The document divides workers into three groups, "core members with accumulated expertise," "highly skilled specialists," and the "flexibly employed." The permanent employment previously guaranteed to almost all male university graduates would now only be continued for a handful of workers with hard-to-replace "accumulated expertise." The other groups are to be utilized in a "flexible" manner. Actually, the Worker Dispatch Law passed in 1985 occasioned some deregulation and it was in the 1990s that more deregulation took off. The proportion of irregular employees has consistently increased from the mid-1990s to the present day.

The corporation-dependent Japanese welfare state had already begun to collapse as corporations pulled out of the system. Employment insecurity after the financial crisis just hastened the fall.

From "Civil-Engineering Keynesian" to "Neoclassical Deregulation"

Until the September 2009 election, the LDP held power, with very few short-term exceptions, for the half century since World War II. The LDP arose in 1955 as an amalgamation of the conservative camps. The Socialist Party was the LDP's rival and largest opposition party, but working from a platform of Marxist-Leninist socialism in the context of the Cold War and the US-Japan alliance effectively left the LDP as the only party with real power in the political system.

However, the LDP did not simply coast along relying on the geopolitics of the day. Theodore J. Lowi (1969) has described the US polity as "interest group liberalism." The LDP successfully used similar conditions in Japan to rationalize their system of power dominance. With "interest group liberalism," decisions regarding distribution and regulation are decided, not in discussions at the Congress or the Diet, but outside the official political process as various interest groups pressure bureaucrats and politicians.[7] Japan is unlike the United States, where the two parties rise and fall with the backing of interest groups. As there was no likelihood of a change in the party in power, the power dynamics among interest groups and political parties in Japan favored the single party with unbroken power—the LDP.

A kind of "Civil-Engineering Keynesianism" is one of the factors that made the LDP the agent of distribution in the context of Japan's "interest group liberalism." President Roosevelt's economic stimulus policies to remedy the Great Depression had two aspects. The public works aspects of his policies are well known. Less attention has been paid (by Japanese economists) to the social aspects of his economic stimulus. Roosevelt also made efforts to maintain effective demand in the economy by guaranteeing people's income with the Social Security Act and a federal minimum wage. After World War II it was the social support policies, the "Keynesian Welfare State," that spread throughout the West to become the prevailing economic policy.

The LDP's "interest group liberalism" can be seen in the same vein as Roosevelt's public works programs of the New Deal, as specialized policies for stimulating effective demand through public works. Stimulus through public works can be seen as an unintended result of the 1950s policy for reconstruction after World War II. After being presented for a period in the 1960s as the "Plan for Doubling the National Income," Kakuei Tanaka, conscious of their role as an economic stimulus, made the policies his own under the title "Building a new Japan; a plan for remodeling the Japanese Archipelago" in 1972, the same year he became prime minister. The "Plan for Doubling the National Income" aimed to achieve full employment through the development of export industries, while at the same time correcting income and development disparities between varied areas in Japan and among the different types of industry. The second group of policies taking aim at disparities in the country were taken and built upon as "Prime Minister Tanaka's plan for remodeling the Japanese Archipelago." Ostensibly to redistribute some of the nation's wealth to the peripheral countryside under the banner of "well-balanced land development," public works were increased with the intensive construction of railroads, highways, and dams.

There are differences of opinion about whether the civil-engineering projects of the "well-balanced land development" policies actually contributed to lessening disparities for underdeveloped areas in Japan. However, it cannot be denied that regular employment in the relatively underdeveloped areas was attained through the public works projects. Even after Kakuei Tanaka's reign as prime minister, his faction utilized their control over the distribution of money for public works to maintain their power and remain the central, authoritative group within the LDP until the 1990s. (The DPJ's secretary-general, Ichiro Ozawa is from the Tanaka faction.)

The large deficits run up by Civil-Engineering Keynesianism led to a debate among the Ministry of Finance and some economists over the need for a shift in policy. The economic slump during "The Lost Decade" of the 1990s after Japan's asset price bubble burst made it clear that the LDP's traditional economic policies had ceased to function. At the same time, the political realignment after the end of the Cold War had the LDP facing, not the Marxist-Leninist Socialist Party as their main rival, but the New Frontier Party at first, and then the DPJ, both made up mainly of former LDP members. As the urban electorate, not benefiting from public project largesse, started voting for these new opposition parties, the LDP began seeking new policies to gain popularity and votes. Representative of this period is the Koizumi administration with the rallying calls of "Destroy the LDP" and "Without reform there will be no growth." Emblematic of the Koizumi administration's shift from Civil-Engineering Keynesianism to neoclassical economic policies was economist Heizo Takenaka's entering into the Koizumi cabinet and taking up the post of economic and fiscal policy minister. The two pillars of these policies were deregulation and privatization.[8]

It wasn't only the LDP shifting from Civil-Engineering Keynesianism to neoclassical policies. When the Koizumi administration made postal service privatization the central issue in the debate for the 2005 election, the DPJ also promoted neoclassical policies. Research into the policies favored by candidates showed the DPJ adhering closer to neoclassical economics.[9]

Since the Koizumi administration, the LDP's economic policies have come about from inner conflicts among factions emphasizing fiscal reconstruction for balanced budgets, and factions emphasizing economic growth via deregulation. After the financial crisis of 2007, this tug-of-war has ended up weaving together Civil-Engineering Keynesianism once again.

The main factor effecting the 2009 change in ruling parties after 50 years was rejection by both the financial sector and the voters as they said "no" to a revival of Civil-Engineering Keynesianism. However, it is difficult to foresee the economic policies that will come out of the coalition government headed by the DPJ as the coalition, and even the DPJ itself, contains a mixture of conflicting ideologies regarding economic policy.

On the one hand, the group coalesced around Ichiro Ozawa (secretary-general of the DPJ when they first took power), along with the People's New Party, seem to have inherited traditional LDP-style Keynesianism. On the other hand, the group around Prime Minister Hatoyama and the ex-Socialist Party fraction in the DPJ have, since the

1990s, been very critical of public works such as dams. However, a principled, consistent direction for an economic policy to replace old-style, pork-barrel Keynesianism is not yet visible. Policies such as the child-care allowance have been justified under the slogan "Shifting from Concrete to People," but were implemented due to a temporary alliance between the two fractions. Also within the DPJ is a third grouping with neoclassical economic designs, which includes members such as Katsuya Okada (foreign minister of the first DPJ cabinet and current secretary-general of the DPJ) and Seiji Maehara (transportation minister of the first DPJ cabinet).

One large problem is that the new policy direction termed "Shifting from Concrete to People" has absolutely no credibility as an economic policy in Japan's public discourse. The vocabulary used in public discourse on economic policy consists merely of "Keynesianism equals old-style pork barrel politics" and "Neo-Classical economics equals reform." Economic debate among reformists is limited to the choice between "economic growth through deregulation" or "fiscal recovery through higher consumption taxes and downsizing the budget." As long as the DPJ doesn't commit to either policy, economists that narrow the scope of the problem to this limited number of choices will criticize the party for "having no economic policy."

We, as advocates of BI have the potential to expand the debate by filling the gap in the vocabulary used for public discourse with regard to economic policy. We can promote BI as a new Keynesian policy. Before developing this point in full, I would like to present an overview of the BI debate in Japan.

Brief Overview of the History of BI Argument in Japan

If we follow the explanation of history given on the BIEN's (Basic Income Earth Network's) website, it would seem that the idea for a BI first appeared in Europe's Leuvain when Thomas More's *Utopia* was published in 1616. However, if we liberate ourselves from the limitation of focusing solely on European history, an embryo of the BI concept may be found in the sixth-century China and the seventh-century Japan. These ancient East Asian regimes sought to provide the "means of livelihood" in a secular way as a precondition for taxation and military service.

Apart from these historical episodes, modern discussions of BI were introduced into Japan between the World Wars though the translations of John Stuart Mill, Bertrand Russell, and C. H. Douglas. Douglas's "Social Credit" enjoyed popularity at one point. Douglas followers labeled themselves as "Douglasite" economists (artists, etc.) to differentiate themselves from Marxist economists (artists, etc.) but the fad didn't last long.

The radical disabled people's movement of the 1970s developed a similar philosophy to that of the Italian social movements of the same period. Although the Italian movements demanded BI, radical currents in the Japanese disabled movement never settled upon an actual BI. Their demands for social security were ignored at the time and forgotten later. More recently in 1990, Italian social movement expert Toshimaru Ogura called for a BI called an "Individual Wage" but there was not much of a reaction.

The serious academic discussion on BI started a decade ago, among social policy researchers and analytical political philosophers. Among them Shuji Ozawa, a Marxian public economist, published a book on BI in 2002. This can be said to be the first Japanese publication in favor of BI (Ozawa 2002). Several academic publications followed (e.g., Takegawa 2008; Yamamori 2002, 2009).

BI first appeared in the media in the beginning of 2007. I contributed an article to the *Mainichi Newspaper* in April, followed a month later, in May, with an article by Shuji Ozawa in the *Asahi Newspaper*. For radio, the first mention must have been my appearance on the Japan Broadcasting Corporation (NHK) station in January of 2008. In December of that same year, a famous IT entrepreneur, Takafumi Horie, spoke of BI on television after being exposed to debates over BI that welled up on the internet. The blog of Hajime Yamasaki, an economic commentator well known in cyber space, must have played a big role as a catalyst for the debate over BI. Yamasaki himself referenced the BI debate from a publication featuring an exchange between myself and the VOL collective, a group of Autonomia intellectuals. After reading Yamasaki's blog referring to our debate, Horie was moved to write in favor of BI on his own blog and even recommended the idea on a TV show. Since 2010, several satellite television (TV) channels have shed light on BI, including my explanation of BI for 40 minutes at TBS Newsbird, BS news channel by one of major TV channels.

The internet debate over BI is developing with a vocabulary from the neoclassical or neoliberal tradition. There are good discussions around these proposals on the internet. One of the good episodes for letting people know the impact of the internet debate might be an internet TV program in February 2010. This program opened with my lecture, followed by discussion with several neoliberalists and one left-wing activist. Even though this program broadcasted after midnight, it was viewed by 50,000 people. Although I cannot sum up the varied discussions, I can say that their main concern is minimizing the administrative costs of government, rather than ensuring a decent life for the disadvantaged. One could say that the discussion in Japan is in line with the neoliberal rationale. Horie's BI advocacy floats in the currents of neoliberalism.

As far as politicians are concerned, as I mentioned at the beginning of this chapter, MPs in the Democratic Party invited me to speak on BI in April of 2009, and it can be seen as one example of a growing interest in the BI proposal. However, it can be said in general that the political will has progressed no further than just "interest." The exception is one small party "Shinto Nippon." The leader of this party (and the only MP from this party) is a famous writer and is fascinated by the idea of BI. He adopted BI in his party's manifesto in the spring of 2009. Iwao Nakatani, an economist that supported the Koizumi/Takenaka reform track but later changed his position to criticize himself and market fundamentalism, has proposed a very small BI in order to reduce regressive elements of a consumption tax. The majority of the internet discussion and mass media mentions for BI are informed by the neoliberal rationale. You might give them the benefit of the doubt and call it neoliberalism with a human face.

The values informing street-level activism for BI are in sharp contrast to neoliberalism. Some single mothers' organizations and women's trade unions call for a BI with pay equity. Some precariat movements call for BI with regulation for labor protection. There are voices in support of BI in the disabled people's movement also. People suffering from underdevelopment in rural areas have also pinned hopes on a BI. For example, the mayor of Nakagawa Village in Nagano Prefecture has voiced support for BI. A proposal to demand a BI was passed in the Kushiro chapter of the Construction Worker's Union convention of June 2009. These are the voices of marginalized people, long excluded from Japan's "welfare society."

How Can We Make Marginalized Voices Heard?: A Strategy

When the mass media airs the voices of those excluded from Japan's welfare society, the discussion is limited to individual tragedies and almost never expanded to cover economic and social policy issues. The media spent a great deal of time on employment insecurity and unemployment after the financial crisis but the coverage was limited to male workers. In the media, the problem was limited to the "winners" in the "Dual System" of the Japanese welfare society. Only the previously secure men that were no longer able to maintain their positions in the middle class had their grievances aired.

Let me introduce a representative case. On December 18, 2009, the *Mainichi Newspaper*, under the headline, "A Prescription to Cure

Poverty?" featured three viewpoints, an economic policy issue specialist's view, a union activist's view, and my view. The economist felt that Japan no longer had the financial resources to maintain antipoverty measures, and that the main issue was improving the poor economy resulting from the financial crisis. He prescribed monetary easing and deregulation for a more flexible labor market. The union representative prescribed secure employment for middle-aged and older men. The choices were deregulation or secure employment, both sides of the debate shared common ground in that they had only the "winners" of the Japanese welfare society (i.e., male workers) in mind. (It goes without saying that I prescribed BI as a cure for poverty.)

Of course, just as not all of the minorities excluded from Japan's welfare society are demanding BI, the BI is not a cure-all prescription for the problem of poverty. However, promoting the BI as a way to get the majority to consider marginalized voices has three points in its favor. The first two points are vital for minorities and the third point is strategic.

The first point is the need to reexamine Japan's work ethic. Why was Japan unable to become like Sweden or the United Kingdom? As I explained in the first section of this chapter, Japan would seem to have the same welfare structures that are found in the Western countries. Then why, with a similar system in place, does Japan have a mere 20 percent take-up rate for social assistance compared with an almost 90 percent take-up rate in the United Kingdom? This discrepancy is in the difference between the number of people seen by society as being unable to work and the number of people that are actually unable to work. One big reason that Japan was unable to become a full and actually functioning welfare state is that, compared to the West, Japanese society is less accepting of people's inability to work. The BI debate has the potential to interrogate Japan's work ethic.

The second point is that, while the BI discussion is criticized for the potential number of "free riders," this criticism raises the possibility of showing how the Japanese welfare society has, all along, had a free ride on the unpaid work of women.

The third point is strategic and brings me back to the economic policies of the government now headed by the DPJ. The government has explained its policy of cutting back public works such as dam construction while implementing a child allowance with the slogan "Investing in People, not Concrete." While the mass media cheers the decrease in public works projects, the child allowance is criticized as not so much an economic policy but as an attempt to curry favor with voters. While working on the 2010 budget, Hirohisa Fujii, the finance minister at the time, countered this criticism saying that, by increasing demand, the policy would result in changes of industry structure from one that relies on exports to one driven by domestic consumption.

The analysis introduced at the beginning of this chapter that linked the logical outcome of DPJ's policies to the BI proposal was Mitsuharu Ito's attempt to lend support to Finance Minister Fujii's argument. Ito, a well-known Keynesian economist, understands the traditional LDP policies of lowering taxes to increase consumption while increasing overall investment with public spending. Now that the DPJ policies have halted the public works stimulus in favor of "direct support for households" he understands the change as intended to stimulate the economy through increased consumption.

At present, there are not many BI proponents using Keynesian arguments. I (Yamamori 2009) may be the only one using Keynes to support the BI proposal. For the most part, people in Japan think that Keynesian policy and BI proposal are mutually exclusive, and that their proponents are on opposite sides of the economic debate. However, if we turn our eyes abroad to international discussions of BI, many proponents, such as James E. Meade, and more recently Antonio Negri, Andrea Fumagalli, and others have been arguing that the BI would be an effective Keynesian stimulus. Now is a crucial time to explain the Keynesian effects of a BI. The new direction policy has taken in Japan, other than the rare exceptions like Ito's paper, has not been justified for its positive economic effects. Keynesian arguments for a BI may reach the mainstream while providing justifications for this shift in policy.

As the DPJ has yet to fully define this new direction in economic and social policy, we have an opportunity to explain their policies as rational and effective and to push these policies toward the BI proposal. It just may be possible to get "dual society" problems and the BI on the agenda both in the media and in policy-making circles.

Postscript

This chapter was written before the change of prime minister in Japan from Yukio Hatoyama to Naoto Kan, which happened in June 2010. Naoto Kan too seems about to resign shortly because of his depleted reputation resulting from his reaction to the recent earthquake and nuclear accident in Fukushima. In spite of these past and upcoming changes to the "front cover" of the DPJ government, it still has, and will most probably continue to have, a Janus face. For this reason I would not change the bottom line of the chapter. The nuclear accident has the potential to make room for environmentalist arguments in Japan's policy discussions, and to give some credibility to environmentalist lines of justification for

BI, to which I am also committed although I have not mentioned these arguments in this chapter.

Notes

*The first draft of this chapter was translated by Brian Small, a lecturer at Minami-Kyushu University, and a participant in basic income activism in Japan. This research has received support from a grant-in-aid for Scientific Research by Japan Society for the Promotion of Science.

1. http://www.gender.go.jp/data/files/z4–4.pdf.
2. Of course there were criticism and struggles among social movements by minorities themselves such as single mothers' activism (see Yamamori 2010). In academics, see Osawa (1993).
3. This last tendency has been supported by the law that discriminates against children born out of wedlock. This law violates international treaties forbidding this kind of discrimination. But I will not discuss this issue here.
4. http://stats.oecd.org/Index.aspx?datasetcode=SOCX_AGG.
5. Eardley, Bradshaw, Ditch, Gough, and Whiteford (1996), p.35.
6. http://www.oecd.org/dataoecd/12/4/35445297.xls.
7. Lowi criticized this and proposed "judicial democracy." See Lowi (1969).
8. Deregulation and privatization began in the 1980s. However, these policies, which were prior to the Koizumi administration, only happned in the area where these policies could weaken the interests of labor unions, but never happened where they would weaken the interest of DPJ on "Civil-Engineering Keynesianism."
9. Taniguch, Uenohara, and Sakaiya (2009).

References

Eardley, Tony, Jonathan Bradshaw, John Ditch, Ian Gough, and Peter Whiteford. 1996. "Social Assistance in OECD Countries." Department of Social Security Research Report No. 46, London: HMSO.

Ito, Mitsuharu. 2009. "Evaluating Ecnomic Policy of the Hatoyama New Government." *World* December 2009. Tokyo: Iwanami Publishing House.

LDP. 1979. *Japanese Style Welfare Society.* The LDP Public Relation Committee Press.

Lowi, Theodore J. 1969. *The End of Liberalism: Ideology, Policy, and the Crisis of Public Authority.* New York: Norton.

Ozawa, Shuji. 2002. *The Welfare Society and Social Security Reform.* Kyoto: Takasuga Publisher.

Tachibanaki, Toshiaki, and Kunio Urakawa. 2006. *Research of Poverty in Japan.* Tokyo: University of Tokyo Press.

Takegawa, Shogo (ed.). 2008. *Citizenship and the Possibility of Basic Income.* Kyoto: Horitu-Bunka-Sha.

Yamamori, Toru. 2002. "Market, Decomodification and Basic Income." In *Transformation of the Welfare State*, edited by Shogo Takegawa and Koichi Ogasawara, 53–71. Tokyo: Toshindo.

———. 2009. *Beginning Basic Income.* Tokyo: Kobunsha.

———. 2010. "Missing Women: The Forgotton Struggles of Single Mothers for Basic Income." In *Sustainable Utopia and Basic Income in a Global Era*, edited by Basic Income Korea Network, 85–103.

CHAPTER 13

Mexico: The First Steps toward Basic Income

Pablo Yanes

In Mexico, discussion surrounding basic income (BI) is relatively new. It is primarily though far from exclusively situated in academic circles, mainly in the sociopolitical circle, serving as indispensable references when thinking about poverty, inequality, and the transformation of social policy in Mexico. It could be noted that there have been many moments and initiatives that have consolidated this discussion in Mexico: the creation of the universal pension for senior citizens (from 2001 onward), the incorporation of BI as part of the electoral platform of one candidate in 2006, the presentation of two initiatives of law for installing BI nationwide in 2007, and the creation and formal recognition of the Basic Income Earth Network's Mexican chapter in 2008. In 2007 and 2010, two seminars on BI were held in Mexico City.

There is also a public radio program on the matter that has been airing weekly since 2008 and a rural pension for citizens aged 70 and over (*Setenta y Más*). BI is now part of the "Letter for the Right to the City of Mexico City." There have been articles, essays, and books by several experts on the matter. This means that the discussion in Mexico has several dimensions: an academic dimension, a publicity dimension, a political promotion one, a legislative one, and a public policies and programs dimension, which all serve as a practical reference for the BI proposal. That is, having references such as the Mexico City citizen's pension or the federal "*Setenta y Más*" program is a peculiar strong point of the Mexican debate, allowing for the proposal to be easily accepted and understood, though not without challenges.

Programs, Laws, and Debates

Without a doubt, the creation of the citizen's pension in 2001 by Andrés Manuel López Obrador, then Mexico City chief of government, was a watershed moment in the country's design of cash transfer programs. Instead of the dominant logic of conditional cash transfer programs such as *Oportunidades* and Progresa, the citizen's pension established the logic of the universal, individual, and unconditional transfer. Mexico, as a country, was presented as a world example of what should be done: targeted conditional cash transfers, temporary and by household. However, Mexico City opened an alternative path: universal cash transfers, lifelong, unconditional, and individual, with three relevant differences in relation to federal programs—the amount of the transfer, coverage, and judicial status. Under *Oportunidades,* the monthly amount of the transfer is $70, whereas, the citizen's pension amounts to $75 per person over 68 years of age in the household. Under *Oportunidades*, because the programs were so targeted, there were many erroneous exclusions and inclusions, while under the citizen's pension, those errors are by definition zero, except for the inclusion of people who live outside the city but still have proof of residence and exclusion errors relating to a lack of access for the population in question. There are also those who voluntarily exclude themselves from the program. Finally, while *Oportunidades* is a government program that may disappear or shrink at any time, the citizen's pension is recognized as a right within the city's judicial framework, guaranteeing its universality and unconditionality as well as the amount, half a minimum wage a month. The philosophical and axiomatic link between BI and the citizen's pension is now evident. In essence, the pension, which was made a guaranteed right in 2003, is a BI for the city's senior citizens. Rigorously speaking it is "not" a universal BI, because it is not given to the entire population, but for those 68 years of age and over, it acts as BI.

It is pertinent to note this, because during the 2001–2003 debates, between its beginning as a program and its recognition as a right, the main battle that the Mexico City government had to win was regarding the legitimacy of a universal and unconditional transfer. In those years, there were accusations of financial unsustainability, that ten years since have been proven unfounded. Nonetheless, the biggest public objection was regarding the universal and unconditional natures of the program.

There were frequent objections—some echoes can still be heard—that universality was regressive, because it gave a pension to those who did not need it, there were proposals for targeting measures, by income level, by lack of social security, or by level of economic problems in the area of residence. The biggest problem, however, was about its being unconditional, noting that there should be no handouts, that the pension should be in exchange for something; even that the elderly needed work, not pensions. Additionally, there were calls to limit the goods purchasable with the money, saying that beneficiaries should not be allowed to buy cigarettes or liquor with the money, limiting the purchases to basic household goods. Such conditions served to undermine the pension aspects of BI and made children out of senior citizens.

These objections quickly gave way to the logic of universality and unconditionality, however, as there was extensive social appropriation and support from senior citizens and their families. It was so strong that even if recognition as a right was achieved in 2003 with votes coming only from members of the then ruling party, in 2008 the expansion of the pension to those aged 68 and over was approved unanimously by the city legislature. No one abstained, no one voted against it.

Because of this, the pension is a great gateway into the discussion regarding BI and its explanation. In Mexico City, the easiest way of explaining BI is "It's like the senior citizen's pension, but for everyone." It is a kind of BI, a guaranteed income that, as of the end of 2011 covers 520,000 people, 98 percent of the people eligible.

It is worth noting that this income is guaranteed by law, and that in Mexico City since 2003, with reforms made in 2008 there exists a law that guarantees the right to a food pension for those aged 68 or older in the city. It is a law that solidifies one of the most important social policy measures in the city and which is defined by its simplicity and brevity. It is only five articles long:

> **Article 1.** Senior citizens aged sixty years or over in Mexico City are entitled to a daily pension of no less than half the current minimum wage in Mexico City.
>
> **Article 2.** The Chief of Government in the City must include in the Budget Project for Mexico City an amount that guarantees, effectively, the right to a food pension for all the city residents who are aged sixty eight years or older.
>
> **Article 3.** The Legislative Assembly of Mexico City must approve, within the Yearly Budget Decree, an amount sufficient for making the right to a food pension effective.
>
> **Article 4.** The way in which the pension will be made valid will be through an electronic card, which will be created by the Mexico City government, and which will be usable in the main authorized shopping centers and marketplaces of Mexico City. The verification of residence, creation and permanent updating of the beneficiary roster and other needs and necessary procedures for the exercise of the right created in this law will be set in the corresponding guidelines.
>
> **Article 5.** All public servants tasked with the execution of this law who do not fulfill the obligation of acting with the principles of equality and

> impartiality in mind, will be liable for a major sanction and will be punished according to applicable legal procedures.[1]

It is within this context that during the 2006 presidential campaign, Andrés Manuel López Obrador proposed the senior citizen's pension for the entire country. The candidates from other parties made proposals for several other forms of cash transfers for senior citizens. The candidate from the small Social Democrat Alternative Party included BI within her platform, marking the proposal's first appearance within a presidential race.

It should be noted, however, that the proposal went by nearly unnoticed, as other matters captured the attention of the public. Nonetheless, that the proposal was included in a presidential platform was still symbolically relevant.

This context served as a reference for the presentation before the National Congress of two initiatives of law for instituting BI on a national level. One, from the members of the Democratic Revolution Party, was a law establishing the right to BI and another proposal from Elsa Conde, Social Democrat Alternative Party, which aimed to include the right to BI into the nation's constitution. The proposals were as follows:

The Democratic Revolution Party Proposal

> An income of this kind would be assigned with no restrictions nor qualifiers. It would be received regardless of gender, religious affiliation, income level or sexual orientation. Its immediate function would be to counteract two nefarious effects of modern capitalism: extensive misery and massive unemployment. The lack of employment or a low salary would no longer be impediments for the normal subsistence of an individual. The two fundamental characteristics of the basic income idea are universality and unconditionality. Even if it is a modest income, the idea that everyone should receive a universal basic income sufficient for subsisting should hardly leave anyone indifferent.
>
> Said income does not substitute paid work but rather, it creates more choices for citizens. It should also be said that guaranteeing this right is equivalent to recognizing the social importance of unpaid work, volunteer activities and activities that are not for profit. Because of this it is a powerful measure for combating the root of poverty, lessening the terrible inequality that assails us and building citizenship and a new social cohesion.[2]

Among its more relevant articles, it notes that:

> **Article 2.** With no distinction, all inhabitants of the United Mexican States are entitled to Basic Income, which guarantees the meeting of basic needs, the broadening of freedoms, of personal autonomy and access to a dignified living.

Article 3. Basic Income is a demandable right. It consists of an individual cash transfer, unconditional, life long and non-taxable that in no case may be less than half the highest current minimum wage in the country. The amount will be determined every five years and adjusted annually for inflation.

Article 4. In order to receive Basic Income, people with a Mexican nationality will only have to show proof of residing within the United Mexican States. People of other nationalities will have to show proof of having resided within the country for at least five years since the establishment of this law.

Article 5. Basic Income will be instituted in a gradual, progressive and cumulative fashion. Full universality will have to be achieved during a period of no more than three years since the establishment of this law.

Article 6. Effective immediately, federal public administration must begin the transformation of its conditional cash transfer programs into Basic Income. Automatically, all people who are beneficiaries of these programs will instead receive basic income.[3]

The Social Democrat Alternative Proposal:

This initiative has as its aim to establish within our constitution, as a guarantee to the right to equality, Basic Income.

Under the Social-Democratic proposal Basic Income consists of the giving, by part of the State, of a sufficient monetary stipend so that each individual may cover his or her basic needs in education, food, housing and health care. It is unconditional, formally lay, egalitarian, permanent and universal. It is the monetary expression of "Basic Staples Per Capita": Said right aims, simultaneously, to give sustenance to the guarantee of equality and with this to make effective the exercise of the individual guarantees established in our Magna Carta. The proposal has social, political, philosophical, material and moral implications of great importance. It means recognizing the social value of all types of unpaid work, and it rebuilds the collective responsibilities and solidarity of all members of society so that nobody, for the mere fact of existing, lacks the basics. It represents, as Luis Villoro says, the possibility of creating material conditions for a more dignified living for women, young people, senior citizens, and all those who are in a situation of discrimination. It also represents the possibility of creating a society where equality is complemented with freedom, and where the creation of community is harmonized with the unleashing of individual autonomy.[4]

Elsa Conde concludes by proposing an addition to the first article of the Constitution, so that it would read:

As a guarantee of the right to equality that this Constitution grants, every individual will enjoy a basic income. For this, the State will provide a

> monetary stipend which will be sufficient to cover the basic individual needs of education, feeding, health care and housing, ensuring that no individual shall suffer conditions of poverty that impede the development of his or her capabilities. It is a demandable, permanent, unconditional and universal right and it may not be suspended, reduced or denied by anything other than the loss of nationality or by being condemned of a crime that merits the privation of freedom.[5]

Both initiatives, the first to be presented in Mexico for recognizing the right to BI, have neither been discussed nor assessed in Congress. They are not expected to be discussed in the near future, but their value resides in the consistency with which they capture the profound meaning of the proposal, not reducing it to an improved version of conditional transfers, but rather linking it to its emancipatory nature, as it seeks to free people from poverty, from the bindings of social domination and subordination, and its transformational power, its ability to broaden autonomy and freedom. Having the BI proposal reach the highest legislative instance in the country is also symbolically valuable, in a country where it seemed that targeted, temporary, and conditional cash transfers were the only model and the most finished proposal in social policy.

Nevertheless, the debate on BI could be relevant in the 2012 electoral campaign because, in a surprising move, one of the presidential precandidates of one of the main political parties in Mexico, Partido Revolucionario Institucional (PRI), Senator Manlio Fabio Beltrones proposed in October 2011 establishing in Mexico what he called in his social policy proposal a *minimal universal income*. This is the first time in Mexico that a powerful politician not coming from the left wing agrees and endorses the BI option.

Oportunidades Program and Conditional Transfers under Scrutiny

The *Oportunidades* program in Mexico has been presented and promoted by the World Bank and the Inter American Development Bank as the emblematic example of poverty fighting programs and, both institutions, have suggested to the governments in the region that they recreate the program in their own countries. According to the Economic Commission for Latin America and the Caribbean (ECLAC) data, in 2011 there are 18 countries with such programs in Latin America and the Caribbean. It can be said that, with *Oportunidades,* Mexico became an exporter of social technology.[6]

This is neither to say that the program, previously called Progresa, which has been progressively applied in Mexico during the last 11 years does not have positive effects on the incomes of families, especially in the short term, nor that it does not help in improving some social indicators. Because of its continuity and coverage and because of the circulation of resources involved, it would be impossible for this not to be the case.

Instead, the important issue is about deciding whether *Oportunidades* or the Targeted Conditional Cash Transfer Program (TCCTP) is the right way to overcome poverty in a sustained manner. At issue in part is whether central hypotheses and operating assumptions of the program are correct: that poverty is a consequence of a lack of human capital in people; that the poor require conditions and a system of rewards and punishment in order to go to school and take care of their health; and that implementation and operation of the program extends the enjoyment of social rights and builds citizenship.

In 2011, the program had a register of 5.8 million families and a budget of $4.8 billion. On average, each household receives a transfer equivalent to $827 annually or $69 monthly.[7] The amount of support for families varies heavily, but the ceiling, when there are scholarships involved for high school studies, is $203 a month per household. Regardless of the fact that its budget is meaningful, it represents a small fraction of the federal budget, around 1.68 percent.

The program has been modified in recent years, with new components that have partially altered its initial design. In 2005, a $20 transfer for people aged 70 or above was implemented within the context of the "The Countryside Can't Take Any More" mobilization and the impact of the universal senior citizen's pension was introduced in Mexico City, a subject I will address later.

A product of social and political pressure, the introduction of the senior citizen dimension was a large shift, even if targeted and conditional. The main objective of breaking the intergenerational transmission of poverty is the reason why the heart of the program consists of scholarships for children aged between 9 and 21 years. It was no longer about addressing the poverty of today's children, but about today's senior citizens. However, this aspect of the program is considerably reduced due to the existence of a program of transfers for senior citizens called *Setenta y Más* (Seventy and Over).

Likewise, there have been two new modifications in recent years. In 2007, the so-called energy component was added, which consists of a cash transfer to homes in order to compensate spending on energy sources (power, coal, wood, fuel, or candles) that, although it could be included in the nutritional dimension of the program, goes beyond it.

The most important change, however, happened in 2010. A new transfer was added, called *Apoyo Infantil Vivir Mejor* (Live Better Child

Support) which consists of a small monthly transfer of little over $8 for every child between zero and nine years of age, with a ceiling of three transfers per family. This transfer, even if it is very small, alters the idea of a program built on the logic of increasing human capital, understood fundamentally as an increase in school enrollment.

Until the year 2010, the cash incentives in *Oportunidades* began in the third grade and nine years of age. This had been strongly criticized as it was noted that the families with the youngest children, those between zero and five years old, are those with the most need for support, but the response was that the program could not be built on incentives for increasing birth rates, assuming that, given a cash incentive, the poor would have more children in order to get more transfers.

It can be said that the refusal to support families with very young children is based more on prejudice than on scientific evidence. However, as the world financial crisis started in 2008 and its acute manifestation as a food crisis amongst poor families, the federal government in Mexico decided to alter the policy and added transfers for children from birth to nine years old.

Oportunidades, without renouncing its nature of conditional and targeted transfers, has had to introduce adjustments that modify its initial concept of only catering to school-age children, of having as a strategic objective of breaking the intergenerational transmission of poverty, and of only granting transfers for children aged 9 to 22. Because of the social and political dynamic, the program now involves children under 9 and adults over 70 years, first within *Oportunidades* and later through *Setenta y Más.*

Both new programs have sizable budgets. In the case of *Apoyo Infantil Vivir Mejor*, the budget exceeds $649.0 million and regarding senior citizens, through *Setenta y Más,* the budget reaches $1.1 billion. Both new components, small children and senior citizens, make up about 25 percent of the program's budget.

The case of *Setenta y Más* is very interesting because it expresses the transition from an individually targeted and conditional program to a territorial targeted program that has no conditions. By 2010, the program had incorporated a little over 2.3 million people in rural areas and small cities. And in the proposed federal budget for 2011 the federal government is asking the Congress to increase the resources for this program by 62 percent. That means around $5.5 billion more. If the Congress agrees *Setenta y Más* will become one of the biggest cash transfers programs in Mexico and Latin America.

That is quite relevant because, as we have seen, the philosophical bases of *Setenta y Más* are closer to the universal and unconditional approach than to the traditional targeted, means tested, and conditional characteristics of *Oportunidades* and the Conditional Cash Transfer (CCT) programs in Latin America.

Rigorously speaking, *Setenta y Más* was not a program designed by the federal government, but decided from within Congress as a response to the peasant mobilizations that demanded a rural pension. It is a program with universal coverage for all people over 70 years of age residing in localities of up to 30,000 inhabitants and, contrary to *Oportunidades*; it has no coresponsibilities or conditions. *Setenta y Más* is a large program in both coverage and resources whose purpose is to keep growing by increasing the size of the locations where it applies. It receives neither the attention nor the publicity that *Oportunidades* does. Both programs suggest that Mexico through the *Secretaría de Desarrollo Social* (Ministry of Social Development) has different paths for transfer policies, that it is possible to go from a model of individual targeting to territorial targeting as a halfway point toward universality and from conditional transfers to unconditional transfers.

Policy Challenges and Paradoxes of *Oportunidades* and *Setenta y Más*

In order to understand the tension inside the federal government's Ministry of Social Development due to the parallel existence of two models for cash transfers, it's useful to compare the operational rules of *Oportunidades* and *Setenta y Más*.

An examination of such rules[8] for the two programs allows one to see, for instance in the chapter on the obligations of beneficiary families,[9] that women are actually charged with additional duties when responsibility is shifted to the families. Far from transforming traditional gender roles, this reinforces them. This can be seen in the following obligations: "Support the scholarship holders in primary education so that they regularly attend class and take better advantage of their education."[10] It is a very vague meaning, to support them so that they attend class, but it is a very delicate thing to make families, understood to be the mother, and responsible for the improvement of schooling, which should be the objective and sole responsibility of the school system and not, essentially, the mother's obligation.

In the same way, it is noteworthy that another obligation is, "Support the scholarship holders in secondary education so that they assist both class and the community workshops on health self-care and to participate in a dynamic manner in activities that mark both the plans and programs of study in each federal entity."[11] It is curious at the least to know that somebody can have the obligation of making young people "dynamic manner in activities that mark both the plans and programs of study" when in reality the subject has more to do with the real offer, the quality, the relevance, and the attractiveness of the education offered to young people.

Likewise, it is stated in the same chapter that another obligation is to "Receive and consume nutritional supplements delivered at the health-care unit for children and pregnant women who are breastfeeding" (Dario Oficial de la Federación 2010: 30). This establishes the amazing obligation of having to consume the supplements that are delivered regardless of will, taste, or flavor.

There is also an obligation with respect to senior citizens that remains in *Oportunidades* rather than in *Setenta y Más*. The obligation consists of "Delivering to the senior citizens the monetary support intended for them" (Dario Oficial de la Federación 2010: 30). As the mother of the small children in the home is, usually, the titular of the transfers in *Oportunidades*, the absurd situation of the money intended for the senior citizens being delivered to the daughter who in turn must deliver it to the senior citizen, ensues. This introduces a lamentable relationship of power within the family nucleus in which the senior citizen is rendered child-like and has no direct access to resources that are her/his by right, and so depends completely on the intervention of the daughter.

Even worse, according to the same operational rules, the support is definitively terminated when "the senior citizen leaves the household" (Dario Oficial de la Federación 2010: 33). So, the possibility of an independent life or at least a separate house is negated. The senior citizen under *Oportunidades* must get her/his support from her/his daughter and will definitively lose it should she/he live in a different home.

This serves to illustrate the contrast between being a senior citizen under *Oportunidades* and under *Setenta y Más*, two federal transfer programs aimed at the same group of people. In the first case, the citizen receives a $25 monthly transfer, in the second, it is $40. In the first program, there are conditions, in the second, there are none. In the first one, she/he must get the money through her/his daughter, in the second she/he gets it directly. In the first program, she/he loses her/his income if she/he leaves the household, in the second one she/he loses it only if she/he moves to a location with over 30,000 inhabitants.

In addition to the central matter of the link between schooling, education, and income, *Oportunidades* or TCCTP also suffer from very important vulnerabilities in their aim to combat poverty and break its intergenerational transmission. Amongst them there are: the exclusion errors that are part of all targeted programs, *ex post* intervention only for the identified poor and thus, a lack of a preventive dimension to keep at risk population from becoming poor. It assumes that the fight against poverty is a straight line, and those who leave it never come back and thus, the policies and programs ignore those who go over the line or threshold of poverty.

However, one of the largest vulnerabilities is the dependence on the effect and impact of these programs on the evolution of the economic cycle. They are procyclical programs that get results, mostly modest ones, in the growth phase of the economic cycle and lose, in one or two years of crisis, all that was gained in the previous years. Seen as midterm trends we cannot say that in Mexico and *Oportunidades*, we have reached a firm and sustained tendency that has found points of no return in the fight against poverty.

There is, on the contrary, more of a roller coaster dynamic, with slow ascents and sudden falls that negate a firm and sustained diminution of poverty. It seems more to head in the direction of a more sustained diminution in the intensity of poverty. That is, the lasting effect is that the poor are less poor, but there are no fewer poor, and the fall into poverty is an ever present danger that is highly dependent on the economic cycle.

Policy Alternatives to *Opportunidades* and *Setenta y Más*

I have highlighted that, in the case of Mexico, at the federal level there are two coexisting models for cash transfers expressed in the existence of the two relevant programs because of the size of the funds they administer and the coverage they reach: *Oportunidades* and *Setenta y Más*. The aforementioned paradoxes and challenges suggest that the time is right for consideration of policy alternatives, models of which can be seen in Mexico at local levels of government and in other countries.

In the case of Mexico, as we have seen, the Mexico City government has a law, signed in 2003 and reformed in 2008 that establishes, as a right, a universal citizen's pension for all citizens over the age of 68 that have lived in the city for the last three years. It is an unconditional transfer that, by law, cannot be less than half a monthly minimum wage. Currently, the pension is equivalent to $75 per person and reaches 520,000 people. Likewise, in Bolivia, the government of Evo Morales built the *Renta Dignidad*, which is also a universal unconditional pension for those over 60 years of age and is financed partly from the income from hydrocarbon sales. Such policies indicate that in Latin America not all programs are *Oportunidades* or TCCTP by design. In this context, it is relevant that ECLAC, in its recent report "Time for Equality: closing gaps—opening trails,"[12] proposes the need to advance toward a system of redistributive citizen cash transfers with an emphasis on homes with small children, senior citizens, and the unemployed.[13]

ECLAC argues that:

> There are, on the other hand, good reasons to defend a basic system of partial guaranteed incomes. The first, as has been previously mentioned, is the equality of social rights that concerns the citizens. The homes that face situations of exogenous shock or biographical changes and that are affected by poverty and vulnerability tend to be de-capitalized beyond the effect of the shock, precisely because they lack guaranteed minimums, or at least instruments that softer the flow of income in the face of adverse situations. In practical terms, and even more in ethical terms, avoiding the collapse of the economies of homes that represent a good part of the population and Latin American production is as necessary as avoiding the collapse of the financial systems (by subsidizing its deficiencies).
>
> (ECLAC 2010: 208)

It is fundamental to frame the discussion in other terms so that it is not the logic of emancipation without poor with obligations but rather citizens with rights and free of poverty that can be opened. Such reframing would also facilitate that social policy—and particularly cash transfers—ceases to be an instrument of social control and becomes an instrument of citizenship building.

It is thus evident that the debate regarding the best way to carry out income transfers to the population is, at its heart, political and axiomatic—and not technical as it is often presented. More precisely, it is a debate regarding the content and manner of executing the rights of the citizenry. And it is this dispute where the BI proposal, which is starting to make inroads in Latin America and other regions, separates itself from the TCCTP. The BI initiative, by being unconditional, universal, guaranteed, individual, and lifelong is shown to be a powerful alternative as it overcomes the problems derived from inclusion and exclusion errors common to targeting; it centers on the person and not on families; and it permits the reordering of social relations based on the expansion of autonomy and individual freedoms.

By implying an important movement of resources, BI would force progressive fiscal reforms that would imply important redistributive processes. Likewise, BI constitutes the way to overcome poverty, not only contain it or diminish it in small or transitory proportions and, above all, it creates a preventive dimension so that those that cease to be poor do not fall back into poverty.

Because of the amounts that BI would involve, it would constitute an effective material support that will permit people to meet basic needs and make long-range plans, even lifelong projects. Because it would be a right, a social guarantee, the dimension of citizenship would be broadened and people could escape the vices of patronage, insecurity, and uncertainty that are common with TCCTP.

Beyond all of this, in the BI initiative there is a proposal for a society and a concept of rights of citizenship that is different from that of the TCCTP. It is not only a technically powerful proposal in effects and results, it is not only an alternative course of action for current social policies and poverty fighting policies (although it also is that), but rather it is part of an emancipation project that seeks to end the social subordination derived from material dependence and the incapability of having a guaranteed material existence. It is because of this that the BI initiative is inscribed within the movement of emergent human rights.[14]

Building Popular Support for BI in Mexico

In such a context, the broadcasting for three years now of a weekly radio show dedicated to BI in Mexico has been an important experience. As Makieze Medina, the shows cohost, has noted, in the almost 160 shows to have been aired since October 2008, the BI proposal has been promoted, this is, an unconditional and universal transfer guaranteed by the state to every member of a territory with the aim of guaranteeing a minimum material income that allows for a dignified living.

The radio show has allowed for an advancement in the promotion of the proposals that have been built on an international level and, fundamentally, those for implementing BI in Mexico, which have been elaborated by academics, public servants, legislators, researchers, leaders, and activists from civil society. That is, it has become a platform for analysis and diffusion for the BI proposal, making it an innovative proposal in the context of BIEN. Likewise, it has served as a bridge with the most diverse demands and movements from popular, civil, social, human rights, and other organizations.

It is also important to note that in 2010, a document entitled "Carta de la Ciudad de México por el Derecho a la Ciudad" (Letter from Mexico City for the Right to the City) was created in Mexico City. It was created by a broad group of civil and social organizations and signed by the chief of government, Marcelo Ebrard. It is not a judicially binding document, but rather a programmatic platform that the chief of government and all signatory organizations proposed as the basis for the (future) creation of the city's Constitution.

The document includes a great many points, one of which is "promoting the establishment of basic income." The importance of this inclusion resides in making the demand for BI part of the political agenda for social movements, and being part of the construction process of and agenda and, in due course, of the discussion and creation of the city's Constitution. It is, in consequence a modest, yet, relevant step.

After the First Steps Come the Most Difficult Ones

There is no doubt that compared with the landscape from a few years ago when the proposal was still a practical unknown, barely recognized, and viewed as a non viable and oddball proposal, the country has come a long way.

Today BI is a proposal that is known, discussed, and debated in public policy debate forums. There are more or less frequent references in the press and in some other media, two initiatives of law, one a constitutional reform, and the other waiting for a hearing in Congress. Further, there are two high coverage social programs that are more or less close to the BI perspective, the senior citizens' pension and the federal *Setenta y Más* program.

These last two programs, and especially the Mexico City one, as it has been instituted as a right, have opened up the possibility of debating BI. Mexico City has made a large contribution by having given legitimacy and a new conceptual place to some principles that seemed to have been defeated in social policy: universality, unconditionality, and permanence. These principles are components of the pension created in Mexico City during the last ten years and are also fundamental concepts in BI. It can even be said that the battle has been won on a national level and today, it seems viable that in the short term the senior citizens' pension can be extended to a national level. The rapid growth of *Setenta y Más* seems to point in this direction.

However, the leap from such pensions to BI is a profound transformation whose social legitimacy is yet to be established, and whose material base and thus, its viability still depend on radical modifications of the tax structure that are not yet imminent unless a new political coalition, with the possibility of ruling the state and affecting the great interests that keep the Mexican State in a condition of fiscal destitution, emerges.

I wish to stress, however, the large cultural battle must still be waged in order to propose true BI. Seen in perspective, it was relatively simple to build social legitimacy for the social pension for senior citizens. The proposal met some resistance initially, but this was rapidly overcome, although it probably won't be as easy with a proposal for people who are still of age for work.

At the core, the debate was around pensions and not BI itself. It was assumed that senior citizens had the right to a social pension due to having worked all of their lives, for having contributed to society and, in the case of women, as retribution for all of the domestic work done for so many years. It is still hard to accept that people are entitled to an income when they are still in their productive years.

There is still strong opposition to the idea of an income that is not linked—and yet complementary to—activities in the labor market. The idea that income can only be derived from paid work or self-employment is still culturally very powerful. In very broad social sectors and overwhelmingly so among the organized political forces the central idea is still rooted in the Bible: he who does not work does not eat and you shall earn your bread with the sweat from your brow.

Because of this, it is highly feasible that the idea of BI continues to advance through unconditional universal transfers for social groups outside the so-called (labor market) productive years, or that are somehow limited in their ability to join the workforce. It is very feasible that in the coming years in Mexico, the expansion of income derived from public transfers, more or less close to BI, will focus on broadening the rights of senior citizens, for example, lowering the age for the pensions (as already happened in Mexico City, where the age has been dropped to 68 years, or as in the most populous delegation in the city, Iztapalapa, where the age was reduced to 65 years, although at a lower amount), broadening the reach and coverage of *Setenta y Más* in rural areas and taking it to urban areas or creating unconditional transfers for people with disabilities, creating a BI for children and teenagers, or broadening protection programs with monetary transfers for the unemployed. It may even be possible to make the conditions in *Oportunidades* more flexible.

There is the risk, however, that the current process of expansion of coverage for public transfers stops and that a great transfer system covering broad social sectors but still limited to poverty or certain age groups is created. It seems that the main challenge in Mexico will not be to expand the programs that are close to BI but limited to certain social groups but rather to broaden the debate. Such debate would be about the desirability of a true BI, instead of a fragmented society, where on the one hand are those with a guaranteed income outside of paid work, and on the other, those still in their productive years who will have no other income, in the middle of the crisis facing the wage society. This will likely be the most profound debate facing the Mexican society in the coming years.

Thus, it is very feasible for public transfers to continue their process of expansion and that they continue, as I have pointed out, to broaden the extent of resources that will be the material base for BI in Mexico, and to strengthen the legitimacy within society of this kind of income and transfer, with which the eventual implementation of BI appears as a necessary, logical step. In this way, BI could be paradoxically reached through universal, but targeted, transfers, through a long detour that would start with age groups and progressively expand, that is, by stealth.

Notes

1. GACETA OFICIAL DEL DISTRITO FEDERAL (FEDERAL DISTRICT OFFICIAL GAZETTE). 18 de Noviembre de 2008. Distrito Federal, México.
2. Proyecto De Ley Sobre El Ingreso Ciudadano Universal En México (Project of Law on Basic Income in Mexico). Salón de sesiones de la Comisión Permanente, a 4 de julio de 2007. Partido de la Revolución Democrática. Mimeo, México, p. 2.
3. Ibid., pp. 7–8.
4. Iniciativa Con Proyecto De Decreto Por El Que Se Adiciona El Tercer Párrafo Del Articulo Primero De La Constitución Política De Los Estados Unidos Mexicanos A Cargo De La Diputada Elsa Conde Rodríguez, Del Grupo Parlamentario De Alternativa Socialdemócrata (Initiative with a project for a decree that adds to the third article of the Constitution of the United Mexican States, under the care of the Congresswoman Elsa Conde Rodriguez, from the Social Democrat Alternative Parliamentary Group), Palacio Legislativo de San Lázaro, Ciudad de México, México. 27 de abril de 2009. Mimeo, pp. 1–2.
5. Ibid., pp. 15–16.
6. Many of the following ideas were originally developed in my essay "Mexico's Targeted and Conditional Transfers," published in *Economic and Political Weekly*, May 21–27, 2011, Mumbai, India. I really appreciate the permission to use it.
7. All calculations are based on an exchange rate of 12 Mexican pesos for one American dollar.
8. *Diario Oficial de la Federación* (2010): "*Reglas de Operación del Programa de Desarrollo Humano Oportunidades*" (Operational Rules for the Oportunidades Human Development Program), December 31.
9. Ibid., p. 30.
10. Ibid.
11. Ibid.
12. ECLAC (2010): "*La hora de la igualdad. Brechas por cerrar, caminos por abrir*"(Time for Equality: closing gaps—opening trails*)* Thirty-Third ECLAC Session Period, Brasilia, Brazil. May 30–June 1.
13. Ibid., pp. 208–222.
14. In November of 2007, within the framework of the Forum of the Cultures held in Monterrey, México, a declaration titled "Declaración Universal de los Derechos Humanos Emergentes" ("Emerging Human Rights Universal Declaration") was approved. In the third point or its first article reads as follows: "The right to basic income which assures all the individual, independently of their age, sex, sexual orientation, civil status or employment status, the right to live under

worthy material conditions. To such end, the right to an unconditional, regular, monetary income paid by the state and financed by fiscal reforms, is recognised as a right of citizenship, to each resident member of society, independently of their other sources of income, and being adequate to allow them to cover their basic needs."

References

Diario Oficial de la Federación (*Official Journal of the Federation*). 2010. "Reglas de Operación del Programa de Desarrollo Humano Oportunidades" (*Operational Rules for the Oportunidades Human Development Program*). December 31.

ECLAC. 2010. "La hora de la igualdad. Brechas por cerrar, caminos por abrir" (*Time for Equality: closing gaps—opening trails*). Thirty-Third ECLAC Session Period, Brasilia, Brazil. May 30–June 1.

ECLAC Social Development Division of the Economic Commission for Latin America and the Caribbean, Noncontributive social program database in Latin America and the Caribbean 2010. Available at, http://dds.cepal.org/bdptc/.

CHAPTER 14

The United Kingdom: Only for Children?

Malcolm Torry[*]

The United Kingdom already has an unconditional and nonwithdrawable income—for children. I shall therefore tell the story of how Family Allowance came about, how it became Child Benefit, and how it fares today; and at each stage of the story I shall seek reasons for why things happened as they did. Beyond hearings by parliamentary committees, there has been no legislative process relating to an unconditional and nonwithdrawable income for every adult citizen, but during the early 1970s there was an attempt to legislate a Tax Credits scheme that bore some resemblance to a Negative Income Tax. I shall draw lessons from that attempt. The Tax Credits proposal of the early 1970s should not be confused with the last Labour government's means-tested wages supplement, which it erroneously and confusingly called "Tax Credits." I shall then study parliamentary committee discussions of universal benefits for adults and a recent proposal for something like a citizen's pension; and finally I shall discuss the factors that might determine whether the United Kingdom will ever legislate for a Citizen's Income (CI).

Child Benefit is not the only universal aspect of the welfare state in the United Kingdom. In 1948, the previous patchwork of charitable, local authority, insurance-based– and private health care provision was subsumed into the state-run National Health Service (NHS). The ways in which the NHS is organized have changed since then, and they are still changing, but the service still offers high-quality health care, is very good value for money, and is still free at the point of use. No government that wished to be reelected would change that. Until the 1950s, prescriptions, dental care, false teeth, and spectacles were free. That is now the case for selected groups only, but visits to a general practitioner, stays in hospital, and all inpatient and outpatient treatment remain free. The NHS is a rare and remarkable example of universality.

Education in state-run schools is free; pensioners over 75 years old get free television licenses; schoolchildren used to receive free milk at school; and everyone on any kind of state pension receives the same winter fuel payment.

While important, none of these universal aspects of the United Kingdom's welfare state will be the subject of this chapter. What this chapter *will* be about is universal cash benefits, whether paid to a demographic group, such as children, or to every citizen.

Terminology

Spicker defines "universal benefits" as "given to whole categories of a population, like children or old people, without other tests" (Spicker 2011: 117); but this leaves open the question as to whether contribution records that determine the level of payments count as a "test." In this chapter, I shall take "universal benefits" to mean "unconditional and nonwithdrawable cash payments made to every individual citizen as a right of citizenship." Child Benefit is not universal in this sense because it is restricted to children, but otherwise it fits the definition because equal amounts are paid to every main carer of the same number of children regardless of that carer's income, employment status, household structure, or any other factor. There is another sense in which Child Benefit is not universal: a main carer only receives Child Benefit for a child up to 19 years of age if that child remains in full-time education—so, strictly speaking the benefit is only universal for children below the statutory minimum school leaving age. Michael Hill prefers to call Child Benefit a "contingent" benefit because only children receive it (Hill 1990: 82–83), but I shall call it "universal" because every child who fulfills certain residence requirements gets it unconditionally and nonwithdrawably.

In the context of this book, a more important terminological point is that in the UK context, we need to avoid "guarantee" language. There are two reasons for this:

1. The previous government enacted a "Minimum Income Guarantee," later called a "Guarantee Credit" (Spicker 2011: 80), for pensioners: a means-tested payment to bring their household income up to a prescribed level. This is as far from a universal benefit as it is possible to get.
2. The academic literature uses the term "minimum income guarantee" for a prescribed level of net income to which a household is raised by a payment dependent on the level of earned income. For

instance, James Meade formulates his Modified Social Dividend proposal in terms of a universal benefit (a "Social Dividend") and an additional means-tested payment to bring an individual up to a "minimum income guarantee" (Meade 1978: 269–279).

In the United Kingdom, the normal term for an unconditional, non-withdrawable income for every citizen is a "CI" or a "Basic Income." In English as used in the United Kingdom, the word "basic" can have derogatory overtones, so in this chapter I shall employ the CI terminology. (I shall leave to one side the important questions as to whether children are, can be, or should be, regarded as citizens. For the purposes of this chapter, they are citizens.)

"Allowance" is another word over which care needs to be taken. "Child allowance," "family allowance," or simply "allowance," refer to payments made (in the case of child allowances, on behalf of the child to the main carer). "Income Tax allowance" refers to an amount of earned income on which tax is not levied, tax only being levied on income above the "tax threshold."

Eleanor Rathbone's Family Endowment Society

The early history of social security benefits in the United Kingdom is one of a locally administered means test. The more recent history is mainly one of social insurance benefits topped up by means-tested benefits and increasingly replaced by them. The single universal benefit, Child Benefit, which evolved from Family Allowance, is therefore significant.

In 1796, the prime minister, William Pitt, wanted to make benefits "where there are a large number of children a matter of right and honour, instead of a ground for opprobrium and contempt. This will make the large family a blessing, and not a curse" (Macnicol 1980: 4). It did not happen, but in 1909, the chancellor of the exchequer, Lloyd George, established child tax allowances. During the First World War, the amount paid to a serviceman's family at home included an amount for each child. Those payments continued for six months on demobilization. In 1918, Beatrice Webb, a significant social commentator, called for the payments to continue beyond that point (Macnicol 1980: 5–10). During the 1890s, the Independent Labour Party had called for the "endowment" of motherhood (Thane 1996: 63–64), and Seebohm Rowntree, on the basis of his survey of poverty in York, had proposed a national minimum wage sufficient for a family with three children, and child allowances for the fourth and subsequent children. In this context, Eleanor Rathbone's 1911 pamphlet suggesting that children were society's responsibility, and her 1917 argument that a man's wage could not be expected to support a large family, contained nothing new. What *was* new was her establishment in 1917 of the Family Endowment Society, and then of the Children's Minimum Council, to pursue the cause of payments to mothers to enable them to care for their children (Macnicol 1980: 10, 20–23; Thane 1996: 202).

In 1924, Rathbone wrote *The Disinherited Family*, questioning the wisdom of expecting the same wage to be adequate for every family, whatever its size, especially as there was always a question over how much of a man's wage reached his wife. Rathbone discussed other countries' child allowances and the possibility of occupational schemes, and called for a universal state scheme in order to reduce class envy (Rathbone 1986 [1924]: 139, 167, 353).

William Beveridge and His Report

William Beveridge wrote this in his epilogue to the 1949 edition of *The Disinherited Family*: "I suffered instant and total conversion" (William Beveridge as cited in Rathbone 1949: 270). He had read the book in 1924, when he was director of the London School of Economics (LSE). In 1925, Beveridge chaired a Royal Commission on the mining industry and recommended child allowances, paid by employers, as a way of both providing for miners' families and not increasing the general level of wages. The general strike intervened and the moment was lost, but not at the LSE, where child allowances were soon being paid.

In 1934, Beveridge was asked to sit on the Unemployment Insurance Statutory Committee, which reported on the state of the Contributory Unemployment Benefit schemes fund. Child allowances were paid with unemployment benefits, which concerned Beveridge, as it meant that when someone returned to employment on low wages they could suffer a loss of income if they had a large family. Child allowances for every child was the only solution (Beveridge in Rathbone 1949: 271), so when Beveridge was asked to chair an interdepartmental committee on the future of social insurance, he was already sure that child allowances should be recommended in the report. The fact that universal benefits were not part of his brief did not perturb him: he simply made child allowances an assumption on which the rest of the report's findings were based (Beveridge 1942: 154).

The reasons that Beveridge gave for assuming child allowances were that they would achieve a national minimum for families, that income out of work would not be higher than income in work, and that a decline in the birth rate would be arrested (Beveridge 1942: 154). Rathbone would have wanted the emancipation of women from dependence on men in the list of reasons, but it was not, though another of her arguments had persuaded Beveridge: that a child allowance was "an expression of the community's direct interest in children" (Beveridge 1942: 155).

Beveridge based his report on *three* assumptions:

1. Full employment
2. Everyone "will be covered for comprehensive medical treatment and rehabilitation and for funeral expenses"
3. "Children's allowances, which will be paid from the National Exchequer in respect of all children when the responsible parent is in receipt of insurance benefit or pension, and in respect of all children except one in other cases" (Beveridge, 1942: 10: cf. 158, 163, 177)

It is surely significant that two of the three foundations that Beveridge thought essential to his social insurance edifice are universal benefits.

Beveridge argued that child allowances should be universal because "little money can be saved by any reasonable income test" (Beveridge 1942: 157), and that adjustments to child tax allowances could ensure that wealthier people would receive no net benefit from child allowances. The chancellor of the exchequer agreed that a flat-rate- and universal payment would be cheap to administer and were therefore desirable (Land 1975: 193). Beveridge wanted the child allowances to be paid "at rates averaging 8/- a week" (Beveridge 1942: 177). (8/- means 8s.: Until 1971, there were 20s. to the pound and 12d. to the shilling, so 8s. would have been equivalent to 40p if today's currency had been in use then). Beveridge had to compromise and to agree not to pay an allowance for the first child in order to achieve this figure: but the Family Allowances Act of 1945 stipulated a payment of just 5s. [25p]. The Treasury achieved another victory: Family Allowance rather than child allowance prevailed. The chancellor had argued that child allowance would lead to the argument that sufficient should be paid to maintain a child, whereas Family Allowance could be an allowance to assist in the support of a family, and no one would expect the government to pay all of a family's subsistence costs (Macnicol 1980: 193). What survived the debate was the universality of the payment, and in 1945, the Family Allowance Act was passed with all party support.

The Family Allowance Act 1945: Why Did It Happen?

As Hilary Land suggests: "In three years family allowances had gained the attention and the interest of the government that twenty years of campaigning by the Family Endowment Society had failed to achieve" (Land 1975: 195). Here are just some of the reasons for that success:

1. *Poverty in large families*: The argument that the wage system did not and could not provide for the subsistence needs of large families had become widely accepted, and the 1930s had provided plenty of surveys of poverty that Rathbone could publicize (Macnicol 1980: 93). She and her Family Endowment Society had taken every opportunity, in and out of Parliament, to make the point that only child allowances could keep large families out of poverty, and the argument had finally been accepted by policymakers.
2. *Opposition from trades unions had melted away*: In 1928 and 1929, the Trade Union Congress (TUC) had discussed child allowances but had decided that it preferred child tax allowances: not surprisingly, given that most members of trades unions were men, that wage-earning men benefited from child tax allowances, and that their wives might benefit from child allowances. The 1930 TUC conference accepted from a working party the *minority* report, which advocated child tax allowances rather than child allowances (Land 1975: 169).

   The next time the TUC discussed child allowances was during the Second World War. By then, more women were members of trades unions, and there were Labour ministers in the coalition government. The TUC therefore felt less isolated. The Labour Party had called both for child allowances and for a living wage, and had recognized that no realistic living wage would be able to keep large families out of poverty without child allowances being paid, particularly during the war. At its 1941 conference, the TUC found itself more favorable toward the idea of family allowances (Thane 1996: 226).
3. *Population decline*: In 1936, the government's Population Investigation Committee had expressed concern about the falling birth rate, as it could foresee a growing elderly population with too few younger adults to do the necessary work. The need to maintain the birth rate in all social classes, and not just amongst the poor, argued for universal rather than means-tested child allowances (Land 1975: 173).
4. *The state of young adults*: Army recruitment officers had expressed concern about the state of health of young adults, and child allowances were seen as a means of ensuring that the next generation would be better nourished (Land 1975: 174).
5. *Disincentives in the labor market*: Beveridge was particularly keen to ensure that someone in work did not experience net income

less than someone not in employment with the same size family. Only child allowances for those in work could achieve that (Thane 1996: 228). Larger tax allowances could *not* achieve it because the low paid often did not earn enough to benefit from their existing tax allowances (Land 1975: 196).

6. *Fear of inflation*: Economist John Maynard Keynes was an unpaid advisor to the cabinet during the Second World War. A major aim was controlling inflation, which was achieved through price controls and rationing. Wage control remained voluntary (Thane 1996: 225–226), but there was concern that after the war wages might rise rapidly as price controls eased. Keynes argued for child allowances as a way of keeping large families out of poverty without wages having to rise (Macnicol 1980: 176).
7. *A better Britain*: Members of the different political parties continued to offer the arguments that we might expect: the Conservatives that the government should not interfere in a family's financial arrangements, and some Labour members of Parliament (MPs) that child allowances were a means of keeping wages low; but a general desire for a new start after the war meant that a comprehensible policy such as child allowances could gain considerable approval both across party lines in Parliament and among the general public. The fact that child tax allowances increased the incomes of the wealthy more than they increased those of the poor was beginning to be understood, and child allowances were beginning to look more in tune with the kind of country in which people wanted to live once the war was over (Land 1975: 179).

The Parliamentary Debate

The 1943 parliamentary debate on Beveridge's report was rather fraught, and the Conservatives' opposition to its ideas might well have been one of the reasons for their defeat in the general election of 1945; but the child allowances assumption underlying the report attracted widespread support (Land 1975: 205). The Treasury then employed delaying tactics (Macnicol 1980: 191), but in 1945, the Family Allowances Act was passed.

An important question raised during the debate was whether the allowance should be paid to the father or to the mother. Rathbone threatened to vote against the Act if the allowances were paid to the father, a free vote was offered, and the amendment to pay the allowance to the mother was passed (Land 1975: 221; Macnicol 1980: 193). The first Family Allowances were paid on August 6, 1946.

A significant aspect of the debate in Parliament was that there was little discussion of the *objectives* of child allowances (Land 1975: 221).

This might have been because each MP could find something to like in child allowances (whether the relief of poverty, the suppression of wages, the reduction of labor-market disincentives, or possibly for some Conservatives a hope that to increase working-class incomes might increase their share of the vote at the next general election): but they all knew that other members had very different reasons for wanting them and didn't want to risk a fractious debate that might risk losing child allowances. The government's aim was to keep wages down (Macnicol 1980: 172, 202). It certainly was not to improve the status of women.

In her biography of Eleanor Rathbone, Mary Stokes writes,

> Family Allowances...could be approached from so many directions, with such an infinite variety of emphasis and application. It could be handled as a problem of vital statistics, housing administration, minimum wage legislation, child nutrition, national insurance, teachers' salary scales, coal-mining economics, feminism, social philosophy or pure finance. That is perhaps one reason why Eleanor's handling of it never became...tedious by repetition.
>
> (Mary Stokes' [1949] *Eleanor Rathbone: A Biography* quoted in Freeman 1998: 2)

This insight offers us a clue to Rathbone's success in getting child allowances onto the statute book. She was able to persuade individuals and groups of the advantages of the idea in relation to their own interests. Child allowances were part of the solution to a wide variety of problems: hence, a level of support could be built which was able to submerge objections from trades unions, and also the generally unspoken objection that child allowances paid to the mother would reduce her dependence on the father (Land 1975: 227).

Crucial were two particular conversions, Beveridge's and Keynes'. Beveridge saw that child allowances would reduce disincentives in the labor market, and Keynes that they would help to keep inflation under control (Land 1975: 227).

So why did Family Allowances happen? The reasons are as follows:

1. Persistent campaigning over a long period of time
2. One good book
3. Accidental convergence of different interests on a single policy change
4. Two crucial conversions

The only connection with reducing inequality and empowering women was that these were amongst *Rathbone's* aims. They were essential to the process because they motivated her.

The Rediscovery of Poverty during the 1960s, and the Birth of Child Benefit

Beveridge eventually got his National Insurance Acts passed in 1946, and in 1948, a National Assistance Act was passed to provide means-tested benefits for people with insufficient contributions records. However, National Insurance benefits were generally paid at levels below National Assistance levels, largely because National Assistance took into account housing costs and National Insurance benefits did not. The United Kingdom, therefore, found itself still mired in a largely means-tested system (Atkinson 1969: 24). The situation was not helped by government neglect of Family Allowances, which by 1960 were paying only 8s. [40p] per week for the second child and 10s. [50p] per week for each subsequent child in a family (Townsend 1979: 162–163). By the mid-1960s, this was a serious problem because a family on means-tested benefits could claim benefits for *every* child, and the payments were age related, with payments for older children being significantly higher than those for younger children. Fourteen percent of families in work with six children or more were living below National Assistance levels, and half of all families below that level had three or fewer children (Atkinson 1969: 24).

A serious problem was that child tax allowances were worth more to families on higher incomes. (The allowance reduced taxable pay, which for someone paying higher-rate tax reduced the amount of earned income taxed in the higher-rate–tax rate band; whereas, for someone who didn't pay higher-rate tax, the allowance reduced the amount of pay taxed in a lower-rate–tax rate band. A compounding factor was that some people's pay was only just over, or in some cases was below, the tax threshold. The child tax allowance therefore made little or no difference to their net income.) The problem had to some extent been ameliorated by a "claw back" mechanism that reduced the tax allowance by an amount for each child for whom Family Allowance was in payment. The significance of this seemingly insignificant piece of history is that it marked the first direct relationship between the tax and benefits systems (Banting 1979: 95).

An important context for the next stage in the development of universal benefits in the United Kingdom—the transition from Family Allowance to Child Benefit—is the flurry of social scientific study of poverty that occurred during the early 1960s. Significant books were Richard Titmuss's (1962) *Income Distribution and Social Change*, and Brian Abel-Smith and Peter Townsend's (1965) *The Poor and the Poorest: A New Analysis of the Ministry of Labour's Family Expenditure Surveys of 1953–54 and 1960*. Their close study of official statistics, including family expenditure data, revealed substantial income inequality and almost one in five families on incomes below half the average. More important for public understanding of the realities of poverty was the television play *Cathy Come Home*, broadcast in 1966, which tells the story of a family in which the male breadwinner is injured and loses his job, leading to unemployment, homelessness, and the removal of the family's children into the care of the Social Services.

This "rediscovery of poverty" gave birth in 1965 to the Child Poverty Action Group (CPAG), which argued for a Family Allowance for the first child in a family and for the child tax allowance to be abolished in favor of higher Family Allowances (Hill 1990: 41). In 1968, Family Allowance was raised to 15s. [75p] for each child, and then to 18s. [90p] (Atkinson, 1969: 85). Families out of work had amounts equal to their Family Allowance deducted from their benefits, and instead received age-related child allowances. Family allowance of 90p per week was only 74 percent of the means-tested allowance for a child under five years of age, and 50 percent of the means-tested allowance for a child aged between 11 and 13 years (Atkinson 1969: 86), meaning that if a parent with a large family returned to work then they could experience a considerable loss of income. A compounding factor was that Family Allowance was taxed, whereas means-tested benefits were not.

There was thus considerable logic in CPAG's campaign for the abolition of child tax allowances (which didn't benefit the lowest earning families) and payment of child allowances for every child in a family at a rate higher than that of the current Family Allowance. That such a change would improve labor-market incentives was an important argument (Atkinson 1969: 141). By 1968, child allowances for every child in the family had been termed "Child Benefit" and had gained considerable support in government, but then the Labour administration was replaced by Edward Heath's Conservative government.

By the time of Labour's return to power in 1974, there was a consensus that a universal Child Benefit (that is, a payment for every child) would be useful, and that it should be accompanied by the phasing out of child tax allowances. The bill received a second reading in May 1975, but no start date was given. The next year cabinet minutes leaked to Frank Field, director of CPAG, and published in *New Society* on June 17, 1976, revealed government concern that to abolish tax allowances and to pay a Child Benefit higher than Family Allowance would reduce net incomes of men and thus cause wage inflation; and that the change from tax revenue foregone to an increased payment to the mother would look as if public expenditure had increased even though it had not (Spicker 2011: 118).

CPAG convened a "Child Benefit Now" campaign, trades unions gave their support (particularly those with high numbers of women members), Barbara Castle MP (from 1974 secretary of state for Health for Social Services, but consigned to the back benches when James

Callaghan replaced Harold Wilson as prime minister in 1976) gave parliamentary support, and, whilst both trades unions and the government remained divided, Child Benefit was eventually established (McCarthy 1986: 274).

Why Did Child Benefit Happen?

Again, individuals were significant: Margaret Herbison MP (a former minister of social security) gathered support for Child Benefit amongst MPs and journalists; Barbara Castle was far from silent on the matter; Frank Field campaigned consistently; and the cabinet mole was crucial. As time went by, and ministers came and went, the balance within the cabinet shifted against those wanting a means-tested approach to poverty in working families, and the Labour Party's historic suspicion of means tests eventually defeated the critics of Child Benefit (Banting 1979: 102–103). (Many Labour Party members could still remember the 1930s household means test, which took the assets and income of everyone living in the household fully into account when benefits were calculated.) Equally significant of course was 20-years' positive experience of Family Allowance and a resultant growing understanding that universal benefits experience high take-up, that they are simple and therefore cheap to administer, that they don't attract stigma, that the mother is more likely to spend money on the children than is the father (so a universal benefit paid to the mother will on average be of more value to the children than a tax allowance or a means-tested benefit paid to the father), and that universal benefits ameliorate the poverty and unemployment traps (because they do not reduce the net effect of additional earnings in the way that taxation and means tests do) (Barr and Coulter 1991: 279–280; Spicker 2011: 119).

Child Benefit entered the statute book because enough MPs could find reasons to support it, because a successful public campaign and the leaked cabinet minutes had reduced opposition, and because the trades unions now contained more women members and opinion amongst trade union members was therefore more divided. The pursuit of greater equality for women was a motivator for some of those involved (Barr and Coulter 1991: 295), and was therefore significant, but more important was an understanding that poverty in working families mattered and that something had to be done about it.

Preserving Child Benefit

From 1979 to 1997, there was again a Conservative government, and from 1979 Child Benefit was uprated in line with prices rather than wages (Hill 1990: 57). In 1985, the secretary of state for Social Security, Norman Fowler, reviewed social security benefits. The government replaced Family Income Supplement (a means-tested in-work benefit that the previous administration had established) with the more generous but still means-tested Family Credit, whereas Child Benefit was frozen. The result was a marked shift toward means testing (Barr and Coulter 1991: 282). "Targeting" was the aim, but unfortunately, means-tested benefits constitute a less efficient form of targeting than universal benefits accompanied by a progressive tax system.

CPAG joined in the debate by publishing research on mothers' experience of Child Benefit:

> [Child Benefit] is essential to a large majority of mothers in providing for the needs of their children . . . [and] it is a reliable payment made reliably and directly to them . . . A large majority of mothers supports the continuation of the universal payment of child benefit for each child.
>
> (Walsh and Lister 1985: 42)

The late 1980s saw Conservative voices questioning the future of Child Benefit. CPAG was vigorous in its defense: "The government should not be asking how much can be 'saved' from Child Benefit, but how this valuable multi-purpose benefit can be maintained and improved as an investment in the future into the twenty-first century . . . The case for more emphasis on Child Benefit is, in part, the case against *over*-use of means-tested benefits, because of their defects" (Brown 1988: xiii, 15)—especially their labor-market disincentive effects. Child Benefit was much to be preferred to means-tested provision because it provides a secure floor to a family's income, and it recognizes the whole community's responsibility for the care of the next generation (Brown 1988: 20, 35, 43; Brown 1990: 15). CPAG complained, as others had before, that Child Benefit was counted as public expenditure whereas child tax allowances were not, which skewed the argument toward regressive tax allowances and away from universal and thus progressive Child Benefit (Brown 1988: 63), despite the fact that when Child Benefit was phased in there was cross-party agreement that it should be viewed as similar to a tax allowance, and that the 1979 Conservative government viewed it as similar to a tax credit (Brown 1988: 25). Holly Sutherland and Hermione Parker, working at the LSE, showed that from the point of view of claimants, administrators, and taxpayers, Child Benefit was preferable to child tax allowances, and also concluded that a CI would be preferable to means-tested benefits (Parker and Sutherland no date: 133). Child Benefit survived, and when John Major became prime minister, his first act was to unfreeze it.

At the Conservative Party conference in 2010, the chancellor of the exchequer announced that Child Benefit would be withdrawn from every household containing at least one higher-rate taxpayer. The administrative mechanism for achieving this still seems to be undecided, but the government's current proposal is to expect the child's main carer in a household containing a higher-rate taxpayer not to claim Child Benefit, or for the higher-rate taxpayer to declare their household's Child Benefit in their tax return. Sanctions have been promised for those who do not declare receipt, suggesting that a new investigative department is envisaged. Any attempt by Her Majesty's Revenue and Customs to work out which Child Benefit recipients are in households containing a higher-rate taxpayer would involve considerable administrative complexity, additional civil servants, and thus additional costs: costs that could easily wipe out any revenue saved (Spicker 2011: 120). What seems particularly unjust in the proposal is that a household containing two earners, both just under the higher-rate threshold, would still receive Child Benefit, whereas an identical household with just one earner just over the threshold would not. We are hoping that the chancellor has now informed himself of Child Benefit's efficiency, and that he will shelve his proposal—though, as we shall suggest later, the fact that the proposal would require the establishment of new investigative or administrative systems, and thus additional civil servants, might result in departmental enthusiasm that could help to propel the proposal onto the statute book.

Tax Credits

We have studied Child Benefit: a legislated universal benefit that is still with us. We now turn to proposals that did not make it into the statute book, and first of all to the Heath government's Tax Credit proposals, not because they constitute a universal benefit (though they share some of their characteristics) but because the attempt to establish a Tax Credits scheme in the United Kingdom offers lessons to those who might wish to see a CI established.

The reader is reminded that the Tax Credits scheme of the early 1970s was for genuine tax credits. Households (and not individuals) would have been awarded tax credits. These would have replaced tax allowances, would have been paid in full if earned income dropped to zero, and would have been withdrawn at a specified rate as earned income rose. As earned income continued to rise, the tax credits would have ceased to be paid out and the worker would have started to pay tax. (The Labour government's recent "Tax Credits" scheme, introduced in 2003, is a means-tested benefit, it is not tax credits, it should not have been called tax credits, and it should not be confused with the genuine article.)

As the Heath government's consultation paper says,

> The tax credit system is a reform which embodies the socially valuable device of paying tax credits, to the extent that they are not used against tax due, positively as a benefit... [so as to] bring together what people pay and what they receive... Fewer people will be means-tested and others means-tested less often, and for the community there will be a large saving in administrative staff.
>
> (Her Majesty's Government 1972: iii)

Not everyone would have benefited from the scheme. Anyone self-employed or employed and earning less than £8 per week would have been excluded. Also excluded would have been employed married women (Her Majesty's Government 1972: 5). In 1971, a married woman was given the right to have her income assessed separately for income tax, rather than her earnings being included on her husband's tax return along with her income from other sources. A married man received a tax allowance higher than that for a single person, and a married woman received a single person's allowance to set against her earnings. The result was a financial advantage for married men. The Tax Credits consultation paper maintained this position by granting a £4 per week tax credit to each single person, a £6 tax credit to a married man, and a continuing tax allowance to each married woman (Her Majesty's Government 1972: 18).

The number of people in the scheme would have risen over time because someone already in the scheme who became unemployed would have had their tax credit paid through the Department of Health and Social Security or through the Department of Employment (Her Majesty's Government 1972: 3), but otherwise all tax credits would have been calculated by the employer who would have deducted tax from all earned income at 30 percent and set the tax credit against the tax due. A major difference between tax credits and income tax allowances was that tax credits would have operated on a weekly basis, whereas tax allowances operate on an annual basis, so no longer would the employer have had to manage complex ongoing calculations to ensure that by the end of the year the right amount of tax had been deducted. A major advantage of the scheme was that poorer families would have benefited from it, whereas they often didn't earn sufficient income to benefit fully from tax allowances (Her Majesty's Government 1972: 28).

The parliamentary select committee that examined submissions to the consultation recommended that the withdrawal rate for Tax Credits should be 30 percent (whereas the withdrawal rate for the means-tested Family Income Supplement was 50 percent), that additional Tax Credits should be allocated for such conditions as blindness, that married women should receive a single person's Tax Credit rather than a tax allowance, that a married woman should be able to transfer half of her Tax Credit to her husband if he did not qualify for one, and that Child Tax Credits should be paid to the mother (or to whoever had care of the children) as cash payments at the post office (Her Majesty's Government 1972: 5, 20–24). Family Income Supplement would have been abolished, but not other means-tested benefits, which would still have been needed (House of Commons Select Committee on Tax-Credit 1973: 7): though as the Tax Credits scheme had matured fewer families would have had need of means-tested benefits.

A minority report suggested that, as only Family Income Supplement would be replaced, it would be preferable to solve the problem of working poverty by establishing a National Minimum Wage and increasing tax allowances (House of Commons Select Committee on Tax-Credit 1973: 74): but the majority of the committee members recommended acceptance of the Tax Credits scheme because it appeared "to offer the possibility of improving the amount of income retained from increased earnings... The effect of the scheme [was] to give the same treatment to the very large majority of the population, with scope for differential treatment by giving selective help to those in greatest need and levying differential taxation on the highest paid" (House of Commons Select Committee on Tax Credit 1973: 7).

The Conservative government was defeated in the 1974 general election, and a new Labour administration preferred Family Income Supplement to Tax Credits. Since then we've had Family Credit (minor revisions of Family Income Supplement) and Gordon Brown's "Tax Credits" (further revisions of Family Income Supplement but now administered by Her Majesty's Revenue and Customs rather than by the Department of Social Security).

Why did Tax Credits not happen? There was an enthusiast, Sir Arthur Cockfield, and there were sufficient reasons for supporting the proposals to enable MPs with a variety of interests to support them. The Tax Credits scheme would have reduced working poverty, provided a greater incentive to increase earned income, and increased administrative efficiency. Even though the scheme was not entirely a tidy one, it would clearly have met these objectives. If the Heath government had survived its difficulties with the trades unions in 1972 then we might now have had nearly 40-years' experience of genuine tax credits. Admittedly, the scheme was not a universal one, and it was not entirely individualized. Nonetheless, increasing numbers of people would have found themselves within it. The Tax Credits scheme would have provided an additional paradigm alongside Child Benefit, contributory benefits, and means-tested benefits, and it would have enabled a more informed debate to take place on the extent to which the tax and benefits systems should and could be integrated with each other and on the relative advantages and disadvantages of the tax credit and universal benefit approaches to integration. In particular, experience of tax credits might eventually have enabled the government to ask about different options for recording in the national accounts revenue foregone and benefits paid out.

Genuine tax credits did not entirely disappear from the agenda. In 1979, Philip Vince developed for the Liberal Party a scheme of "tax-free credits, some of them universal and some withdrawn as other income rises" (Vince 1986: 5); and in 1983, Richard Wainwright MP presented an uprated version of the scheme to the Treasury and Civil Service Committee's enquiry into "the Structure of Personal Income Taxation and Income Support" (Parker 1989: 168–189; Vince 2011). The tax credit scheme was party policy, but it was the policy of a party with few MPs and little influence. During the early 1990s, a CI was Liberal Democrat Party policy, and the same reason meant that nothing happened.

Juliet Rhys Williams' Minority Report

Just as Tax Credits did not get onto the statute book, CI scheme also has not. A CI has never been the subject of a government green paper (consultation document), but it has been discussed by parliamentary select committees, and there are lessons to be learnt from understanding those discussions.

The UK debate about a CI arguably goes back to the eighteenth century and to Thomas Paine and others like him who recognized every citizen's natural right to a subsistence income: a right, because all citizens are of "one degree . . . all men are born equal and with equal natural rights" (Paine 1992: 273–276; Claeys 1989: 125). On this basis, Paine developed a scheme for incomes for the poorest (Paine 1992: 198). It was left to others to draw the conclusion that equal natural rights meant equal incomes.

Amongst those, were Mabel and Dennis Milner and Bertram Pickard, all Quakers, who established the State Bonus League to campaign for a "state bonus" of 9s. for each citizen (Macnicol 1980: 9; Van Trier 1995: 31–142). The Labour Party Executive Committee discussed the idea in 1921 and rejected it.

When William Beveridge presented his report on *Social Insurance and Allied Services* in 1942, Lady Juliet Rhys Williams, secretary of the Women's Liberal Federation (Harris 1981: 258), issued a minority report, subsequently published in a more developed form as *Something to Look*

Forward to (Rhys Williams 1943). Her concern was that a combination of social insurance and means-tested benefits would involve high marginal-deduction rates as earned income rose, and would therefore provide little incentive to earn a living. Coercion would therefore be needed to get people to work, and "once the power of the State is made use of as a means of making a man work against his will" (Rhys Williams 1943: 13), other coercions could easily follow. "The hope of gain is infinitely preferable to the fear of punishment and the fear of want as a motive for human labour...The real objection to the Beveridge scheme does not lie in its shortcomings in respect of the abolition of want, which could be made good, but in its serious attack upon the will to work" (Rhys Williams 1943: 45, 141). In particular, part-time labor must be possible in industries that require less labor, but part-time employment did not provide a subsistence income and would have made a man unavailable for other work and so unable to receive national insurance unemployment benefit.

Rhys Williams proposed a new contract: "The State owes precisely the same benefits to all of its citizens, and should in no circumstances pay more to one than to another of the same sex and age, except in return for services rendered...Therefore the same benefits [should be paid] to the employed and healthy as to the idle and sick...The prevention of want must be regarded as being the duty of the State to all its citizens and not merely to a favoured few" (Rhys Williams 1943: 139, 145). In Rhys Williams' scheme, there would have been "no more adult dependents" (Rhys Williams 1943: 151), and women would have received an income in their own right, though interestingly 19s. [95p] per week rather than the 21s. [£1.05] for men. The result would have been that workers would have received "the whole benefit of wages (less taxation)" (Rhys Williams 1943: 147). To cope with differential housing costs Lady Rhys Williams recommended different levels of payment in different regions.

This really was meant to be a *contract*, the scheme required visits to the Labour Exchange for anyone not in employment, and any work offered would have to have been accepted. This provision reintroduced fear (of losing the state income) into employment incentives (Rhys Williams 1943: 167), but Rhys Williams clearly expected the reduced marginal-deduction rates to be sufficient incentive to people to look for and accept any employment on offer.

In 1953, Rhys Williams listed the advantages of her equal payment for all citizens: administrative simplicity, raised employment incentives, the avoidance of means testing, increased possibilities for useful activity during periods of unemployment, and an improvement in married women's status (Rhys Williams 1953: 138). As H. S. Booker suggested in relation to the scheme, "Is there anything fundamentally wrong with a subsidy on wages if there are appropriate safeguards?" (Booker 1946: 232); and what better safeguard than *not* losing the state's contribution to one's income when earned income rises? Under the National Insurance Act, a man, wife, and child could earn £3 per week and be only 5s. [25p] better off. Under Rhys Williams' scheme, they would have been £1 16s. [£1.80] better off.

Like Mother, Like Son

Juliet Rhys Williams' son Sir Brandon Rhys Williams was a Conservative MP, and when in March 1973 a select committee evaluated the Tax Credits proposal, he was a witness (House of Commons Select Committee on Tax-Credit 1973). In 1982, a Treasury and Civil Service Committee Sub-Committee heard evidence on "the Structure of Personal Income Taxation and Income Support," and, as well as considering the Liberal Party's tax credits scheme, it received from Sir Brandon Rhys Williams a memorandum recommending a "Basic Income Guarantee": that is, a CI. ("Guarantee" here means that the citizen is guaranteed to receive an unconditional income. This was before the use of "guarantee" for a guaranteed net-income level, so its use did not cause any confusion.) "Every British Citizen should be awarded a personal allowance of a value related to personal status, not to resources" (House of Commons Treasury and Civil Service Committee Sub-Committee 1982: 423; cf. Rhys Williams 1989).

Sir Brandon Rhys Williams also submitted a synopsis of the scheme from his colleague, Hermione Parker: "Every citizen would be entitled to a personal basic income or PBI. These guaranteed basic incomes would replace virtually all existing benefits and allowances" (House of Commons Treasury and Civil Service Committee Sub-Committee 1982: 425; cf. Parker 1982, 1989, 1995). The committee examined Brandon Rhys Williams (BRW) on the proposals. The final exchange is instructive:

> *Chairman (C)*: There seem to me to be many benefits of this system.
>
> *BRW*: There are.
>
> C: Clearly, you are expressing them very eloquently. Clearly, they would go a long way toward easing the unemployment and poverty traps.
>
> *BRW*: There would not be any unemployment under these schemes. You would not need to register as unemployed. There would be people who were not in full-time work but they would not need to have themselves labeled as unemployed. If they got an opportunity of work or casual work they could take it and nobody would have to know.
>
> C: Are you saying that the unemployment benefit trap would be virtually eradicated by this?

BRW: Certainly.
C: Also, it would be administratively much simpler.
BRW: Yes, it would.
C: I wonder what degree of redistribution of resources there would be or is that one of the matters that could be flexible within the system?
BRW: This is optional. This is why I have not put figures in my paper because you could make the scheme do what you liked. If you want to help people on low wages or low incomes you can tilt the tax and benefit structure in such a way that it is redistributive in certain directions.
C: May I say that you will observe that owing to pressure of other engagements we have lost our third member and are now therefore non quorate. Thank you very much."

(House of Commons Treasury and Civil Service Committee Sub-Committee 1982: 459)

The committee recommended that the government should consider a Basic Income as an option for reform, but that more work needed to be done on the idea: "We recommend that the Government should put such work in hand," (House of Commons Treasury and Civil Service Committee 1983: para 13.35; as cited in Parker 1989: 100).

There is no evidence of this happening.

Committees of Enquiry

In 1984, the Basic Income Research Group (BIRG) was convened by Peter Ashby, an employee of the National Council for Voluntary Organisations. BIRG subsequently helped to establish the Basic Income European Network (BIEN), became a charitable trust, and in 1994 became the Citizen's Income Trust (CIT). For the past 27 years it has promoted debate on CI, published a regular journal (originally the *BIRG Bulletin*, now the *Citizen's Income Newsletter*), organized meetings, maintained a library and website, and responded to requests for information. During the past few years, perhaps its most significant activity has been to contribute evidence to parliamentary committees.

In 2007, the trust submitted evidence to the House of Commons Work and Pensions Committee's enquiry into benefits simplification. Its submission, a fully costed and revenue neutral CI scheme, was printed as evidence in the committee's report (House of Commons Work and Pensions Committee 2007: Ev 84–90), but no witnesses from the trust were called. During the committee's discussion with witnesses, Donald Hirsch explained that the Joseph Rowntree Foundation had estimated that a CI would require a basic tax rate of 46 percent. (He did not say whether this included National Insurance Contributions.) "We did not think the country was quite ready for that particular form" (House of

Commons Work and Pensions Committee 2007: Ev 14). The CIT's carefully calculated tax rate of 33 percent (22 percent Income Tax + 11 percent National Insurance Contribution) did not get a mention, suggesting that none of the committee members had read the submission.

In 2010, Iain Duncan Smith MP became secretary of state for Social Security. While in opposition, he had established a Centre for Social Justice (CSJ) with which the CIT exchanged a certain amount of correspondence, particularly in relation to the CSJ's publication *Dynamic Benefits* (Centre for Social Justice 2009). That report's main recommendation was for "Universal Credits," a means-tested benefit to replace several existing means-tested benefits in such a way as to reduce the overall marginal-deduction rate. "The Universal Credit system is one benefit, with a work-focused component and living costs component, withdrawn at a uniform rate above an earnings disregard, which is determined by household type" (Centre for Social Justice 2009: 265). This idea found its way into the new coalition government's consultation paper, *21st Century Welfare* (Department for Work and Pensions 2010a): "The Universal Credit would gradually be reduced as post-tax household incomes rose...A single withdrawal rate would make it clearer and simpler to calculate the financial gains from work and for people to be confident of being better off by taking a job and progressing to more hours and higher pay once in work" (Department for Work and Pensions 2010a: 21). Legislative proposals followed with *Universal Credit: Welfare That Works* (Department for Work and Pensions 2010b): "As earnings rise, we expect Universal Credit will be withdrawn at a constant rate of around 65 pence for each pound of net earnings" (Department for Work and Pensions 2010b: 13). At each stage the CIT has participated in the debate: by corresponding with the CSJ, by sending a submission in response to the consultation, and by commenting on the draft legislation; and it has published its contributions in the *Citizen's Income Newsletter* (Citizen's Income Trust 2010, 2011; Miller, 2011). The message has been that a Universal Credit is a useful few steps along the road to a CI, and it will take only a few more steps to create a CI and secure the benefits that it would offer in terms of income security, employment incentives, poverty reduction, and social cohesion. Another possibility, of course, is that the Universal Credit will make means-tested benefits more acceptable by reducing marginal-deduction rates, thus postponing debate on whether we need a new income-maintenance structure.

(It is a pity that the unified benefit has been termed "Universal Credit." While the "credit" usage is consistent with Gordon Brown's use of the term for *his* "Tax Credits," it is not consistent with the use of "credit" for the 1972 Heath government's proposal for genuine tax credits. It would have been better to term the means-tested payment a "benefit." It's also a pity that it's been called "universal." It is not. "Unified Benefit" would have been a far better description of the proposal.)

In 1994, the Labour Party's Commission on Social Justice, chaired by Sir Gordon Borrie, issued its report: *Social Justice: Strategies for National Renewal*. Like the CSJ, the commission studied the difficulties experienced by the existing tax and benefits system, and explored options for change. The commission's report gave a CI an honorable mention: "It would be unwise . . . to rule out a move towards Citizen's income in future: if it turns out to be the case that earnings simply cannot provide a stable income for a growing proportion of people, then the notion of some guaranteed income, outside the labor market, could become increasingly attractive" (Commission on Social Justice 1994: 263–264). It also commented favorably on a "Participation Income": an income conditional on participating in some way in society (Commission on Social Justice 1994: 264–265). Just as nothing happened following the 1982 Select Committee's hearing to which Brandon Rhys Williams gave evidence, so also the Labour Party did nothing further on the CI. What did happen when Labour came to power in 1997 was a National Minimum Wage. This was a good thing in itself, but it did little to sort out the complexities and disincentives of means-tested benefits.

Citizen's Pension

At the end of 2010, Steven Webb, minister for pensions in the coalition government, proposed a single flat-rate state retirement pension; on March 8, 2011, Iain Duncan Smith expressed approval of the plan for a basic state pension of £140 per week; and in April 2011, one of the options contained in a Department for Work and Pensions consultation document, *A State Pension for the 21st Century*, was a single-tier state pension of £140 per week for every individual with a 30-year National Insurance Contribution record (Department for Work and Pensions 2011: 10, 29–35). This is not strictly a Citizen's Pension, but it would only take the substitution of a residence condition for the contribution record condition for it to become one.

The current pattern of state pension provision is composed of two contributory elements, one of which is earnings related, and an additional means-tested element for individuals whose income in retirement does not reach a stated minimum. This structure makes it difficult for people to know what level of state pension they will receive when they retire, and thus difficult for them to plan for the future, so there is little incentive for those on low incomes to take out private pensions; and because savings are taken into account in the calculation of means-tested pension supplements, in a somewhat complex way, there is little incentive for those on low incomes to save in other ways for their retirement. A genuine Citizen's Pension would take no account of savings, or of private or occupational pensions, and so would encourage people to take out private pensions and to save in other ways; and for everyone with a 30-year-contribution record the proposed single-tier state pension would have the same effect because it would already be above the level of the current guaranteed retirement income.

Steven Webb is no newcomer to a CI. In 1990, he published a book on the subject with Samuel Brittan, *Beyond the Welfare State: An Examination of Basic Incomes in a Market Economy*: "A Basic Income is a payment received by every person or household adequate to provide a minimum income, based only on age and family status, but otherwise unconditional" (Brittan and Webb 1990: 1). (Because the proposed payment was to be calculated on a household basis, and not on an individual basis, it was not strictly a CI. If it had been individualized then it would have been one.) In 2004, the Pensions Policy Institute studied New Zealand's Citizen's Pension (O'Connell 2004; James and Curry 2010), so the idea had already received a certain amount of public debate: debate in which the CIT participated (Citizen's Income Trust 2004). Therefore, the new pension proposal hasn't come from nowhere—it has come from an interested individual and from existing debate: a pattern that we've seen before.

The CIT will of course be making a submission to the consultation on *A State Pension for the 21st Century* and will publish its submission in a future edition of the *Citizen's Income Newsletter*.

Discussion

So why did nothing follow Juliet Rhys Williams' minority report? Here we had a significant book, and a context of debate about the future of the tax and benefits system. Moreover, why did nothing happen following Brandon Rhys Williams' interventions? Here we had thorough research and a feasible scheme. In the case of the Universal Credit proposal, we have a ministerial champion and thorough research, and similarly with Steven Webb's pension proposal. In both cases, we have identifiable problems that need to be fixed (high marginal-deduction rates, and disincentives to save for retirement). In the case of Universal Credit, the parliamentary champion is a secretary of state who has persuaded the chancellor of the exchequer that in the medium term, his scheme will save money even though it might cost money to establish it. Universal Credit is going to happen. Steven Webb is a junior minister and a member of the junior party in the coalition, but his secretary of state understands and has backed his plan. The first of two options listed in *A State Pension for the 21st Century* retains the current structure of first and second state pensions and increases the rate at which the second pension will become flat rate. The second option is the single-tier state pension. The consultation document is clear that the first option doesn't meet the department's own reform criteria as well as the second option does. A flat-rate single-tier state pension for everyone with a 30-year-contribution record is likely to happen.

Recent CI contributions to parliamentary committee debate have been only that, and have lacked parliamentary champions. Neither Juliet Rhys Williams nor Brandon Rhys Williams were ministers. This might suggest that major reform requires a ministerial champion. However, there is another distinction to be drawn: Both Juliet and Brandon Rhys Williams were attempting to change the entire benefits system, whereas the Universal Credit and a single-tier state pension are for particular demographic or contingency groups—for people on means-tested benefits, and for the elderly. Similarly, Family Allowance and Child Benefit were only for children. It is somewhat challenging to have to recognize that the last major overhaul of the United Kingdom's benefits structure occurred after a serious recession and during a major war. In such a context, the apparent difficulties faced by major fiscal reform fade into insignificance beside other national difficulties. The question for us is this: Is that the only context in which we might expect reform of the system as a whole?

Clearly, no such change will ever occur without some previous discussion of the issues that the system faces, and of the options for change. That condition has been met to some extent: although it has to be said that debate has taken place mainly amongst those professionally and academically interested, rather than among policymakers. Since the mid-1980s, there has been exponential growth in the volume of academic debate on income-maintenance reform proposals: Negative Income Tax, Tax Credits, and a CI. Some of this interest has been generated from within academic departments because the originally rather thin field has offered plenty of opportunity for theses and dissertations and for the publication of books and articles. Some of the debate has been generated by think tanks. We have already mentioned the CSJ, but some general-purpose think tanks have also occasionally dabbled in the field; and the CIT has, of course, played its own part in promoting and publicizing debate on CI. One of the reasons for interest in academic departments is that universal benefits can be the subject matter for research and debate in a wide variety of disciplines: economics, social policy, sociology, moral philosophy, theology, and more. A rather narrower field of disciplines will be of interest to policymakers.

Here is not the place to rehearse the numerous arguments both for and against universal benefits, though more *systematic* work on those arguments, and on the ways in which arguments in different fields do or do not connect, would be welcome. Here our task is to ask whether there is any possibility that the United Kingdom's policy-making process will ever turn research and debate into additional legislated universal benefits, and perhaps to ask the rather more pressing question as to whether the universal aspects of the welfare state that we currently possess (Child Benefit and the NHS) will survive the current government.

General political trends will be an important factor. The proposed changes to Child Benefit are part of a general trend toward conditionality. This trend is evidenced in both the Conservative and Labour Parties, particularly in relation to increasingly onerous conditions placed on Job Seeker's Allowance recipients, on recipients of Incapacity Benefit, and now on households in receipt of Child Benefit.

Another factor which might determine whether further universal benefits reach the statute book, lies in Harris's suggestion as to why Juliet Rhys Williams' scheme never happened: "Like most schemes for abolishing bureaucrats, Lady Juliet's proposals met with an official wall of silence" (Harris 1981: 258). Family Allowances did not abolish anything, and so added to the total number of civil servants. Child Tax Allowances disappeared when Child Benefit was established, but there were plenty of other tax allowances for Inland Revenue staff to administer. Whether this factor had any influence over the process which led to Family Allowance and Child Benefit is difficult to determine, but it is clearly possible. The two Rhys Williams' proposals would have shrunk the number of staff administering Income Tax, National Insurance Contributions, and means-tested benefits. This might have been a reason for the proposals being ignored. Civil servants' attitudes to proposed legislation clearly color the ways in which those civil servants might formulate a reform proposal, recommend it to ministers, or fail to recommend it, and calculate its costs and benefits: though how significant this factor might be in any particular case will of course be difficult to determine. It is not obvious that the 1970s Tax Credit scheme would have reduced the number of civil servants. Civil servants were therefore content to facilitate the project. Universal Credit will rationalize to some extent the current patchwork of means-tested benefits, and will reduce marginal-deduction rates. It might or might not reduce civil-service numbers. Because the proposal for a single-tier state pension retains contribution records, any reduction in staff numbers resulting from the change will be small. The government's proposal to deprive households containing higher-rate taxpayers of their Child Benefit is more likely to increase the number of jobs in Her Majesty's Revenue and Customs than to decrease it.

A further significant factor, which we have already mentioned, is this: Our national accounts count benefits payments as public expenditure, but do not count as public expenditure the tax foregone by the government through the mechanism of tax allowances. This means that any proposal to shift income-maintenance policy from tax allowances to cash payments will suffer from a disadvantage, and any proposal to shift policy in the opposite direction will experience a positive advantage. This is entirely irrational.

This accounting difficulty poses no problem to the current state pension proposal, of course. Public expenditure will be affected very little, the second option in *A State Pension for the 21st Century* would tackle some recognized problems in the current system, there is existing debate and research on the proposal, and it has a ministerial champion. It will probably happen.

Things are rather different for a CI, which is by definition payable to every citizen. The CI itself would take little administration, whereas fewer people would be on means-tested benefits, and so fewer civil servants would be required. Personal tax allowances would be turned into cash payments, so Her Majesty's Revenue and Customs would require fewer staff. The national accounts would show higher public expenditure even though revenue foregone through tax allowances would decline by the same amount that benefits payments increased. It doesn't look good for CI.

One hope for a CI in the United Kingdom is for a significant parliamentary champion to emerge who understands the tax and benefits system and its disincentive effects, who is willing to put the arguments for universal benefits in and out of parliament, and who has sufficient influence to persuade colleagues that the tax and benefits system matters and that it is high time for a radical change.

A rather different hope is that Child Benefit will survive as a universal benefit; that a Citizen's Pension will be enacted as a natural extension of the current proposal for a single-tier pension; that a "universal grant" will be established for young adults to encourage education and training; that a universal "mature worker's grant" will be established to encourage flexible labor-market patterns amongst the over fifties; and that filling the 25 to 50-year-old gap will then seem obvious.

A possibly impossible task is to persuade the British public that a CI is a good idea. Research by D. V. L. and Smith Associates in 1991 showed that "few respondents had a clear understanding of the UK system of pensions and benefits" (D. V. L. Smith and Associates 1991: 5) and that many people could not comprehend reform options when they were explained (D. V. L. Smith and Associates 1991: 29). Debate amongst apparently intelligent members of the Conservative Party about the government's current proposals for depriving some families of Child Benefit ("They don't need it") showed a woeful ignorance of the efficiency and incentives advantages of universal benefits, of the context of a progressive tax system (which withdraws from wealthy families far more than they receive in Child Benefit), and of the disadvantages of means testing.

What *is* required is rational debate amongst ministers in the Treasury and the Department for Work and Pensions about the way in which we keep our national accounts, about the administrative waste of means testing, and about the increased employment incentive and social cohesion that a CI would deliver. We also, of course, need a chancellor of the exchequer who is able to understand these things. The CIT's research suggests that there would be parliamentary support for a major review of income-maintenance policy and for serious consideration being given to a CI (Citizen's Income Trust 2007), and Bochel and Defty have found a diversity of views on social policy issues amongst Conservative MP, and an interesting willingness to question previous policy positions (Bochel and Defty 2007; Bochel 2011: 13). It is therefore possible that a minister who decided to consult on an extension of universal benefits might find more of a welcome in Parliament than they might expect.

Notes

* I am grateful to all of those who have read and commented on a first draft of this chapter, and particularly Professor Hartley Dean, Dr. Tony Fitzpatrick, Professor Ruth Lister, Ms Anne Miller, and Mr. Philip Vince. Any opinions expressed in this chapter are not necessarily those of the Citizen's Income Trust, and any remaining mistakes remain entirely my own.

References

Abel-Smith, Brian, and Peter Townsend. 1965. *The Poor and the Poorest: A New Analysis of the Ministry of Labour's Family Expenditure Surveys of 1953–54 and 1960.* London: Bell.

Atkinson, A. B. 1969. *Poverty in Britain and the Reform of Social Security.* Cambridge, UK: Cambridge University Press.

Banting, Keith G. 1979. *Poverty, Politics and Policy: Britain in the 1960s.* London: Macmillan.

Barr, Nicholas, and Fiona Coulter. 1991. "Social Security: Solution or Problem?" In *The State of Welfare: The Welfare State in Britain since 1974*, edited by John Hills, 274–337. Oxford, UK: Clarendon Press.

Beveridge, Sir William. 1942. *Social Insurance and Allied Services.* London: Her Majesty's Stationery Office. Cmd. 6404.

Bochel, Hugh. 2011. "Conservative Approaches to Social Policy since 1997." In *The Conservative Party and Social Policy*, edited by Hugh Bochel, 1–22. Bristol: Policy Press.

Bochel, Hugh, and Andrew Defty. 2007. *Welfare Policy under New Labour.* Bristol: Policy Press.

Booker, H. S. 1946. "Lady Rhys Williams' Proposals for the Amalgamation of Direct Taxation with Social Insurance." *The Economic Journal* 56: 230–243.

Brittan, Samuel, and Steven Webb. 1990. *Beyond the Welfare State: An Examination of Basic Incomes in a Market Economy*. Aberdeen: Aberdeen University Press.

Brown, Joan. 1988. *Child Benefit: Investing in the Future*. London: Child Poverty Action Group.

———. 1990. *Child Benefit: Options for the 1990s*. London: Save Child Benefit / Child Poverty Action Group.

Centre for Social Justice. 2009. *Dynamic Benefits: Towards Welfare That Works*. London: Centre for Social Justice.

Citizen's Income Trust. 2004. "Further Support for a Citizen's Pension." *Citizen's Income Newsletter* 2004 (2): 1–2. London: Citizen's Income Trust.

———. 2010. "A Response to *21st Century Welfare*." *Citizen's Income Newsletter* 2010 (3): 3–9. London: Citizen's Income Trust.

———. 2007. "Both the House of Commons and the House of Lords Support a Citizen's Income Approach to the Reform of Tax and Benefits." *Citizen's Income Newsletter* 2007 (2): 1–2. London: Citizen's Income Trust.

———. 2011. "With Apologies to 'Yes, Minister.'" *Citizen's Income Newsletter* 2011 (1): 16. London: Citizen's Income Trust.

Claeys, Gregory. 1989. *Thomas Paine: Social and Political Thought*. Boston: Unwin Hyman.

Commission on Social Justice. 1994. *Social Justice: Strategies for National Renewal*. London: Vintage.

Department for Work and Pensions. 2010a. *21st Century Welfare*. London: The Stationery Office. Cmd. 7913.

———. 2010b. *Universal Credit: Welfare That Works*. London: The Stationery Office. Cmd. 7957.

———. 2011. *A State Pension for the 21st Century*. London: The Stationery Office. Cmd. 8053.

D. V. L. Smith and Associates. 1991. *Basic Income: A Research Report*. Prepared for Age Concern England.

Freeman, Chris. 1998. *Family Allowances, Technical Change, Inequality, and Social Policy*. The Eleanor Rathbone Lecture, 1996. Liverpool: Liverpool University Press.

Harris, J. 1981. "Some Aspects of Social Policy in Britain during the Second World War." In *The Emergence of the Welfare State in Britain and Germany, 1850–1950*, edited by W. J. Mommsen, 247–262. London: Croom Helm.

Her Majesty's Government. 1972. *Proposals for a Tax-Credit System*. London: Her Majesty's Stationery Office. Cmd. 5116.

Hill, Michael. 1990. *Social Security Policy in Britain*. Aldershot: Edward Elgar.

House of Commons Select Committee on Tax-Credit. 1973. *Report and Proceedings of the Committee*. Session 1972–1973, Volume I. London: Her Majesty's Stationery Office. HC 341–I.

House of Commons Treasury and Civil Service Committee. 1983. *Enquiry into the Structure of Personal Income Taxation and Income Support*. Third Special Report, Session 1982–1983.

House of Commons Treasury and Civil Service Committee Sub-Committee. 1982. *The Structure of Personal Income Taxation and Income Support: Minutes of Evidence*. London: Her Majesty's Stationery Office. HC 331–ix.

House of Commons Work and Pensions Committee. 2007. *Benefit Simplification*. Seventh Report of Session 2006–2007. London: The Stationery Office. HC 463.

James, Sean, and Chris Curry. 2010. *A Foundation Pension: A PPI Evaluation of NAPF* [National Association of Pension Funds] *Proposals*. London: Pensions Policy Institute.

Land, Hilary. 1975. "The Introduction of Family Allowances: An Act of Historic Justice?" In *Change, Choice and Conflict in Social Policy*, edited by Phoebe Hall, Hilary Land, Roy Parker, and Adrian Webb, 157–230. London: Heinemann.

Macnicol, John. 1980. *The Movement for Family Allowances, 1918–1945: A Study in Social Policy Development*. London: Heinemann.

McCarthy, Michael. 1986. *Campaigning for the Poor: CPAG and the Politics of Welfare*. London: Croom Helm.

Meade, J. E. 1978. *The Structure and Reform of Direct Taxation*. Report of a committed chaired by Professor J. E. Meade. London: George Allen and Unwin, for the Institute for Fiscal Studies.

Miller, Anne. 2011. "*Universal Credit: Welfare That Works*: A Review." *Citizens Income Newletter* 2011 (1): 4–10. London: Citizen's Income Trust.

O'Connell, Alison. 2004. *Citizen's Pension: An Introduction*. London: Pensions Policy Institute.

Paine, Thomas. 1992. *The Rights of Man*. Indianapolis: Hackett. First published 1791–1792.

Parker, Hermione. 1982. *The Moral Hazard of Social Benefits: A Study of the Impact of Social Benefits and Income Tax on Incentives to Work*. London: Institute of Economic Affairs.

———. 1989. *Instead of the Dole: An Enquiry into Integration of the Tax and Benefit Systems*. London: Routledge.

———. 1995. *Taxes, Benefits and Family Life: The Seven Deadly Traps*. London: Institute of Economic Affairs.

Parker, Hermione, and Holly Sutherland. No date. *Child Tax Allowances? A Comparison of Child Benefit, Child Tax Reliefs, and Basic Incomes as Instruments of Family Policy*. London: Suntory-Toyota International Centre for Economics and Related Disciplines, London School of Economics and Political Science.

Rathbone, Eleanor. 1986. *The Disinherited Family*. Bristol: Falling Wall Press. First published 1924.

———. 1949. *Family Allowances*. London: George Allen and Unwin. (A new edition of *The Disinherited Family* with an epilogue by William Beveridge).

Rhys Williams, Brandon. 1989. *Stepping Stones to Independence: National Insurance after 1990*. Aberdeen: Aberdeen University Press.

Rhys Williams, Juliet. 1943. *Something to Look Forward to*. London: MacDonald and Co.

———. 1953. *Taxation and Incentives*. London: William Hodge and Co.

Spicker, Paul. 2011. *How Social Security Works: An Introduction to Benefits in Britain*. Bristol: Policy Press.

Stokes, Mary. 1949. *Eleanor Rathbone: A Biography*. London: Gollancz.

Thane, Pat. 1996. *Foundations of the Welfare State*. 2nd edition. London: Longman.

Titmuss, Richard. 1962. *Income Distribution and Social Change*. London: Allen and Unwin.

Townsend, Peter. 1979. *Poverty in the United Kingdom*. Harmondsworth: Penguin.

Van Trier, Walter. 1995. *Every One a King*. Leuven: Departement Sociologie Katholieke Universiteit Leuven.

Vince, Philip. 1986. "Basic Incomes: Some Practical Considerations." *BIRG Bulletin* (Spring 1986): 5–8. London: Basic Income Research Group.

———. 2011. Correspondence to the author, dated April 6, 2011.

Walsh, Alison, and Ruth Lister. 1985. *Mother's Life-Line*. London: Child Poverty Action Group.

CHAPTER 15

United States of America: GAI Almost in the 1970s but Downhill Thereafter

Richard K. Caputo

The United States's experiences with guaranteed annual income (GAI) schemes suggest that linking them to resolving specified social problems increases the political acceptance of the idea, although it by no means ensures adoption and implementation. Alternatives more aligned with existing programs and policies of social welfare provisioning tend to be taken more seriously by the public at large and policymakers in particular. This chapter, which in part synthesizes related material from a much broader work of mine that examines social welfare policy transitions in the United States from the 1980s through the first years of the Obama administration (Caputo 2011), discusses how a GAI proposal was seriously considered and nearly adopted by the US Congress when deliberating about how to best reform its major welfare program designed primarily for low-income families, especially single-mother families with young children. It highlights the centrality of reciprocity and priority given to labor force attachment as contributing to the loss of popular support for the idea of an unconditional basic income guarantee and shows how alternative policies such as the Earned Income Tax Credit were adopted that fit more readily into a cluster of values and an existing array of social welfare provisioning associated with individual responsibility.

The chapter also briefly highlights the Alaska Permanent Fund, the subject of another book in the Palgrave Exploring the Basic Income series (Widerquist and Howard forthcoming). Dividends from the Alaska Permanent Fund are distributed annually to all citizens of Alaska meeting a basic-residency requirement, but otherwise unconditionally (Butler

2005). Finally, the chapter discusses attempts in the first decade of the 2000s to get a basic income scheme back on the political agenda. It concludes that any such ideas or concrete proposals are political nonstarters in the United States for the foreseeable future, despite the annual income that citizens of the state of Alaska get as dividends from the Alaskan Permanent Fund and regardless of how the issue is framed.

Reducing Poverty in the 1960s

The idea of guaranteeing citizens an annual income in the United States gained ascendency in the 1960s in the form of negative income tax (NIT) proposals and related experiments (Steensland 2008). In a review essay of Michael Harrington's *The Other America*, activist and scholar Dwight MacDonald (1963) contended that some form of GAI policy was the solution to poverty. He called for income security as a basic right of citizenship. At that time, GAI was not new to the US experience. Variations have been promoted intermittently: Thomas Paine's 1779 *Agrarian Justice*, Cornelius Blatchley's 1829 *Causes of Popular Poverty*, Thomas Skidmore's 1829 *The Rights of Man to Property*, and Orestes Brownson's 1840 *Brownson's Defense* (Caputo 2006). Although mentioned briefly earlier in the twentieth century (e.g., Stigler 1946), the idea of a guaranteed income, in general, and the NIT, in particular, generated little political traction until 1960s when economists Milton Friedman (1962) recommended and Robert Lampman (1965, 1969) advocated for the NIT as the means of alleviating poverty (Moffitt 2004).

The idea of a citizen's right to an adequate income was included in a report entitled, "The Triple Revolution," produced by a group of well-known scholars and writers collectively known as the Ad Hoc Committee on the Triple Revolution (1964). President Lyndon Johnson, the minority and majority leaders of the House and Senate of the US Congress, and the secretary of labor each were sent copies. The 1966 report of the Council of Economic Advisors (CEA) noted, "the institution of uniformly determined payments to families based only on the amount by which their incomes fall short of minimum subsistence levels" would be a viable alternative approach (to the welfare program targeting low-income women with children) already under scrutiny "by many scholars" (*Economic Report of the President* 1966: 115). In 1968, some 1,300 economists at approximately 150 institutions urged Congress by a signed petition to adopt a "national system of income guarantees and supplements" ("Economists Urge Assured Income" 1968). The President's Commission on Income Maintenance Programs (1969) had recommended adoption of NIT in its final report. Family allowances, payments based on the number of children in a family regardless of income, competed with the NIT as a form of guaranteed income. Both types of guaranteed income schemes, the NIT favored by economists and family allowances favored by social workers and sociologists (e.g., Gans 1968; Schorr 1966) were discussed within the Johnson administration, although neither was adopted (Steensland 2008).

Several NIT experiments were launched in the 1960s and the early 1970s. The most prominent among them were the New Jersey-Pennsylvania Negative Tax Experiment (Cogan 1983; Garfinkel 1974) and the Seattle-Denver Income-Maintenance Experiment (SIME-DIME) (Spiegelman and Yaeger 1980), with related experiments in Gary, Indiana (Moffitt 1979). These experiments, however, had little impact on the welfare reform efforts of the Richard M. Nixon administration, which had proposed the Family Assistance Plan (FAP) first in 1969 and again in 1972. Results of the SIME-DIME experiments were published primarily in various issues of the *Journal of Human Resources* throughout the 1970s and most extensively in the autumn 1980 issue. The NIT experiments' impact, particularly those showing greater levels of marital dissolution and diminished work effort among income recipients vis-à-vis control groups, though subsequently questioned (Widerquist 2005), was highly influential in welfare reform debates during the Jimmy Carter administration at the end of the 1970s (Steiner 1981: 104–110) and the Ronald Reagan administration throughout the 1980s (Murray 1984), culminating in 1988 with the passage of the Family Support Act (Caputo 1989, 2008). Suffice it to say that in addition to costs, the effects of such programs on work effort, especially on working poor males who were outside the framework of the existing welfare system (Spiegelman and Yaeger 1980), but who were nonetheless benefited from the spillover effects from welfare rights legitimizing rationale (Reich 1964) and advocacy efforts (Cloward and Piven 1966; Steensland 2008), were a main driving concern of political feasibility during the Nixon and Carter administrations.

Reforming Welfare: The Nixon Administration's FAP

When Richard M. Nixon announced his FAP on August 8, 1969, it was one of several different income guarantee-like schemes that varied by coverage, cost, and portended consequences. As summarized by Cavala and Wildavsky (1970: 352–354), the series of proposals embodied four characteristics: (a) assistance was to be made only on the basis of need; (b) need and entitlement to public assistance would be objectively and uniformly measured throughout the nation; (c) assistance should be cash;

and (d) any tax placed on income earned in addition to that provided by the supplement should be less than 100 percent. Milton Friedman's (1962) proposal set the guaranteed minimum income to 50 percent of the unused personal exemptions of a family minus its minimum standard deduction ($3,000 for a family of four, the break-even point), with a projected cost at that time of $10 billion. Economist Robert Theobald's (1963) proposal set the guaranteed income equal to $1,000 for each adult, $600 for each child, with an offset rate at 90 percent (a family kept 10¢ of every dollar it earned up to a break-even point, $3,556), with a projected cost of $30 billion. Edward Schwartz's (1964) scheme set the guaranteed minimum income equal to $4,000 for a family of four, with no offsetting tax on other income, with a projected cost of $23 billion. Senator George McGovern's 1969 proposal (as cited in Cavala and Wildavsky 1970: 353) paid $10 a month to every dependent child, with a projected cost of $8 billion. Robert Lampman's (Green and Lampman 1967) proposal set variable rates and amounts of subsidies determined by the amount by which the respective incomes fell below a break-even point, with projected costs of $8 billion. James Tobin's plan (1965) was that the government pay $400 a year for each member of the family to each taxpayer below the $6,000 break-even point for a family of five, reducing the allowance by 33.3¢ for every dollar the family earned above $6,000, and had a projected cost of $12–$15 billion.

In regard to portended effects, Cavala and Wildavsky (1970: 330) surmised that Schwartz's and Theobald's plans would leave no one worse off than being under the then current welfare or public assistance system, thereby targeting poverty as the social problem to be alleviated. Friedman's, Tobin's, and Lampman's plans, however, would not reduce the cost of public assistance by a politically visible amount without making the poor of several states worse off than before, thereby having mixed antipoverty and antiwelfare results. Cavala and Wildavsky concluded that income by right was not politically feasible in the near future. Though sympathetic of FAP, the political columnist Tom Wicker (1973) doubted any reasonable chance of Congress adopting a GAI scheme, contending that the guaranteed income was "an idea whose time had not come" and that FAP "had little chance in the 90th and 91st Congresses, no matter what Mr. Nixon did or said." Nonetheless, the prospect of nationalizing federal-state public assistance programs resonated to some degree with the public and politicians.

President Nixon's FAP left provisions for federal assistance to the aged, blind, and disabled unchanged, while establishing a monthly income floor of $65 for all such recipients (Woolley and Peters 2011b). Under FAP, the public assistance program primarily for low-income single mothers, formally known as Aid to Families with Dependent Children

(AFDC) and informally referred to as "welfare," would be abolished. A minimum annual sum of $1,600 would be paid to each family of four, with additional earned income taxed at 50 percent, but the first $720 of income would not reduce the initial subsidy. The break-even point for a family of four as per this plan was $3,920. FAP excluded single adults who were not handicapped or aged as well as married couples without children. It nonetheless allowed payments to families headed by unemployed males. FAP was also work related: recipients had to accept training opportunities and suitable work when offered. Mentally and physically incapable persons were exempt from these work requirements, as were mothers of preschool children. Refusal to participate in work requirements would result in loss of his portion of the benefit. The remaining funds for mother, children, or both were to be made available through a local welfare agency (Cavala and Wildavsky 1970: 354). In his August 8, 1969, address to the nation, President Nixon differentiated FAP from unconditional guaranteed income schemes. He put the issue this way (Woolley and Peters 2011a):

> This national floor under incomes for working or dependent families is not a "guaranteed income." Under the guaranteed income proposal, everyone would be assured a minimum income, regardless of how much he was capable of earning, regardless of what his need was, regardless of whether or not he was willing to work.
>
> Now, during the presidential campaign last year, I opposed such a plan. I oppose it now and I will continue to oppose it, and this is the reason: A guaranteed income would undermine the incentive to work; the family assistance plan that I propose increases the incentive to work.
>
> A guaranteed income establishes a right without any responsibilities; family assistance recognizes a need and establishes a responsibility. It provides help to those in need and, in turn, requires that those who receive help work to the extent of their capabilities. There is no reason why one person should be taxed so that another can choose to live idly.

As Cavala and Wildavsky (1970) and Steensland (2008) noted, by the time Nixon assumed office poverty was no longer a social problem that had to be addressed. Poverty had not been eliminated: 13 million working poor were to benefit from FAP had it been passed. Poverty rates, however, had declined from 22 percent in 1960 to 13 percent in 1970 (Jencks 1985). Further, the 23 million poor persons in 1973 were one-third less than at the start of the Johnson administration's War on Poverty in 1964, diminishing national interest in the subject (Arnold 1974). The War on Poverty was nonetheless viewed as a failure, signified by urban riots and increasing AFDC or "welfare" caseloads, both tinged with racial friction.

In his memoirs, Nixon (1978: 425–426) acknowledged his determination to reform welfare, that is, AFDC, to end what he viewed as the inefficiencies and inconsistencies of the Great Society. It irked Nixon among other things that AFDC payments to equivalent families could range from $263 a month in one state to $39 a month in another; that higher payments were often made to fatherless families; that a sizable majority (93 percent) of the families added to the welfare rolls between 1961 and 1967 had absent fathers; and that loopholes made it possible to earn more on welfare than working for the minimum wage, violating the principle of less eligibility. As noted by Jencks (1985) even the prospect of providing a nonworking–able-bodied mother with an income from AFDC that was more than some other non-AFDC recipient-working mothers was morally and politically unacceptable in principle.

President Nixon's unhinging welfare reform from poverty reduction was one of several major stumbling blocks FAP faced. Several of the aforementioned GAI schemes were aimed primarily at poverty reduction. Their advocates had little or no voice in the Nixon administration, including Milton Friedman whose GAI scheme would have abolished the social welfare system.

With vilification of the social welfare system, in general, and the AFDC program, in particular, by President Nixon and others, the much debated conundrum among policymakers and political pundits was whether the enjoinment of both the nonworking and the working poor into one overarching or comprehensive program would in effect result in an expansion of the AFDC program. It was estimated that the Nixon administration's plan added about 13 million persons to the welfare or AFDC rolls. According to Steensland (2008), the stigma associated with the AFDC program was so great that, through a process of "symbolic pollution," the moral standing of the working poor would be severely compromised and, hence, rejected by many even among those who would nonetheless gain economically. In short, if the AFDC or welfare system was as morally repugnant and programmatically faulty as President Nixon deemed it, doubling its roles by extending the reach of dependency on government beneficence to working poor families would be even more morally reprehensible.

Although "symbolic pollution" entered into discussions of the merits of guaranteed income plans in general, its relative weight in the eventual demise of FAP was questionable (Caputo 2010). Writing during this period, Cavala and Wildavsky (1970) made a more nuanced point about stigma, though not about AFDC recipients but about the working poor, that went to a core American value of equal opportunity vis-à-vis equality of result: "In America the stigma of poverty," they wrote (1970: 332), "lies less in the fact of being poor than in the implication that one is lacking in those abilities which are rewarded." An income floor, such as that proposed in FAP and other GAI schemes, modified this implication, suggesting that poor persons were not completely responsible for their fate and may have lacked opportunity to participate in the race for economic gain. "But to say that the losers in the race will not starve" they continued "is very different than saying that the race itself is not a worthy one." To the extent that income inequality remained, stigma associated with the working poor would remain.

Maintenance of the distinction between deserving and undeserving poor that historically played an important role in the development of social policy in the United States was deemed important to policymakers and the public at large. Since its creation as part of the Social Security Act of 1935, public assistance programs invariably targeted those who were not expected to work, recipients were deemed deserving, and their moral worth was not in question. That changed in the 1960s when the AFDC caseloads increased more sharply than in previous decades, and the composition shifted disproportionately to unwed black mothers. Hence, AFDC recipients lost some moral standing and were subject to two stigmatizing characteristics: race and marital status. This was due to the disproportionate numbers of blacks and unwed mothers. Added was a third stigmatizing characteristic: no labor-force attachment. Able-bodied persons were viewed as undeserving of cash assistance unless it was tied to work-related efforts (Peck 2001). By reaching out to the working poor, many of whom were white, Nixon's FAP held the promise of expanding the deservedness category for cash assistance, eclipsing the three stigmatizing characteristics of AFDC. The stigma associated with working poverty per se may have remained, as Cavala and Wildavsky (1970) contended. That type of stigma seemed of a higher order of moral worthiness than what had befallen AFDC cash recipients throughout the 1960s. Making cash assistance available for working poor families as deserving, necessitated a conceptual shift, one that might have occurred during the Nixon administration had the president tied welfare reform more directly or even secondarily to poverty reduction. The treatment of employable persons on the same moral basis as unemployable persons made little sense to the US public, in general, and the US Congress, in particular, unless employable or able-bodied persons were willing to look for and accept employment as a condition of receiving benefits (Harris 2005; Rogers 1981).

On the whole, FAP had more going against it than for it from those on both the political left and right of the political spectrum. A combination of cultural, institutional, and pragmatic factors eroded its initial support and in large part accounted for its demise, first in 1970 and again in 1972. Collapsing AFDC poor and working poor persons and the cultural factor challenging the work ethic that many on the political right found unacceptable could not be reconciled with the pragmatic factor of "trying to contain the fiscal burden of [AFDC] welfare," which was particularly acute for many state and city governments (Handler and Hasenfeld 1991: 149). As initially proposed, FAP was estimated to add $2.8 billion to the then current AFDC public assistance program (Cavala and Wildavsky 1970: 354). As part of the Nixon administration's overall revenue-sharing scheme, FAP would have afforded all states savings or minimal losses. This included a high AFDC-paying state like New York, which would lose $14 million for their AFDC programs, but would nonetheless gain $9.8 million when considering federal expenditures for adult programs for the aged, blind, and disabled (Caputo 1994: 497, n. 37). However, in 1971 Nixon unhinged FAP from state-related revenue enhancement by proposing a delay in the effective start date of FAP. The support of many otherwise previously supportive governors evaporated, contributing to the demise of FAP when it was considered a second time by the Congress.

Political conservatives contended that there was a moral hazard associated with the potential erosion of the work ethic among the working poor and potential discouragement of nonworking AFDC poor from seeking work. Political liberals and other more strident activists also opposed FAP. The National Welfare Rights Organization (NWRO), whose constituency included mostly AFDC recipients, contended that work requirements in FAP amounted to slave labor and that the initially proposed cash benefit of $1,600 (subsequently raised to $2,400) minimum for a family of four was too low. NWRO wanted a minimum of $5,500, an amount that got additional support from the National Association of Social Workers and the National Conference on Social Welfare.

Had FAP been passed, AFDC recipients in 15 southern states would have seen an increase in the economic standing since maximum welfare benefits fell below $2,400. The prospect of improving the economic standing of poor blacks in southern states presented a formidable challenge to the political hegemony of Congressional Southern Democrats as well as Southern governors who for the most part opposed FAP (Jimmy Carter of Georgia who was elected president of the United States in 1976 was an exception) and to the Southern economy that relied on a pool of low-income black labor. By equalizing earnings at the bottom of the wage scale between men and women and between whites and blacks, FAP would have released many Southern black able-bodied adults from the necessity of accepting the lowest wage work and empowered them politically (Quadagno 1990; White and Long 1972).

FAP also found initial opposition by organized labor (American Federation of Labor—Congress of Industrial Organizations [AFL-CIO]).

From the vantage point, with the AFL-CIO increased numbers of non-working but employable AFDC recipients added to the pool, low-income workers would intensify competition for a fixed number of jobs and exacerbate low-wage employment. Over time, low-wage rates in the subsidized sector would depress wage rates in the nonsubsidized sector. The AFL-CIO also feared that the proposed training programs in FAP would undermine the union's autonomy over skilled craft jobs, allowing workers to enter the protected segments of manufacturing and skilled trade. Both AFL-CIO objections were addressed in the 1971–1972 version of FAP, and labor withdrew its opposition. However, it was too late, especially as previously noted, after Nixon proposed delaying the revenue-sharing part of FAP that led to the loss of support of governors and local officials (Caputo 1994, 2011).

The Earned Income Tax Credit (EITC)

Three years after FAP's demise, Congress approved the EITC as part of a larger tax cut package drafted primarily by Congressional Democrats in 1975 during the administration of Gerald Ford (Caputo, 1994; Howard, 2007). The EITC provided tax-filing poor families with at least one child, a tax rebate of 10 percent of earned income up to $4,000 (phased and finally eliminated on wages between $4,000 and $8,000). By providing a cash subsidy to low-income workers with children, EITC reaffirmed the importance Congress placed on continued labor force participation.

The EITC became permanent during the Carter administration as part of the Revenue Act of 1978. It matured as an antipoverty strategy during the Reagan administration as part of the Tax Reform Act of 1986 when Congress raised the maximum EITC benefit, which had fallen by 35 percent in real terms, to the 1975 level, increased the phase-out level to near the 1975 level, and indexed it for inflation (U.S. Joint Committee on Taxation, 1987; Ventry, 2000). The EITC was preferred to raising the minimum wage as an antipoverty strategy in part because it better targeted low-income household heads rather than low-wage earning students or teenagers, and it accounted for family size (Lang 1999; Ozawa 1995).

From 1975 through 1987, the number of EITC claimants ranged between 6,000 and 9,000; in 1988, more than 11,100 individuals claimed the credit (Hotz and Scholtz 2003). By 1997, 19.4 million tax filers received the credit, amounting to a loss of $30.4 billion to the US Treasury Department; in 2009, the most recent year for which data are available, 25.9 million tax filers received the credit, amounting to a US Treasury loss of nearly $57.9 billion (Internal Revenue Service 2011).

The Alaska Permanent Fund Dividend

Two items about the Alaska Permanent Fund are noteworthy for purposes here (Smith, P. 1991), given as previously noted that it is the subject of another book in Palgrave's Exploring the Basic Income series (Widerquist and Howard forthcoming). First, its creation required a constitutional amendment since the state constitution held that Alaska's natural resources are owned by the people of Alaska (not the state) and it had prohibited creation of a dedicated fund, affording some protection from legislative shenanigans like pork-barrel projects. Second, the social welfare objective of providing citizens a dividend from the fund played little or no role in deliberations about the objectives of the fund. The idea of a Permanent Fund in Alaska originated in the 1970s when the state of Alaska received and quickly spent $900 million from the sale of Prodhoe Bay leases, imparting the lesson that large sums of money could easily vanish if state spending were not restrained by some mechanism. Initially, the fund idea had only limited support primarily from Governor Jay Hammond who wanted to offset the highest cost of living in any of the states and who seemed genially surprised at the relative ease with which the measure to amend the constitution was adopted by the state legislature and put up to the citizens of Alaska for voting accordingly (Hammond 1994: 251; Rose 2008).

In 1976, the citizens of Alaska voted by a two-to-one margin to amend their state constitution specifying creation of a Permanent Fund resulting from at least 25 percent of all mineral leases, royalties, royalty sales proceeds, federal mineral-revenue sharing payments, and bonuses received by the state and leaving the objectives of the fund to be determined by the state legislature. The amendment excluded severance taxes, thereby reducing to 10–11 percent of the amount going into the Permanent Fund from the state's petroleum revenues (Rose 2008: 129). It took three years for objectives of the fund to be ironed out by the Alaskan state legislature, with the key struggle being between economic development and savings. Savings won out—in large part to moderate revenue fluctuations brought on by volatile oil prices by investing in diversified portfolios. Bereft of a state income tax and a state sales tax, about 85 percent of state government revenues were generated by the petroleum industry (Brown and Thomas 1994).

It was only in 1982 when the legislature, primarily to improve accountability of the fund, required that part of the fund's earnings be distributed as dividends both to ensure that all Alaskans of all ages receive a share of the oil wealth and to encourage greater public scrutiny over the fund's management. Greater public scrutiny over the funds can be viewed as in the common interest or good, though some political pundits like Olson and O'Brien (1990), Brown and Thomas (1994), and the *Economist* (One State's Free Lunch 2004) have claimed that the public is not necessarily served as a whole to the extent that the fund cannot be tapped to meet collective and long-term needs, such as financing schools or roads or reducing chronic state debt (Anderson 2002). In 1982, checks for the amount of $1,000 were distributed to each Alaskan, with amounts varying each year thereafter, ranging from a low of $331.89 in 1984 to a high of $2,069 in 2008, which excludes an additional rebate of $1,200 (Permanent Fund Dividend Division 2011). No other state has adopted the idea of creating and using such a fund for distributional social welfare purposes. It is worth noting that although the fund is permanent, for at least as long as the oil is produced and profitable, this is not the case for the distribution of annual dividends which could end theoretically, if not politically, once the fund has fulfilled the function of helping the state to preserve a portion of its oil wealth (Rose 2008: 157–158).

Recent Attempts to Adopt Basic Income Plans

Since the 1980s, economically conservative or free market think tanks have come to dot the American political landscape, bringing together like-minded–multidisciplinary scholars and fellows to analyze and advocate for policies aimed at influencing national legislation (Smith, J. 1991). American enterprise scholar and self-identified libertarian Charles Murray (2006) proposed a basic income plan to eliminate poverty and nearly the entire welfare state that called on the US Federal Government to offer individuals 21 years of age or older an intermittently adjusted amount of $10,000 a year, of which $3,000 would go to health care coverage. Murray was under no delusion that politicians would take his plan seriously: "Today's politicians would not build it," he declared among the Ground Rules of the book (2006: xv). He was correct, despite a spate of reviews in popular outlets such as *The New Republic* (Klein 2006), *National Review* (Ponnure 2006), and the *University of Pittsburgh Law Review* (Delgado 2007) among others. In *Coming Apart,* Murray (2012) proposed his basic income plan again as a solution to the growing income inequality and fraying of the social fabric in the United States and found some support in the popular press (Ferguson 2012). Commentators and reviewers of *Coming Apart*, however, focused more on his analysis of cultural and social trends and either ignored (Confessore 2012) or characterized his guaranteed income prescription as "weird" (Noah 2012) or impractical (Douthat 2012).

Another idea that got some attention as contrasted with Murray's plan focused on assets, say a $10,000 lump sum at birth rather than income, with parents managing the money until the child turns 18 years of age, similar to Tony Blair's Baby Bond program in Britain (Conley 2006). As a presidential contender and senator from New York, Hillary Clinton was reported to have claimed that she liked "the idea of giving every baby born in America a $5,000 account that will grow over time, so when that young person turns 18, if they have finished high school they will be able to access it to go to college" (Jones 2007; The Associated Press 2007). This idea too got nowhere politically.

"The Tax Cut for the Rest of Us Act," was introduced into the 109th US Congress in 2006 by California Congressman Bob Filner and cosponsored only by Illinois Congressman Jesse L. Jackson. The Congressional bill got nowhere other than getting referred to the House Committee on Ways and Means where it languished (Sheahen 2008). "The Tax Cut for the Rest of Us Act" would have provided $2,000 for the taxpayer, $2,000 for the spouse of the taxpayer, and $1,000 for each dependent to those individuals who did not itemize deductions, affecting about 70 percent of all tax filers (Toder and Rosenberg 2007). Scholar and activist Steven Shafarman (2008) acknowledged the futility of efforts to gain political tractability for basic income legislation leading up to the US presidential campaign of 2008, which Barack Obama won. Shafarman saw little hope to reverse an antipathetic public sentiment: "The main obstacle we see is the general sentiment that it is somehow wrong to give people money," a sentiment that crystallized over the past two decades and seems unlikely to change any time soon.

On September 21, 2011, Rep. Dennis Kucinich (D-Ohio) introduced a monetary reform bill known as the National Employment Emergency Defense Act (H.R. 2990) that, in addition to providing money for direct funding of infrastructure, called for "an initial monetary [tax-free] dividend to citizens" (Section 507: 45). The intent was to provide liquidity to the banking system at the commencement of the Act before governmental expenditures for infrastructure had a chance to circulate in the economy. Presumably, this was intended as a one-time measure, although no time frame was specified in the bill. H.R. 2990 also called for a study of the effects of the dividend on production, consumption, prices, morale, and other economic and fiscal factors (Kucinich 2011). The bill was immediately referred to the House Committee on Financial Services and a month later sent to the Subcommittee on Financial Institutions and Consumer Credit, where inlanguished without further action (U.S. Congress 2012).

Most recently, Stuart Alexander, the presidential nominee of the Socialist Party USA (SPUSA), has endorsed a basic income guarantee for everyone 20 years of age and over (Lomibao 2011; Stewart Alexander for President 2012 Campaign Committee 2011). A longtime supporter of basic income guarantee, Alexander's plan would index a livable basic income to inflation. SPUSA, however, is a minor political party in the United States, a mere shadow of the Socialist Party of Eugene V. Debs prior to World War I and of Norman Thomas prior to World War II (Deininger 1963; Mann 1971; Thomas 1948). The likelihood of favorably influencing a national level debate of the issue is remote.

References

Ad Hoc Committee on the Triple Revolution. 1964, April. "The Triple Revolution." *Liberation*: 9–15. http://educationanddemocracy.org/FSCfiles/C_CC2a_TripleRevolution.htm.

Anderson, Jonathan. 2002. "The Alaska Permanent Fund: Politics and Trust." *Public Budgeting and Finance* 22 (2): 57–68.

Arnold, Mark. R. 1974, September 29. "The Good War that Might Have Been." *New York Times Sunday Magazine*: 56–66 and 71–73. http://query.nytimes.com/mem/archive/pdf?res=FA0A12F63A5D127A93CBAB1782D85F408785F9.

Brown, William S. and Clive S. Thomas. 1994. "The Alaska Permanent Fund: Good Sense or Political Expediency?" *Challenge* 37 (5): 38–44.

Butler, Sean. 2005. "Life, Liberty and a Little Bit of Cash." *Dissent* 52 (3): 41–47.

Caputo, Richard. K. 1989. "Limits of Welfare Reform." *Social Casework* 70(2): 85–95.

———. 1994. *Welfare and Freedom American Style II: The Role of the Federal Government, 1941–1980.* Lanham, MD: University Press of America.

———. 2006. Review of *The Origins of Universal Grants*, edited by John Cunliffe and Guido Erreygers. *Basic Income Studies* 1(1): article 14.

———. 2008. "U.S. Welfare Reform Links Assistance to Work, 1971–2000." In *Great Events from History: The 20th Century*, edited by Robert. F. Gorman, 2215–2217. Pasadena, CA: Salem Press.

———. 2010. Review of *The Failed Welfare Revolution: America's Struggle Over Guaranteed Income Policy*, by Brian Steensland. *Eastern Economic Journal* 36: 423–426.

———. 2011. *U.S. Social Welfare Reform: Policy Transitions from 1981 to the Present.* New York: Springer.

Cavala, Bill and Aaron Wildavsky. 1970. "The Political Feasibility of Income by Right." *Public Policy* 18: 321–354.

Cloward, Richard. A. and Frances Fox Piven. 1966, May 2. "The Weight of the Poor: A Strategy to End Poverty." *The Nation*: 510–517.

Cogan, John. F. 1983. "Labor Supply and Negative Income Taxation: New evidence from the New Jersey-Pennsylvania Experiment." *Economic Inquiry* 21: 465–485.

Confessore, Nicholas. 2012, February 10. "Tramps Like Them," review of *Coming Apart: The State of White America, 1960–2110*, by Charles Murray. *The New York Times Sunday Book Review*: BR9.

Conley, Dalton. 2006. "Charles Murray's New Plan," review of *In Our Hands: A Plan to Replace the Welfare State*, by Charles Murray. *Boston Review* 31 (5): 39–40.

Deininger, Whitiker T. 1963. Review of *Eugene V. Debs: Socialist for President*, by H. Wayne Morgan. *The Political Science Quarterly* 16 (2): 509–510.

Delgado, Richard. 2007. "The Myth of Upward Mobility," review of *In Our Hands: A Plan to Replace the Welfare State*, by Charles Murray. *University of Pittsburgh Law Review* 68 (4): 879–913.

Douthat, Ross. 2012, February 11. "Can the Working Class Be Saved?" *The New York Times Sunday Review*: SR11.

Economic Report of the President. 1966. http://fraser.stlouisfed.org/publications/ERP.

"Economists Urge Assured Income." 1968, May 28. *The New York Times:* 1, 22. http://select.nytimes.com/mem/archive/pdf?res=FA0E12F7355D147493CAAB178ED85F4C8685F9.

Ferguson, Niall. 2012, January 23. "Rich America, Poor America." *Newsweek*: 42–47.

Friedman, Milton. 1962. *Capitalism and Freedom*. Chicago: University of Chicago Press.

Gans, Herbert. J. 1968. *People and Plans: Essays on Urban Problems and Solutions*. New York: Basic Books.

Garfinkel, Irwin. 1974. "The Effects of Welfare Programs on Experimental Responses." *Journal of Human Resources* 9: 504–529.

Green, Christopher and Robert J. Lampman. 1967. "Schemes for Transferring Income to the Poor." *Industrial Relations* 6 (2): 121–137.

Hammond, Jay. 1994. *Tales of Alaska's Bush Rat Governor: The Extraordinary Autobiography of Jay Hammond Wilderness Guide and Reluctant Politician*. Fairbanks, AK: Epicenter Press.

Handler, Joel F. and Yeheskel Hasenfeld. 1991. *The Moral Construction of Poverty: Welfare Reform in America*. Newbury Park, CA: Sage.

Harris, Robert. 2005. "The Guaranteed Income Movement of the 1960s and 1970s." In *The Ethics and Economics of the Basic Income Guarantee*, edited by Karl Widerquist, Michael. A. Lewis, and Steve Pressman, 77–94. Burlington, VT: Ashgate.

Hotz, V. Joseph and John. K. Scholtz. 2003. "The Earned Income Tax Credit." In *Means-Tested Transfer Programs in the United States*, edited by Robert A. Moffit, 141–197. Chicago, IL: University of Chicago Press.

Howard, Christopher. 2007. *The Welfare State Nobody Knows: Debunking Myths about U.S. Social Policy*. Princeton, NJ: Princeton University Press.

Internal Revenue Service. 2011, January 3. *Earned Income Tax Statistics*. http://www.irs.gov/individuals/article/0,,id=177571,00.html.

Jencks, Christopher. 1985, May 9. "How Poor Are the Poor?" review of *Losing Ground: American Social Policy, 1950–1980*, by Charles Murray, *New York Review of Books* 32 (8). http://yulib002.mc.yu.edu:2888/articles/archives/1985/may/09/how-poor-are-the-poor/.

Jones, Athena. 2007, September 28. "Clinton Talks 'Baby Bonds.'" *MSNBC* http://firstread.msnbc.msn.com/archive/2007/09/28/385053.aspx.

Klein, Ezra. 2006. "Mr. Big: Charles Murray's Nuttiest Idea Yet," review of *In Our Hands: A Plan to Replace the Welfare State*, by Charles Murray, *The New Republic* 234 (13): 12–13.

Kucinich, D. 2011. "National Emergency Employment Defense Act of 2011. H.R. 2990." 112th Congress, 1st Session. Washington, DC: U.S. Congress. Retrieved from http://www.gpo.gov/fdsys/pkg/BILLS-112hr2990ih/pdf/BILLS-112hr2990ih.pdf.

Lampman, Robert J. 1965. "Approaches to the Reduction of Poverty." *American Economic Review* 55 (1/2): 521–529.

———. 1969. "Expanding the American System of Transfers to Do More for the Poor." *Wisconsin Law Review* 1969 (2): 541–549.

Lang, Susan S. 1999. "Income Tax Credits, Not Minimum Wage Hike, Will Benefit the Working Poor." *Human Ecology Forum* 27 (4): 3.

Lomibao, L. 2011, December 16. "Election 2012: SPUSA Candidate Alexander Calls for a Basic Income Guarantee (BIG)." San Francisco Bay Area Independent Media Center. Retrieved from http://www.indybay.org/newsitems/2011/12/16/18702851.php.

MacDonald, Dwight. 1963, January 19. "Our Invisible Poor." *The New Yorker* 38: 82ff, 126–132.

Mann, Arthur. 1971. Review of *Pacificist's Progress: Norman Thomas and the Decline of American Socialism*, by Benard K. Johnpoll. *The American Historical Review* 76 (5): 1619.

Moffitt, Robert A. 1979. "The Labor Supply Response in the Gary Experiment." *Journal of Human Resources* 14 (4): 477–457.

Moffitt, Robert A. 2004. "The Idea of a Negative Income Tax: Past, Present, and Future." *Focus* 23 (2): 1–8.

Murray, Charles. 1984. *Losing Ground: American Social Policy, 1950–1980*. New York: Basic Books.

———. 2006. *In Our Hands: A Plan to Replace the Welfare State*. Washington, DC: American Enterprise Institute. http://www.aei.org/docLib/9780844742236.pdf.

———. 2012. *Coming Apart: The State of White America, 1960–2010*. New York: The Crown Publishing Group.

Nixon, Richard M. 1978. *RN: The Memoirs of Richard Nixon*. New York: Grosset & Dunlap.

Noah, Timothy. 2012, February 20. "The Two Americas," review of *Coming Apart: The State of White America, 1960–2110*, by Charles Murray. Online review at *The New Republic*. http://www.tnr.book/review/charles-murray-white-america.

Olson, Dennis O. and Patrick O'Brien. 1990. "The Great Alaskan Money Give Away Program." *Economic Inquiry* 28 (3): 604–615.

"One State's Free Lunch." 2004. *Economist* 374 (8405): 28–32.

Ozawa, Martha N. 1995. "The Earned Income Tax Credit: Its Effects and Significance." *Social Service Review* 69 (4): 563–582.

Peck, J. 2001. *Workfare States*. New York: Guilford Press.

Permanent Fund Dividend Division. 2011. "Dividend Amounts." http://www.pfd.state.ak.us/dividendamounts/index.aspx.

Ponnure, Ramesh. 2006. "A Better Deal," review of *In Our Hands: A Plan to Replace the Welfare State*, by Charles Murray, *National Review* 58 (6): 46–48.

President's Commission on Income Maintenance Programs. 1969. *Poverty Amid Plenty: The American Paradox*. Washington, DC: Government Printing Office.

Quadagno, Jill. 1990. "Race, Class, and Gender in the U.S. Welfare State: Nixon's Failed Family Assistance Plan." *American Sociological Review* 55 (1): 11–28.

Reich, Charles A. 1964. "The New Property." *Yale Law Journal* 73 (5): 733–787.

Rogers, Charles S. 1981. "Work Tests for Welfare Recipients: The Gap between the Goal and the Reality." *Journal of Policy Analysis and Management* 1 (1): 5–17.

Rose, Dave. 2008. *Saving for the Future: My Life and the Alaska Permanent Fund*. Kenmore, WA: Epicenter Press.

Schorr, Alvin. 1966. *Poor Kids: A Report on Children in Poverty*. New York: Basic Books.

Schwartz, Edward E. 1964, July 9. "A Way to End the Means Test." *Social Work* 9: 3–12.

Shafarman, Steven. 2008. "The Basic Income Campaign in the United States, 2008." Paper presented at the Twelfth BIEN Congress, Dublin, Ireland, June 20–21, 2008. http://www.basicincome.org/bien/papers.html

Sheahen, A. 2008. "The Rise and Fall of a Basic Income Guarantee Bill in the United States Congress. *USBIG Discussion Paper No. 179*. http://www.usbig.net/papers.php?Search=Sheahen&Sortby=Date+DESC.

Smith, James A. 1991. *The Idea Brokers: Think Tanks and the Rise of the New Political Elite*. New York: The Free Press.

Smith, Peter J. 1991. "The Politics of Plenty: Investing Natural Resource Reserves in Alberta and Alaska." *Canadian Public Policy* 17 (2): 139–154.

Spiegelman, Robert. G. and K. E. Yaeger. 1980. "Overview." *Journal of Human Resources* 15: 463–479.

Steensland, Brian. 2008. *The Failed Welfare Revolution: America's Struggle over Guaranteed Income Policy*. Princeton: Princeton University Press.

Steiner, Gilbert. Y. 1981. *The Futility of Family Policy*. Washington, DC: The Brookings Institution.

Stewart Alexander for President 2012 Campaign Committee. 2011. "Social Safety Net." Stuart Alexander and Alex Mendoza 2012 Socialist Party USA Presidential Ticket. New York: Socialist Party USA. Retrieved from http://stewartalexanderforpresident2012.org/issues/social-safety-net/.

Stigler, George J. 1946. "The Economics of Minimum Wage Legislation." *American Economic Review* 36 (3): 358–365.

The Associated Press. 2007, September 29. "Clinton Proposes $5,000 'Baby Bonds.'" *The New York Times*: A11. http://www.nytimes.com/2007/09/29/us/politics/29bond.html.

Theobald, Robert. 1963. *Free Men and Free Markets*. New York: Clarkson N. Potter.

Thomas, Norman. 1948. "Do Left-Wing Parties Belong in Our System?" *Annals of the American Academy of Political and Social Science* 259 *Parties and Politics: 1948*: 24–29.

Tobin, James. 1965. "On the Economic Status of the Negro." *Daedalus* 94 (4): 878–895.

Toder, Eric J. and Carol Rosenberg. 2007. "The Share of Taxpayers Who Itemize Deductions Is Growing." Washington, DC: The Tax Policy Center. http://www.urban.org/UploadedPDF/1001054_Share_of_Taxpayers.pdf.

U.S. Congress. 2012. H.R. 2990. Latest Major Action. Washington, DC: Author. Retrieved from http://thomas.loc.gov/cgi-bin/bdquery/z?d112:HR02990:@@@D&summ2=m&.

U.S. Joint Committee on Taxation. 1987. "General Explanation of the Tax Reform Act of 1986." http://www.jct.gov/jcs-10–87.pdf.

Ventry, Dennis J. 2000. "The Collision of Tax and Welfare Politics: The Political History of the Earned Income Tax Credit, 1969–1999." *National Tax Journal* 53 (4): 983–1026.

White, Gerald B. and Burl R. Long. 1972. "The Welfare Reform Bill and Its Effects in the South." *Southern Journal of Agricultural Economics* 4(1): 221–227.

Wicker, Tom. 1973, March 22. "Who Crushed Nixon's Revolution?" review of *The Politics of a Guaranteed Income: The Nixon Administration and the Family Assistance Plan*, by Daniel Patrick Moynihan, *New York Review of Books*. http://yulib002.mc.yu.edu:2888/articles/archives/1973/mar/22/who-crushed-nixons-revolution/.

Widerquist, K. 2005. "A Failure to Communicate: What (If Anything) Can We Learn from the Negative Income Tax Experiments?" *Journal of Socio-Economics* 34: 49–81.

Widerquist, Karl and Michael Howard. Forthcoming. *Alaska's Permanent Fund Dividend: Examining Its Suitability as a Model (Basic Income Guarantee)*. New York: Palgrave Macmillan.

Woolley, John T. and Gerhard Peters. 2011a. Richard M. Nixon. "Address to the Nation on Domestic Issues. August 8, 1969." *The American Presidency Project* [online]. Santa Barbara, CA: University of California (hosted), Gerhard Peters database. http://www.presidency.ucsb.edu/ws/index.php?pid=2191.

———. 2011b. Richard M. Nixon. "Special Message to the Congress on Reform of the Nation's Welfare System. August 11, 1969." *The American Presidency Project* [online]. Santa Barbara, CA: University of California (hosted), Gerhard Peters database. http://www.presidency.ucsb.edu/ws/index.php?pid=2194.

Other Countries

CHAPTER 16

Iran: A Bumpy Road toward Basic Income

Hamid Tabatabai

Iran's experience with basic income is paradoxical. The concept is virtually unknown in the country and almost entirely absent from the public discourse. And yet, since December 2010, all Iranians residing in the country have been entitled to, and nearly all receive, a monthly cash transfer of Rl 455,000 (about $45)[1] per person from the government. These unconditional transfers are officially known as "cash subsidies," since they replace price subsidies that are being phased out. The scheme falls short of a basic income as commonly conceived in the literature, but it comes far closer to it than any other large-scale cash transfer scheme in the world. It is in effect a de facto basic income that is unique not only in its scope and size, but also in its provenance and prospects. Indeed, as a potential model for replication, it may claim certain advantages over some alternative pathways to a basic income, not least the fact that it is already in place as it approaches its first anniversary.

The story of how this de facto basic income came into being is recounted elsewhere (Tabatabai 2011) and is summarized below. The transfers are an integral part of a subsidy reform that went into effect on December 19, 2010. The early results of this reform are now beginning to show. As these consequences come to light and are more widely known, debate is picking up as to how the process should be managed henceforth, particularly the cash transfer component. This chapter takes stock of this unfolding experience, in particular the challenges it is facing, and draws some preliminary insights that might be of interest in the basic income debate.

The chapter is structured as follows. First, a brief account of Iran's reform of price subsidies is provided, focusing on how its cash transfer component came to resemble a nationwide basic income. Key provisions of the Subsidy Reform Law and the modalities of its implementation are then highlighted. Early results of the reform are presented next, followed by a discussion of the main issues that now preoccupy the country and of the prospects of a national basic income. The final section concludes.

From Price Subsidies to Cash Subsidies

Iran is a major producer and exporter of oil, and as such, its fortunes—and misfortunes—have been closely tied to this "filthy, foul-smelling liquid that squirts obligingly up into the air and falls back to earth as a rustling shower of money" (Kapuscinski 1986: 34). For decades, the government's easy access to oil revenues has financed development efforts and current expenditures, but it has also spawned a resource management culture that often favors short-term expediency over long-term transformation. As a result, the well-known structural weaknesses of the economy have persisted and intensified, notably its dependency on an exhaustible, primary product.

A major manifestation of this lax culture was the cheap fuel policy in the domestic market. In November 2010, just before the recent reform was launched, fuel prices in Iran were the lowest of any country in the world, except for Venezuela.[2] Gasoline costs 10¢ a liter and diesel fuel only 1.6¢ throughout the country. Gas, water, and electricity were similarly cheap, as were a few staple foods such as bread. The result was overconsumption, inefficient production, waste, pollution, smuggling to neighboring countries, and, last but not least, a lopsided distribution of benefits as the bulk of the subsidies went to the better-off sections of the population who consumed more. By official estimates, price subsidies in recent years have been costing some $100–120 billion annually, of which 70 percent went to only 30 percent of the population, mostly in the urban areas.[3]

The widely perceived mismanagement of the oil wealth prompted over the years a variety of proposals to turn this "curse" into a blessing by managing it differently to lay the foundations of a strong economy and to bring about a more equitable sharing of the benefits. Initially, the focus of these proposals was on revenues from oil exports alone but they increasingly encompassed the potential revenues that could be derived from a more rational pricing policy for domestic use as well. Of particular interest in the context of this chapter are those proposals that would distribute a large portion of the actual and/or potential revenues to the population in cash. Lacking political support, none of these proposals made much headway in influencing state policy. The sole one that was politically significant was that of Mehdi Karrubi, a reformist presidential candidate in 2005.[4] Karrubi's election platform pledged to distribute to every adult Iranian the equivalent of $50 a month, financed from oil exports, savings in the national budget, reduced consumption of gasoline, and replacement of some other transfers.[5] The payments were to be regular and unconditional, with no means testing or work requirement. It is unclear as to what extent this particular pledge of a basic income for adults contributed to Karrubi's 5.3 million votes, but it was widely dismissed at the time as populist election *avaamfaribi* (demagoguery) that would turn every Iranian into a beggar. With his election loss, the proposal became moot and was forgotten.

The reform of price subsidies too has been a long-standing concern, with successive governments trying to take up the challenge as best they could in the light of political, economic, and social realities they faced. During the presidency of Mohammad Khatami (1997–2005), for example, it was decided to raise the price of gasoline by 20 percent a year for five years to reach the Persian Gulf price. However, barely a year into the process, a new parliament dominated by a rival political current reversed the increase and mandated stable prices for energy and government services—an action billed as a New Year gift to the nation! While this reversal was publicly defended on the grounds of protecting the more vulnerable sections of society, the motive was more political than economic or social. The same forces that thwarted Khatami's reform toed the line under the next president, Mahmoud Ahmadinejad, who came up with a far more radical plan in 2008 that entailed raising subsidized prices not by a modest percentage but severalfold. The support of Iran's supreme leader, Ayatollah Ali Khamenei, was instrumental in ensuring the approval of the parliament.

The outline of Ahmadinejad's plan was publicly unveiled in June 2008, with more details emerging gradually. Part of a larger package of reforms covering various sectors of the economy, the subsidy reform consisted of abandoning the cheap fuel policy and, in compensation, returning the net proceeds from higher prices to the public in the form of cash. The "cash subsidies" would thus replace the implicit and explicit price subsidies that Iranians had been enjoying for decades. The reform would also extend to electricity and water services, transport, bread, and some other items, but over 90 percent of the subsidies concerned fuel products.

Several issues dominated the prolonged discussions and debates that followed, particularly in the parliament where the debate was intense. There was little disagreement that the system of price subsidies needed reform, a need that had long been recognized by the political class and experts, even by many ordinary citizens. Nor was there much dispute about the need to compensate the lower-income people with cash transfers, which are fairly well established in Iran through various programs.

Some critics questioned the timing of the reform, arguing that prior work was needed to contain the existing inflation and kick-start the anemic economy. Others doubted the implementation capacity of the government. The most widespread concern, however, was the fear of inflationary pressures that would be unleashed following massive price increases and their implications for the livelihood of the lower deciles of the population. Alarming predictions were made by various observers, including influential members of parliament, of runaway inflation that could derail the economy and endanger social peace and stability. The anxiety was deep and widely shared, notwithstanding government assurances that this would not happen.

Less controversial was the targeting of cash transfers. While views varied as to whether the transfers should cover the lowest two deciles of the population, five, seven, or even the entire population, the issue was overtaken by events when the government tried to put in place a targeting mechanism very early on, long before the reform plan was to be considered by the parliament. To this end, heads of households were invited toward the end of 2008 to apply for the transfer by filling out a Household Economic Information Form, which, apart from demographic information, inquired about the socioeconomic status of household members, in particular their incomes and assets. With about 70 percent of the population earning less than the average national income, a methodology was developed to identify three groups of households: (1) the bottom four deciles that would be entitled to the highest transfer amount per person; (2) the middle three deciles that would receive somewhat less; and (3) the top three deciles that would not receive any. The results, however, did not please everyone and there were many who objected to their group assignment. Overtime, the chorus of protests grew loud enough for the government to abandon the exercise and declare everyone eligible for the transfer. This about-face was billed as a temporary expedient and the door was left open to revive targeting at some future date when the government could develop a more satisfactory methodology for the identification of the target population.

Universal coverage also heralded the uniformity of transfer amount for all. Although, the amount could in principle vary by such easily ascertainable criteria as age or region of residence—higher amounts for the more deprived provinces was one of the options considered—in the end the simplest option of uniform payment was adopted. As regards the transfer amount, no official figure was available until the reform was launched but speculation was rife, with less speculative estimates hovering around $10–25 per person per month, depending on the underlying assumptions. Such estimates were generally based on specifics of the Subsidy Reform Law to which we now turn.

The Subsidy Reform Law and Its Implementation

It was against this background that the parliament formally took up the discussion of the reform bill toward the end of 2009. The debates led to a patchwork of compromises that, while allowing the passage of the law, made implementation problematic. The Subsidy Reform Law was enacted in January 2010, despite government objections to some of its provisions.[6]

The main provisions of the law authorize the government to reform prices of fuel, electricity, water, transport, and postal services as well as of some subsidized food items over the five-year period of the Fifth Development Plan, March 21, 2010—March 20, 2015. Domestic sale prices of gasoline, diesel fuel, and other fuels are to be raised gradually to reach at least 90 percent of Persian Gulf Free On Board (FOB) prices.[7] For natural gas, domestic prices should be increased to eventually exceed 75 percent of average export price, and for electricity and water to reach their full cost price. In the case of wheat, rice, cooking oil, milk, sugar, air and rail transport, and postal services, arrangements are to be made for the gradual elimination of subsidies over the same five-year period.

The net revenues thus generated would be used to compensate the population for price rises and to facilitate the structural transformation of the economy. The law authorizes the government to spend up to 50 percent of the net proceeds for (1) cash and noncash subsidies payable to all households countrywide, taking into account the level of household income; and (2) implementing a comprehensive social security system for the targeted population. Cash payments would be made through the banking system to the head of each eligible household, or another eligible person as determined by the government. The payments would be exempt from income tax.

The law also sets aside 30 percent of the net proceeds to help producers adopt energy saving technologies, to compensate part of losses to companies and municipalities providing utility services, to develop and improve public transport, and to promote non-oil exports. The remaining 20 percent of the net proceeds, commonly known as the government share, would be used to compensate the impact "on spending and the acquisition of capital assets," with no further specification. The government may modify the 50–30–20 percent shares up to a maximum of 10 percentage points within each year, but not over the entire implementation period of five years.

The imposition of five years for the implementation process, instead of three that the government wanted, was aimed at ensuring a more gradual pace of reform and dampening its inflationary effects. This gradualist intent was reinforced further by limiting the net proceeds from higher prices in the first year to $10–20 billion, a provision that the government vigorously opposed as unrealistic, demanding a cap of $40 billion instead.

Having failed to persuade the parliament to go along with its wishes, the government took a different tack and delayed launching the reform for nine months beyond the start date implicit in the law. The delay was ostensibly to allow for more thorough preparation but it served to vastly accelerate the pace of reform as the government then tried to generate a good part of the revenues authorized for the first year in only its final quarter. The scale of price increases, from 75 percent to 2,000 percent depending on the item, thus went far beyond what would have been necessary to collect the authorized revenues over a 12-month period. Such acceleration was of course what the government wanted all along, since more drastic changes in relative prices would have more of an impact on the behavior of consumers and producers and more rapidly. The main reason for the delay, however, was to allow the transfer amount to be set at a much higher level than it would have been possible otherwise, since the "inflated" revenues collected over three months would also be distributed over the same three months. The transfer amount was thus set at $45 per person per month, nearly three times the maximum amount consistent with strict adherence to the provisions of the law, which is about $17.[8] This seems to have been regarded by the government as necessary to bring about a more rapid transformation of the economy and ensure public support. A cash subsidy of about $17 per month—only 5 percent of the minimum wage—would have had little incentive effect and might well have scuttled the reform from the start.

Cash transfers to households started at the same time that price increases went into effect on December 19, 2010. The payments are made during the second week of each month. But while payments to households have been regular, those destined for businesses and the government have been anything but regular, and for good reason. Once household payments are made, there is rather little left for businesses and the government.[9] The universality of payments, their rather high level (relative to revenues collected), and, to make matters worse, the apparent overestimation of expected revenues seem to have thrown the finances of the reform program into disarray. It is thus not surprising that most observers view the implementation process as sharply at variance with that envisaged in the law. Ali Larijani, the speaker of the parliament, echoed that feeling by lamenting that the parliament never imagined that the government would implement the law in the way it did.[10] However, whether or not the government was justified in its approach, the consequences have been far-reaching, as we shall see below.

Some Early Results

By November 2011, nearly a year into the reform process, some evidence had begun to emerge on the consequences. The reliability and precision of the evidence may be variable but the overall picture is consistent with what one might expect.[11]

As noted before, the fear of inflation was the most controversial issue about the reform. Official figures suggest that while the initial shock to overall prices was relatively contained, it left a continuing mark. According to the Central Bank, the annual rate of urban inflation in the months preceding the reform was 9–10 percent.[12] With the launch of the reform on December 19, 2010, this rate started climbing by about 1 percentage point a month to reach 18.3 percent in September 2011.[13] The acceleration appears to have been entirely due to price reform. In July 2011, when the rate of inflation was 16.3 percent, 4.5 percentage points of it were attributed to the direct impact of the subsidy cuts and 1.9 percentage points to their indirect impact through other prices.[14] The relatively subdued impact on overall inflation—when subsidized prices had been raised severalfold—was due in part to price controls that were intensified when the reform was launched. Price controls were subsequently relaxed but not entirely withdrawn. The bank expected the rate of inflation to continue rising for some more months but at a decreasing rate.

One of the main objectives of the reform was to reduce excessive consumption of goods and services, notably of fuel. This seems to have been achieved, perhaps even to excess. According to the government, there was a considerable decline in the consumption of fuel products, gas, electricity, and bread flour. During the first 6–7 months of the reform, the consumption of various types of fuel fell by 3.4 billion liters, or about 17 million liters a day. The daily consumption of gasoline, more specifically, fell by 9 percent from 60 to 55 million liters while it had been growing at a comparable rate before the reform. Fuel smuggling also dropped sharply, although some still went on given the continuing price differences across national borders. Electricity consumption fell by 8 percent, compared to an increase of 10 percent in the previous year. The consumption of wheat and bread flour plunged by an estimated 28 percent. Such huge drops in consumption had their mirror image in production, particularly in the small business sector. For example, industry sources reported that about 30 percent of traditional bakeries wanted to close down. The dairy industry was facing similar problems as well. Given the importance of such basic items in the nation's diet, there is widespread concern about the wisdom of removing subsidies on them.[15] Caught between higher input prices, lower consumer demand, and price controls, small businesses felt the pinch and many of them found it hard to operate profitably in the new environment. The evidence on impact on productive sectors is too limited to draw reliable conclusions and the government and its critics sharply differ in their assessments of the situation. What is clear though is that cash transfers tended to favor consumers more than the producers who did not get their envisaged share of 30 percent in the proceeds from subsidy cuts.

Another main objective of the reform was to reduce income inequality. The cuts in subsidies affect household incomes in proportion to their consumption of subsidized goods and services. While some food items were among them, the cuts overwhelmingly concerned energy products whose consumption correlates positively with income. The compensatory transfers are, however, the same for everyone, and hence, the short-term impact of the reform on income distribution can only have been egalitarian, although the extent of it is not known since no hard data are available. The Statistical Centre of Iran expected the Gini coefficient in urban areas to fall from 0.379 to 0.358 in the year following the reform. The corresponding decline in rural areas is from 0.361 to 0.345.[16]

Finally, it may be useful to consider selected results of an opinion poll on the reform carried out by an unidentified official agency. It covers Tehran, the capital city, and sheds some light on the hopes and anxieties of the public soon after the reform was launched.[17] As might be expected, the state-owned Radio and TV network was the main source of information about the reform for most people (76 percent), with the rest getting their information from friends and acquaintances (9 percent), newspapers (8 percent), and the Internet (4 percent). The transfers were about as likely to be spent as saved. Of the 77 percent of the respondents who had received the transfer,[18] 41 percent had spent it all, 37 percent had saved it all, with the remaining 22 percent having divided it up between consumption and saving. Nonetheless, a majority (62 percent) were of the opinion that most people would not be able to cover the extra expenses due to higher prices despite the transfer and even if they reduced their consumption. Some 33 percent thought that they could do so. A similar majority (65 percent) felt that the reform would help "correct" the consumption pattern, although others (28 percent) had little confidence that it would. Perhaps most importantly, the respondents were split down the middle between those who had much or very much confidence that the reform program would be a success (40 percent), and those who had little or very little confidence in the same (39 percent). And more people rated the chances of the transfers continuing as little or very little (42 percent) than those who rated these chances as high or very high (36 percent). It should be noted that public opinion in rural and other urban areas that are less privileged than Tehran is likely to be more favorable to the reform as price subsidies tend to favor the better off whereas cash subsidies are the same for everyone.

From Cash Subsidies to Basic Income?

What is the future of Iran's cash transfer program? Will it remain as is, evolve toward a full-fledged basic income, move away in a different direction with ad hoc adjustments as circumstances may dictate, or even disappear altogether? In examining this question, it is fairly safe to assume that the price reform that gave birth to the transfers would not be rolled back. There is a general consensus that the old system of price subsidies was untenable and had to be transformed. The most difficult first stage of the reform process, namely the massive initial shock, passed off reasonably smoothly thanks to the cash subsidies, long preparation, and an effective public information campaign.[19] The authorities appear determined to press ahead with the subsequent phases of the reform, a determination that is bolstered by the favorable assessments of international organizations (none of which has been directly involved) and the interest shown by other countries. The International Monetary Fund (2011) welcomed the strategy, observing in particular that the cash transfers were instrumental in supporting domestic demand, improving income distribution, and reducing poverty. Similarly, the World Bank (2011) found that, according to preliminary estimates, the transfer program had reduced poverty and regional income disparities significantly. Are the IMF and the World Bank singing the praises of a de facto national basic income?

There is no unique definition of basic income but Philippe Van Parijs captures its essence by defining it as "an income paid by a political community to all its members on an individual basis, without means test or work requirement" (Van Parijs 2006: 4). Elaborating further, he adds that this income is paid in cash, at regular intervals, and by the government out of publicly controlled resources (Van Parijs 2006: 4–5). Van Parijs and most other proponents of basic income also tend to view it as an economic right that should be enjoyed indefinitely. This income may or may not be sufficient to ensure a minimal standard of living. It may or may not be provided to (long-term) residents who are not citizens. While the details may vary, the fundamental characteristic of a basic income is the legal entitlement of the recipients to an income stream that provides a certain level of economic security.

As discussed in detail in Tabatabai (2011), Iran's cash subsidies in their current form (as of November 2011) come sufficiently close to meeting the necessary criteria to be regarded as a de facto basic income. The main difference is that the transfers for members of a household are not paid out to them individually but are paid instead to the head of the household on their behalf. The reason is simple: the transfers are a form of compensation for subsidy cuts and thus go to the person who pays the higher bills, which is normally the head of the household. However, the advantages attributed to individualized payments are not entirely lost. A basic income "is paid on a strictly individual basis, not only in the sense that each individual member of the community is a recipient, but also in the sense that how much (s)he receives is independent of what type of household she belongs to" (Van Parijs 2006: 8). The practice in Iran satisfies the latter proviso—the amount received does not depend on whether one is living alone or belongs to a household—but not the former one. Van Parijs goes on to argue that "[p]recisely because of its strictly individualistic nature, a basic income tends to remove isolation traps and foster communal life" (Van Parijs 2006: 8). But this is true for Iran's case as well. That said, it is conceivable that over the longer term the situation might evolve as more is learned about the impact of payments on intrahousehold distribution of welfare. In the interest of expanding people's choices, a step in the right direction might be to allow households to express a preference between payment to household head or to adults individually (children's share would of course go to the parents or guardians).

The important question at this juncture, however, is not whether cash subsidies in their current form constitute a basic income or not, but whether they will continue, and if so, how they might evolve. The cash transfer program, while popular, does not enjoy universal support. Some experts have called for it to be stopped and the resources redirected to other priorities, for example, job creation or expansion of public goods and services.[20] That is unlikely to be feasible anymore, socially or politically, regardless of any economic merit the idea might have. Others are less categorical and would support a certain portion of the funds being distributed in cash to lower income groups.[21] The government itself initially intended to cover seven deciles of the population but dropped the idea as the identification of the target population proved to be technically challenging and socially unpopular. The universality of coverage thus came about for lack of a practical alternative. It had few advocates per se and may yet prove to be short lived, even if retreating from it may be harder after it has been firmly in place for some time. The revival of targeting is one of the options under continuing consideration to deal with the apparent resource constraints facing the program.[22]

It is not clear how serious the resource constraints are. The finances of the transfer program have become a highly controversial issue with divergent assessments from the government, institutions with oversight responsibilities, and other observers. While the government denies there are any serious problems, skepticism abounds and appears to be confirmed by the ad hoc measures taken from time to time to maintain the payments. What is certain is that the financing provisions of the law have been put on the back burner. Household payments amount to $40 billion a year. Revenues of around $67 billion would be needed if the household share were to be no higher than the maximum of 60 percent provided in the law, an amount that was not forthcoming. The annual budget for Iranian year 1390 (March 21, 2011—March 20, 2012) acknowledged this reality by anticipating revenues at $54 billion, which may still be optimistic.[23] Such uncertainty about the finances of the program is feeding speculation about its sustainability in its present form.

This anomalous financing situation is variously blamed on the overestimation of potential revenues from higher prices, the universal coverage of the population, and/or the high level of the transfer.[24] To some extent the program appears to have become a victim of its own success, or that of the reform more generally. On the one hand, the shortfall in revenues might be due in part to the more than expected decline in the consumption of goods and services concerned, particularly fuel. On the other hand, the sharp rise in participation in the early months of the program was no doubt a reflection of its growing popularity, particularly because of the relatively generous amount of the transfer.

To elaborate on the latter point, it may be noted that at the start of the reform in December 2010, only about 80 percent of the households had completed the formalities required to qualify for the transfer, which involved filling out the registration form and supplying a bank account into which the payment would be deposited. Of the 20 percent of households that did not participate, about half had not applied at all, most likely because they did not wish to report their incomes and assets, were not impressed with the transfer amount likely to be involved—which was not known at registration time before the launch of the reform—or were simply unaware of the program. The other half had filled out the registration form but chose to suspend their participation by withholding bank account details. This gesture followed government appeals to those who were better off to forego their entitlement voluntarily so as to leave more funds for those who needed the transfer.

However, the situation evolved once the cash started to flow. In the first few months of the program the number of participants rose from 60 million to 72.5 million, or from 80 percent of the country's population of 75.3 million to 96 percent.[25] Several factors may explain this evolution. First, with targeting abandoned, the information on incomes and assets was no longer relevant to eligibility and the concern about scrutiny of these by the government may have eased or disappeared.[26] Second, the bureaucratic registration process was simplified, giving way to registration through the Internet. Third, with the transfer program already operational, the more skeptical people who were biding their time during the uncertain preprogram period may have been encouraged to put in their claims. And fourth, the sense of solidarity that motivated some people to stay away may have evolved with the realization that charitable purposes could be served just as well or better privately by the beneficiaries themselves rather than through the government.

The most significant factor, however, may well have been the amount of the transfer that, as discussed before, turned out to be much higher than anticipated, just as price rises were. Once the new prices and the transfer amount were known, many nonparticipants must have felt that staying away had become too costly and joined the program, which should not be surprising. The public was assured that the amount of the transfer would remain unchanged at about $45 per person per month until at least March 2012. Subsequently, it would be expected to rise in line with further price increases in later stages of the reform process. In fact, noting that the subsidy bill was around $120 billion, only a third of which had already been converted to cash transfers, the president observed at one point that "it would be appropriate to triple these transfers."[27] The possibility cannot be ruled out over the medium term as later phases of the reform kick in. A key relevant factor is the impact of inflation on the transfers. Given the relatively high and accelerating rate of inflation—hovering around 20 percent although some believe it to be higher—the government's easiest option to reduce the burden of transfers might be to let inflation erode their real value.

Finally, as regards the duration of the program, there have been contradictory reports as to where policymakers stand on the matter but there is little discussion of it in public.[28] Since the subsidies are being removed permanently, there might be an expectation that the compensatory cash transfer program would be equally permanent, at least as long as Iran is producing enough fuel for its domestic requirements.

Concluding Observations

In chapter 4, Guy Standing, one of the founders of Basic Income Earth Network (BIEN), identifies three main lines of thinking that have dominated the basic income conversation: (1) first, that is broadly philosophical and libertarian, stressing the appeal of a basic income as a right and as a stand-alone matter; (2) second, that sees basic income as one component of a redistributive political and economic strategy; and (3) a third line that is becoming increasingly important, namely the potential of a basic income as a means of enhancing a more gendered and ecologically viable future. In the case of Iran, it is clearly the second that has been the dominant influence. The first and third lines played little or no part, although the ecological factor did figure in to some extent since one key objective was to reduce the consumption of fuel products. However, even the significance of the distributional objective should be seen in context. It was only part of a broader policy agenda that aimed to correct the long-standing problem of mismanagement of Iran's most important natural resource. Put differently, Iran's version of basic income became a reality not on its own merit alone but because it helped facilitate the resolution of a larger issue of national concern.

Another critical consideration is that this de facto basic income is not putting a new burden on public finances (national budget or oil export revenues) but is financed through a redistribution of existing household incomes. This model of financing a basic income has not been much discussed in the literature but may make basic income more of a realistic proposition and in more countries.[29]

But as discussed above, there have been many challenges along the road to a basic income in Iran and more lie ahead. Its future is by no means guaranteed. While its existence in reality may have created conditions for the development of a strong constituency to maintain it, the best guarantee for its continuation would be to show convincingly that the larger price subsidy reform of which it is an integral part is indeed working reasonably well and could work better still. That calls for comprehensive and systematic evaluation of the impact of the reform on a continuing basis. The lessons, positive or negative, will help resolve the outstanding policy issues, improve the functioning of the program, and help make it less vulnerable to shifting political currents. This social experiment on a grand scale may also provide a model that some other countries could adapt to their own circumstances.

Notes

1. The Iranian currency, rial, is subject to a managed floating exchange rate regime that has effectively kept it pegged to the US dollar for years at rates hovering around US$1 = Rl 10,000. For the sake of simplicity, rial figures in this chapter are given in equivalent dollar terms using this exchange rate. All references to dollar are to the US dollar.
2. GIZ, "International fuel prices, 2010/2011, data preview," January 2011:4–5. http://www.gtz.de/de/dokumente/giz2011-international-fuel-prices-2010–2011-data-preview.pdf.
3. It should be noted that the subsidies are mostly implicit, not financed by oil exports or the budget. They arise because domestically produced oil and gas (the sector is nationalized) are sold cheaply in the local market.

4. Karrubi, a cleric once regarded as a pillar of the regime, was the speaker of the parliament twice, 1989–1992 and 2000–2004. He finished third in the first round of presidential elections in 2005, just behind Tehran mayor Mahmoud Ahmadinejad, who went on to win the second round against the former president Akbar Hashemi Rafsanjani.
5. Interview with Mehdi Karrubi, published on http://sharifnews.ir /, May 4, 2005. The website is no longer operational but the interview may be found at http://60000000.blogfa.com/post-2404.aspx, May 5, 2005.
6. For the full text of the law in English, see Guillaume et al. (2011), Appendix I.
7. The government is authorized to keep domestic energy prices unchanged for consumers as long as Persian Gulf FOB prices fluctuate within a range of 25 percent. If price fluctuations exceed this range, domestic prices will be adjusted accordingly.
8. If 60 percent of the first year revenues of $20 billion (two maximums allowed under the Law) were to be distributed equally among the 60 million participants who joined the program from the start, they would each be entitled to about $17 per month over the year.
9. In the first three months of the program, for example, revenues amounted to $8.6 billion (http://www.iraneconomist.com/economic/bazaar-money-stock/43594–8600 – – – -.html, August 23, 2011), while $8.1 billion was paid out to households ($45 per person per month X 3 months X 60 million participants in early months), far above the household share of 50 percent (maximum 60 percent for the year) authorized under the law.
10. http://www.fararu.com/vdca0mna.49ny015kk4.html, July 22, 2011.
11. Over the past couple of years, there have been increasing complaints about the lack of official statistics on key economic indicators and/or their reliability. Some critics accuse the government of "managing" the flow of information to minimize unfavorable publicity and criticism of its policies.
12. The annual rate of inflation at any given month is the percentage change of prices for the 12-month period ending in that month relative to the same period a year earlier.
13. http://www.iraneconomist.com/economic/ecnomy-bazzar /45513 – – 183 – .html, October 10, 2011. Alternative data from the Statistical Centre of Iran put the similarly defined rate of inflation for September 2011 at the higher figure of 22.4 percent for urban and rural areas combined. See, http://jahannews.com /vdcfxxdytw6d1ma.igiw.html, October 11, 2011.
14. http://www.fararu.com/vdcfmedc.w6deyagiiw.html, August 29, 2011.
15. See http://alef.ir/1388/content/view/112298/, July 29, 2011; http:// www.hamshahrionline.ir/news-143823.aspx, August 23, 2011; http://www.farsnews.com/newstext.php?nn=13900525151256,

September 23, 2011; http://www.ayandenews.com/news/36010/, September 7, 2011; and http://www.salamatnews.com/viewNews.aspx?ID=33295&cat=5, September 20, 2011.

16. http://www.fardanews.com/fa/news/161242/%D9%81%D8%B1%D8%B2%DB%8C%D9%86-%D9%8A%D8%A7%D8%B1%D8%A7%D9%86%D9%87-%D9%86%D9%82%D8%AF%DB%8C-%D9%85%DB%8C%E2%80%8C%D8%AA%D9%88%D8%A7%D9%86%D8%AF-3-%D8%A8%D8%B1%D8%A7%D8%A8%D8%B1-%D8%B4%D9%88%D8%AF, September 10, 2011.
17. http://www.ayandenews.com/news/34168/, August 10, 2011. It should be noted that opinion polls in Iran are rare, and the publication of their results rarer still, particularly on sensitive issues. If they are conducted, it is usually to allow the sponsoring institution, often an official body, to gauge the mood of the public on some issue, keeping the results confidential. The results of this poll were leaked to the press, perhaps only selectively.
18. In the early months of the reform, when this poll was carried out, only 80 percent of the population was covered by the cash transfer program nationwide; see below.
19. For a good account of the public relations campaign that preceded the introduction of the reform, see Guillaume et al. (2011).
20. See, for example, interview with Professor Hamid Dayheem, secretary of the Society of Iranian Economists, http://www.thebankers.ir/news/NewsDetail.aspx?Newsid=2044128557, August 5, 2011.
21. See, for example, interview with Professor Djavad Salehi Esfahani, http://www.donya-e-eqtesad.com/Default_view.asp?@=223148, September 12, 2010, and with Professor Ali Rashidi, president of the Society of Iranian Economists, http://parlemannews.com/?n=15696, October 30, 2011.
22. http://iraneconomist.com/economic/ecnomy-bazzar/40794–2011–06–14–08–22–24.html, June 14, 2011, and http://www.fararu.com/vdcd9n0j.yt0k96a22y.html, August 6, 2011.
23. http://www.mellatonline.ir/index.php/negah/79-news/7170–60-, August 17, 2011.
24. The information on finances of the program is sketchy, in particular data on revenues collected through subsidy cuts. Some observers contend that revenue shortfalls are being met from other budgetary resources whose legality is questionable. The government denies the claim. http://khabaronline.ir/news-172817.aspx, September 12, 2011.
25. http://www.fararu.com/vdcd9n0j.yt0k96a22y.html, August 6, 2011.
26. Such information continues to be required of new applicants as part of an effort to build up a socioeconomic profile of the nation. In this connection, it should be noted that the receipt of cash subsidies is subject to households providing accurate information. If the information proves to be inaccurate, the law calls for legal action to be taken by the government to recover the amounts so paid and

discontinue future payments. It does not appear that this provision is being enforced.

27. http://www.donya-e-eqtesad.com/Default_view.asp?@=268669, September 9, 2011.
28. http://www.iraneconomist.com/economic/economic-articles /45249-2011-10-04-09-59-14.html, October 4, 2011.
29. See Van Parijs (2010) and Tabatabai (forthcoming).

References

Guillaume, Dominique, Roman Zytek, and Mohammad Reza Farzin. 2011. "Iran—The Chronicles of the Subsidy Reform," IMF Working Paper No. WP/11/167. Washington, DC: International Monetary Fund. https://www.imf.org/external/pubs/ft/wp/2011/wp11167.pdf.

International Monetary Fund. 2011. "IMF Executive Board Concludes 2011 Article IV Consultation with the Islamic Republic of Iran," Public Information Notice (PIN) No. 11/107, August 3, 2011. http://www.imf.org/external/np/sec/pn/2011/pn11107.htm.

Kapuscinski, Ryszard. 1986. *Shah of Shahs.* London: Picador / Pan Books.

Tabatabai, Hamid. 2011. "The Basic Income Road to Reforming Iran's Price Subsidies" *Basic Income Studies* 6 (1): Article 3. http://www.bepress.com/bis/vol6/iss1/art3.

———. Forthcoming. "From Price Subsidies to Basic Income: The Iran Model and Its Lessons." In *Exporting the Alaska Model*, edited by Karl Widerquist and Michael Howard. New York: Palgrave Macmillan.

Van Parijs, Philippe. 2006. "Basic Income: A Simple and Powerful Idea for the Twenty-First Century." In *Redesigning Distribution: Basic Income and Stakeholder Grants as Cornerstones for an Egalitarian Capitalism*, edited by Bruce Ackerman, Anne Alstott, and Philippe van Parijs. London and New York: Verso.

———. 2010. "BIEN 2010 Congress: A Brief Personal Account." *BIEN NewsFlash* 62: 2–4. http://www.basicincome.org/bien/pdf/Flash62.pdf.

World Bank. 2011, September. "Iran Country Brief." http://go.worldbank.org/KQD2RP3RX0.

Notes on Contributors

Richard K. Caputo is professor of social policy & research and the director, PhD program in social welfare, at the Wurzweiler School of Social Work, Yeshiva University, in New York City. He has authored five books and edited a sixth. His most recently published book is *U.S. Social Welfare Reform: Policy Transitions from 1981 to the Present* (2011). He is the associate editor of the *Journal of Family and Economic Issues* and serves on the editorial boards of the *Journal of Poverty*, the *Journal of Sociology & Social Welfare*, and *Families in Society.*

David Casassas is a postdoctoral fellow in sociology and political theory at the University of Barcelona. He is the secretary of the Basic Income Earth Network (BIEN) and vice president of Red Renta Básica. He is an associate editor of the journal *Basic Income Studies.* He is the author or coauthor of several articles on republicanism and basic income (BI).

Michiel van Hasselt, a sociologist, participates in the Dutch association of basic income as a member of the board. He wrote BI relevant books *The state of simplicity* (1998) and *Social security: an alternative*! (2004); and more recently, wrote an article in the scientific Tijdschrift voor Arbeidsvraagstukken *Policy elite misinterpretes labour market* (2009). In 2011, he published a book *Politics in the Dutch Welfare State: Misrepresentation and Civil Reconstruction.*

Seán Healy is director of Social Justice Ireland. For more than 25 years he has been active on issues of socioeconomic policy in Ireland. Before that, he worked for more than 10 years in Africa. He has a PhD since 1984. He has been a member of the National Economic and Social Council (NESC) for more than a decade. He has worked on many government task forces dealing with a wide range of social and economic policy issues. Together with the Social Justice Ireland's other director, Brigid Reynolds, Seán has written or edited 27 books on public policy as well as three books on spirituality for social engagement (2004, 2006, and 2008). Their most recent publications are *A New and Fairer Ireland: Securing Economic Development, Social Equity and Sustainability* (2011—authors) and *Sharing Responsibility in Shaping the Future* (2011—eds.). Their book *Social Policy in Ireland* (published in 1998 and revised in 2006) has become a standard textbook on social policy in Ireland.

Markku Ikkala served several years as an organizational leader. Further, he continues his work in real estate management business as an entrepreneur. Simultaneously, he has studied political science and business management in the University of Jyväskylä where he earned his MSc (Soc. Sc.) degree. His subject of research in political science is "Basic Income discussion in Finland," for which he has collected a wide material and on which he has lectured in Finland and also in the BIEN congress 2008, in Dublin. His research in business management has also touched BI as far as questions of motivation at work are concerned. He has actively participated in BIEN congresses and is a life member of BIEN.

Sascha Liebermann is PhD in sociology and MA in philosophy. His research focus has been as follows: political sociology, welfare state, economic sociology, theory of professions, sociology of socialization, and qualitative methods. He has worked as assistant professor at Ruhr-University Bochum; visiting fellow at the Swiss Federal Institute of Technology (ETH) Zurich (Switzerland); and founding member of "Freedom not Full Employment" (www.freiheitstattvollbeschaeftigung.de) (in 2003), a group of German citizens arguing for an unconditional BI.

James P. Mulvale, PhD, RSW, is an associate professor in the Faculty of Social Work at the University of Regina, Canada. He teaches in the areas of social welfare policy and work and economic security. His research interests include guaranteed income or BI, and Aboriginal approaches to economic and community development. He chairs the Basic Income Canada Network / Réseau Canadien pour le Revenu Garanti, an affiliate of the BIEN. He is also a member of the steering committee of Poverty Free Saskatchewan.

José A. Noguera is associate professor in the Department of Sociology at the Universitat Autònoma de Barcelona, and director of the Analytical Sociology and Institutional Design Group (GSADI). He holds a PhD in sociology from the Universitat Autònoma de Barcelona and has been a visiting researcher at the University of California, Berkeley and at the London School of Economics and Political Science. He has been the principal investigator of several GSADI projects funded by the R & D Spanish National Plan since 2006. José A. Noguera's research covers sociological theory, philosophy of social science, social policy, and normative social theory. He is a member of the European Network of Analytical Sociologists, and serves on the International Advisory Board of the BIEN. José A. Noguera is coeditor of *Papers. Revista de Sociologia*, and an editorial board member of *Revista Española de Investigaciones Sociológicas* and *Basic Income Studies*.

Daniel Raventós teaches at the University of Barcelona and is chairman of Red Renta Básica. His last book is *Basic Income. The Material Conditions of Freedom* (2007). He is a founding member of the international political review *Sin Permiso* (www.sinpermiso.info).

Brigid Reynolds is director of Social Justice Ireland. For more than 25 years, she has been active on issues of public policy in Ireland. Before that, she worked for more than 10 years in Africa. She has worked on many government task forces dealing with a wide range of social and economic policy issues. Together with the Social Justice Ireland's other director, Seán Healy, Brigid has written or edited 27 books on public policy as well as three books on spirituality for social engagement (2004, 2006, and 2008). Their most recent publications are *A New and Fairer Ireland: Securing Economic Development, Social Equity and Sustainability* (2011—authors) and *Sharing Responsibility in Shaping the Future* (2011—eds.). Their book *Social Policy in Ireland* (published in 1998 and fully revised and updated in 2006) has become a standard textbook on social policy in Ireland.

Guy Standing is professor of economic security at the University of Bath. He is a founder of the BIEN and has published several books and numerous articles related to economic security and basic income guarantees. His most recent publication is *The Precariat: The New Dangerous Class* (London: Bloomsbury Academic, 2011).

Eduardo Matarazzo Suplicy, a native of São Paulo, Brazil, studied at the Escola de Administração de Empresas de São Paulo, FGV, becoming a professor of economics in 1966. He completed his Master (1968) and PhD (1973) in economics at Michigan State University, USA, with the thesis: "The Effects of the Mini-Devaluations of the Exchange Rate on the Brazilian Economy." In 1972, a visiting scholar at Stanford University, he offered a seminar on the Brazilian economy. In 1978, he was elected state representative in São Paulo. On February 10, 1980, he was one of the cofounders of the Workers' Party becoming, in 1982, federal representative. In 1988, he was elected city councilman and president of the City Council of São Paulo. In 1990, 1998, and 2006 he was elected senator for three eight-year terms. As a senator, he approved the law to institute, step-by-step, under the executive's criteria, starting with those most in need, a citizen's basic income. His main book is *Renda de Cidadania. A Saída é pela Porta* (2004).

Hamid Tabatabai was a senior economist at the International Labour Office, Geneva, Switzerland, until his retirement in 2010. His main areas of work related to employment, poverty, income distribution, child labour, and cash transfers. He did his postgraduate studies at the London School of Economics and at Cornell University, Ithaca, New York, USA, where he obtained a PhD in economics in 1982. He is an Iranian and lives in France.

John Tomlinson's PhD examined the political obstacles to the introduction of a guaranteed minimum income in Australia. He worked as a commonwealth government social worker and a community worker with low-income earners in Queensland and the Northern Territory from 1964 until 1975. He taught at a several Australian universities and colleges. From 1987 until 1993, he was the director of the Australian Capital Territory (ACT) Council of Social Services. In the period 1993–2007, he was senior lecturer in social policy and community work at the Queensland University of Technology. His best-known books are *Is Band-Aid Social Work Enough?* (1978) and an e- book *Social Insecurity: The Basic Income Alternative* (2003).

Malcolm Torry is director of the Citizen's Income Trust and a visiting senior fellow in the Social Policy Department at the London School of Economics.

Yannick Vanderborght teaches political science at the Facultés universitaires Saint-Louis (Brussels), where he currently directs the Research Centre in Political Science (CReSPo). He is also a member of the Hoover Chair (Louvain), of the executive committee of the BIEN, and an associate editor of *Basic Income Studies.* He coauthored with Ph. Van Parijs *L'allocation universelle* (2005), and has published several articles on BI and related issues. He is the coeditor (with K. Widerquist, J. Noguera, and J. De Wispelaere) of *Basic Income: An Anthology of Contemporary Research* (Blackwell, forthcoming).

Julie Wark is a Barcelona-based translator, independent researcher and author of *Manifiesto de derechos humanos* (The Human Rights Manifesto, forthcoming 2012). She is member of the Red Renta Básica—the Spanish basic income network.

Jurgen De Wispelaere is a senior research fellow at CRÉUM (Centre de Recherche d'Éthique de l'Université de Montréal) and a visiting scholar at UAB (Universitat Autònoma de Barcelona). His published work on BI has appeared in *Analyse und Kritik*, *The Political Quarterly*, *The Social Service Review*, *Policy and Politics*, and the *International Social Security Review*. He is a founding editor of the journal *Basic Income Studies* and coeditor of *The Ethics of Stakeholding* (Palgrave Macmillan, 2003); *Recognition, Equality and Democracy* (Routledge, 2007); and *Basic*

Income: An Anthology of Contemporary Research (Blackwell, forthcoming). He is currently completing a book on *Republicanism* (Continuum, 2012), coauthored by David Casassas.

Toru Yamamori is a professor of social policy in the faculty of economics at Doshisha University, Kyoto, Japan. He is also the secretary-general of the Basic Income Japan Network. His *Beginning Basic Income* has sold more than 20,000 copies since it was published from Kobunsha, Tokyo in 2009. His works in English include "Constructive Universalism: Sen and Sensitivity to Difference" in *La revue Éthique et économique*, vol.1. His research interests include the philosophical foundations of economics, feminist economics, multiculturalism, and social movements by welfare claimants.

Pablo Yanes has a bachelor's degree in economics and a master's degree in government and public matters, both from the National Autonomous University of Mexico. He has made presentations on social policies, inequality, poverty, human rights, and indigenous rights in Chiapas, Puebla, Queretaro, San Luis Potosi, Oaxaca, Durango, Hidalgo, Zacatecas, San Diego California, Barcelona, Bilbao, Madrid, Dublin, Quito, Guatemala, San José, Costa Rica, Santo Domingo, Bogotá, Santiago de Chile, Montevideo, Belem do Pará, Brasilia, Sao Paulo, Buenos Aires, Mendoza, and Cape Town, South Africa. From 2002 until December 2006, he was general director of equity and social development for the Mexico City government. Since February of 2008, he has been general director of the social development evaluation council of Mexico City. He was an active participant in the design of and in the legislative process that lead to the creation of the council.

Index

Act to Eliminate Poverty in Canada, An (2011), 185
administration of BI, 24–27, 34n6, 148n12, 221; simplicity of, 251, 253, 259
affordability of BI. *See* funding BI; piecemeal BI schemes
agency, 18–19, 20–21; discrete and diffuse, 7, 19, 20, 27, 29
Aid to Families with Dependent Children (AFDC) (U.S.), 268–273
Alaska Permanent Fund, 8, 13, 34n11, 265–266, 274–275; Brazil and, 44–45, 50, 52
Alexander, Stuart, 276–277
Althaus, Dieter, 86–87, 99n6
Andersson, Jan-Otto, 4–5, 66
AOW (Algemene Ouderdoms Wet) (Dutch pension law, 1956), 126, 127, 128–129, 132
Apoyo Infantil Vivir Mejor (Live Better Child Support) (Mexico), 223–224
Arajärvi, Pentti, 67, 68, 71, 74
Australia, 10–11, 153–173; blind pension in, 155, 173; competing ideologies in, 157–159; Gillard government in, 169–170, 172; Howard government in, 165, 167–168, 169–170, 172, 173; income guarantees in, 159–163; as liberal welfare state, 178; in 1901–1910, 154–155; in 1980s and 1990s, 165–166; obstacles to BI in, 170–173; Poverty Inquiry and, 153, 160–161, 164, 171; Rudd government in, 169–170, 172; superannuation in, 11, 153, 162, 165, 166–167, 171–173; unemployment in, 156, 159, 164–165, 166; widows' pension in, 156, 158, 159–160, 163; Woodhouse inquiry and, 162–163, 164; *See also* disability benefits (Australia); pension (age-related in Australia); welfare programs/system (Australia)

Basic Income Canada Network/ Réseau Canadien pour le Revenu Garanti (BIEN affiliate), 195
Basic Income Earth Network (Basic Income European Network) (BIEN), 7, 83, 141–142; BI definition by, 64; BIRG and, 253; Canada and, 191, 195; inception of, 3–4; Japan and, 57, 210; Mexico and, 217, 229; name change of, 3–4, 56–57; Network BI and, 86; Standing and, 3, 8, 10, 12, 60, 296; symposiums and, 137, 141; 25th anniversary of, 55–60; Van Parijs and, 50, 51, 73, 132, 142, 293–294; VBi and, 131–132
Basic Income Japanese Network (BIJN), 57
Basic Income Research Group (BIRG) (UK), 253
behavioral feasibility of BI, 7, 8, 18, 21, 29–32, 33
Belgium, 5, 42, 73, 132, 187, 195n1

Beveridge, William, 238–241, 242, 243, 250–251
Beveridge Report, 204, 238–239, 241, 250–251
BI. *See under* basic income
Bildu (Basque political party), 147
BIRG (Basic Income Research Group) (UK), 253
Bloc Québécois, 184, 185
Bolsa Família Program (Brazil), 43, 45, 46–48, 50, 51, 52
Brazil, 7, 41–53; BIEN and, 57, 60; Bolsa Família Program and, 43, 45, 46–48, 50, 51, 52; Brazil without Poverty Program, 46, 49; CBI in, 44–45, 49, 50; EITC (U.S.) and, 8, 42–44, 51–52; funding BI in, 50–52; minimum income in, 45, 47, 50, 51
"Building a new Japan: a plan for remodeling the Japanese Archipelago" (Tanaka policy proposals), 208
Bündnis 90/ Die Grünen (Green Party) (Germany), 88, 90, 99n10
bureaucracy, 49, 70; BI implementation and, 25–26, 72, 148n12
Bürgerinitiative bedingungsloses Grundeinkommen Berlin (Citizens' Group BI Berlin), 88

Callaghan, James, 244–245
Canada, 3, 177–197; Alberta, 182, 186–187; BI and civil society and, 188–193; BI and politics in, 3, 182–188, 193–195; British Columbia, 186, 197n26; GAI in, 177–178, 183–190, 193; income inequality in, 178, 179, 180; Manitoba, 177, 184, 191; minimum income in, 179, 186, 187, 189; Newfoundland and Labrador, 180; NIT in, 31, 177–178, 182–185, 188, 190; poverty in, 178, 179; Quebec, 180, 181, 183, 184, 185, 186–188, 189, 192, 194; Saskatchewan, 180; senior citizens in, 178, 181, 182, 186, 190, 192; social assistance in, 179–181; unemployment in, 42, 186; welfare programs in, 11, 177, 178–182, 186, 188, 189, 191; Yukon Territories, 186, 197n25
Canada Assistance Plan (CAP), 180, 193
Canadian Feminist Alliance for International Action (FAFIA), 192–193
Canadian Labour Congress (CLC), 188–189
Cap and Dividend proposal (Brazil), 51
Cartão Alimentação (Food Card) (Brazil), 45
Casassas, David, 10
cash subsidies (Iran), 13–14, 285–287, 289, 290, 293–294, 299n26
cash transfer programs: in Iran, 285–286, 287, 288, 290, 292, 293–294, 296; in Mexico, 12, 49, 59–60, 218, 220, 221, 228, 231; *Oportunidades,* 12, 49, 218, 222–227, 231; TCCTP and, 223, 226, 227, 228–229
Castle, Barbara, 244–245
Castonguay-Nepveu report (1971) (Canada), 183, 187
Catalan parliament, 137, 140, 144
Cavala, Bill, 267, 268, 269, 270, 271
CDA (Christelijk Democratisch Appel) (Dutch Christian political party), 130–131, 132
Center Party (KESK) (Finland), 65, 73, 74
Centraal Planbureau (CPB) (Dutch economic planning agency), 128–129, 132
Centre for Social Justice (CSJ) (UK), 254–255, 257

Centre Party (Finland), 69
Child Benefit program (UK), 11, 12–13, 235–247, 249, 257–260; Beveridge Report and, 238–239, 241; evolving from Family Allowance, 235, 237, 243–245; household payments and, 245, 247, 258; parliamentary debates leading to, 241–242; preservation of, 245–247; Rathbone endowment and, 237–238; terminology and, 236–237; universality and, 235, 236, 237
child benefit programs: in Australia, 156, 159; in Canada, 11, 182, 194; in Germany, 91, 100n14; in Ireland, 115, 116, 122; in Japan, 210, 213; in Mexico, 223–224; in U.S., 275–276
child care, 92, 96–97, 101n23. *See also* unpaid work
children, 114, 179, 223; Bolsa Família and, 43, 45, 46–48, 50, 51, 52; Dutch social benefits and, 126; education of, in Germany, 91–92, 99n10; EITC and, 42–43; FAP and, 13, 183, 267–273; FFQ and, 192; Henderson Poverty Inquiry and, 161; of single mothers in Japan, 205, 215n3; widows' pension and, 156, 158, 159–160, 163; *See also* Child Benefit program (UK); families; mothers
Chrétien, Jean, 177, 190
Christelijk Democratisch Appel (CDA) (Dutch Christian political party), 130–131, 132
Christlich Demokratische Union (CDU, Christian Democratic Party) (Germany), 86–87, 88, 99n6
Citizen's Basic Income (CBI) (Brazil), 44–45, 49, 50
Citizen's Income (CI) (UK), 13, 235, 237, 246, 252–257, 259–260; Tax Credits and, 247, 250
citizen's pension: in Mexico, 217, 218–220, 223, 227, 230–231; in UK, 235, 255–256, 259; *See also* pension(s)
Civil-Engineering Keynesianism (Japan), 207–210, 215n8. *See also* Keynesianism
Clark, Charles, 110–115
Coalition Party (Finland), 5, 65, 70, 72, 74–75, 77
Coalition pour l'avenir du Québec (Coalition for the future of Quebec, CAQ), 188, 197n33
"Committee for reforming social protection" (SATA Committee) (Finland), 75–77, 78
Conde, Elsa, 12, 220–221
conditionality/conditional programs, 33n6, 59–60; of Australian welfare programs, 10–11, 162–163, 164, 165, 173; CAP and, 180, 193; citizenship and, 92–93; citizen's pension in Mexico and, 217, 218–220, 223, 227, 230–231; disability benefits in Canada and, 190; education requirements and, 91–92, 97, 225; in Finland, 9, 63–64, 76; in Germany, 9, 91; in Ireland, 109; job seeking and, 126–127; in Mexico, 218; in the Netherlands, 10, 126; *Oportunidades,* 12, 49, 218, 222–227, 231; PI and, 25–26, 27–28, 34n8; *Setenta y Más* and, 12, 217, 223, 224–227, 230, 231; in Spain, 139; *See also* means testing/means-tested programs
Confederação Nacional da Indústria (CNI) (Brazil), 41, 42
Congress, U.S., 265, 266, 268, 271–272, 273, 276
Conservative Party (Canada), 185, 186
Conservative Party (UK), 241–242, 244, 245–247, 249, 252, 258–260

conservatives: in Australia, 157–158, 159; in Canada, 177, 183–184, 185, 186, 194; in U.S., 272
Consolidation Act (1947) (Australia), 157, 160
constraints, 18, 19–21; discrete and diffuse, 7; prospective and retrospective, 20, 21, 24, 27, 29; psychological feasibility and, 28–29
CORI Justice (Ireland), 109–110, 111, 112
CPB (Centraal Planbureau) (Dutch economic planning agency), 128–129, 132
C/QPP (Canada/Quebec Pension Plan), 181, 192
CSN (Confederation of National Trade Unions) (Canada), 189
CUT (Central Única dos Trabalhadores [Workers' Central Union]), 41

Democratic Party of Japan (DPJ), 203, 209–210, 213–214, 215n8
Democratic Revolution Party BI proposal (Mexico), 220–221, 222
demogrants, 160, 182–183, 190
deservingness principle, 28, 29, 33
De Wispelaere, Jurgen, 7
dignity, 49, 52, 119, 122; women and, 97
Dilma, Rouseff, 41, 46–47
disability benefits: in Canada, 179, 181, 184, 186, 190–191, 196n12; in the Netherlands, 128, 130
disability benefits (Australia): for blind people, 155, 173; Henderson proposal and, 160–161; Howard government and, 168, 169, 172; means testing and, 153, 155, 163–165; 1908 legislation of, 153, 154–155; Woodhouse Commission and, 162; work search obligations for, 159; *See also* Australia
discrete and diffuse agency, 7, 19, 20, 27, 29
Douglas, C. H., 210–211
DPJ (Democratic Party of Japan), 203, 209–210, 213–214
D66 (Dutch political party), 125, 129, 132
Dutch Association for Basic Income (VBi), 131–132
Dutch welfare state, 125–126, 128, 132

Earned Income Tax Credit (EITC) (U.S.), 13, 265, 273; Brazil and, 8, 42–44, 51–52; Mexico and, 49
Economic and Financial Affairs Council (ECOFIN) (Spain), 136
Economic and Social Research Institute (ESRI) (Ireland), 108, 110, 122n2
Economic Commission for Latin America and the Caribbean (ECLAC), 222, 227–228
economic crises: Canada and, 195; Germany and, 98; global, 6, 195, 224; Japan and, 203, 207, 209, 212–213; Mexico and, 224; the Netherlands and, 128, 130; Spain and, 10, 135–136, 141, 145–146
education, 121; in Australia, 164–165; Bolsa Família and, 51; in Brazil, 45, 51; in Germany, 91–92, 99n10; in Ireland, 112; means testing and, 91–92, 97, 225; in Mexico, 222; in UK, 236
Esping-Andersen, Gøsta, 178, 196n5
Esquerra Republicana de Catalunya (ERC [Republican Left of Catalonia]), 137, 140, 144, 147
European Union (EU), 8, 131; BI policy for, 77, 98; debt in, 136
Existenzgeld (Subsistence allowance) (Germany), 85, 89

families: AFDC and, 268–273; Alaska Permanent Fund and, 44; in Australia, 159, 161, 170; Bolsa Família Program (Brazil), 43, 45, 46–48, 50, 51, 52; in Canada, 194; consumption by, 146; EITC and, 42–43; FAP and, 13, 183, 267–273; fathers and, 241, 245, 269; FFQ and, 192; in Germany, 96–97, 101n23; in Japan, 205; means testing and, 225; middle class welfare and, 172; single-mother, 13, 163, 172, 205, 212, 215n3, 265, 268–269; size of, 237–238, 240, 241, 244, 273; widows' pension and, 156, 158, 159–160, 163; *See also* Child Benefit program (UK); children; mothers
Family Allowance program (Canada), 182
Family Allowance program (UK), 12, 239, 257, 258; CPAG and, 244–245; evolving into Child Benefit, 235, 237, 243–245; parliamentary debates on, 241–242; *See also* Child Benefit program (UK)
Family Allowances Act (1945) (UK), 239–241
Family Assistance Plan (FAP) (U.S.), 13, 183, 267–273
Family Credit (UK), 246, 249
Family Income Supplement (UK), 246, 249
Family Support Act (1988) (U.S.), 267
Family Tax Credit (2000) (UK), 42
Federação das Indústrias do Estado de São Paulo (FIESP), 41, 42
Federal Bureau of Statistics (Statistiches Bundesamt) (Germany), 95
La Féderation des femmes du Québec (FFQ), 192
Federation of Labour (FTQ) (Canada), 189
feminism, 11, 159, 192–193, 205, 242. *See also* gender/gender equality; women
Field, Frank, 244, 245
Fifth Development Plan (Iran), 289
Filner, Bob, 276
financial crises. *See* economic crises
Finland, 4, 63–78; BI adoption in, possibility of, 64; BI political debates in (1990s and 00s), 68–70; BI researchers and, 70–72; citizens' salary in, 70, 72; history of BI in, 66–68; parliamentary election of 2007 in, 73–75; parliamentary election of 2011 in, 77–78; political appeal of BI in, 8–9; political system of, 64–66; SATA committee and, 75–77, 78; social security in, 63–64, 69–70, 72, 76; unemployment in, 42, 63, 69; *See also* Green movement (Finland); Soininvaara, Osmo
Finnish Christian Democrats (KD/KRIST), 65
Foget report (1986), 183
Forget, Evelyn, 191
Fréchette report (1978) (Canada), 187
Freiheit statt Vollbeschäftigung (Freedom, not Full Employment), 84–85
French Minimum Insertion Income, 156–157
Friedman, Milton, 59, 191, 266, 268, 270
fuel prices (Iran), 286–287, 289
Fujii, Hirohisa, 214–215
full employment: in Germany, 84, 86; in Japan, 208; in the Netherlands, 10, 127, 128, 130; in UK, 239
funding BI, 23, 31–32; in Australia, 171–173; in Brazil, 50–52; in Canada, 185; in Finland, 70; in Germany, 97; in Ireland, 110, 112, 114, 115–116; in Mexico, 218; in the Netherlands, 128; in Spain, 135, 142–143, 144; *See also* piecemeal BI schemes

Garantiertes Grundeinkommen (Guaranteed Income) (Opielka and Vobruba), 89
gender/gender equality, 90, 96–97, 121; in Australia, 154, 159; in Japan, 205–206, 207; men and, 207, 269; in Mexico, 225; in UK, 242, 245; See also women
Genug für alle (Enough for all) (*attac* subdivision), 85, 92
Germany, 5, 83–101, 132; BIEN criteria for BI in, 83; BI precursors in 1980s in, 89–90; citizenship in, 89, 92–93, 98, 100n17; current BI debates in, 91–97; EU BI and, 98; history of current BI debates in, 83, 84–89; income inequality in, 179; Liebermann and, 9, 84–85; media in, 84–85, 86–89, 90; unemployment in, 84, 85, 101n22
Gillard, Julia, 169–170, 172
Glaeser, Edward, 50–51
Götz W. Werner—Grundeinkommen für alle (Basic Income for all) (film), 87
Grass, Günter, 9, 85
Great Britain, 6, 154, 206, 276. *See also* United Kingdom
Green League (VIHR) (Finland), 8, 65
Green movement (Finland), 5; BI debates and, 68–70, 78; citizens' salary and, 70, 72; early support of BI by, 67; parliamentary elections and, 72–75, 77–78; Soininvaara as leader of, 66, 68
green papers (consultation documents): in Canada, 184; in Ireland, 111–112; in UK, 13, 250
Green political parties, 22; in Australia, 157; in Canada, 178, 185–186; in Finland, 8; in Germany, 88, 90, 99n10; *See also* Green movement (Finland)
Groot, Loek, 4–5
Guaranteed Annual Income (GAI): in Canada, 177–178, 183–190, 193–194; in U.S., 265–266, 268, 270–271
Guaranteed Income Supplement (GIS) (Canada), 178, 182, 192
Guaranteed Livable Income (GLI) (Canada), 185–186

Hammond, Jay, 44, 274
Hancock Committee (Australia), 162–163, 164
Hartz, Peter, 84
Hatoyama, Yukio, 209–210, 214
Hawke Labor government (Australia), 165, 166
Hayden, Bill, 163, 164
Hayek, Friedrich, 58–59
Healy, John, 110, 112–115
Healy, Seán, 5, 9–10, 110
Heath government (UK), 244, 247–248, 249, 254
Henderson, Ronald, 153, 160–161, 163, 173
Henderson Poverty Inquiry (Australia), 153, 160–161, 164, 171
Her Majesty's Revenue and Customs (UK), 247, 249, 258, 259
Herrera, Joan, 140–141
Hirsch, Donald, 253–254
Holland. *See* the Netherlands
Honkanen, Pertti, 72, 73
Horie, Takafumi, 211–212
Household Economic Information Form (Iran), 288
House of Commons (Canada), 11, 178, 184, 185
Howard, John, 165, 167–168, 169–170, 172, 173
human rights, 100n18; BI eligibility and, 92–93; BI in Mexico and, 229, 232n14; BI in Spain and, 141–142

Ikkala, Markku, 8–9
implementation of BI, 24–27; "all-at-once" strategy to (Ireland), 9, 112, 113; "by-groups" strategy to (Ireland), 9, 112, 113–114, 115–116
incentives, 32, 63–64; behavioral feasibility and, 29–32; "free money" and, 78; Irish BI studies and, 111–112
income, 90, 92; EITC and, 8, 13, 42–44, 49, 51–52, 265, 273; income-maintenance and, 5, 160, 161, 164, 254, 257, 259, 260, 267; PI and, 25–26, 27–28, 34n8; *vs.* wages, 93–94; *See also* minimum income/wage
income inequality, 6; in Australia, 154; in Canada, 178, 179, 180; in Germany, 179; in Iran, 14; in U.S., 179
income-maintenance policy, 5, 266–267; in Australia, 160, 161, 164; in UK, 254, 257, 259, 260
income tax: in Finland, 72; in Germany, 95–96; in Ireland, 107–115, 117–118, 120; IRPF and, 142, 143; *See also* taxes/taxation
In fromf Iniciativa per *the Margins* (Canadian Senate report), 184
Iniciativa per Catalunya-Verds (ICV [Initiative for Catalonia Greens]) (Spain), 137, 144, 147
institutional feasibility of BI, 7, 18, 21, 24–27, 29, 30, 32–33
International Monetary Fund (IMF), 136, 145, 293
Iran, 8, 60, 285–300; cash subsidies in, 13–14, 285–287, 289, 290, 293–294, 299n26; cash transfer programs in, 285–286, 287, 288, 290, 292, 293–294, 296; consumption in, 14, 286–287, 291–292, 295, 297; household income in, 288, 289, 292, 297, 299n26; household payments in, 289, 290, 293–294, 295, 298n9, 299n26; minimum income in, 290; price subsidies in, 14, 285–287, 293, 297; Subsidy Reform Law in, 286–293
Ireland, 6, 23, 107–123; "all-at-once" approach to BI implementation in, 9, 112, 113; "by-groups" approach to BI implementation in, 9, 112, 113–114, 115–116; Clark and John Healy's study of BI in, 110, 112–115; Commission on Taxation in, 108, 113; CORI Justice approach to BI in, 109–110, 111, 112; ESRI study of BI in, 108, 110, 122n2; funding BI in, 110, 112, 114, 115–116; "gradual" approach to BI implementation in, 9, 113, 114–115; green papers in, 111–112; Healy, Seán and Reynolds and, 5, 9–10; Honohan's study of BI in, 108; household income in, 108, 109, 110, 118; implementation of BI in, 112–122; income tax in, 107–115, 117–118, 120; minimum income in, 118, 120; piecemeal BI schemes in, 109–110, 113–114; poverty in, 110–111, 118, 120–122, 123n6; studies of BI in, 107–115; tax credit system in, 10, 115, 116–119, 120, 122; unemployment in, 42, 109, 111–112, 120–121; Ward's study of BI in, 109–110; welfare programs/system in, 9–10, 107–115, 117–118, 120–122; working groups' study of BI in, 110–111
IRPF (Spanish Personal Income Tax), 142, 143

Japan, 10, 11–12, 203–215; BIJN and, 57; deregulation in, 207–210, 213, 215n8; history of BI debates in, 210–212; "Japanese Welfare Society" and, 204–207; Keynesianism and, 12, 207–210, 214; media in, 12, 203, 206, 211–213
Japan Broadcasting Corporation (NHK), 211
Japanese Business Federation (Nikkeiren), 207
"Japanese-style Management...and the concrete measures entailed" (Nikkeiren manifesto), 207
jobs. *See* work/employment
Job Seeker's Allowance (UK), 258
Johnson, Lyndon, 266
Johnson, Patrick, 189
Johnson administration (U.S.), 267, 269
Joseph Rowntree Foundation (UK), 253
JUTTA (BI simulation model), 72, 73

Kalevi Sorsa Foundation (Finland), 4
Kansalaispalkka. Ken elää sen syömänkin pitää (Citizens' Salary. Who Lives Must Also Eat) (Lahtinen), 67
Karrubi, Medhi, 286–287, 298n4
Keating, Paul, 166, 167, 172
Keating Labor government (Australia), 166
Keynes, John Maynard, 241, 242
Keynesianism, 169, 173; in Japan, 12, 207–210, 214
Kingdom of Spain. *See* Spain
Koizumi administration (Japan), 209

Laberge, Louis, 189
labor market, 29, 32, 91–92, 240–241, 242; in the Netherlands, 42, 127, 129, 130, 133n3, 134nn5,6; workfare programs and, 180; *See also* unemployment
Labor Party (Australia), 157, 164, 165, 166, 169, 172, 173; Consolidation Act and, 160
Labour government (UK), 235, 237, 240–241, 244, 245, 249, 255, 258
Lahtinen, Ilpo, 67, 71
Lampman, Robert, 266, 268
Land, Hilary, 239–242
Landry, Bernard, 187–188
LDP (Liberal Democratic Party) (Japan), 203, 204–205, 207–209, 214
Left Alliance (VAS) (Finland), 65
Leftist League (Finland), 69, 70, 75
Lehto, Markku, 75, 76
Liberal Democratic Party (LDP) (Japan), 203, 204–205, 207–209, 214
Liberal Party (Canada), 183, 184, 185
Liberal Party (UK), 250, 252
LICO (Low Income Cut-Off) (Canada), 179, 180, 184, 185, 196n8
Liebermann, Sascha, 9, 84–85
Die Linke (the Left) (German political party), 88, 92
London School of Economics (LSE), 238, 246
López Bulla, José Luis, 137
Lowi, Theodore, 11, 207, 215n7
Lula da Silva, Luia Inácio, 45

Mabo High Court Judgment (Australia), 166
Macdonald, Donald Stoval, 183, 185, 189
Macdonald Commission (Canada), 183, 188, 189, 190, 194
Major, John, 246
Malcolm Fraser Liberal-Country Party Coalition (Australia), 11
Marxists/Marxism, 158–159, 207, 209, 211
Meade, James E., 214, 237

means testing/means-tested programs, 51, 52; Australia and, 153, 155, 157, 162, 163–165; Canada and, 179–181; Child Benefit program (Ireland) and, 116; Dutch tax credits and, 126; education and, 91–92, 97, 225; in Finland, 64; in Germany, 90, 91, 100n12; the Netherlands and, 126; pension in Ireland and, 116; PI and, 25–26, 27–28, 34n8; Tax Credits (UK) and, 13, 235, 246, 247–250, 252, 254, 257–258; in UK, 236, 244–246; *See also* conditionality/conditional programs; disability benefits (Australia); pension (age-related in Australia)
media: in Australia, 169, 171; in Canada, 187, 193; in Germany, 84–85, 86–89, 90; in Iran, 292; in Japan, 12, 203, 206, 211–213; in Mexico, 12, 217; radio programs, 12, 21, 86, 137, 217, 229, 292; in Spain, 137; television and, 244, 292; in UK, 243–244, 254; See also under specific media source
Medina, Makieze, 229
Menzies government (Australia), 159–160
Mexico, 11, 217–233; BI law in, 219–220; cash transfer programs in, 12, 49, 59–60, 218, 220, 221, 228, 231; citizen's pension in, 217, 218–220, 223, 227, 230–231; Democratic Revolution Party proposal in, 220–221, 222; household payments in, 218, 223, 226; media in, 12, 217; minimum income in, 218, 219, 221, 227, 229; *Oportunidades* and, 12, 49, 218, 222–227, 231; popular support for BI in, 229–230; poverty in, 220, 222, 223, 227–229; *Setenta y Más* and, 12, 217, 223, 224–227, 230, 231; unemployment in, 42, 220, 227, 231
Mexico City citizen's pension, 217, 218–220, 223, 227
Mincome experiment (Canada), 191
minimum income/wage, 28, 29; in Australia, 153, 154–155, 160–161, 162, 164; in Brazil, 45, 47, 50, 51; in Canada, 179, 186, 187, 189; EITC and, 43, 273; in Germany, 5, 86, 88, 93–94, 97, 100n12; in Iran, 290; in Ireland, 118, 120; in Mexico, 218, 219, 221, 227, 229; in Spain, 143; in UK, 236–237, 242, 249, 255–256; in U.S., 43, 208, 268, 269, 270, 273; *See also* income
mothers, 126, 246; child payments to, 241, 245, 249; FAP and, 13, 183, 267–273; fathers and, 241, 245, 269; single, 13, 163, 172, 205, 212, 215n3, 265, 268–269; *See also* children; families; women
Mulroney, Brian, 183
Mulvale, James P., 11, 191
Murray, Charles, 275

Namibia, 23, 60, 132
National Action Committee on the Status of Women (NAC) (Canada), 192
National Anti Poverty Organization (NAPO) (Canada), 189–190
National Assistance (UK), 243
National Board of Social Welfare (Finland), 67
National Child Benefit (NCB) program (Canada), 182
National Coalition Party (KOK) (Finland), 5, 65, 70, 72, 74–75, 77
National Council of Welfare (Canada), 180
National Department of Work (Germany), 88

National Economic and Social Council (NESC) (Ireland), 107–108
National Health Service (NHS) (UK), 235–236
National Injury Insurance scheme (Australia), 173
National Insurance Acts (1946) (UK), 243, 252
Native Title Act (Australia), 166, 167–168
natural resources, 44, 50, 97, 171; in Canada, 179, 186; Iran's oil revenue and, 286–287, 297n3; *See also* Alaska Permanent Fund
negative income tax (NIT), 34n8; in Australia, 161, 164; in Canada, 31, 177–178, 182–185, 188, 190; EITC as, 8, 13, 42–43, 44, 49, 51–52, 265, 273; experiments in implementation of, 31, 267; in Finland, 63–64; in Germany, 5, 86, 90; in Ireland, 118–119; in UK, 235, 257; in U.S., 31, 266–267; *See also* refundable tax credits
Negri, Antonio, 214
Negt, Oskar, 9, 85
neoliberals: in Australia, 157–158; in Canada, 194–195; in Japan, 211–212
the Netherlands, 125–133, 179; BIG-favorable and -unfavorable developments in, 126–129; government debt in, 128; labor market in, 42, 127, 129, 130, 133n3, 134nn5,6; piecemeal approaches of income support in, 4, 8, 10, 125, 126, 129, 132; retrenchment plans in, 130–131; unemployment in, 42, 127, 128, 133n3; van der Veen and Groot and, 4–5, 125; VBi and, 131–132
Netzwerk Grundeinkommen (Network BI), 85–86
New Democratic Party (NDP) (Canada), 184, 185, 186, 195
New Frontier Party (Japan), 209
Niinistö, Ville, 73, 78
NIT. *See* negative income tax (NIT)
Nixon, Richard, 13, 183, 267–273
Noguera, José Antonio, 7
Northern Territory Intervention (Australia), 168, 169, 170

Obama, Barack, 42, 45, 52, 265, 276
obligations. *See* conditionality/conditional programs; means testing/means-tested programs
Obrador, Andrés Manuel López, 218, 220
OECD (Organisation for Economic Co-operation and Development) countries, 8, 10, 178, 179, 188, 205. *See also* Australia; Canada; Mexico; Japan; United Kingdom; United States
Offe, Claus, 84–85
Oireachtas Committee on Social and Family Affairs (Ireland), 118
Opielka, Michael, 85, 89
Oportunidades (Mexican cash transfer program), 12, 49, 218, 222–227, 231

paid work, 63–64, 130, 220. *See also* unpaid work; work/employment
Paine, Thomas, 250, 266
parents. *See* families; mothers
Parker, Hermione, 246, 252
Participation Income (PI), 25–26, 27–28, 34n8
Partido Popular (PP [People's Party]) (Spain), 147
Partido Revolucionario Institucional (PRI) (Mexico), 222
Partido Socialista de Catalunya ([Catalan Socialist Party—PSC]), 144
Partij van de Vrijheid (PVV) (Dutch populist political party), 131, 132
Parti Québécois (PQ), 187–188

Partnership 2000 (1996) (Ireland), 110–111
Pay As You Earn (PAYE) tax credit (Ireland), 117
pension (age-related in Australia), 170–171; Hancock report and, 162–163; Henderson proposal and, 160–161; Howard government and, 168; means testing and, 153, 155, 162, 163–165; 1908 legislation of, 153, 154–155; superannuation and, 11, 162, 165, 166–167, 171–172; *See also* Australia
pension (disability-related in Australia). *See* disability benefits (Australia)
pension, widows' (Australia), 156, 158, 159–160, 163
pension(s), 34n8; in Canada, 178, 181, 186, 192; citizen's, in Mexico, 217, 218–220, 223, 227, 230–231; citizen's, in UK, 235, 255–256, 259; in Finland, 76; in Germany, 101n23; in Ireland, 115, 116, 122; in Japan, 204, 205; in the Netherlands, 126, 127, 128–129; *Setenta y Más* and, 12, 217, 223, 224–227, 230, 231; in UK, 235, 236, 255–256, 259; *See also* retirement
People's New Party (Japan), 209
PI (Participation Income), 25–26, 27–28, 34n8
piecemeal BI schemes, 5; in Brazil, 8; in Finland, 72, 73; in Germany, 86; in Ireland, 109–110, 113–114; in Mexico, 228; in Namibia, 132; in the Netherlands, 4, 8, 10, 125, 126, 129, 132; in Spain, 135
"Plan for Doubling the National Income" (Japan), 208
political feasibility of BI, 17–34; behavioral, 7, 8, 18, 21, 29–32, 33; institutional, 7, 18, 21, 24–27, 29, 30, 32–33; psychological, 7, 8, 18, 21, 27–29, 30, 33; strategic, 7, 18, 21–24, 27, 28, 30, 32
poverty: in Australia, 163; BI simulation models and, 71; in Canada, 178, 179; in Finland, 63, 69–70; in Ireland, 110–111, 118, 120–122, 123n6; in Japan, 206–207, 213; in Mexico, 220, 222, 223, 227–229; in the Netherlands, 130–131; in Spain, 138, 146, 148n12; in UK, 240–241, 243–245; in U.S., 266–267; War on, 269
Poverty and Rupture of the Welfare State (Heikkilä and Karjalanen), 71
poverty line: in Canada (LICO), 179, 180, 184, 185, 196n8; Henderson Poverty Inquiry and, 160; in Ireland, 111, 118, 123n6; in Spain, 138, 140; U.S., 43
PP (Partido Popular [People's Party]) (Spain), 147
Precariate movements (Japan), 12
price subsidies (Iran), 14, 285–287, 293, 297
Priorities Review Staff (Australia), 161–162, 163, 164, 171
Programa Renda Cidadã (Citizen's Income Program) (Brazil), 47
Programa Solidário, 48–49
Progresa (Mexican cash transfer program), 49, 218, 222. *See also* *Oportunidades* (Mexican cash transfer program)
PSOE (Partido Socialista Obrero Español [Spanish Socialist Party]), 135, 137, 147
psychological feasibility of BI, 7, 8, 18, 21, 27–29, 30, 33
public expenditure: in Ireland, 109, 111; in Japan, 208, 210, 213–214; in the Netherlands, 127, 130; in Spain, 136; in UK, 244, 246, 258–259

public opinion, 25, 98, 131; polls in Iran on, 292–293, 299n17; psychological feasibility and, 7, 8, 18, 21, 27–29, 30, 33
PVV (Partij van de Vrijheid) (Dutch populist political party), 131, 132

Quebec, Canada, 180, 183, 186–188, 189, 194; Bloc Québécois and, 184, 185; C/QPP and, 181, 192
Québec Solidaire (QS), 188

race, 154, 159, 168, 169, 170; in U.S., 272
Rassemblement pour l'alternative progressiste (RAP) (Canada), 187–188
Rathbone, Eleanor, 237–238, 240, 241–242
Raventós, Daniel, 10
Reagan administration (U.S.), 267, 273
reciprocity norm, 8, 9, 13, 28–29, 33, 265
Red Renta Básica (Spanish Basic Income Network—RRB) association, 136, 137, 143, 145
refundable tax credits, 51, 100, 182; in Ireland, 10, 115, 116–119, 122; *See also* taxes/taxation
Renta Dignidad (Bolivian pension program), 227
retirement, 167, 168, 255–256. *See also* pension (age-related in Australia); pension(s)
retrospective constraints, 7, 20–21, 24, 29
Reynolds, Brigid, 5, 9–10
Rhys-Williams, Brandon, 13, 252–253, 255, 256–257
Rhys-Williams, Juliet, 13, 250–252, 256–257, 258
rights, 231; of citizens, 89, 120, 228, 236; human, 92–93, 100n18, 140–142, 229, 232n14; to income, 90, 92; to work, 92
Royal Commission on the Economic Union and Developments Prospects (Macdonald Commission) (Canada), 183, 188, 189, 190, 194
Rudd, Kevin, 169–170, 172

SATA Committee (Finland), 75–77, 78
Schröder, Gerhard, 84, 85, 87, 91
Seattle-Denver Income-Maintenance Experiment (SIME-DIME), 267
Segal, Hugh, 11, 178, 185, 186
SEO (Stichting voor Economisch Onderzoek) (Dutch foundation for economic research), 132, 133n3
Setenta y Más (Mexican rural pension program), 12, 217, 223, 224–227, 230, 231
Shinto Nippon political party (Japan), 12, 212
single mothers, 13, 163, 172, 212, 265, 268–269; in Japan, 205, 215n3; *See also* mothers
Smith, Iain Duncan, 254, 255
Snyder, Linda, 180–181
Social Democrat Alternative Party (Mexico), 220
Social Democrat BI proposal (Mexico), 221–222
Social Democratic Party (SDP) (Finland), 5, 65, 69, 73–75; BI debates and, 67, 78; Wahlroos' proposal and, 70
Social Democratic Party (SDP) (Germany). *See Sozialdemokratische Partei Deutschlands* (SPD, Social Democratic Party)
social insurance: in Canada, 181–182; in Ireland, 109, 116; in Japan, 204; superannuation in Australia and, 166–167; in UK, 237, 238, 239, 250–251

Social Insurance and Allied Services (Beveridge report), 204, 238–239, 241, 250–251
Social Insurance Institution of Finland (Kela), 71–72
Socialist Party (Japan), 204, 207, 209
Socialist Party USA (SPUSA), 276–277
socialists (Australia), 158
Social Justice Ireland, 109, 116, 118–119
social welfare. *See* welfare programs/system
Soininvaara, Osmo, 66, 67, 71, 73–76, 78; BI debates and, 68, 73; as minister of health and social services, 69–70; *See also* Finland
Something to Look Forward to (Juliet Rhys-Williams), 250–251
Sozialdemokratische Partei Deutschlands (SPD, Social Democratic Party), 88
Sozialhilfe (social assistance) (Germany), 89, 100n12
Spain, 6, 135–149; austerity in, 136; Basic Income Symposium in (2001), 137, 141; BI as human right in, 141–142; citizenship in, 138–140, 142, 144, 148n12; debates on BI in, 143–145; economic crisis in, 10, 135–136, 141, 145–146; funding BI in, 135, 142–143, 144; grassroots support of BI and, 146–147; legislative bills for BI in, 137–141; minimum income in, 143; RRB and, 136, 137, 143, 145; unemployment in, 136, 145
Spanish Basic Income Network (RRB), 136, 137, 143, 145
Spanish Personal Income Tax (IRPF) system, 142, 143
Spanish Socialist Party (PSOE [Partido Socialista Obrero Español]), 135, 137, 147
Standing, Guy, 3, 8, 10, 12, 60, 296
State Contributory Pension (Ireland). *See* pension(s)
State Pension for the 21st Century, A (Department for Work and Pensions), 255, 256–257, 259
Steensland, Brian, 269, 270
Stichting voor Economisch Onderzoek (SEO) (Dutch foundation for economic research), 132, 133n3
stigmatization, 28; CBI and, 49; Family Allowance and, 245; in Spain, 138, 148n12; of unpaid work, 95–97; of welfare recipients in U.S., 270
strategic feasibility of BI, 7, 18, 21–24, 27, 28, 30, 32
Subsidio ao Emprego (Brazil), 49
Subsidy Reform Law (Iran), 286–293
Suomi 1980-luvella (Finland in the 1980s) (Soininvaara and Lampinen), 66
superannuation (Australia), 11, 153, 162, 165, 166–167, 171–173
Suplicy, Eduardo, 8, 10
surfer effect, 8, 30–31
Swedish People's Party (RKP/SFP) (Finland), 65, 75
Switzerland, 84, 132, 195n1

Tabatabai, Hamid, 13–14, 293
take-up rates for social assistance, 206, 213, 245, 295–296
Targeted Conditional Cash Transfer Program (TCCTP) (Mexico), 223, 226, 227, 228–229
tax credits, 29; in Australia, 161; EITC, 8, 13, 42–43, 44, 49, 51–52, 265, 273; in Ireland, 10, 115, 116–119, 120, 122; in the Netherlands, 126, 129, 131; refundable, 10, 51, 100, 115, 116–119, 122, 182; in UK, 13, 235, 246, 247–250, 252, 254, 257–258; *See also* refundable tax credits

taxes/taxation: BI simulation models and, 71–72; Commission on Taxation (Ireland), 108, 113; on consumption, 97; on environmental polluters, 50; in Finland, 70; in Germany, 89, 95–96, 97, 99; integration of with social security system (Australia), 160–161, 163; integration of with welfare system (Ireland), 107, 110, 120, 122; in Iran, 289; Ireland BI funding and, 110, 112, 114; IRPF and, 142, 143; marriage and, 117, 248, 249; payroll, 41–42, 43; tax credit system (Ireland), 10, 117–118, 119, 120, 122; in UK, 243; *See also* income tax; refundable tax credits; tax credits

Tax Policy Investigation Committee (DPJ) (Japan), 203

television: in Iran, 292; See also media

TNS Gallup Oy (research group), 72

Tobin, James, 268

Tomlinson, John, 10–11, 158, 166

Torry, Malcolm, 12–13

trade unions, 22; in Australia, 165, 167, 168; BI simulation models and, 71; in Canada, 177, 188–189; in Finland, 66, 69, 70, 71, 74, 75–76; in Germany, 84, 93; in Japan, 212, 213; SATA Committee and, 75–76; in Spain, 136, 137; in UK, 240, 242, 244–245, 245, 249; in U.S., 272–273

True Finns (PER), 65, 77

Tuomala, Maati, 68–69

UK. *See* United Kingdom

unconditionality. *See* conditionality/conditional programs

unemployment, 6, 95–96, 120–121; in Australia, 156, 159, 164–165, 166; in Belgium, 42; in Canada, 42, 186; in Denmark, 42; in Finland, 42, 63, 69; in France, 42; in Germany, 84, 85, 101n22; in Ireland, 42, 109, 111–112, 120–121; in Japan, 204, 212; in Mexico, 42, 220, 227, 231; in the Netherlands, 42, 127, 128, 133n3; in New Zealand, 42; in Spain, 136, 145; in Sweden, 42; in UK, 42, 84, 238; in U.S., 84; *See also* labor market; work/employment

United Kingdom, 10, 12–13, 235–260; Beveridge report and, 238–239, 241, 250–251; CI in, 13, 58, 235, 237, 246, 247, 250, 252–257, 259–260; Citizen's Pension in, 235, 255–256, 259; committees on enquiry in, 253–255; Family Allowances Act in, 239–241; Great Britain, 6, 154, 206, 276; "guarantee" language in, 236–237; health care in, 235–236, 239; household payments in, 245, 247, 256, 258; Japan and, 204, 206, 213; minimum income in, 236–237, 242, 249, 255–256; parliamentary debate in, 241–242; poverty in, 240–241, 242–245; Rathbone endowment and, 237–238, 242; Rhys-Williams, Brandon and, 252–253; Rhys-Williams, Juliet report and, 250–252, 256; social assistance expenditures in, 206; tax credits in, 235, 246, 247–250, 252, 254, 257–258; unemployment in, 42, 84, 238; *See also* Child Benefit program (UK); Citizen's Income (CI) (UK); Family Allowance program (UK); Ireland

United States, 3, 6, 10, 178, 265–277; Alaska Permanent Fund and, 8, 13, 34n11, 44–45, 50, 52, 265–266, 274–275; BI adoption in, recent attempts, 11, 275–277; Congress of, 266, 268, 271–272, 273, 276; EITC and, 8, 13, 42–43,

44, 51–52, 265, 273; FAP in, 183, 267–273; GAI debates in Congress and, 265–266, 268, 270–271; income inequality in, 179; Japan and, 206, 208; minimum income in, 43, 208, 268, 269, 270, 273; NIT experiments in, 31, 266–267; poverty in, 266–267; social assistance expenditures in, 206; unemployment in, 84; USBIG and, 57, 191; welfare programs/system in, 13, 265, 267–273, 274–275; workfare in, 58, 181
United States Basic Income Guarantee (USBIG), 57, 191
Universal Child Care Benefit (UCCB) (Canada), 182
Universal Declaration of Human Rights, 92, 100n18, 141
Universal Income Security Program (UISP) (Canada), 183, 185
universalism/universality, 93, 230; Beveridge report and, 238–239, 240; of cash payments in Iran, 294–295; Child Benefit program (UK) and, 235, 236, 237; of citizen's pension (Mexico), 218–219; Family Allowance and, 245; NHS and, 235–236
unpaid work, 101n21; BI as respectful of, 121; child care and, 92, 96–97, 101n23; domestic duties as, 112; in Germany, 92, 95, 96–97, 101n23; in Mexico, 220, 231; stigmatization of, 95–97; women and, 112, 213; *See also* paid work; work/employment

Vanderborght, Yannick, 5, 11
van der Veen, Robert J., 4–5, 125
van Hasslet, Michiel, 10
Van Parijs, Philippe, 50, 51, 73, 132, 142, 293–294
Vereniging Basisinkomen (VBi) (Dutch Association for Basic Income), 131–132
VIVANT (Belgian political party), 5
VVD (Volkspartij voor Vrijheid en Democratie) (Dutch political party), 125, 130, 132

wages, 93–94, 97, 100n20, 241. *See also* income
WAO (Wet op de Arbeidsongeschiktheid) (Dutch disability benefits law), 126, 128, 133
Ward, Seán, 109–110
Wark, Julie, 10
Webb, Beatrice, 237
Webb, Steven, 255–256
welfare programs/system, 7, 28, 87, 91–92; in Brazil, 48; in Canada, 11, 177, 178–182, 186, 188, 189, 191; in Finland, 9; in Germany, 9, 84, 91; integration of with tax system (Ireland), 107, 110, 120, 122; in Iran, 294; in Ireland, 9–10, 107–115, 117–118, 120–122; in Japan, 11, 204–207, 212–213; in the Netherlands, 125; in U.S., 13, 265, 267–273, 274–275; *See also* conditionality/conditional programs; means testing/means-tested programs
welfare programs/system (Australia), 154, 170, 172; conditionality and, 10–11, 162–163, 164, 165, 173; extension of, 157, 160; politics and, 153, 157–159, 166, 169, 173; simplification of, 161–162; *See also* Australia
welfare recipients: in Australia, 157–158, 169; in Germany, 85, 86; in Ireland, 117; responsibility and, 6; in U.S., 270, 271; *See also* stigmatization
welfare reform, 4–5, 6; in Canada, 181, 183; in Finland, 75–76; in Germany, 84; in Ireland, 114, 120; in U.S., 265, 267–273
Werner, Görtz W., 86, 97, 100n20, 132

Whitlam Labor government (Australia), 11, 158, 160, 163–164, 165
widows' pension (Australia), 156, 158, 159–160, 163
Wildavsky, Aaron, 267, 268, 269, 270, 271
women, 96–97, 121; in Australia, 154, 172; child allowances in UK and, 238–239, 242; Child Benefit (UK) and, 245; FAP and, 13, 183, 267–273; feminism and, 11, 159, 192–193, 205, 242; in Germany, 90; in Japan, 205–206, 207, 215n3; men, 207, 269; in Mexico, 225, 231; pension eligibility in Ireland of, 116; Rhys-Williams, Juliet and, 251; unpaid work and, 112, 213; widows' pension and, 156, 158, 159–160, 163; *See also* gender/gender equality; mothers
Woodhouse National Compensation Scheme (1974) (Australia), 162–163, 164
Work Choices legislation (Australia), 168, 169
work/employment, 120, 251; education and, 91–92; full employment, 10, 84, 86, 127, 128, 130, 139, 208; job loss and, 145; job seeking and, 126–127, 159; job training and, 51, 96, 121; paid, 63–64, 130, 220; reduction of hours of, 93–94, 97; reemployment business and, 127, 133n3; *See also* unemployment
work ethic(s), 9; AFDC and, 272; behavioral feasibility and, 29–32; in Japan, 213; reciprocity norm and, 28–29
workfare programs, 25, 32; in Canada, 180–181; in Germany, 84, 85, 88; in U.S., 58, 181
Working Income Tax Benefit (WITB) (Canada), 182
WRR (Wetenschappelijke Raad voor het Regeringsbeleid) (Dutch scientific council for government policy), 125, 133
WW (Wet werkeloosheid) (Dutch unemployment benefits law), 126, 128, 133
WWB (Wet Werk en Bijstand) (Wet Water and Bread) (Dutch social benefit scheme), 126–127, 133, 133n3

Yamamori, Toru, 11–12, 203, 211–212, 214
Yanes, Pablo, 12
Young Finnish Party, 8, 69

Zapatero, José Luis Rodríguez, 135, 136